INHABITED WILDERNESS

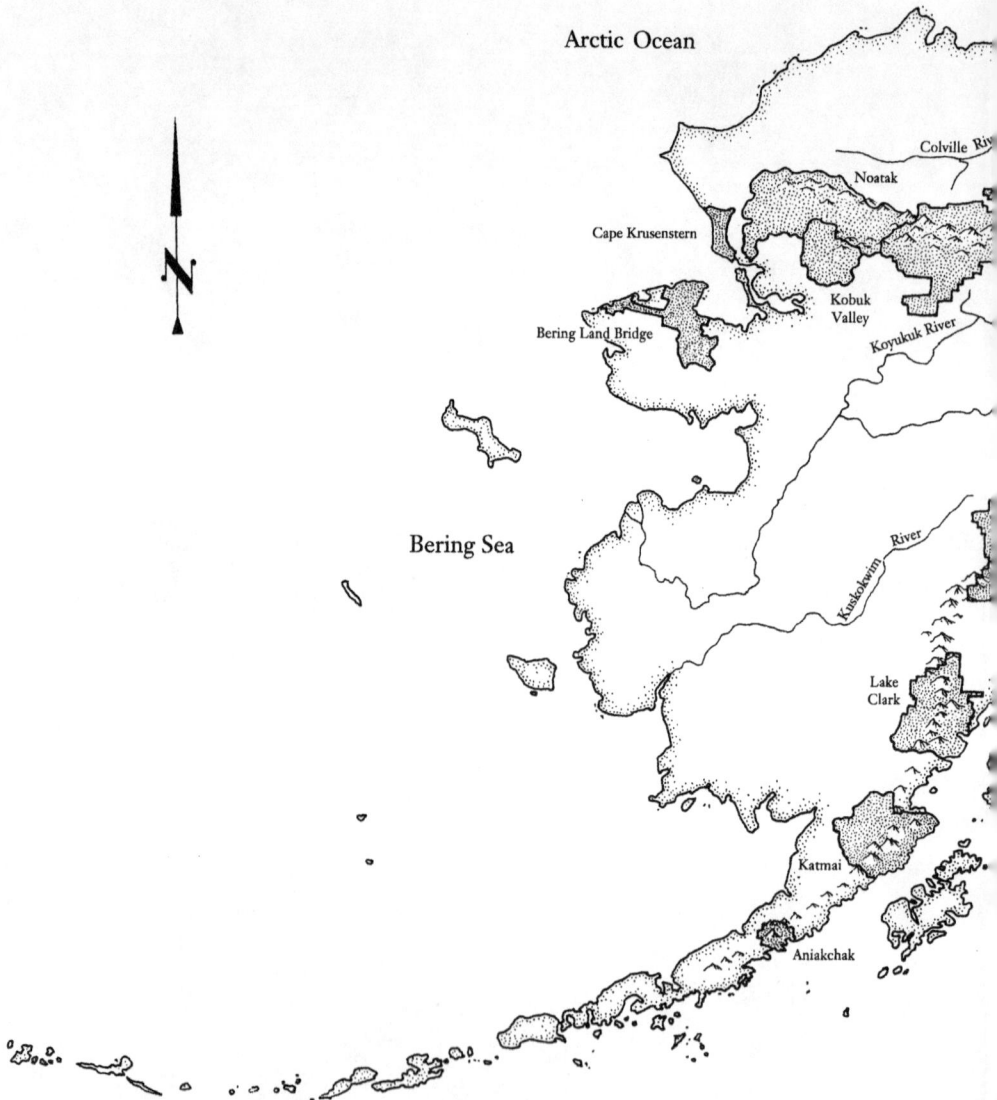

Arctic Ocean

Colville Riv

Noatak

Cape Krusenstern

Kobuk
Valley

Bering Land Bridge

Koyukuk River

Kuskokwim River

Bering Sea

Lake
Clark

Katmai

Aniakchak

N

Gates
of the
Arctic

Yukon River

Yukon-Charley Rivers

Tanana River

Denali

River

Wrangell-Saint Elias

Kenai Fjords

Glacier Bay

Gulf of Alaska

| 0 | 200 Kilometers |
| 0 | 200 Miles |

NATIONAL PARKLANDS IN ALASKA

THEODORE CATTON

Inhabited Wilderness

INDIANS, ESKIMOS, AND NATIONAL PARKS

IN ALASKA

NEW AMERICAN WEST SERIES

ELLIOTT WEST, GENERAL EDITOR

↓   ↓   ↓

University of New Mexico Press Albuquerque

ISBN-13: 978-0-8263-1827-5

© 1997 by The University of New Mexico Press
FIRST EDITION

Library of Congress Cataloging-in-Publication Data
Catton, Theodore.
Inhabited Wilderness : Indians, Eskimos, and National Parks in Alaska /
Theodore Catton. — 1st ed.
p.   cm. — (New American West series)
Includes bibliographical references (p.   ).
ISBN 0-8263-1826-6 (cloth). — ISBN 0-8263-1827-4 (pbk.)
1. Glacier Bay National Park and Preserve (Alaska) — History.   2. Denali
National Park and Preserve (Alaska) — History.   3. Gates of the Arctic
National Park and Preserve (Alaska) — History.   4. National parks and
reserves — Alaska — History — 20th Century — Case studies.   5. Indians of North
America — Alaska — Government relations — History — 20th century — Case studies.
6. United States. National Park Service — History — Case studies.
I. Title.   II. Series.   F912.G5C37   1997
979.8' 2 — dc21 97-4873
CIP

For Kristi

Contents

Illustrations

Maps

↓

Foreword

On a recent trip to Thailand my family and I visited the Koh Kradan National Park, an extraordinary green gem of an island in the Andaman Sea. As the four of us waded ashore — there are no docks or wharves — our first sight was a simple sign beside a palm. Beneath an inscription in Thai was an English translation: "Please Keep the Nature."

It seems that the impulse to preserve something of the "natural world" from the onslaughts of contemporary change can be found in many settings across the planet. In the United States, however, this desire is more powerful than in most societies. It is also more culturally resonant. For more than two centuries European Americans have made an imagined wilderness part of their national identity, an essential element of whatever it is that has set them apart from their mother cultures. But by conceiving wild nature a part of our national character, it turns out, we have gotten more than we bargained for. By carrying this impulse into modern America, we have also inherited a series of contradictions regarding ourselves, our continent's history, and the nature of "nature."

In *Inhabited Wilderness: Indians, Eskimos, and Alaska's National Parks*, Theodore Catton offers us a fascinating look at some of those contradictions and their origins. He also describes how, on what many call our "last frontier," a grappling with those contradictions has begun.

Catton's book inaugurates the New American West series. Our advisory board and the editors at the University of New Mexico Press believe this series will be a forum for new voices in a field that has enjoyed a remarkable invigoration during the past fifteen years. We hope this project will encourage fresh ideas and new approaches that build on distinguished work of the

recent and more distant past. The most influential works in western studies
have usually bridged the standard boundaries — perhaps barriers would be a
better word — between academic disciplines. The New American West series will feature innovative studies that range among history, economics,
anthropology, environmental sciences, psychology, and other fields. Ideal
candidates will be those that frustrate the most thoughtful attempts to fit
them cleanly into one category or another.

Inhabited Wilderness fits that standard nicely. Catton has something to say
to specialists in political science, public policy, anthropology, and Native
American studies as well as to political, environmental, cultural, and intellectual historians. His book is about the making of some of our largest and
most splendid national parks, but in a deeper sense he writes about an ancient longing of Europeans, and their American descendants — their aching
dream of finding a lovely land scarcely touched by humans and their history. Many believed they had found their Eden in the magnificent mountains, huge deserts, vast snowfields, and dense forests of the far West. As the
West was filled and transformed by an expanding society and its institutions, this "wild" country came to be seen as a spiritual resource. Some
parts, it was felt, must be set aside and preserved as recollections of the
timeless pockets of land close to their pristine condition before history's
clock started ticking. The preservationist movement was born. Its most
visible creations have been our national parks.

But from the start there was a problem. What has been called wilderness
is some of the oldest inhabited land in North America. Before they became
national parks, Yosemite, Yellowstone, and Glacier had been the homes and
workplaces of native peoples. Over the millennia these places had been the
seats of culture for dozens of societies, which had used and shaped the land
and, in turn, had been changed by it. Until recently, avoiding that contradiction was simple enough. Native Americans were taken up and moved
somewhere else, and their former homes were re-imagined into pristine
parks. Illusion was maintained — except, of course, among the evicted.

Lately, however, this approach has begun to change. One of the most
interesting, and largely unrecognized, shifts in public land policy has been
played out in the creation of new national parks in Alaska and the revision of older ones. These evolving policies have recognized the rights of
occupation and use by native peoples — as well as by descendants of earlier
European-American settlers. These changes tell us a lot about much that
has happened in the West of the century. Among other things, they show
the continuing adaptation of Indian peoples, in this case into shrewd and
effective political infighters and publicists capable of holding their own.

Behind such developments, however, are signs of a far more fundamental shift in the perception of the land itself, a rethinking of the most basic assumptions of our true birthright and our obligations in the old and complicated place we call "the West."

Theodore Catton tells the story of the evolution in both public policy and its intellectual underpinnings. He does so with a direct, engaging style and a clarity of exposition. The result is a book that readers will find a revelation on several levels. As such, *Inhabited Wilderness* is a welcome addition to the literature on the modern West and a foretaste of what we hope will be an important new series in western history and life.

ELLIOTT WEST

Preface

I am not an Alaskan. I am, however, a wilderness enthusiast and a deep admirer of the national parks. My interest in Alaska's national parks began in 1991 when, as a graduate student at the University of Washington, I was given the opportunity to write an administrative history of Glacier Bay National Park and Preserve for the U.S. National Park Service (NPS). At the initial briefing for that project a fascinating issue was brought to my attention. The indigenous people of Glacier Bay are denied the privilege to hunt and fish for their subsistence within the park, while in most of Alaska's other national parks subsistence use is permitted by law. That troubling inconsistency between Glacier Bay and other Alaskan parks raised broader questions in my mind. For instance, I wondered how the modern subsistence hunter fits into the national park scheme for preserving nature and how the national park concept of preservation meshes with the cultural values of Alaska's native peoples. I found the NPS to be open to an analysis of these issues. Subsequently, I explored the problem of native subsistence use in Glacier Bay in a seminar taught by Richard White, and I examined the problem of subsistence in the wider context of Alaska's national parks in my Ph.D. dissertation. In the meantime, from 1993 to 1995, I was employed by the NPS regional office in Seattle, a position that enriched my understanding of NPS policy and agency culture.

Hunting of any kind in national parks invites scrutiny. As anyone familiar with the national park system knows, it is a matter of longstanding principle that national parks are sanctuaries for wildlife. The hunting prohibition is more than a matter of aesthetics; it is, and always has been, embedded in the larger purpose of preserving these areas in a natural condition. Hunting in the national park context is usually perceived as an intrusion on nature, a taking from the ecological community, a consumptive use of resources that might be equated with logging or mining. Clearly, the accommodation of subsistence hunters in Alaska's national parks required some rethinking of these basic assumptions. It implied a different conceptualization of humankind in nature.

Subsistence use itself is controversial — whether it occurs in Alaska's national parks or anywhere else. The basic assumption underlying this practice is that it is primal, compared with other kinds of resource use, and therefore ought to be given priority. Subsistence use is an outgrowth of aboriginal culture, but it is not the same thing as aboriginal hunting and fishing. It takes form in relation to other types of hunting and fishing around it: market hunting, sport hunting, commercial fishing, sport fishing. However, as subsistence users adopt the technology commonly employed in these other types of hunting and fishing, the primal quality of subsistence use becomes increasingly obscure. Sportsmen and commercial fishermen — and in the national park context, preservationists — grow more skeptical about the subsistence users' privilege.

The subsistence user's new technology becomes a lightning rod for criticism. It is argued that the technology dramatically increases the subsistence user's effect on the environment; the subsistence user retorts that it is not the technology itself but how it is used that matters. In the national park context, aesthetic as well as environmental consequences of the new technology are debated. The sight and sound of caribou hunters riding all-terrain vehicles across the arctic tundra, even the tracks that those vehicles leave behind, may destroy a park visitor's wilderness experience.

Subsistence users are sometimes upbraided for demanding legal protections on the one hand, while strongly objecting to legal definitions of subsistence on the other, but their conflicting desires are less fickle than they first appear. Subsistence users know from experience that legal definitions are devised to fix and circumscribe their privilege as well as protect it. They object to limitations on their subsistence privilege because change and adaptation are at the very heart of subsistence; indeed, these are basic attributes that subsistence shares with the aboriginal hunting and fishing patterns from which it is descended. Moreover, subsistence users chafe at legal definitions because they resent the loss of privacy that comes with enforcement. The more precisely subsistence is defined, the more searching the questions become concerning the hunter's cultural identity, personal motivation, and economic need.

I believe that the marrying of subsistence use to the national park idea is the outstanding feature in the story of Alaska's national parks. This is not a simple marriage of convenience, but something far more interesting, creative, tumultuous, and compelling. The marriage of the two concepts is officially recognized in nine of ten new national parks, preserves, and monuments that were established in Alaska in 1980, and in the large additions made to Denali and Katmai National Parks under the same act. Since this unique land management scheme still lacks an official designation, I have called it "inhabited wilderness."

Alaska's national parklands are enormous. They comprise some 51 million acres, or more than half of the total land area in the national park system. It is difficult to appreciate the size of these parks when viewed on a map of Alaska, because the forty-ninth state itself is so disproportionately large compared with the lower forty-eight. Consider that the greatest Alaskan park, Wrangell–Saint Elias, equals the combined area of Massachusetts, Connecticut, and New Jersey, while one glacier in the park is larger than the state of Rhode Island. Alaska's national parklands are also geographically diverse, ranging from Glacier Bay in the temperate, mountainous, southeastern panhandle of Alaska to Cape Krusenstern on the Arctic coast; from Yukon-Charley Rivers in the forested interior to Aniakchak on the storm-swept Aleutian Peninsula.

This book examines the making of Alaska's national parklands through case studies of Glacier Bay, Denali, and Gates of the Arctic National Parks. Glacier Bay National Park constitutes a de facto inhabited wilderness, a place in which the indigenous people (the Hunas) and the NPS have struggled for more than fifty years to reach an accommodation. In Glacier Bay we find the longest, sharpest dialogue between wilderness preservationists and inhabitants to have occurred anywhere in Alaska.

The second case study focuses on the origins of Denali National Park and its early administration through 1928, an era in which miners and prospectors enjoyed the legal privilege to hunt for their subsistence within the national park. In Denali, the former Mount McKinley National Park, we discover the roots of the inhabited wilderness idea in Alaska's unique frontier experience.

Finally, the third case study involves one of the ten new national parks established in 1980. While almost any of the new national parks in Alaska could serve as a focal point for examining the modern conception of inhabited wilderness embodied in these areas, Gates of the Arctic deserves notice for a number of reasons. First, the central Brooks Range has the distinction of being the place that beckoned the wilderness explorer and philosopher Bob Marshall in the 1930s. Marshall became the first preservationist to propose setting aside Alaska wilderness on a massive scale, as well as the first preservationist to think systematically about the long-term interests of the area's inhabitants; he played a pivotal role in this story. Second, the central Brooks Range was one of the battlegrounds for wilderness preservation and oil development in the 1970s. The Trans-Alaska Pipeline traverses the range directly east of the park. The making of Alaska's new national parks cannot be understood apart from the contemporary influence of Alaska's oil boom. Third and finally, the central Brooks Range is home to the caribou-hunting Nunamiut Eskimos, whose village of Anaktuvuk Pass lies in the heart of the 8-million-acre Gates of the Arctic National Park and Preserve. The Nunamiuts' experience in the making of this wilderness park presents an illuminating comparison with the Hunas' experience in Glacier Bay.

I am grateful to many people for giving me help and encouragement while writing this book. Darryll Johnson first introduced me to the topic of subsistence in Alaska's national parks and subsequently enriched my understanding of the phenomenon from a sociological perspective. William E. Brown provided me with an NPS historian's insights on the national park system in Alaska at an early stage in the project. Professor Richard White read through multiple drafts of all the chapters, usually, it seemed, while flying from one conference or symposium to another, and still found time between trips to discuss the project with me in his office. John Findlay, Richard Kirkendall, Bruce Hevly, James Karr, Stephen Haycox, Polly Dyer, David Louter, Elliott West, Larry Durwood Ball, and Carla Homstad read all or portions of the manuscript and offered valuable criticism.

I want to thank the staff of Historical Research Associates, Inc., and particularly its president Alan Newell, for providing a most congenial setting for the completion of this project. Computer programmer Rich Poitras turned his wizardry to converting all of the text files from my dissertation to a more versatile software program. Cass Williams cheerfully formatted and reworked the manuscript, and Brad Letzig helped with the maps. Archeologists Weber Greiser and Milo McLeod shared their photographs and memories of two field seasons in Anaktuvuk Pass.

I am indebted to Amy Marvin, Mary Rudolph, and Al Dick of Hoonah for sharing some of their personal and community experiences relating to their dispossession from Glacier Bay.

I am grateful to the editors at the University of New Mexico Press—especially Larry Durwood Ball and Louise Cameron—who patiently saw the book to completion.

My wife, Kristi, deserves more of my thanks than anyone, for without her love and generous spirit I could not have enrolled as a returning student at the University of Washington six years ago, when we had three young sons to raise. For giving me that gift I dedicate this book to her. I am also indebted to my parents for the wonderful financial assistance that made my late educational experience possible, and to my sons Walt, Ben, and Eli, who made the experience so pleasurable.

ALSEK RANGE

CHILKAT RIVER

TAKHINSHA MOUNTAINS

Muir Glacier

MUIR INLET

FAIRWEATHER RANGE

GLACIER BAY

BRADY ICEFIELD

Ranger
Station

Gustavus

EXCURSION INLET

TAYLOR BAY

DUNDAS BAY

ICY STRAIT

GULF OF ALASKA

North

0.1   5   10   15 Kilometers
0   5   10   15 Miles

CROSS SOUND

Hoonah

GLACIER BAY REGION

CHICHAGOF ISLAND

Introduction

The national parks are a proud American tradition. Since the establishment of Yellowstone National Park in 1872, these designated areas have served to highlight the nation's extraordinary endowment of natural wonders and scenic beauty. As historian Alfred Runte has shown, Americans have exhibited a kind of "scenic nationalism" in the making of national parks. As Americans explored and toured the West in the nineteenth century, they felt compelled to compare their country's national splendors with Europe's famous landscapes and architectural works. They likened the Rocky Mountains to the Swiss Alps, the time-hewn canyons and monuments of the Southwest to Europe's antiquities. National parks confirmed in Americans their belief that the United States possessed in natural scenery what was lacking in cultural monuments.

While extolling the natural wonders and beauty to be found in the national parks, Americans have also pointed with pride to the democratic principles enshrined in the national park idea. The primary object of national parks, it has often been said, is to preserve outstanding examples of America's natural and cultural heritage in public ownership for the use and benefit of all the people. The making of national parks has served to protect such lands from ruinous exploitation by a small minority, and, further, to consecrate these areas as places where all Americans can go for pleasure and inspiration. For generations of Americans the national park system has presented a satisfying contrast to the landed heritage of Europeans, where wildlands were originally set aside for the pleasure of the king and a few noblemen. As one longtime publicist for the NPS asserted, national parks are distinctly an American idea, "a definite expression of the highest in our American code of government — equality for all."[1]

Americans invested their national parks with another cultural significance as well: the parks came to memorialize America's wilderness heritage. The earliest national parks were created around so-called natural wonders — the geothermal splendors of Yellowstone, the glacier-hewn Yosemite Valley, massive Mount Rainier, Crater Lake, the Grand Canyon. Other national parks, coming into the system somewhat later, were inspired simply by the scenic grandeur of the area. Examples include Glacier, Rocky Mountain, Great Smoky Mountains, and Olympic National Parks. Yet no matter what the original attractions of the area were, each acquired added significance as soon as it was set aside. They became protected remnants of a wilderness that had once spanned the continent. By the 1930s, one of the stated goals of national park management was to preserve the indigenous flora and fauna and primitive feeling of these places so that they would provide glimpses of North America as it had looked when the white man first explored it. Thus, national parks fulfilled a cultural need associated with the closing of the frontier: they were windows to America's past, keepsakes of a once-virgin land.

In the 1960s the American people began to consider the future of the public domain in Alaska. When Alaska attained statehood in 1959 it had a population of around 225,000. This amounted to a little more than 0.1 percent of the U.S. population in a state that accounted for 16 percent of the U.S. land area. Moreover, the state of Alaska contained a great deal of scenic magnificence: mountains, glaciers, pristine rivers and lakes, and interesting wildlife. A land that nineteenth-century politicians and newspapers had once caricatured as "Seward's Folly," "Icebergia," "Walrussia" — that is, an American possession of doubtful worth — now struck many Americans as being a treasure trove of wilderness. If Alaska's northern climate still seemed harsh and strange to most Americans, the state's claim to being the nation's last frontier struck a sympathetic chord with them. In certain symbolic ways, Alaska wilderness had become a touchstone for all Americans. A Maine newspaper editorial put it best during the congressional debate over Alaska lands in 1980: "Alaska is our ultimate wilderness, the last remnant of what the New World used to be. If we lose the freshness and the beauty there, something essential to North America will have died out forever."[2] It was enough for most Americans to know that such a place still existed in the United States. They did not have to go to Alaska to feel that they had a stake in it.

To preserve this heritage for present and future generations, Congress enacted the Alaska National Interest Lands Conservation Act, or ANILCA, on December 2, 1980. It was a landmark act in the history of conservation. ANILCA designated more than 100 million acres, or 28 percent of the state, as new national parks, forests, wildlife refuges, and wild and scenic rivers. It added ten new units to the national park system alone. The new parklands in Alaska had a combined area of more than 51 million acres, 13 percent of the state, an area greater than the entire state of Washington. These were the first new national parks to be established in Alaska in more than fifty years, or since the creation of Mount McKinley National Park in 1917, Katmai National Monument in 1918, and Glacier Bay National Monument in 1925.

The creation of Alaska's national parks also forced a critical reevaluation of two old and cherished tenets of America's national park tradition: (1) that the national parks were democratic, and (2) that they preserved vignettes of primitive America. In the first instance, these lands were inhabited by native peoples who made a substantial part of their living by hunting, trapping, and fishing with nets — activities that were normally excluded from national parks. Unlike Indians in the American West, Alaska natives had not been forced to give up their lands and remove to reservations. Although Congress finally extinguished Alaska natives' aboriginal land title in 1971, the law protected their right to make continued "subsistence use" of the public domain. When Congress passed ANILCA nine years later, therefore, it duly provided for the continuation of "customary and traditional" subsistence use in the new national park areas. This important adaptation of national park policy extended to rural, white Alaskans who practiced a "subsistence lifestyle," too. Today, local Eskimos, Indians, and whites hunt animals for food in most of the new parks. In the winter, trappers work their traplines and occupy cabins within the national park boundaries. In the summer, families or heads of families come and establish fish camps. One permanent Eskimo village, Anaktuvuk Pass, is situated within Gates of the Arctic National Park. In the formation of Alaska's national parks one important principle gradually emerged: American democracy would not be well served if the national parks oppressed this small minority. The process involved a search for balance and commonality between the interests of preservationists and those of resident peoples.

In the second place, as the science of ecology developed new models for explaining the dynamics of nature and the process of ecological succession, it became increasingly clear that ecological change was too ubiquitous and complex to allow national parks ever to fulfill their stated purpose as historical vignettes. Alaska's national parks occupied a special place in this rethinking. The attention given to Alaska native subsistence use underscored the fact that national parks in the lower forty-eight were in fact missing a vital part of their earlier biological communities: man the hunter. Now preservationists reasoned that to prohibit subsistence hunting by Alaska natives in the new national parks would not only be undemocratic, it would in fact disturb the very natural conditions that the national parks were intended to preserve. Consequently, the NPS would have to manage subsistence use both as a minority right and as a part of nature.

Superficially, at least, this innovative concept for Alaska's new national parks harkened back to one of the earliest antecedents of the national park idea. In 1832, the artist George Catlin, concerned about the destructive effects of the American frontier on the Plains Indian culture and wildlife that he had observed on the upper Missouri, suggested that the two might be preserved "by some great protecting policy of government . . . in a magnificent park. . . . A nation's park, containing man and beast, in all the wild[ness] and freshness of their nature's beauty!"[3] What Catlin had in mind was infeasible, for the artist wanted to freeze the Plains Indian culture in time, as though capturing it on a canvas. The crucial difference between Catlin's vision and the new national park scheme in Alaska was that the latter made no pretense about preserving an aboriginal way of life. The very term "subsistence use" recognized that the hunting and gathering done by contemporary Alaska natives was a complex blend of the traditional and the modern. Yet the romantic appeal of Catlin's vision did not lie far beneath the surface of the legal language set forth in ANILCA's subsistence provisions. The law's insistence that subsistence use must be "customary and traditional" came perilously close to a denial of the intrinsic need of cultures to evolve. It was that tension between the rights of native peoples to be masters of their own cultural evolution on the one hand, and the desires of preservationists to retain the primitive feeling of Alaska's national parks on the other, which made the new parks so interesting and yet so fraught with difficulty.

The unique provision for subsistence use in Alaska's national parks gives them a significance in today's world that goes beyond their impressive extent and the extraordinary quality of their scenic and scientific resources. The amount of land protected in national parks and equivalent reserves worldwide approximately doubled during the 1970s. This was an encouraging development in many respects, but it carried a moral burden. Indigenous or resident peoples were often displaced by the creation of national parks in an effort to give full protection to wildlife populations. Many developing nations, in their effort to demonstrate the legitimacy of their conservation programs and to boost tourism, sought to create national parks on the traditional American model where no hunting or residency was permitted. As environmental historian David Harmon tartly put it, "Every country . . . want[ed] to have its Yellowstone, and the consequences be damned."[4] After the human costs of the new reserves came to be understood more clearly, the same nations began casting about for alternative models.[5] Whether or not Alaska's new national parks will prove to be worthy of emulation, it seems likely that future national parks will be closer in design to them than to the traditional Yellowstone model.

The significance of Alaska's national parks is that they are attempting, on an unprecedented scale, to correlate cultural and ecological change. The new Alaska parks are striving (1) to protect native cultures; (2) to satisfy wilderness preservationists; (3) to treat resident peoples justly; and (4) to maintain pristine environments for ecological study — all at the same time. Not surprisingly, the 200-page law that brought these parks into being has been characterized as a mass of contradictions and compromises. But it is much more than that. ANILCA's bold premise was that these objectives had to work together for they would not work separately. Preserving ecosystems without their human constituents or creating wildernesses at the expense of native cultures would be hollow achievements and ultimately self-defeating.

A decade and a half after its passage, ANILCA still stands as the climactic event in the Alaska land debate and as the foundation for Alaska's new national park system. The purpose of this study is to reexamine ANILCA in historical perspective, to trace the origins of the inhabited wilderness idea. Eventually, ANILCA will be seen as but another in a long series of negotiations between wilderness preservationists and wilderness inhabitants over humankind's place in nature.

It might be said that the negotiations commenced more than a hundred years ago, when the people of the native village of Hoonah in Southeast Alaska encountered Alaska's first wilderness preservationist. His name was John Muir.

ONE

Land Reborn

✦

John Muir had a rare passion for glaciers. Like so much else that stirred the famous naturalist's imagination, glaciers appealed to Muir on two levels: as things of wondrous beauty and as objects for scientific study. From the tiny remnant glaciers that he sought in the High Sierra to the massive namesake Muir Glacier that he discovered in Alaska, glaciers inspired him like no other phenomenon in nature.

Muir's intellectual hero was the preeminent glacial theorist of his day, Louis Agassiz. Agassiz's glacial theory revolved around two main postulates: that glaciers move and are a force of erosion, and that changes in the earth's climate had produced one or more ice ages. Muir devoted much of his own energy as a scientist to demonstrating the truth of these central ideas. Muir's first article, "Yosemite Glaciers," published by the *New York Tribune* in 1871, aimed to show that ice-age glaciers, not an earthquake, had created the incomparable Yosemite Valley. Muir eagerly sought out all kinds of evidence of past glaciation in his beloved Yosemite: glacier-polished rock surfaces, glacier-born alpine lakes, glacier-hewn canyons, and glacier-tilled meadows. In both the High Sierra and Alaska, he drove rows of stakes into glaciers and recorded their movements.[1]

In a time when scholars and lay people still doubted the ice-age theory on the grounds that it contradicted the Bible, Muir believed that evidence of past glaciation only increased the glory of God's creation. "A day and eternity are as one in His mighty workshop," Muir liked to tell Yosemite tourists. "I can take you where you can see for yourself how the glaciers have labored, and cut and carved, and elaborated, until they have wrought out this royal road."[2] As Muir groped toward his eventual vocation of writing and lecturing about nature, he developed what he called the "glacial gos-pel," the belief that glaciers could spark in people an abiding awe of nature, and that by studying and exploring nature people could be transformed. They could be born again.[3]

In 1879 Muir went north to study Alaskan glaciers. He passed most of the summer in and around Fort Wrangel, at the southern end of the Alaskan panhandle, where he was enthralled as much by the expanse of primeval forest — never "wasted by fire" nor "touched by the ax of the lumber-man" — as by the tidewater glaciers. But his Indian guides kept telling him of an inland bay to the north whose glaciers were larger than anything he had yet seen. In October, with the rain already turning to sleet and new ice forming on the surface of sheltered inlets, Muir set out for this bay with a missionary friend and four Indian guides in a 35-foot dugout canoe.[4] As the large bay did not yet appear on any charts, Muir would later be credited with its discovery.[5]

Muir and his companions took several days exploring the numerous in-lets and arms of Glacier Bay. Not far into the bay the dense forest gave way to a weird landscape of bare, rounded rock scapes. With his keen eye for glaciated landforms, the terrain could mean but one thing to him: the basin, filled from one end with seawater, was the scene of a remarkably fast and expansive glacial recession. In Geikie Inlet, which Muir named after the Scots geologist, he found glacial striations within the tidal zone — tracks of the retreating glacier so fresh that they were not yet warn away by wave action. Camping on the beach, the men burned "fossil wood" from a pre-glacial forest, and when the whistling wind died down they heard the thun-der of icebergs breaking off the glaciers up bay, testimony to the glaciers' continuing swift retreat. Climbing alone to the top of a ridge above camp, Muir made a sketch in his journal of his first general view of Glacier Bay: "a stern solitude of ice and snow and raw, newborn rocks, dim, dreary, myste-rious."[6] In Glacier Bay Muir had discovered a unique setting for con-templating how the land might have looked as it emerged from the ice ages.

Muir's responses to Glacier Bay were significant because they would eventually find expression in the establishment of Glacier Bay National Monument nearly half a century later. Muir's fascination with glaciers and the phenomenon of glacial recession would be shared to some degree by virtually every visitor who came after him. Muir's "glacial gospel" would be institutionalized in the NPS's educational program as park interpreters sought to give tourists not only a bit of scientific knowledge about what they were seeing, but to inculcate an environmental ethic as well. Unfortu-nately Muir had a blind spot that would work its way into the national park scheme, too; he treated the native presence in the area as something of no consequence to the land.

Muir's dismissal of the native presence sprang directly from his views on humankind and nature. Nature for Muir was the embodiment of the divine spirit, beautiful, harmonious, pristine, the fundamental source of human inspiration. Humankind, meanwhile, dwelling for the most part in squalid towns and cities, was spiritually adrift from nature. Indeed, wherever the "Lord Man" went, it seemed to Muir, he was hell-bent on befouling nature. Civilized human beings could commune with nature only by entering the natural landscape as observers, conscientiously leaving all natural processes alone. Here in Glacier Bay, cresting the wind-whipped waves in the cedar canoe, Muir looked upon the surrounding mountains as reflections of a divine perfection, infinitely enhanced by the very absence of humanity. "After witnessing the unveiling of the majestic peaks and glaciers and their baptism in the down-pouring sunbeams," he wrote, "it seems inconceivable that nature could have anything finer to show us."[7] This was a land reborn from the ice, pristine, free of the footprint of "Lord Man."

Contrary to Muir's perspective the Tlingits did not separate themselves from the natural world; indeed, they drew their cultural identity from their connection with the land. Their name for themselves was "the people whose table is set when the tide is out." To a later generation of Huna Tlingits Glacier Bay was "the Hoonah breadbasket," or "the main place of the Hoonah people."[8] The Tlingits' relationship to the environment was rooted in a seasonal pattern of resource extraction for their subsistence needs and interpreted through oral traditions describing their ancestors' long association with particular places and totem animals.

The Tlingits who accompanied Muir formed a curious impression of the man they called the "Great Ice Chief." As the party proceeded up the bay under lowering skies, Muir would order the canoe to shore, stuff his knapsack with notebook and woolens, and set off scrambling up the glacier-scoured slopes. Returning to camp with eyes aglow, he would appear almost feverish with excitement to reach the next wild vista. He was strangely indifferent to the rain and sleet. When the Tlingits tried to place Muir's behavior within their own frame of reference, they concluded that he was communicating with the evil spirits that resided in the mountains. One damp night when the missionary in the party tried to explain to the Tlingits that his naturalist friend was seeking knowledge, one of them grumbled, "Muir must be a witch to seek knowledge in such a place as this and in such miserable weather."[9]

Muir, for his part, found in his Indian companions a kind of devotional attitude toward nature that resonated warmly with his own animistic philosophy. "To the Indian mind all nature is instinct with deity," he wrote approvingly in his journal on a later visit to Glacier Bay.[10] But he also took the conventional nineteenth-century view that Indians were considerably far back on a cultural continuum of savagery and civilization. He found these Indians "afflicted" with a multitude of superstitions in much the same way that "all wild, or rather ignorant, peoples are sunk."[11] The natives seemed to display an exaggerated fear of the forces of nature, which made them as much the intruders, the exotics, in Glacier Bay as he. In writing his lyrical account of the trip for *The Century Magazine* a few years afterwards, Muir tended to picture the natives in opposition to the natural world around them: huddled together in a circle of firelight, crowded inside a smoky hut at a seal hunting camp, fleeing the breaking icebergs in their canoes. This contrasted with Muir's solitary wanderings on the bare slopes high above camp where, symbolically at least, he was closer than they to God and nature.[12]

Considering that the Tlingits of the nearby village of Hoonah would one day lose their best hunting and fishing grounds by the creation of Glacier Bay National Monument, it is ironic that this people had such an intimate encounter with America's premier preservationist. Before Muir, the missionary, and the four guides entered Glacier Bay, they took the precaution of stopping in Hoonah and taking on board the most esteemed seal hunter of the village. Certainly, neither Muir nor the Huna seal hunter showed great interest or ability in understanding the nature-thought of the other, and their communications were crude at best. The missionary Young later recalled how Muir conveyed to the Tlingits his sensibility about killing wild animals. Whenever the party saw a deer grazing along the shoreline or a flock of ducks passing overhead and his guides tried to draw a bead on them, Muir would "take pleasure in rocking the canoe." The natives, Young wrote, reacted to these antics with "some annoyance and a great deal of astonishment."[13] It was an odd foreshadowing of the Huna Tlingits' modern predicament, which no one in the canoe could possibly have predicted.

Aboriginal use and occupation of Glacier Bay is documented through a variety of sources including archeological surveys, ethnographic accounts, and correlations between the oral traditions of Huna Tlingits and the geological and climatological record. Together these sources indicate that ancestors of the Tlingits had winter village sites in what is now Glacier Bay prior to the last cycle of glacial advance and retreat. Huna Tlingits used most of the area now embraced by Glacier Bay National Park during the past century and a half or more.

In this glacier country the archeological record is thin. The advance and retreat of so much ice over the millennia caused the land alternatively to sink under the weight and rebound, so that the ancient shorelines where people made their camps were subsequently drowned below sea level or lifted tens of feet above the high-tide mark and covered by dense forest. A survey of the Glacier Bay region by archeologist Robert E. Ackerman during three field seasons in the 1960s uncovered one prehistoric site at Ground Hog Bay near Point Couverdon on the north shore of Icy Strait. This site indicated human occupation of the area 9,000 years ago by an earlier culture. Nearby, at a place called Grouse Fort, Ackerman found evidence dating from 500 to 900 years ago that revealed the development of a material culture more like that of the Tlingits of the historic period.[14]

The most intriguing evidence of past occupation comes from the now-famous "Glacier Bay story" of Hoonah's Tcukanadi clan. The clan legend recalls a time when the basin held a glacier and freshwater lake at one end, from which a large river flowed to the sea. Geologists have found evidence of such a lake in what is now the east arm of Glacier Bay, while ecologists have discerned from relic tree stumps the prior existence of a lowland spruce and hemlock forest.[15] The legend tells of an ancestral village in this valley where the Tcukanadi, together with three other clans, enjoyed an abundance of all types of salmon. Their occupation of this place came to a swift end when a teenage girl of the village, weary of her confinement during menstruation, whistled through some charmed fish bones to beckon the glacier's spirit. Once set in motion, the glacier was unstoppable. The people held a council and decided that they must abandon their village while the girl, Kaasteen, would remain as a sacrifice. According to Huna elder Amy Marvin's rendering of the story, they waited till the end to depart, sitting in their canoes while water flooded the village, and the house that contained Kaasteen "slid downward to the bottom of the sea before their eyes." At that moment the clan chief sang a song with the refrain "pity my house" and "pity my land." The four clans separated, and while three established villages at points along Icy Strait, the fourth clan, the Tcukanadi, went to the present site of Hoonah.[16] The Glacier Bay story, handed down from generation to generation by oral tradition, makes no pretense of dating these events. It seems that the Tcukanadi possess a cultural memory of a distant time before the Little Ice Age, several centuries ago.

Geologists and plant ecologists now estimate that this recent glaciation reached its maximum extent in the eighteenth century, completely filling the bay and giving the channel to the south its name of Icy Strait. The first European explorer to chart this shoreline was Captain George Vancouver, who recorded in 1794 a slight indentation "terminated by a solid, compact mountain of ice, rising perpendicularly from the water's edge." By the time of John Muir's exploration in 1879, the ice mass had receded about fifty miles up the bay, now split into two main glaciers and numerous lesser ones, exposing a terrain largely denuded of vegetation and deserted of land mammals but rich in marine resources. Hair seal congregated near the face of the glaciers, feeding on the shrimp that flourished in the upwelling glacier meltwater and finding sanctuary from killer whales on the icebergs. Seabirds nested on the islands of the bay, while the tides washed edible seaweeds onto the gravelly beaches. In the lower part of the bay where approximately a hundred years had passed since the ice had melted, new vegetative growth included berry bushes and other edible plants. The vegetation provided ground cover and forage for new populations of marmot, mountain goat, and deer. Freshwater streams supported new salmon stocks. Huna Tlingits would later recall that their parents and grandparents regarded Glacier Bay as "a kind of storehouse for the people of Hoonah." Huna families built numerous smokehouses for seasonal use and stayed at these locations for several weeks at a time.[17] There is abundant ethnographic evidence that by the end of the nineteenth century Glacier Bay was the recognized hunting and gathering territory of the Tcukanadi clan of Hoonah. Other clans of the same winter village claimed neighboring areas around Excursion Inlet, Dundas and Taylor Bays, and the outer coast — all in what would eventually become the national park.

The Tlingits were a trading people. The island and mainland villages had access to different resources, and the people went on long trading expeditions in their large canoes. Moreover, the coastal environment generally provided such an abundance of resources, particularly salmon, that the Tlingits could build up stores of food each year and pass most of the dark, wet winters in their snug houses. Thus, they were sedentary gatherers with a relatively high population density, some specialization of labor, and a rich material culture. The wealthier Tlingits owned slaves until the late nineteenth century.[18]

When stores ran low in early spring, a Tlingit family group would pack the canoe and venture out of the village, beginning with a seal hunting expedition of several weeks' duration. By April, the group could be gathering green plants and edible roots or the potatoes they had planted on some sunny hillside the previous year.[19] In May they might go on a trading expedition, followed in June by berry picking and gathering birds' eggs. In late June and July, during the first salmon run, the men fished and hunted seal while the women dried meat and seal skins and rendered the seal oil.

August was devoted to more food storage, and in September they followed the second salmon run. Late fall was the time for hunting and trapping. Finally, as winter approached, they returned to the village for a season of potlatches, trading expeditions, craft work, and repairing of fishing gear.[20]

The Tlingits' view of nature was essentially animistic. All physical objects — glaciers, mountains, heavenly bodies — had spirits. Human beings made their way in the world by treating these spirits respectfully, communicating with the spirits either directly or through their shamans. Animals had a prominent place in this spirit world; they possessed souls essentially like those of human beings in that they inhabited the body and could be reincarnated after death. The ethnologist Frederica De Laguna wrote in her magisterial work on the Yakutat Tlingits:

> The world of animals, to an even greater extent than that of plants and the rest of personified nature, was part of man's moral world. Through the relationship between sib and totem, many species were also drawn into the human social order and were, in a sense, members of the sibs that claimed them as "friends." Particular species also played distinctive roles because of their importance in shamanism, in foretelling the future, or because they were supposed to possess some other special character or power.[21]

It was in their relationship to animals, particularly the animals they hunted, that Tlingits most clearly demonstrated a religious or devotional view toward nature, and their relationship to animals is worth examining, because it would lie at the heart of their long contest with the NPS after the creation of Glacier Bay National Monument.

Ethnohistorians have tried to reconstruct how various Indian groups' religious beliefs affected their exploitation of natural resources. The problem is a difficult one. There is always a disparity between what human societies preach and what they practice. Moreover, the earliest ethnographic records come from fur traders and missionaries whose presence among the Indians already heralded a time of change, if not upheaval, in aboriginal societies. By the time John Muir recorded his impressions of his native companions in 1879, the Tlingits had been in contact with Russian, British, and American traders for more than three generations; they had been ravaged by several epidemics; and they had been introduced to Christianity, first by the Russian Orthodox Church, then by American Presbyterians. The most important consequence of European contact was the dependent relationship that Tlingits gradually developed with the fur companies as they became accustomed to modern manufactures. To earn the cash with which to purchase European and American manufactures, Tlingits hunted sea otter, hair seal, deer, and other animals for the commercial value of their furs and hides.

These economic pressures notwithstanding, the Tlingits' moral relationship to the natural world predisposed them to patterns of resource use that whites would misconstrue as conservationist in a modern sense. For example, whites often observed that Tlingits tried to use all parts of the animals they killed and to kill only what they could consume — admirable conduct to those who advocated a sportsman's code as well as laws for the conservation of game. But the Tlingit practices were not guided by concern about the supply of game and the public welfare; rather the Tlingit hunter sought to earn the animals' favor in order to bring himself luck and future success in hunting. Another Tlingit practice that was misconstrued as conservationist was the enforcement of rules against visiting certain seal or sea otter hunting grounds during the spring pupping season. Whites assumed that this was to conserve the new crop of pelts for subsequent harvesting in the fall, but the Tlingits were actually motivated by concern that the herds could easily scare at this time of year and permanently leave the area.[22]

While some whites were impressed by the Tlingits' restraint in hunting, others reported numerous instances of wanton slaughter of game by the Indians of Southeast Alaska. The hide and fur market introduced economic incentives for hunting animals in larger numbers. Native hunters may have had no compunction about killing mass quantities as long as they still met their ritual obligations to the animals. One American traveler reported that Indians who hunted the great Alaska brown bears never brought in the head or claws, presumably out of respect for the animal, even though this considerably reduced the market value of the hides at the store.[23] In other instances, Tlingit hunters may have adapted their traditional rites to meet the changing economy. As deer hides began selling for ten to twenty cents apiece in Southeast Alaska, natives and whites together slaughtered hundreds of deer for the hides alone. In 1902, a field agent for the New York Zoological Society reported how native and white hunters cruised among the islands in small boats hunting the deer with jack-lights or running them into the water with dogs where they were shot while swimming. The field agent found the bodies of deer "piled up on the wharves like cord-wood."[24]

In terms of commercial value the sea otter overshadowed all other resources in Southeast Alaska in the nineteenth century. Tlingits readily competed with Aleut hunters in obtaining the furs and selling them to Russian, British, and American buyers. After Russia sold Alaska to the

United States in 1867, American schooners were known to cruise the Inside Passage laden with muskets, cloth, liquor, and other manufactured goods to exchange for sea otter pelts at the various Tlingit villages. Tlingits also went to Sitka by canoe to trade with the Americans. In 1880 the ranking American officer in Sitka commented that the Hunas had killed 127 sea otter in a single expedition to the outer coast that spring. With the pelts selling for $50 to $200 each, Captain L. A. Beardslee thought the 600 to 800 people of Hoonah would be "kept very comfortable from this resource alone."[25]

Like native hunting of big game for the market, the extermination of sea otter throughout most of the animal's range in Alaska in the nineteenth century flew in the face of the Tlingits' "conservationist" practices. It was a dubious legacy, a classic example of overexploitation, what historian Calvin Martin termed in his study of Indians and the fur trade in eastern Canada, "a monumental case of improvidence." Martin assumed that the fur-trading Indian had some knowledge of wildlife population dynamics, that the Indian "was simply too skilled a hunter to overlook the ultimate consequences of wildlife overkill."[26] If this were true, it was indeed a paradox.

The Tlingits, however, had other explanations for the abundance or scarcity of animals. In their view the supply of fish and game depended on how respectfully the hunters treated the hunted animals and how obliging the hunted animals were in return. There is no evidence to indicate that Tlingit hunters anticipated the extermination of the sea otter. While white fur traders could apprise themselves of the annual harvest records maintained by the U.S. Bureau of Fisheries and, more importantly, could comprehend sea otter hunting in a wider context of fur trading on the frontier, Tlingit hunters operated under different cultural assumptions. These ideas persisted up to the waning years of the sea otter trade, as evidenced in a speech by Chief Koogh-see of Hoonah to the Governor of Alaska on December 14, 1898. "We make our living by trapping and fishing and hunting, and white men take all these places away from us; they constantly interfere with us," Koogh-see told the governor.

> Now not very far from where I live is Lituya Bay, where our people, our ancestors, used to go hunting for sea otters and hair seals. Now that place is taken away from us. Great many schooners going there. White camp, they make lots of smoke. That scare animals, sea otters especially. That ground is very good for sea otter hunting. We went up there, 20 or 30 canoes and hunted around all summer and did not get any. The smoke scares the animals away. And when we talk to those

white men they say the country does not belong to us, belongs to
Washington. We have nothing to do with that ground. All our people
believe that Alaska is our country.[27]

In Koogh-see's mind, whites were occupying the land and driving away the
sea otter through ignorance or lack of respect. Wood smoke, not overhunt-
ing, was the cause of the animals' disappearance.

After the sea otter the hair seal was the most valuable marine mammal to
the Tlingits at the end of the nineteenth century. Tlingits sold seal oil in
Sitka for twenty-five cents per gallon and made sealskin moccasins for sale
in the new tourist trade. The meat and oil from the seal accounted for a
large part of the Tlingits' subsistence, especially among the Hunas, who
were renowned for their stealth in the seal hunt. Huna Tlingits sometimes
camouflaged their canoes with white sheets draped over the gunwales. In
the 1920s and 1930s, Frank O. Williams hunted hair seal at every place in
Glacier Bay where the animal was found. Interviewed in 1946, he recalled
how the hunters would lie in their small boats amidst the pan ice when the
ice unpacked in the spring. Albert Greenewald, whose father was German
and mother was Huna, remembered hunting hair seal in Geikie, Tarr, and
Muir Inlets and north of the Beardslee Islands, all in Glacier Bay. In Muir
Inlet there was a pupping ground where the hunters went ashore and killed
the seals by clubbing.[28]

Ethnologist George B. Grinnell described the seal hunters he observed
in Yakutat Bay in 1899. The men hunted in pairs in small, light canoes. The
man in the prow was armed with a gun or spear. After stealing as close to a
seal as they could, the hunters waited patiently until it dived into the water,
then paddled toward the spot and waited for it to surface. If the seal sur-
faced within range and the shot was good, the men would paddle furiously
to reach the animal before its lungs filled with water and it sank.[29]

Grinnell reported that while the men hunted, the women skinned, butch-
ered, and cooked the seal. First they removed the skin and pinkish white
blubber from the carcass. Then, spreading the hide hair-side-down on a
board, the women stripped the blubber by rolling it into one large piece.
They cut the blubber into strips and slowly rendered it into oil in a large
cooking pot. They stretched the hide over a wooden drying frame, and
dried the ribs, flippers, intestines, and other parts of the seal carcass over a
fire. The Tlingits consumed every part of the seal, including the brain.
Grinnell wrote that the seal hunting ground at Yakutat Bay was shiny with
grease and littered with the bleached bones of previous seasons' kills. He
counted some 500 seal carcasses from the current hunt.

While sea otter pelts were the Tlingits' largest commercial crop and hair seal provided them with meat, oil, and hides for sale or their own consumption, it was salmon that formed the mainstay of the Tlingits' subsistence economy. Traditionally the Tlingits fished for salmon near the stream mouths during the spawning runs in early and late summer. They caught most of their fish with traps placed in the stream, weirs built across the stream to obstruct the salmon, gaff hooks, or spears. Each clan house owned a salmon stream, and the head of the house group usually owned a smokehouse in which the salmon were dried during inclement weather. Men caught the fish, and women prepared the fish for smoking or drying. There were numerous smokehouses in lower Glacier Bay, Dundas Bay, and Excursion Inlet where the house groups made their summer camps or sheltered out of the weather during their seal hunting expeditions. There was a custom whereby the leader of a clan house could forbid fishing for a time in order to ensure that a certain number of salmon went upstream to spawn.[30]

Beginning with the construction of the first two canneries in Southeast Alaska in 1878, commercial salmon fishing began to exert a growing influence upon Tlingit culture and land use patterns. Next to their hunting of marine mammals, the Tlingits' involvement in commercial fishing would be the second most important facet of their cultural evolution in relation to their conflict with the NPS over Glacier Bay. It was the rise of the commercial fishing industry in Southeast Alaska that brought out the differences between white and native concepts of land ownership. Although commercial fishing in Glacier Bay itself was not an issue, the industry shaped Tlingit relations with white society and the federal government in the twentieth century.

In the early days of the industry, cannery operators acknowledged Tlingit clan ownership of the various streams by paying the headman of the clan for their use. The canneries procured salmon the easiest way possible, by throwing a few logs across a nearby spawning stream and blocking the salmon run. As the salmon gathered beneath the barricade it was a simple job to dip them out into a scow and transport them to the cannery, although the result could be the extinction of that particular salmon stock. By 1889, when thirty-seven canneries were operating in Southeast Alaska and the total salmon pack had grown to 700,000 cases, the destructiveness of this method became so apparent that Congress passed a law making it illegal to build obstructions in any of the rivers of Alaska for the purpose of impeding the run of salmon to their spawning grounds.[31] This law, the first conservation act in Alaska, was intended to reorient Southeast Alaska's commercial fishery to open-water fishing in order to protect the salmon spawn, but the law also ignored Tlingit claims to the various streams and effectively out-lawed the natives' use of weirs or fences for catching salmon.

For about a decade the Tlingits still fished the streams according to their traditional methods and sold salmon to the canneries directly from their canoes, thus blending their subsistence fishing with some marginal involve-ment in the commercial fishery. Around the turn of the century Tlingits began working alongside Chinese, Filipinos, and Italians in the canneries and with Americans from California, Oregon, and Washington on fishing boats. These activities gradually supplanted their traditional pattern of going to fish camps and berrying grounds for the summer.[32] The wealthier Tlingit men built their own fishing boats and purchased outboard motors and nets on credit from the cannery operators.[33] By World War I, most Tlingit men worked each summer on commercial fishing boats, while a substantial number of Tlingit women and children worked each summer in the canneries. A government study estimated the total Tlingit cash income from the commercial fishing industry in 1913 at $225,000, or about $50 per capita. With the sea otter now practically exterminated, this amounted to 91.5 percent of their total cash income. Conservative estimates of their cash income from other sources were as follows: labor, $10,000; furs, $7,000; basketry, $4,000—a total of $21,000, or 8.5 percent of their total cash income.[34]

Huna Tlingits worked in the canneries at Excursion Inlet, Dundas Bay, and Hoonah and seined salmon in Icy Strait and Cross Sound. Relatively little commercial fishing took place in Glacier Bay. The more time they put into commercial fishing, the less time they had for traditional hunting and gathering in Glacier Bay. Although no hard data exist on levels of resource use for this period, the amount of time that natives spent in Glacier Bay certainly declined in the first three decades of the twentieth century, par-ticularly during the summer season. Nevertheless, many Huna Tlingits continued to use their clan hunting and fishing grounds in Glacier Bay; to maintain their smokehouses; to run their traplines; to gather gull eggs, seaweed, and berries; and, here and there, to cultivate a vegetable garden. The country remained, in their minds, the "Huna breadbasket."[35]

Tourists who visited Glacier Bay in the 1880s and 1890s perceived a radically different landscape. American tourists' enthusiasm for Southeast Alaska's glaciers was a striking example of what historian Alfred Runte has termed "monumentalism" in the development of the national park idea. Nineteenth-century Americans, Runte contends, felt a compulsion to com-pare their country's natural splendors with Europe's famous landscapes and architectural masterpieces. Runte argues that monumentalism influenced how Americans appreciated nature in the nineteenth century and that the latent nationalism in this kind of nature appreciation encouraged the creation of national parks.[36]

Early visitors to Glacier Bay described the scenery on a monumental scale. John Muir boasted that all the glaciers of Switzerland could not equal the immense volume of ice that had so recently occupied Glacier Bay. One tourist compared the face of the Muir Glacier to "a great castle whose towers and turrets had fallen to ruin," another to "the workshops and laboratories of the elder gods." The favorite metaphor for the Muir Glacier was "a frozen Niagara." John Burroughs wrote of the Muir Glacier: "We realized that here is indeed a new kind of Niagara. Probably few more strange and impressive spectacles than this glacier affords can be found on the continent."[37] The comparison is significant given the fact that preservationists in the nineteenth century made the ugly commercialization of Niagara Falls the most notorious example of what could befall the nation's scenic treasures if they were not protected.

By 1890, the Pacific Coast Steamship Company had three vessels, the *George W. Elder, City of Topeka*, and *Queen*, sailing fortnightly from Tacoma and Portland to Southeast Alaska during the excursion season of May through September. By the end of the decade, the Alaska Steamship Company's *Spokane, Dolphin*, and *Olympian* were also visiting the bay. The package tours included a night in Victoria, British Columbia, followed by twelve days on board the steamer. The regular steamship service from Northwest ports to Glacier Bay provided easy access for scientists, and during the 1880s and 1890s no fewer than five prominent scientists in the field of glacial geology made field studies of the Muir Glacier. Their published works increased the area's renown, which in turn brought more tourists.[38] Boosters echoed one another in proclaiming that the grandest sight of all came when the excursionist was brought "face to face with the Muir Glacier."[39]

Tourist accounts often described the thunderous calving of icebergs into the bay as the most memorable spectacle of the whole trip. In the 1880s and 1890s, the Muir Glacier presented an ice wall nearly 300 feet high above the water line and two to three miles across. It was undoubtedly more active then than any tidewater glacier in Glacier Bay today. The biologist C. Hart Merriam recorded the scene in his diary on June 9, 1899:

> We arrived a little before 5 P.M., just in time to see the birth of one of the largest icebergs that ever came off from Muir Glacier. The terrible event began by the fall of ordinary ice masses, weighing perhaps a few thousand tons, which in some way disturbed the equilibrium of other

and vastly larger masses until it seemed as if a great part of the face of
the glacier was sinking into the sea. The huge blocks of ice, 200 f[ee]t
in height above the water and no one knows how thick below, at first
slid & sank gradually, then faster & faster until they shot down with a
thundering roar & disappeared under the water, to reappear and rise
half their height & disappear again, & then dance and roll & finally
shoot into the current to move steadily down the bay. The wave caused
by the first great plunge of the iceberg was one of the most impressive
things I ever saw.[40]

Tourists and scientists alike came in search of the unusual and the spectacular. Not surprisingly, by the time they reached Glacier Bay they gave the
Indians little notice.

This early period of mass tourism in Glacier Bay ended abruptly in
September 1899 when an earthquake shook the Yakutat Bay region, apparently weakening the floating terminus of the Muir Glacier even though
it lay more than a hundred miles from the quake's epicenter. When the
steamships went north the next summer, their captains found Glacier Bay
choked with such a mass of icebergs that they could no longer get close to
the fronts of the glaciers. By the time the upper bay was navigable again
several years later, the steamship companies were marketing sightseeing
excursions to two other tidewater glaciers, the Davidson and Taku, instead.
Scientific interest also shifted from the Muir to these two glaciers, located
east and south of Glacier Bay. This pointed up another difference in the
way whites and natives viewed the landscape; for tourists and even for some
glaciologists, Southeast Alaska's inlets and tidewater glaciers were all so
phenomenal as to be virtually interchangeable with one another.[41]

For one young ecologist named William S. Cooper, however, Glacier
Bay was still without peer as a laboratory for scientific research. Cooper is
central to the story of Glacier Bay because he led the campaign to make
Glacier Bay a national monument in 1922–25. Between this public campaign and his scientific works on the bay, Cooper was as influential as any
man since Muir in shaping the way white people experienced the area.

Cooper made his first trip to Glacier Bay in 1916 — thirty-seven years
after Muir. Yet the two men's connections to the area were much closer
than the passage of time would suggest. Both men were drawn to Glacier
Bay by the combination of its breathtaking mountain scenery and its potential to teach them something about the end of the ice ages in their home
country (the High Sierra for Muir, the Minnesota pinelands for Cooper).
Both men artfully combined careful nature study in the scientific tradition

with aesthetic nature appreciation in the romantic tradition. Both viewed nature study as in some sense a spiritual quest for nature's intrinsic harmony, and both were fervent preservationists. Although Cooper's first trip to Glacier Bay came thirty-seven years after Muir's, the obscuring effects of the 1899 earthquake made Cooper, like Muir, a pathfinder in opening up a wilderness to tourism. And to the ultimate detriment of the area's indigenous people, both men did not really grapple with the native presence in the area. Whereas Muir had portrayed the natives as being out of their natural element and fearful of glaciers, Cooper screened the natives out of his view of the environment entirely.

Cooper traced his love of nature to one boyhood summer with his father in the Blue Ridge and Adirondack Mountains. Later, as an undergraduate at Alma College in Michigan, he began rounding off each year of academic studies with a summer mountain-climbing trip to the Colorado Rockies. With his passion for mountaineering, Cooper's intellectual interests shifted back and forth between the science of ecology and a kind of nature writing, which, according to a friend, was "strongly reminiscent of that of John Muir." Torn between these different callings, Cooper dabbled in graduate studies at Johns Hopkins University, drifted from botany courses into an elementary geology course taught by the glaciologist Harry Fielding Reid, and finally transferred to the University of Chicago by way of another mountain-climbing trip to Colorado. Twice during that year, first while climbing in the Rockies and several months later in Chicago, Cooper experienced chest pains and black-outs, which led him to think that he had a weak heart. Deciding that the strenuous life of a mountaineer–nature writer was not to be his, he set his course on becoming a professor of ecology.[42]

At the University of Chicago, Cooper studied under one of the masters, Professor Henry Chandler Cowles. Cowles' seminal work on ecological succession in plant communities in the Lake Michigan sand dunes had helped establish the new school of "dynamic ecology." The central tenet of dynamic ecology was that plant communities succeeded one another in an orderly, predictable fashion. The process of ecological succession led to a "climax community," or steady state of nature. When an area was disturbed, the process of ecological succession began anew. Cowles discovered a vivid example of this principle on the shifting Lake Michigan sand dunes, where "a pattern of ecological development *in space* paralleled the development of vegetation in time."[43] A person could walk inland from the lake shore and observe, in order, water-tolerant plant communities on the beach, increasing varieties of grasses clinging precariously to the dunes, then pines, and finally the edge of the mature oak forest — a climax community — on the far side. Walking his graduate students vicariously through these dunes in his classroom instruction, Cowles planted a seed that would eventually germinate in Cooper's study of plant succession in Glacier Bay.

After graduating from the University of Chicago, Cooper traveled to the Canadian Rockies and Alaska with his old climbing partner, John V. Hubbard. This trip started him on a search, he later said, "for a situation where vegetational change and development were proceeding so rapidly that they could be studied with fair completeness in the span of a lifetime." The one limitation of his mentor's study of the sand dunes was its reliance on inference rather than direct observation, for the ecological succession on the Lake Michigan shore spanned much more than a single human lifetime. Glacier Bay would provide Cooper with just the kind of rapid ecological succession for which he was looking. Returning to Minnesota, Cooper read about Glacier Bay in the literature on glacial recession and in Muir's newly published *Travels in Alaska*. On his second trip to Alaska with Hubbard two years later, Cooper hired a Juneau boat pilot and went to have a look. It was 1916; Cooper was thirty-two, beginning his second year on the faculty of the University of Minnesota.

Cooper's next action may have been the most influential development in the history of Glacier Bay. Using the previous work of geologists to determine the "subaerial age" of various sites around the bay — that is, the length of time that the sites had been exposed to the air after the ice covering had melted away — he established nine permanent one-meter quadrats of sample vegetational growth. Cooper's intention was to return to the quadrats approximately every five years and plot each one's changing soil and plant composition. These sample plots would test one of the central hypotheses of ecology in that era: that ecological succession in any given climatological environment followed a predictable pattern. Ecological successions were ubiquitous in nature, but most were "secondary successions," proceeding from some local disturbance, such as a forest fire, or a plowed and abandoned field, which left many of the original species still present. The ecological succession occurring in Glacier Bay was what ecologists called a "primary succession." Glacier Bay would become one of the premier outdoor laboratories in the world for studying this phenomenon in its entirety, beginning with the formation of soils and ending with a mature forest. Eventually, perhaps after Cooper was gone, the sample quadrats would reveal the whole story "from pioneers to climax."[44]

The idea of making Glacier Bay into a national park followed naturally from Cooper's work. Cooper's study highlighted the fact that a recently deglaciated basin presented an unusual natural phenomenon, namely, the colonization of a virtually barren landscape by successive communities of plants and animals. From this standpoint, Glacier Bay stood apart from all the other mountain and glacier scenery of southern Alaska. Making Glacier Bay into a national park would not only celebrate this natural phenomenon, it would also protect the area from human actions that could potentially disturb the ecological succession.

Cooper first broached the idea of a national park with his colleagues in the Ecological Society of America in 1922. The Society formed a committee to pursue the idea and appointed Cooper its chairman. Another committee member, Robert F. Griggs, who had worked on the recent campaign to establish Katmai National Monument in Alaska, suggested that they try for the establishment of a national monument rather than a national park, as the former could be created by presidential proclamation while the latter required an act of Congress. There was little other substantive difference between the two designations. Cooper agreed with Griggs and began gathering information and comments from other Glacier Bay scientists and various agency officials.[45]

Cooper's main worry was that many Alaskans and the U.S. Geological Survey (USGS) would oppose the monument because of the area's potential mineral values. In proposing approximate boundaries for the monument, Cooper came up with two alternatives: a larger area that extended from the Gulf of Alaska on the west to Lynn Canal on the east, and a fallback position that included only the basin around Glacier Bay. He noted that the Treadwell Mining Company was prospecting around Lituya Bay on the outer coast, "which might produce difficulties."[46]

The Ecological Society of America also adopted a moderate approach after hearing the committee's report at the next annual meeting in Cincinnati. The Society passed a resolution recommending the establishment of a national monument "for permanent scientific research and education, and for the use and enjoyment of the people." Significantly, the Society claimed that the area was useless for any other purpose; preservation would not impair Alaska's economic growth. The Society sent copies of the resolution to President Calvin Coolidge, the secretary of the interior, the NPS, the Smithsonian Institution, and the governor of Alaska.[47]

The Society's pragmatic, businesslike approach may have been realistic, given the importance of mining in Alaska's economy. A few years earlier, Congress had made unusual provision for mining and prospecting in the Mount McKinley National Park Act of 1917. The Society's statement that the land around Glacier Bay was useless for any other purpose merely echoed the rhetoric of most congressional debate on national park bills. This was a political reality that historian Alfred Runte dubbed the "worthless lands" argument for creating national parks.[48] Nevertheless, the liability of this argument soon became manifest as mining interests requested that geological surveys of the highly mineralized shoreline areas be made before the monument was proclaimed. Mining companies would not undertake this effort for themselves, but they had a powerful advocate in the USGS.

Mineral development was central to the federal government's plan for making the territory of Alaska worth the cost of administration. Following the chaotic years of the Alaska gold rush, the USGS had promoted a more efficient development of Alaska's mineral wealth, fielding a staff of geologists and topographers to assist the mining industry with mineral investigations and surveys.[49] Hardrock mining of gold ore accounted for most of Alaska's mineral production in the early 1920s. By far the largest producer in the territory was the Alaska Juneau Gold Mining Company, whose workings honeycombed Mount Juneau within a stone's throw of the territory's capital. Other mining companies operated on Chichagof and Admiralty Islands south of Glacier Bay, and in the mining districts around Ketchikan and Sitka. In the immediate vicinity of Glacier Bay prospectors had already staked claims on Lemesurier Island in Icy Strait and on Francis Island in the bay itself.[50] When the USGS's Alaska expert, Alfred H. Brooks, heard from Cooper about the proposed monument, he wrote back: "I do not think it is possible or advisable to establish a park in Alaska from which the prospectors are shut out."[51] Brooks sent his man A. F. Buddington to examine Glacier Bay. Buddington talked to prospectors on Lemesurier and Francis Islands. On the basis of their information and a few assays of some quartz veins, he reported molybdenum, silver, and gold in the area.[52]

Meanwhile, the Ecological Society of America's proposal garnered endorsements from several conservation organizations, including an important endorsement from the Council on National Parks, Forests, and Wild Life at its annual meeting in New York on March 4, 1924. The council represented twenty-eight large organizations and many smaller ones, and often came to the defense of national parks by organizing letter-writing campaigns and by lobbying congressmen. Eventually the Ecological Society of America received letters from more than eighty groups reporting that they had conveyed their support for a national monument to the Department of the Interior.[53]

On April 1, 1924 Secretary of the Interior Hubert Work announced that the area around Glacier Bay from the Gulf of Alaska to Lynn Canal was withdrawn from entry pending a study by the Interior Department on the merits of the monument proposal. The withdrawal brought howls of protest from the white citizens of Southeast Alaska. Chambers of commerce in Juneau, Haines, and other towns sent indignant letters to the Coolidge administration. The editor of the *Alaska Daily Empire* branded the withdrawal "a monstrous crime against development and advancement."[54] A handful of homesteaders who had occupied the marshy plain at the entrance to Glacier Bay wrote to the Department of the Interior: "Your petitioners have located their homesteads and toiled for years in anticipation that settlers would gradually enter and develop this great scope of rich farming country." The withdrawal "would blight all such hopes."[55] This latter protest from Alaskan settlers was an unexpected snag. In June, Cooper wrote to the department that parts of the area of the withdrawal could be omitted from the monument if it would otherwise "cause injustice to the settlers."[56]

The man whom Secretary Work sent to survey the proposed monument was George A. Parks. An Alaskan resident and civil engineer for the General Land Office since 1907, Parks had begun his career surveying coal claims and had recently been appointed the assistant supervisor of surveys for Alaska. He would shortly become the territory's next governor. Sensitive to Alaskans' attitudes toward land and the federal government, Parks knew how to recognize potential mineral and agricultural areas when he saw them.[57]

Parks canvassed homesteaders, fox farmers, miners, and foresters about the natural resources contained in the area. His report, submitted in August 1924, consisted largely of an inventory of the area's economic values according to the most optimistic estimates. The boundaries of the temporary withdrawal embraced about a tenth of the land area of Southeast Alaska and practically all of the public domain in that region outside of the Tongass National Forest. Some 4 billion board feet of marketable timber stood along the 600 miles of shoreline. There were numerous islands within Glacier Bay that were suitable for raising foxes for the fur market; some were already developed. The area contained several patented homesteads, mining claims, canneries, fish traps, and native land allotments. The small plain at the entrance to Glacier Bay — an alluvial outwash plain left by the great glacier that had filled the bay less than two hundred years earlier — comprised the only large level area of arable land in Southeast Alaska. The federal government had already surveyed about a quarter of it and was actively "extending wagon roads through this land to aid in its development." The inclusion of this area in the monument would be tantamount to confiscation of these homesteads, Parks argued, because they would be rendered valueless if the community could not grow and obtain schools, transportation links, and mail service.

Parks spoke for prevailing Alaskan opinion when he concluded that the area did not merit preservation as a national monument anyway because human activity could not deface glaciers. Such was the limitation of monumentalism as a basis for preservation. Cooper's more subtle assertion of biological values failed to make much impression. Parks concluded that the "glaciers and other objects of interest," if they must be preserved in a national monument, could be separated from the areas that were "potentially valuable for future development." He proposed a boundary that enclosed the east and west arms of Glacier Bay and the surrounding drainage, but omitted roughly the lower half of the bay and its flanking mountains, as well as the far slopes of the Fairweather and Chilkat Ranges from the mountain crests to the Gulf of Alaska and Lynn Canal respectively.[58]

Cooper made one last appeal for the preservation of some mature forest within the monument. On January 8, 1925, he wrote to the Department of the Interior saying that the Ecological Society of America was "exceedingly desirous" to have an area included on the east side of Glacier Bay "for the preservation of certain features of great scientific interest, and for the provision of a suitable site for future administrative headquarters." This letter succeeded; President Coolidge's proclamation of Glacier Bay National Monument on February 26, 1925 described a boundary that followed Parks' recommendation with the addition of the Beartrack Creek drainage and all the shoreline area between.[59]

The proclamation of the monument was a victory for conservation, even if the monument's boundaries were considerably reduced by compromise. Encompassing 1,820 square miles, the monument was one of the largest areas in the national park system. Together with Katmai National Monument, established in 1918, these two Alaskan preserves redefined the scope of the national monument designation from small areas centered upon archeological ruins or specific geological features to large natural areas that were essentially the same as national parks. Unfortunately, the truncated boundaries of 1925 still left much to be desired. The monument was too far up the bay, rugged, and inhospitable to attract any tourists. Many Southeast Alaskans would later claim that its very existence was soon forgotten. The monument did not encompass the full continuum of postglacial ecological succession, from bare rock at the glaciers' snouts to mature forest along the shores of the lower end of the bay. Nor did it include the rain forest along the outer coast. And while the original proclamation made no concession to mining interests within the monument, an act of Congress in 1936 soon opened the area to mining and prospecting—over the protests of Cooper, the Ecological Society of America, and a large coalition of conservation groups.[60]

What no one recognized or acknowledged in 1925 was that this victory for conservation was a defeat for the natives of Hoonah, whose aboriginal territory and contemporary hunting and fishing grounds extended the full length of Glacier Bay. Neither Cooper and the conservation organizations who led the campaign for the monument nor anyone in the Department of the Interior gave thought to the natives of Hoonah and their seasonal use of the area for food gathering. Parks' report of August 1924 made fleeting reference to native allotments, but that was all. The Bureau of Education, which had jurisdiction over Alaska native affairs at this time, was not consulted and had nothing to say on the matter.

That the campaign for Glacier Bay National Monument virtually ignored the native claim in Glacier Bay was not really surprising. Conservation groups were experienced in battling agricultural, mining, and timber interests, but seldom had they vied for Indian lands. By the time the preservation movement gathered momentum at the turn of the century, virtually all Indian groups in the trans-Mississippi West had been forced onto Indian reservations, having ceded most of their former homelands or lost them in war with the United States. On most of the rugged and scenic lands that comprised the national park system in 1925, several decades had elapsed since local Indian peoples had ceded the lands. There were a few exceptions—portions of Grand Canyon and Glacier National Parks, for example—but most national parks were created from public domain or national forest lands many years after the federal government had extinguished what was known as "aboriginal" or "Indian title." Only in Alaska did the federal government establish national parklands (Mount McKinley in 1917, Katmai in 1918, and Glacier Bay in 1925) *before* extinguishing aboriginal title.

What was more ironic, perhaps, was the fact that Cooper, the Ecological Society of America, and other natural science and conservation organizations summarily dismissed the natives' role in the ecology of Glacier Bay even while they touted the scientific study of ecological succession as one of the major reasons for establishing the monument. The scientists who were familiar with Glacier Bay knew that natives exploited its resources. They knew that aboriginal Indians had occupied the area for a long time—perhaps since before the latest cycle of glacial advance and retreat—and more germane to the problem of ecological succession, they knew that Tlingits had been extracting resources from the area over the past hundred years or more with increasingly potent technology and market incentives. Yet no one addressed the ecological consequences of prohibiting or countenancing contemporary native use of the area. The position taken by the American Association for the Advancement of Science (AAAS) was characteristic of the preservationist viewpoint. Noting the "undisturbed" condition of the coastal forest and regenerative plant growth around Glacier Bay, the AAAS declared that the most suitable purpose for this land was that it be "permanently preserved in an absolutely natural condition."[61] One could infer from the AAAS's resolution and numerous other statements in support of the monument that natives had come and gone in Glacier Bay without leaving the slightest impression on the environment.[62] This was a philosophical incongruity that these conservationists left for a later generation. As with the problem of the native land claim, conservationists' inexperience with Indian lands was telling. Unable to fit native use of the area into their frame of reference, they simply disregarded it.

The natives of Hoonah left no record of their reaction to the creation of Glacier Bay National Monument. It is not even clear that they were informed of it. With their limited command of the English language in 1925, it is conceivable that many Huna Tlingits remained ignorant of the monument, or else assumed that it was of no consequence to them. While federal regulations prohibited the taking of wildlife in national parks and monuments, the NPS gave no indication that it intended to station someone in Glacier Bay to enforce the law. A young glaciologist who chartered a boat in Juneau and explored the monument in the summer of 1926 was told that "in the spring, seal hunters from Hoonah still visited the Bay."[63] Whether these natives hunted seals in ignorance of the monument's existence and the NPS law or in contempt of the NPS's paper jurisdiction is unclear, but they certainly ran no risk of arrest in the 1920s.

In the next decade, the NPS enlarged both the size and significance of Glacier Bay National Monument in ways that, once again, neglected Huna uses of the area. On a clear September day in 1932, an NPS biologist, an official of the U.S. Forest Service, and the chief of the U.S. Biological Survey flew over Glacier Bay, the outer coast, and Chichagof and Admiralty Islands in a seaplane, then returned to Glacier Bay via the Forest Service boat *Forester* for a four-day survey of brown bear habitat. They were there in response to public demand for assurance that the Alaskan brown bear would not be exterminated. Their purpose was to recommend either the establishment of a wildlife sanctuary or national park on Admiralty Island, or an extension of the boundaries of Glacier Bay National Monument.

Debarking from the boat at several points in lower Glacier Bay, Dundas Bay, Excursion Inlet, and elsewhere along Icy Strait, they inspected bear tracks on the beaches and cautiously followed bear paths into the alder thickets and spruce forest. Actual brown bear sightings were limited to one pair ambling across a meadow in Beartrack Cove, but the men found tracks everywhere. The three agency representatives agreed that the boundaries of Glacier Bay National Monument could be redrawn to enclose a large population of brown bears, while Chichagof and Admiralty Islands, thick with bears though they were, lacked sufficient scenic grandeur to make a separate national park.[64]

After lengthy maneuverings between the NPS and the Forest Service, the two agencies finally reached an agreement in 1939 for the transfer of more than 1,000 square miles of land from the Tongass National Forest to Glacier Bay National Monument. In exchange for this transfer, the Forest Service received assurances that the NPS would develop tourist accommodations in Glacier Bay and would oppose the creation of a national park on Admiralty Island, leaving this area to the Forest Service to develop for pulpwood production.[65] Both President Franklin D. Roosevelt and Secretary of the Interior Harold Ickes gave the boundary revisions strong support, the latter visiting Glacier Bay himself in August 1938.[66] On April 18, 1939 Roosevelt signed a proclamation that almost doubled the monument's size, bringing the boundary down to Icy Strait on the south and over the Fairweather Range to the outer coast on the west. It made Glacier Bay National Monument larger than Yellowstone — indeed the largest unit in the entire national park system.

The extension of the monument was a triumph for those in the NPS who were advocating a greater emphasis on biology in national park management. A small but influential number of scientists in the NPS, centered in the agency's Wild Life Division in Berkeley, California, were promoting new approaches to management with a view toward preserving wildlife habitat. The suggestion in the early 1930s that Glacier Bay National Monument might serve for the protection of brown bear habitat gave them their first big opportunity to put their ideas into practice. The Wild Life Division's Dr. Joseph S. Dixon, who had represented the NPS on the interagency inspection of Glacier Bay in 1932, teamed up with the NPS's chief forester, John D. Coffman, who inspected the area himself in 1938, in writing the final proposal that led to the presidential proclamation. The aim of the extension, according to Coffman and Dixon, was to make the monument "into a biotic unit representative of the flora and fauna from the bare glaciers to the mature forests of the seacoast, and with the special purpose in mind of preserving the Alaska bears." The authors listed Alaskan brown bear, three species of grizzly bear, black bear, and the rare "blue" or "glacier bear" as inhabiting the area.[67] They noted other mammal life: mink, marten, ermine, otter, lynx, red fox, wolverine, wolf, coyote, mountain goat, and Sitka deer. The coyote and deer were both recent colonists. Whales, porpoises, and harbor seals could be commonly observed in Glacier Bay and nearby waters.[68]

The strong ecological orientation of the authors was evident too in their forceful recommendation to include the surveyed lands near Point Gustavus where a few homesteads were located. The small amount of farming and stockraising there created competition and conflict between humans and bears. Coffman and Dixon seemed to think these few residents would soon sell their holdings to the government if the surrounding unpatented lands were included in the monument; otherwise, the community and the amount of human-bear conflict might grow.[69]

For all of their concern over habitat, however, Coffman and Dixon still operated within the framework of the NPS's essential mission to provide for the public's enjoyment of nature. In order to make Glacier Bay's wildlife visible to the public, Coffman and Dixon envisioned that the NPS would build a number of boat docks so that visitors could land at selected observation points for "viewing the bears when they are attracted to the salmon streams by the salmon run or for observing and studying other wildlife, vegetation, and glaciers."[70]

There was an incipient conflict here between the desire of the NPS to present tourists with an opportunity to observe bears at close range unmolested by people, and the customary use of the same salmon streams by Huna Tlingits. Both Coffman and Dixon were well aware of native use of the area. In 1932, Dixon had encountered a native family catching and smoking sockeye salmon at Berg Bay and three native families gathering wild strawberries and catching coho salmon on the Dundas River. In 1938, Coffman was informed by the Forest Service's regional forester that natives of Hoonah trapped extensively in the area that he and Dixon proposed as an addition to the monument. Both men observed cabins and smokehouses at the mouths of numerous salmon streams, yet they played down the native presence in their report.

In the first place, Coffman and Dixon distorted the natives' place in the ecology of the area. They well knew that Glacier Bay's brown bear population, together with the salmon stocks that sustained it, were of recent origin; this was a land reborn from the glaciers. It should have been apparent to them that the Hunas, with their adaptation to sea travel, had extended their hunting and fishing territory into the deglaciated basin well before brown bears, walking overland, had recolonized the area. Insofar as the Hunas and the bears were in competition for a limited number of salmon streams, it was inaccurate to represent native families as encroaching on the brown bears' former domain. Yet Coffman and Dixon clearly regarded the fauna as indigenous and the natives as relatively new arrivals — itinerant ones at that. "The Indians come over from Hoonah in late summer and early fall to catch and dry salmon for winter," Dixon remarked in his field notes taken at Point Carolus on September 10, 1932. "This formerly was a good bear stream but is not so good now owing to the presence of Indians." And, later, at Excursion Inlet he wrote: "There is a fine large stream coming into the head of the inlet but we found only old bear tracks. The presence of people here doubtless tends to keep the brown bears under cover."[71]

Coffman and Dixon demonstrated their bias toward the native presence in the way they denigrated native landholdings. While listing at the end of their report several "Indian fish camps" together with one trapper's cabin, two fox farms (one under Forest Service permit, the other not), two white residences (both under Forest Service permit), and two unpatented mining claims, Coffman and Dixon did not venture how the native property would be dealt with. The mere fact that the "fish camps" were placed at the end of a list titled "Other Land Occupancy," this list itself following another list of patented homesteads and approved Indian allotments titled "Alienations," indicates that the authors accorded native use of the area low priority. The authors did indicate that "certainly no trapping can be permitted within a national park or monument, and it will be necessary for the Indians to adjust their trapping areas elsewhere so as to make room for the few who may be excluded from areas used by them in the past within the proposed boundaries."[72] However, there was no discussion of this between the NPS and the people of Hoonah or the Bureau of Indian Affairs prior to the president's proclamation on April 18, 1939.

The NPS was naturally wary of the problems for management that arose when it acquired jurisdiction over a natural area that was pock-marked by private holdings. Inholders had certain legal prerogatives. They could use their land in ways that undermined the public purpose of the surrounding national parkland. Coffman and Dixon recognized that the native families who made customary use of cabins and smokehouses in Glacier Bay did not own property in the ordinary sense that inholders owned property, so they gave them little mind. They did not consider that the Huna Tlingits might have a legal claim based on aboriginal rights.

Coffman and Dixon also failed to see that in stressing inholdings over native property, they were inadvertently creating a false impression of the human record in Glacier Bay. Their appraisal of the native inhabitants' legal standing in the area led Coffman and Dixon and other NPS officials to a false perception of the Tlingits' place in nature. This, of course, was not new. By literary technique, John Muir had misrepresented the natives as being out of their natural element in Glacier Bay, for in Muir's mind Glacier Bay was an uninhabited wilderness. And William S. Cooper and the AAAS had, by implication, dismissed the native presence in the area prior to 1925 as of no ecological consequence. Cooper and the AAAS ignored native resource use for essentially the same reason as Muir had: because they wanted Glacier Bay to be a "pristine" and "undisturbed" preserve for the advancement of science. Now, for its part, the NPS embarked upon its own construction of the natural history of Glacier Bay with much the same purpose: to allow tourists an opportunity to have intimate encounters with wildlife in a natural setting, free of competition from human hunters. In doing so, the NPS began to treat the Tlingits as the ecological equivalent of squatters.

If the NPS had a naive understanding of the native claim in Glacier Bay in 1939, it soon became aware that the problem was much more perplexing than was first anticipated. Standing by its premise that a native presence in Glacier Bay would be contrary to the purpose of the national monument, the NPS maintained that native hunting could only be justified as a temporary expedient, never a permanent feature, of its management of the area. Despite its philosophical certitude, the NPS would still face two insurmountable problems during and after World War II: first, a lack of resources with which to establish any sort of law enforcement in Glacier Bay; and second, a lack of clear title as the Tlingits began to press their aboriginal claim. Meanwhile, the Hunas' place in nature continued to evolve.

A TIDEWATER GLACIER, GLACIER BAY

The glacier terminus floats on seawater, "calving" icebergs into the bay.

(Photograph courtesy W. S. Cooper Collection, University of Minnesota.)

MEMBERS OF THE E. H. HARRIMAN EXPEDITION, GLACIER BAY, 1899
John Muir is on the left.
(Photograph courtesy E. H. Harriman Collection, RBD 0201–74, Alaska and Polar Regions Department, University of Alaska, Fairbanks.)

HUNA SEAL HUNTING CAMP, GLACIER BAY, 1899
(Photograph courtesy E. H. Harriman Collection, RBD 0201–37, Alaska and Polar Regions Department, University of Alaska, Fairbanks.)

VILLAGE OF HOONAH, CHICHAGOF ISLAND, CA. 1900
(Photograph courtesy Case and Draper Collection, NA-2475, Special Collections Division, University of Washington Libraries, Seattle.)

WILLIAM S. COOPER

The plant ecologist from the University of Minnesota headed the movement to establish Glacier Bay National Monument.

(Photograph courtesy W. S. Cooper Collection, University of Minnesota, Minneapolis.)

THE PARK SERVICE'S MV *NUNATAK* IN GLACIER BAY

(John Kauffmann photograph, courtesy National Park Service, Washington Office.)

THE *SEACREST*

The concessioner's first daily tourboat began operating between the Glacier Bay Lodge and the glaciers in 1966. The advent of tourists increased pressure on the NPS to end native seal hunting.

(Photograph courtesy Robert E. Howe Collection, Glacier Bay National Park and Preserve.)

Hair seals are the most abundant large mammal in Glacier Bay. They are a pleasing sight to park visitors.

(Photograph courtesy National Park Service, Washington Office.)

TWO

The Privileged and the Dispossessed

✦

The Hunas' relationship to Glacier Bay after 1939 cannot be understood apart from the efforts of whites to impugn it. When the NPS sent two officials that summer to reconnoiter the monument and inform all residents of the area's new status as a nature sanctuary, the two men found no lack of support among the white population for ending native use of the area. While there was much continuity in the Hunas' relationship to Glacier Bay after 1939, henceforth that relationship would be fundamentally oppositional. It would be under assault not only from the NPS but from local whites who vigorously opposed any native privileges in the area.

Before tracing the evolution of that relationship it would be helpful to summarize the principal arguments of those who believed the Hunas should be prohibited from hunting and trapping in the monument. Taken all together, the arguments formed a devastating critique of Huna land use practices. They went roughly as follows:

1. Natives were integrated into the wage economy and were as prosperous as whites.
2. As native participation in the wage economy had increased, native dependence on wild foods had decreased.
3. Natives' use of modern technology for hunting, trapping, and fishing signified that they had lost their traditional cultural outlook on the natural world.
4. Natives' misuse of modern technology was leading them to exterminate the wildlife.

5. Natives who hunted seals for the bounty scalped the seals and left the rest of the animal to rot, proof that they had lost whatever native conservation ethic they once had.
6. The natives' aboriginal claim was opportunistic and hypocritical. They should not have been allowed United States citizenship and special hunting privileges at the same time.

In recent decades, analyses of Alaska native land use patterns have used a different starting point. Rather than fixing the native culture somewhere along a time line between pre-contact with Europeans and full assimilation, the analysis begins with an inventory of what the community consumes and how it gets it. The term "mixed economy" is applied to those Alaska villages in which a significant number of the inhabitants makes a living both by harvesting wild foods and by earning a cash income. The harvesting of wild foods in this context is called "subsistence." Subsistence is the linchpin in this modern native relationship to the environment.

The most straightforward example of subsistence is when an individual brings home wild plant or animal foods and exchanges or consumes them without ever assigning them a cash value. Subsistence may coexist with wage work, and subsistence foods may be consumed alongside store-bought foods. However, a mixed economy is not simply the existence of one type of economy alongside the other, with households or communities making some sort of division of time and energy between the two. Rather, in a mixed economy the two economic sectors act upon each other so that a new, third system is created. Cash earnings enable the subsistence user to acquire guns, traps, outboard motors, modern fishing gear, all of which increase his harvest capabilities. The subsistence user can then harvest more than he needs for his own use and turn the excess into cash earnings. Some, if not most, cash earnings (whether derived from hunting, trapping, and fishing, or from wage work) are plowed back into the subsistence sector in order to buy and maintain technology — to purchase ammunition, gasoline, engine parts, and so on. Subsistence hunting and fishing, meanwhile, act on the cash sector by allowing the subsistence harvester to engage in wage work only seasonally or intermittently. Most jobs in a mixed economy are part time or seasonal and relatively low paying.

Subsistence is sometimes called Alaska's hidden economy because it is difficult to track and quantify, but much has been learned about this hidden economy in the past decade as researchers have interviewed hundreds of randomly selected heads of households in many Alaska villages. The purpose of these studies has been to assist resource managers in the conservation of fish and wildlife and the prioritization of subsistence over nonsubsistence harvesters.[1]

What is beginning to be recognized today that was not acknowledged in 1940, or even in 1970, is that a growth in cash earnings of a given household or community does not necessarily indicate a commensurate decline in the subsistence sector of that household or community economy.[2] Rising income levels, rather than indicating increasing independence of the household or community from reliance on its subsistence base, may simply indicate increasing dependence of the household or community upon a job base linked to the larger regional economy. This crucial distinction points up one of the most important, if subtle, misconceptions about the mixed economy. For decades NPS and other federal officials in Alaska mistakenly assumed that native harvesting of wild foods would decline as native employment in the wage economy grew.

Officials of the Bureau of Indian Affairs (BIA) and Bureau of Fisheries began to study both halves of Alaska's mixed economy as early as the 1930s and 1940s. The statistical reports from this period are cursory. Some of the data used here pertain to the community of Hoonah, other data to the whole Tlingit population. Nevertheless, they do give a sense of what the Tlingits' mixed economy was like in the ten-year period surrounding the expansion of Glacier Bay National Monument in 1939.

The cash sector of the Tlingits' mixed economy in the 1930s was dominated by seasonal employment on fishing boats and in canneries. In the "Juneau District" (roughly the northern half of Southeast Alaska) in 1935, fifteen canneries paid a total of $149,319.55 to Tlingit seiners (fishermen) and $46,787.09 to Tlingit cannery workers. Among a total native population in the district of 2,444, some 862 individuals worked on seiners and 795 worked in canneries.[3] This meant average seasonal earnings of $172.41 for the seiner and $61.38 for the cannery worker, or combined earnings of $233.79 for a household where the husband worked on a fishing boat and the wife in a cannery, as was often the case. Figures for 1936 were higher: average seasonal earnings of $440.74 for native gill netters, $250 to $400 for seiners, and $64.30 for cannery workers.[4] These earnings were sometimes augmented by sales of foods, furs, and crafts, and bounties paid on hair seal. (Beginning in 1931, the territory of Alaska paid a bounty on seals because they are predators of salmon.) Averaged out over the whole village population, however, these sources of income were small; over a twelve-month span in 1939–40, for example, Huna Tlingits earned $2,955 from seal bounties, or approximately $20 to $30 per household.[5]

A 1938 census of Hoonah provides another glimpse of the Huna Tlingits' mixed economy in this period. The census reported a total population of 832, of whom 734 were Tlingit, 92 white, 2 Japanese, 2 Filipino, 1 Chinese, and 1 Mexican. The standard BIA census form for Alaska natives at the time asked for type and size of dwelling; whether the dwelling was owned or rented; values of the dwelling, household equipment, furniture, personal effects, boats, nets, livestock, dogs, foxes, and other property; and total worth of the household. Most residents lived in small frame houses; a few still lived in clan houses. A majority of Huna Tlingits owned boats, and the boats were generally the most valuable asset. One individual who was representative of the poorer class rented a house, owned $10 worth of furniture, $90 in personal effects, and no boat, for a total household worth of $100. This man was middle-aged with four dependent children. An individual who fairly represented the wealthier class of Huna Tlingits as recorded by this census owned a $2,500 boat, a $1,000 net, an $800 house, and personal effects valued at $1,000. The average total worth of most Tlingit households in the census was on the order of $2,000.[6]

The cash earnings and material wealth of the Tlingits increased significantly during World War II. According to BIA estimates, Huna Tlingits had an average household income of $1,085.35 during 1940–45.[7] In November 1945, the average household earnings of the natives of Southeast Alaska stood at $1,400; the figure given for Hoonah was $1,387. The Tlingits made these economic gains thanks in part to wartime labor shortages and higher wages, and in part to federal loans with which many Tlingit men bought their own commercial fishing boats. As significant as these gains were, however, they were offset by inflation and high costs of merchandise in Alaska and the fact that many of the seemingly most prosperous Tlingits carried large mortgages on their boats. Their income was still far below the average in the United States — $2,406.63 — and even further below the average income of white Alaskans. This underscored the fallacy that natives were integrated into the cash economy and were as prosperous as whites. BIA officials accurately predicted, moreover, that native employment in wage work would drop after the war as discharged servicemen and laid-off war industry workers reclaimed jobs in the commercial fishing industry.[8]

The subsistence sector of the Tlingits' mixed economy was more difficult to quantify. Much of what each house group produced was used or consumed by the members themselves, or bartered or shared within the community. Some products were bartered outside the community. Furs, arts, crafts, moccasins, and other such native products were generally exchanged for cash. None of this "income" was taxed. For purposes of determining each community's needs, the BIA had a standard printed form with which its field agents were supposed to track this "hidden" economy, assigning various items of food and native products an equivalent market value. These sources of "income" were then added to the total wage earnings and welfare payments that together comprised the cash sector of the economy. On this basis, the BIA estimated the equivalent cash value of the Tlingits' mixed economy and the quantities of food that they harvested. A comparison of these official estimates for the two years 1943 and 1945 suggests that the Tlingits' mixed economy was highly variable and difficult to track (see tables 1 and 2). The omissions from and wide variations between these two statistical reports may reflect that a certain amount of guesswork was involved in their compilation. Nevertheless, they provide a sense of the relative importance of different native foods in the subsistence economy.[9]

Table 1: Cash Income of Huna Tlingits, 1943 and 1945[10]

Source	1943 ($)	1945 ($)
Native food products	21,800.00	8,000.00
Furs and hides	—	9,000.00
Moccasins, arts and crafts	2,000.00	1,000.00
Wages	31,720.00	76,400.00
Welfare	9,300.00	6,250.00
Total Income	64,820.00	100,650.00

Table 2: Food Harvested by Huna Tlingits, 1943 and 1945[11]

Native food	1943	1945
Game animals	22,000 lb	30,000 lb
Seal meat	30,000 lb	5,000 lb
Gull eggs	800 doz	—
Berries and greens	30,000 lb	5,000 lb
Seal oil	1,000 gal	—
Fish	60,000 lb*	12,000 lb
Other	—	5,000 lb

*Includes 40,000 lb sold and 20,000 lb for home use.

Walter R. Goldschmidt and Theodore H. Haas, surveying Tlingit and Haida villages in the summer of 1946 to determine their possessory rights, found a mixed economy "compounded of aboriginal land uses and modern industrial practices." They noted that both of these economic sectors were based on exploiting the same natural resources. In terms of food storage and consumption, Goldschmidt and Haas reported that the Tlingits prepared some food "according to the fashion of their forefathers," and preserved other food by modern means in cans and preserving jars.[12]

Goldschmidt and Haas interviewed several Huna Tlingits about the locations where they and their parents or aunts and uncles had harvested these resources during the first quarter of the century. Their report, *Possessory Rights of the Natives of Southeastern Alaska*, stands as the best evidence available of the Huna Tlingits' historical use of Glacier Bay. Their informants described seal hunting practically throughout Glacier Bay and on the outer coast as far north as Lituya Bay, goat and marmot hunting in the upper reaches of Glacier Bay, gull egg collecting on the islands in Glacier Bay, berry picking around the lower sections of Glacier Bay and Excursion Inlet, trapping around Dundas Bay, and catching and smoking salmon at various locations in the monument.[13]

The Huna Tlingits' statements are corroborated in part by records on the issuance of trapping permits maintained by the Alaska Game Commission and by records of bounty payments to seal hunters kept by the Territorial Treasury Office. Three months after the extension of the monument of April 18, 1939, the Alaska Game Commission furnished the BIA with a list of twenty-two trappers from Hoonah whose applications during the trapping season of 1937–38 had indicated trapping locations within or adjacent to the new monument boundary.[14] In 1940, the Territorial Treasury Office prepared a list of bounty recipients whose reported kills were made in or near the monument. The number of seals killed between March 23, 1939 and August 22, 1940 in this area came to 1,463.[15] Trapping and seal hunting constituted grey areas in the Tlingits' mixed economy that involved cash incentives but were nonetheless quite marginal to the cash economy of Southeast Alaska.

The questions would arise: did Huna Tlingits hunt seals in Glacier Bay only for the bounty, how many seals were shot and scalped and their bodies left to rot, and what did that mean about the Tlingits' place in nature? When two investigating NPS officials, Frank T. Been and Earl S. Trager, posed these questions in 1939, they looked at the bounty in proportion to the total cash value of each seal. They learned from seal hunters in Hoonah that the average income from each seal came to $7.50 ($3.00 for the bounty, $2.00 for the hide, and $2.50 for approximately five gallons of oil rendered from the blubber). Been was told subsequently, however, that a seal yielded

about $7.00 worth of oil, and that eight pairs of moccasins could be made
from a seal hide. It stood to reason that once the investment was made in
killing a seal for the bounty, the hunter would be reluctant to take only its
scalp and waste the rest of the animal. Nevertheless, this did happen. One
white resident of Dundas Bay informed Been: "Last fall a Native killed nine
seals in one day up at the head of Idaho Inlet where I was trolling. He
scalped all nine for the bounty, threw eight overboard and ate the liver of
one."[16]

The problem can be approached in another way by comparing the numbers of seal kills reported to the Territorial Treasury Office with the amount
of seal meat and seal oil consumed by the community. Total seal kills recorded by the Territorial Treasury Office are shown in table 3. Bounties
were only paid in the First and Second Judicial Districts, or roughly along
the southern coast of Alaska from Kodiak Island to the southern tip of the
Alaskan panhandle. Most of the bounties were paid in the First Judicial
District (the Alaskan panhandle) for seals taken in the vicinity of Icy and
Chatham Straits. About 85 percent of bounty payments were made to natives.[17] The size of these harvests and the reported concentration of kills in
the vicinity of Icy Strait suggest that natives took thousands of seals in
Glacier Bay — possibly a thousand or more each year. A seal hunter from
Hoonah told Been in July 1940 that many kills reported from Icy Strait
actually came from Glacier Bay.[18]

Table 3: Seal Kills and Bounty Payments, 1931–45

Biennium	Bounty Each ($)	No. of Seals	Amount ($)
1931–1932	2.00	9,981	19,962.00
1933–34	2.00	17,496	34,993.75
1935–36	2.00	19,749	37,499.50
1937–38	2.00	25,000	50,000.00
1939–40	3.00	19,000	60,000.00
1941–42	3.00	25,015	75,031.00
1943–44	3.00	11,702	35,106.00
1945–46	3.00	5,666	17,004.00

These harvest figures certainly had to exceed what the natives consumed.
One seal yields about sixty-five pounds of meat. Based on the surveys of
Hoonah made in 1943 and 1945, the amount of seal meat in those years

represented something like 462 seals in 1943 and 77 seals in 1945. While these estimates could be quite low, they are given some credibility by the fact that the downward trend from 1943 to 1945 correlates with the drop in the number of bounties paid by the Territorial Treasury Office in 1944–45.

Three conclusions about native seal hunting in this period are in order. First, nowhere near all seals killed and collected upon were consumed; many, perhaps most, were taken only for the bounty. Second, the amount of seal hunting done principally for the bounty declined as opportunities in the salmon packing industry improved; bounty hunting was not the preferred occupation. Third, and most important, the amount of seal meat consumed by the community fluctuated with the amount of seal hunting taking place, even though seal hunters were frequently motivated primarily by a need for cash from the bounty. What this suggests is that there was no distinct class of native bounty hunters whose exploits were unconnected to the subsistence sector of the Huna economy; rather, native seal hunters appear to have harvested the whole animal sometimes and taken only the scalp at other times.

In sum, the Huna seal hunter did not view his occupation in the mixed economy as a juxtaposition of old and new elements, but rather as a synthesis of the two. When whites observed Tlingits hunting with rifles and taking only the scalp of the seal for the bounty, they saw a corruption of aboriginal Indian culture, a grafting of the artificial onto the natural in the Indians' relationship to their environment. Huna Tlingits had no such conception of their seal hunting. The hunter might feel better when he took the animal's meat and hide as well as its scalp, but he did not feel ashamed or degraded when he chose to hunt seals for the cash.

Seal hunting and trapping were not the only pursuits in which the Tlingits' traditional subsistence activities became intertwined with the cash sector of their economy. Cannery jobs often determined where Tlingit women and children made their summer camps, and these encampments in turn became centers of native food gathering activity. From 1935 to 1946, several dozen Huna Tlingits lived seasonally in Excursion Inlet, on the edge of Glacier Bay National Monument, where they caught salmon, hunted mountain goats, harvested edible plants, and secured seasonal jobs in the cannery located there.[19] Beginning in 1935, the Astoria & Puget Sound Canning Company in Excursion Inlet paid more than a hundred Huna Tlingit men more than $100 apiece to make dock and building repairs prior to the fishing season and to dismantle the machinery and winterize the buildings when the season ended. On February 24, 1938 the Company wrote an illuminating letter to Spencer Shotter, a Huna fisherman:

For the past few years there have been more natives coming to the cannery each season until we have far more men around the camp than we can work. The union regulations also make it entirely prohibitive to use natives in trap work. We therefore wish to advise you that we will be unable to give you any work at our cannery this spring. We are also not giving out any credit until fishing season and then only to men who have made arrangements to fish on one of the boats that will be seining for us.[20]

In this brief letter can be seen the growing interdependence of the two sectors of Hoonah's mixed economy, as the location, duration, and size of the natives' seasonal camps became tied up with questions of credit, fishing seasons, and union regulations — and subjects of negotiation with cannery operators.

Increasingly, the Tlingits looked to their political leaders to protect their interests in this mixed economy. By 1939, when the NPS began to take an active interest in the protection of Glacier Bay National Monument, the Tlingits had developed a high degree of political organization in the Alaska Native Brotherhood (ANB). Unfortunately, NPS officials gave no more attention to the political aspirations of the ANB than they did to the harvest data for Hoonah. This is hardly surprising; even BIA officials were slow to catch on to the ANB's significance. When the ANB became involved in labor organizing during World War II, BIA officials were finally jolted awake. One senior official informed Commissioner of Indian Affairs John Collier that the actions of the ANB at its annual convention in 1943 had thrown "brilliant shafts of light on various Alaskan issues."[21] If the NPS had been interested in a dialogue with the Huna Tlingits in 1939 it could have started with the ANB. Instead, NPS officials did not even familiarize themselves with the ANB's political program — a program that revealed as clearly as anything how the Tlingits' integration into the commercial fishing industry was subtly changing their stake in the land.

Founded in 1912 by a number of highly acculturated Tlingit men, the ANB owed something of its origins to the influence of the Presbyterian Board of Home Missions in Alaska native affairs in the 1880s and 1890s, but its political agenda developed in line with the trend of federal Indian policy during the Progressive Era and the 1920s. As historian Frederick Hoxie has shown, after the turn of the century politicians and intellectuals developed a more pessimistic assessment of the ability of Indians (and other minorities) to assimilate fully into American society. This led to a reformulation of what they sought by the "Americanization" of the Indian. They came to expect that Indians, like Hispanics, Asians, and the new immigrants from eastern and southern Europe, would enter American society as less than equal partners.[22]

In Alaska, this new formulation was reflected in a spate of bills recommended by President Theodore Roosevelt and enacted by Congress in 1905–9. The overall effect of these acts was to segregate Southeast Alaskan society into a white managerial class and a native laboring class. A bill for the regulation of Alaska's fisheries placed restrictions on the natives' use of fish weirs or wheels near the mouth of salmon streams and limited their use of nets and seines. An amendment of the federal Alaska Game Law in 1908 allowed natives to kill protected animals only "when in need of food." Alaska's school system became racially divided, with a territorial school system for whites and "civilized Indians" placed under the governor's administration, and a new system of native vocational schools set up and administered by the Bureau of Education under the secretary of the interior. A law passed in 1906 authorized the secretary of the interior to grant native heads of households 160-acre homesteads, provided that the allotments contained no mineral claims.[23] The most far-reaching act of the period was the establishment of the Tongass National Forest by three presidential proclamations of August 22, 1902, September 10, 1907, and February 16, 1909. The national forest took in nearly the entire Alaskan panhandle, offhandedly treating the Tlingits as though they were landless villagers. In this evolving political context, Tlingit villages came more and more to function as ethnic enclaves in Southeast Alaska's essentially urban society, while the ANB looked more and more like a working-class fraternal organization.

Initially, the ANB accepted the progressive program of political equality coupled with social and economic segregation. In the early 1920s, the ANB lobbied the territorial legislature for equal education and the right to vote, and on other matters it self-consciously aligned itself with the political demands of white Alaskans. It has been suggested that the ANB's leaders patterned their efforts after the white fraternal organization known as the Arctic Brotherhood, which lobbied strenuously for Alaskan representation in Congress and other reforms.[24] The ANB's "platform," emblazoned on the masthead of its newspaper, *The Alaska Fisherman*, demanded "Alaska for Alaskans / Abolishment of all Fish Traps / Full Territorial Government / One Nation, One Language, One Flag."[25] A parallel women's organization, the Alaska Native Sisterhood (ANS), stressed social issues, and enjoyed a larger membership than the ANB and became its financial prop. The ANB and ANS formed local camps in each of the thirteen primary native villages in Southeast Alaska. Both organizations had elected officers, rules of order, and regular business meetings.[26]

Most of the ANB's leadership were graduates of Carlisle Indian School in Pennsylvania or had attended universities. William Paul, Sr. of Wrangell, whose father was a missionary and mother was Tlingit, and who himself held a law degree, soon emerged as the preeminent leader of the ANB. In the 1920s, he made it his career, holding all of its modestly salaried positions of president, secretary, and treasurer, while editing *The Alaska Fisherman*. At the same time a rival faction developed under the leadership of Frank Peratrovich of Klawock, whose followers objected to some of Paul's nontraditional methods and lack of deference toward elders. This factionalism became a lasting feature of the ANB's political structure, with Paul alternately leading the ANB or being thrust aside by his opposition.[27]

By the end of the 1920s, the ANB had a strong organization with a wide membership. Admission was open to all Alaska natives who professed the Christian faith; members paid $10 to join and $6 per year thereafter. In addition to its lobbying efforts, the ANB offered sick benefits and assistance with funeral expenses.[28] It also sought to wean the separate villages away from their "wardship" under the Bureau of Education. In 1924, for example, it urged the residents of Hoonah to elect a new school board and solve their problems independently of the federal government's Bureau of Education. ANB president William Paul took the position in *The Alaska Fisherman* that since Indians were now citizens, they should pay their fair share of taxes.[29] It was also during this period that the ANB began to lend active support to a bevy of local fishermen's unions in Southeast Alaska. The ANB's members were looking, in short, for an opportunity to make a fair living and to assimilate into American society according to their own terms. In the process, they were crafting a unique cultural identity as working-class indigenes.

This new identity was revealed in the remonstrations of Hoonah's three delegates to the grand camp of the ANB in 1924. They introduced a resolution objecting to the "hasty marriages" that were transpiring between young native women and male Filipino cannery workers who were being brought north by the salmon packing companies. David Charles of Hoonah gave an impassioned speech on the need for his people "to go very slowly" when such marriages were proposed.[30] Not only did these outsiders compete for a limited number of seasonal jobs available to the Tlingits, but they brought no property or kinship ties to the marriage and community. There was, for example, a problem regarding where the family would go to subsistence hunt and fish, since it was the male partner's clan that traditionally provided such ground. Eventually, Huna Tlingits reached an agreement with the local cannery in Hoonah that only natives would be employed there.[31] At the end of the decade, when the cannery in Kake imported 156 Filipino workers to replace native labor, the ANB appealed to the territorial governor to protect their interests.[32] Similarly, when the ANB objected a few years later to the cannery owners' attempts to contract with agents in San Francisco for Chinese laborers, it insisted that the canneries should employ native women exclusively "in the occupations of sliming, table working and machine filing." These were jobs that paralleled the Tlingit women's traditional work of cleaning and smoking salmon for winter storage. The ANB couched its members' economic interests in terms of their rights as an indigenous people.[33]

The desire of the ANB leadership to protect these inherent rights inspired the ANB's most radical demand in this period: its call for the abolishment of all fish traps in Alaska. Fish traps were owned and operated by outside capital, and by the 1920s were so prevalent in Southeast Alaska that they accounted for the largest share of each season's salmon catch. Because they preempted the local fisherman, they were opposed by many white Alaskans, too. Fish traps had long since been abolished in British Columbia, Washington, and Oregon. They were symbolic of Alaska's quasi-colonial relationship with the rest of the nation. It was widely assumed that the only reason Congress and the Bureau of Fisheries put up with the fish traps was because the Seattle- and San Francisco–based salmon packing industry bribed members of Congress and federal officials. For most Tlingits, the ANB's fight over fish traps with the Bureau of Fisheries formed the core of their education in the politics of conservation. But it was not "conservation" in the sense that whites understood the term that led most Tlingits to call for the abolishment of fish traps. Whether the issue was jobs or fish, their goal was to protect their territories from encroachment by outsiders. Most Tlingits opposed fish traps because they believed that they themselves, not the trap owners, should be catching and selling those fish.[34]

Imported workers and fish traps were the most overt threats to the Tlingits' job and resource base, but in the late 1930s and early 1940s the Tlingits reacted in like manner toward the organizing efforts of big labor in Southeast Alaska. Until 1935, labor unions in the Alaskan panhandle had been local and weak and had formed a series of short-lived coalitions. Following passage of the National Labor Relations Act (NLRA) in 1935, the American Federation of Labor (AFL) and the Congress of Industrial Organizations (CIO) began considerable organizing efforts in Southeast Alaska. Tlingit leaders soon decided that the AFL and CIO were working chiefly for white resident and nonresident fishermen, so in 1937 the ANB began collective bargaining work among its member fishermen and cannery workers in Sitka. After an easy success in Sitka, the ANB extended this effort to all its other local camps. Each local camp became a plant unit, which negotiated fish prices, cannery wage levels, and closed-shop hiring practices with the local cannery operators.[35]

In response to a 1940 ruling by the National Labor Relations Board that fishermen did not constitute employees protected under the NLRA, more than fifty Tlingits from Juneau, Haines, Sitka, and Hoonah formed the Alaska Fishermen's Cooperative Association (AFCA). This organization bargained with the cannery operators for fish prices in conjunction with the plant units that were bargaining for cannery wage levels. The AFCA's avowed purpose was "to promote intelligent and orderly marketing of aquatic products through cooperation; to eliminate speculation and waste; to engage in any activity or loan of equipment related to fishing."[36] As a native organization, the AFCA was able to obtain credit from the revolving loan fund established under the Indian Reorganization Act of 1934. Thus, the AFCA served not only as bargaining agency but as creditor, too, for fishermen who required capital for boat repairs and other contingencies. The AFCA was capitalized at $10,000.[37]

Soon after the creation of the AFCA, however, ANB members began to split over whether cannery workers should now seek affiliation with the AFL or CIO after all. The faction led by Frank Peratrovich argued that the ANB should bow out as the bargaining agent for its members, while that led by William Paul contended that most Tlingits would be unable to afford membership dues to two organizations and the ANB would be undermined. The two factions reached a compromise in 1941. The ANB would seek federation with the AFL on the basis of "complete local autonomy." Natives and whites would belong to separate unions but the union cards would be interchangeable.[38] At the ANB's annual convention in November 1943, however, Paul reversed his position once again and pushed for separation from the AFL, claiming that it was trying to destroy the ANB from within. Now Paul was able to marshal enough votes to have the federation with the AFL rescinded.[39]

It was a short-lived victory, however, as the rise of the CIO eventually overpowered the ANB's hold on native fishermen and cannery workers. In 1944, the CIO challenged the ANB's role as a bargaining agency on the grounds that it discriminated against non-native cannery workers. The National Labor Relations Board reviewed the case and upheld the ANB's right to organize workers, since the ANB's constitution allowed associate membership to non-natives, but in 1946 the CIO succeeded in affiliating with two other Southeast Alaska labor organizations, the Alaska Purse Seiners' and Cannery Workers' Union and the Alaska Marine Workers' Union, which then merged with the CIO-affiliated Alaska Fisherman's Union. In 1947, the ANB resolved at its grand camp meeting in Hydaburg to end its bargaining agency role. Although the longtime ANB president, William Paul, had feuded with the rival faction for years over this issue, he recognized that the ANB was losing its hold on native union members anyway.[40] So ended the ANB's ten-year involvement in labor organizing.

If they had looked into it, NPS officials might have recognized that the ANB's role in collective bargaining said a great deal about the Huna Tlingits' changing relationship to the land. The thirteen ANB locals represented the thirteen primary Tlingit villages, or "kwaans." These kwaans were the traditional social and political groupings of the Tlingit people. Each kwaan possessed well-defined fishing and hunting territories. Thus, the ANB's local plant units and the ANB's grand camp mediated between the Tlingits' stake in the local natural resources and their interest in the larger economy. The purpose of the plant units was largely territorial — to protect the natives' interest in the fish resources that were harvested locally and found their way to the fish processing plants — but it was also assimilative — to strike a bargain with the cannery operators that would induce them to maintain their operation in or near each village and employ native labor. Collective bargaining constituted a "seam" in the Tlingits' new cultural outlook, a seam between their identity as indigenes with aboriginal rights in the land, and their identity as working-class members of a capitalist society.

Although it was not immediately apparent to them, NPS officials had good reason to concern themselves with all of this. In 1929, the ANB voted to pursue aboriginal land claims against the federal government. In 1935, it won an initial success when Congress passed a jurisdictional act authorizing the "Tlingit and Haida Tribes" to bring suit against the United States in the U.S. Court of Claims.[41] The substance of the Tlingit and Haida Indians' case was that the federal government had never extinguished their aboriginal title to the land. The proclamations that had set aside practically all the land area in the Alaskan panhandle as the Tongass National Forest had dispossessed the Indians without due compensation. The management of the fisheries in Southeast Alaska likewise failed to acknowledge aboriginal rights. While the presidential proclamation of April 18, 1939 purported to transfer land from the Tongass National Forest to Glacier Bay National Monument, the Tlingits did not see it that way. Indeed, given the national

monument prohibition against hunting, it was the most overt act of dispossession in their experience.

NPS officials failed to consider that native use of the area might involve a
tribal claim. They glibly assumed that white homesteaders and mineral
claimants in the monument addition would pose greater difficulties for
them than the natives who made only seasonal use of the area. They accepted the Forest Service's characterization of the native presence in the
area. "Various individuals or families among the Indians" claimed ownership of certain places in the monument addition, wrote one Forest Service
official. Arthur E. Demaray, a longtime associate director of the NPS,
passed this information on to Commissioner of Indian Affairs John Collier
two weeks after the president's proclamation, with the blithe suggestion
that native trappers in the area might be compensated by "reasonable adjustments" of native trapping territories elsewhere.[42] About the same time,
the NPS issued instructions to Frank T. Been, superintendent of Mount
McKinley National Park and now coordinating superintendent for Glacier
Bay, to inform all residents of the area that hunting and trapping by all
persons, including natives, was prohibited in the monument. This the superintendent did as he and chief naturalist Earl A. Trager made a thorough
inspection of their new jurisdiction by boat in the summer of 1939.[43]

The BIA was caught unawares by the president's proclamation. "Obviously, this Office should have been consulted before the Department
approved the extension of these boundaries," Assistant Commissioner
William Zimmerman, Jr. wrote to the BIA superintendent in Juneau. He
continued:

> Now that the extension has been made, what should we do? Can
> trapping areas be set aside elsewhere for these Indians? How impor-
> tant to their livelihood are the trapping privileges of which they will
> otherwise be deprived? I shall appreciate a full report.
>
> Although I am annoyed that this Office was not consulted before the
> damage was done, I have no desire to make trouble for the NPS in the
> administration of this area, unless the fishing and hunting privileges
> are vital to the particular Indians effected.[44]

BIA officials made no effort to include Huna Tlingits in the discussions
that followed. Some time toward mid-October, NPS and BIA officials held
a conference in Zimmerman's office and agreed on some preliminary arrangements. The natives were to be permitted continuance of "normal use"
of the wildlife in the monument, with "normal" being defined as the use

they had made of wildlife resources in the area during recent years. This information was conveyed to Superintendent Been at Mount McKinley, who informed the Hoonah school teacher, Wendell Cordle, of it by radiogram on October 31. Four weeks later, on November 27, Cordle sent a radiogram to his superior in Juneau asking for clarification — Been's radiogram had authorized hunting but was silent about trapping. In Juneau the BIA's Charles W. Hawkesworth consulted with the Alaska Game Commission and advised Cordle by radiogram on November 28 that trapping was permissible, too. Hawkesworth at the same time requested a reaction from Been. Been communicated directly with Washington, D.C., soliciting a letter from Director Arno B. Cammerer on December 1 that would serve to clarify the arrangement. According to Cammerer, he and Zimmerman had not intended to extend the natives' privileges to trapping, for they were assuming that "the principal use by the natives has consisted in the taking of hair seals and the collecting of gull eggs."[45] In all of this correspondence, no one suggested that the people of Hoonah should be consulted directly.

It is evident from these communications that both the BIA and the NPS continued to view the problem as something that concerned "various individuals or families among the Indians" rather than a tribal claim. Even when Superintendent Been visited Hoonah in August 1939, he consulted the white school teacher and a few Tlingit seal hunters but held no meeting with Huna Tlingit representatives or the village at large. In the director's communication to Been, Cammerer noted that Zimmerman thought some compensation would be "desired for the Indians if they [were] deprived of any of their former privileges." He also directed Been to inform Cordle that the NPS had "no intention of making any sudden change in the uses which the Indians [had] been accustomed to make of the monument area." The arrangements were temporary "until a definite wildlife policy [could] be determined upon the basis of a field study and a substitute source of income [could] be provided for them."[46]

During the winter of 1939–40, two or three whites who resided in Dundas Bay, within the national monument, began protesting the natives' privilege. This concerned NPS officials, who were anxious not to prejudice local white opinion against the NPS any more than it already had been. In fact, the NPS director instructed Been to give the natives' privileges "as little publicity as possible," in the vain hope that they would go unnoticed by local whites. These instructions soon put Been in a predicament, as Dundas Bay residents Horace Ibach and William Horsman both inquired whether they might be hired by the NPS to serve as rangers in preventing native poaching in the area. Been's fumbling replies to Ibach and Horsman only confirmed their suspicions that the NPS had adopted a discriminatory policy toward whites living in the monument.[47]

The white backlash against the NPS was not confined to Dundas Bay. In April 1940, the Alaska Game Commission's executive officer, Frank Dufresne, met with officials of the NPS and the Biological Survey and questioned whether the privileges accorded the Huna Tlingits were legal. Dufresne alleged that Tlingits sometimes took eider duck eggs in violation of the Migratory Bird Treaty Act, and he noted that the natives' hunting privilege gave them an unfair advantage over whites in hunting seals for the bounty. This, Dufresne warned, would sow racial discord between local whites and the natives of Hoonah.[48]

Although the situation demanded clarification one way or the other, NPS director Arno B. Cammerer's plan to send his chief biologist to the area in the summer of 1940 and formulate a wildlife policy was never implemented. Drastic cuts in the NPS budget during World War II prevented the agency from fielding a biologist in Glacier Bay until the summer of 1945. In the meantime, local whites interpreted the NPS's indecision as their cue to run the natives out of the area themselves. Huna Tlingits complained that their seasonal cabins were smashed and posted with "Keep Out" signs and that they themselves were driven back to their boats by gunshots on more than one occasion.[49] Most of this vigilantism remained anonymous, while the natives' charges remained vague, only surfacing in 1946 when two BIA officials conducted interviews in the village in connection with the Tlingits' aboriginal claims. One incident involved two old natives who lived on Drake Island in Glacier Bay where the Dakdentan clan had a fort and palisade. It was alleged that a resident fox farmer ran the old couple off the island, tore down these structures, and afterwards insisted that the government had given him permission to do these things.[50] Another incident involved a "white man named Wright" in Dundas Bay who allegedly chased Fred Lawrence out of the area with a gun.[51] More incidents were reported to Assistant Secretary of the Interior William E. Warne when he visited Hoonah in 1948. Hoonah's mayor seemed to hold the NPS accountable for this dismal record during the war.[52]

NPS officials were not blameless. Superintendent Been wrote to Dundas Bay resident William Horsman on November 22, 1939, three weeks *after* he was informed that native hunting would be permitted in the area:

> Because you are living in the area the simple expectation is felt that you will want to see that the area is not misused or exposed to damage by others. There is no expectation that you will be held responsible for

damage to the area, but your interest and assistance is requested to help protect the area as any citizen would want to do. Should instances of misuse or damage come to your attention we shall appreciate being notified. Your judgment must dictate the extent to which you may go to remedy personally a possible unsatisfactory situation.[53]

Incredibly, Been wrote these broad instructions to Horsman without informing him of the natives' privileges in the area. He must have had second thoughts about sending Horsman what was virtually a directive to keep natives out of the area, because he related all of his correspondence with Horsman to the NPS director on January 4.

Horsman thought he ought to have a commission, and wrote to various officials seeking a ranger appointment. In April 1940, NPS Biologist C. P. Russell recommended to the director that Horsman be appointed a ranger or custodian for the protection of wildlife in the area, describing him as "a man of fine character, law-abiding and sincerely interested in preserving the country from destructive uses."[54] A month later, embittered and impatient, Horsman wrote to Been:

I lost good, seven hundred Dollars by not being allowed to trap here this past winter, and I don't think that it is right for me to protect this place now, and have someone else get the benefit for it, as they sure will sooner or later, for someone will come in here and make a cleaning, and as long as you leave this place lay as it is now, I think that the people that live here should be allowed to hunt and trap as they have in the past years, and when you start to make this place a Park (if you ever do) then is the time to stop hunting and trapping.[55]

Meanwhile, it was Horsman's neighbor, Stanley "Buck" Harbeson, who took it upon himself to patrol the Dundas Bay area. A game warden remarked that Harbeson had "instilled a healthy respect for the law in many would-be poachers in his vicinity, and has acquired a reputation among the Indians of the Icy Straits area, that is legend."[56] In 1948, the NPS custodian in Sitka, Grant Pearson, was more blunt when he reported that Harbeson had allegedly sent several parties of natives "on their way at the point of a gun." Added Pearson, "If that is true, he is undoubtedly an asset to that area."[57]

If NPS intentions were fickle, the Fish and Wildlife Service (FWS) made its intentions plain when the two agencies entered a cooperative agreement for the patrol of monument waters at the end of 1944. Clay Scudder, the

head of the FWS office in Juneau, advised two Huna Tlingits that if any
man were caught in Glacier Bay with traps on his boat, even if hunting hair
seals, the traps could be confiscated and the owner fined. Moreover, traps
that were stored in the natives' cabins within the monument would be
confiscated.[58] The following winter, a game warden caught Peter Austin,
James Grant, and Robert Carteeti, all of Hoonah, in the act of setting traps
in the monument. The FWS confiscated eighty-seven traps. The men were
tried in the U.S. Commissioner's Court in Juneau on March 29, 1946 and
fined $50 each. A native of Yakutat was arrested that January for trapping in
the coastal rain forest near Lituya Bay and prosecuted.[59]

With this action (ironically, taken by the FWS) it soon became clear that
the NPS had overplayed its hand. Secretary Ickes was informed of the
arrests by the BIA superintendent in Juneau, and NPS officials in Washington, D.C., received copies of a long, impassioned statement by Frank
Sinclair, a 65-year-old Huna Tlingit, who said that the arrests had made
him fearful to visit his own family homestead in Berg Bay.[60] Most importantly, two BIA officials — the bureau's Chief Counsel Theodore H. Haas
and an anthropologist, Walter R. Goldschmidt — arrived in Hoonah that
summer to investigate the Tlingits' aboriginal claims in the area. Both of
them sympathetic listeners, Goldschmidt and Haas found the residents
eager to talk about "their summary expulsion" from Glacier Bay.[61] It was
only in the aftermath of this visit by Goldschmidt and Haas that the record
of vigilantism in the monument during World War II began to come out.

The report by Goldschmidt and Haas, *Possessory Rights of the Natives of
Southeast Alaska*, finally alerted the NPS to the fact that the Huna Tlingits
had a tribal claim in Glacier Bay National Monument.[62] The report defined
three key areas in the monument where the Huna Tlingits could claim
"possessory rights," and placed most of the monument within the area of
their aboriginal claim. After reading the report, NPS Chief Counsel
Jackson E. Price advised the director that the natives' possessory rights
appeared to be a matter of "primary importance," and that the NPS needed
to stay abreast of "future deliberations by the Department . . . to the end
that our interests will not be overlooked."[63] With this report, NPS officials
contemplated the possibility, however dolefully, that native subsistence use
might become a long-term feature of Glacier Bay National Monument.

Following a meeting of BIA and NPS officials in Washington, D.C., on
December 10–11, 1946, a memorandum of agreement was drafted and
endorsed by both agencies on December 18 of that year. Neither was the
agreement nor were the minutes of the meeting preserved in NPS files, but
the gist of the agreement was contained in a letter from the BIA's Walter V.

Woehlke to Director Drury on December 16, 1946.[64] "After considering the needs of the Natives in relation to the existing regulations and the problems of law enforcement, the following recommendations were advanced for your consideration," Woehlke wrote,

1. That the carrying of firearms for human protection be allowed under permit within the Monument during the berry-picking seasons, the procedure for the issuance of firearms to be worked out.
2. That the Natives be permitted to hunt hair seals from the shore within a distance of not to exceed 100 feet from the water line.
3. That these modifications of the Park Service regulations shall continue in effect until 1950 at which time the Park Service and the Indian Service will review the Glacier Bay Monument conditions to determine whether the facts warrant a continuation of the practices or their modification.

NPS officials would later try to characterize this agreement as a temporary expedient, made in light of Hoonah's dire economic situation after World War II. The village had had its worst fishing season in twenty years, and Hoonah's clam cannery had been closed down by the Pure Food and Drug Administration that summer when toxins were found in the clams. This interpretation of the agreement suggested that the Huna Tlingits must demonstrate economic need each time the agreement came due for reconsideration, but this was a deliberate misreading of the circumstances surrounding the agreement. First and foremost, BIA officials had impressed upon the NPS director the likelihood that the Huna Tlingits did indeed have possessory rights in Glacier Bay National Monument.

No sooner than Drury had made the agreement did his subordinates try to get him to lay the groundwork for its reversal. Major Owen A. Tomlinson, who headed the NPS's western regional office in San Francisco, put the matter tactfully but forcibly in a letter to his boss that spring. "While we admittedly are not familiar with what pressure may have been exerted to bring this action about, we are frank to say that we believe the subject is worthy of further consideration," Tomlinson wrote. "It is probably too late to rescind the decision without embarrassment, but we believe a thorough investigation of the situation should be made before the agreement is extended beyond 1950."[65] Three of Tomlinson's staff—regional naturalist Dorr G. Yeager, landscape architect A. C. Kuehl, and biologist Lowell Sumner—convinced him that the allowance of firearms in the monument would endanger the seal population as well as the monument's population of mountain goat and bear. Sumner and Kuehl each had some firsthand knowledge of the area and a reel of movie footage of the seal herds from brief trips in 1945 and 1946. Tomlinson directed Sumner to study and report back on the native hunting privilege in Glacier Bay the next summer.

Sumner's cursory investigation and report of August 5, 1947 displayed the NPS's strong predisposition to ban native hunting in the monument. Sumner's few days in Glacier Bay in late June allowed only a brief appraisal of the effects of native hunting and egg collecting on the animal populations in the monument, much less a reliable assessment of population sizes and trends of the various species that most concerned the NPS. The biologist probed into the inlets of the upper bay in search of hair seals, scanned the slopes of Mount Wright for mountain goats, and landed on North Marble Island to inspect bird colonies. His contacts with Huna seal hunters were minimal. His report contained a scant seven pages of text. Nevertheless, it was a strongly worded condemnation of the present policy. Tomlinson gave Sumner's report his full support. In a cover letter to Drury he wrote, "We have considered this question carefully and have completed a study of the biological problems involved." Kuehl jotted on the file copy, "Excellent report."[66]

The report was, in fact, flawed in many respects. Sumner's biological assessments were weak, drawing conclusions about animal population trends based on ludicrously inadequate field data. "The National Park Service inspection party of 1947 made a special effort to count the seal population of Glacier Bay," Sumner wrote, "but only a dozen were found, as compared with the scores observed at close range the preceding year. The animals were much wilder and more secretive than previously." Not only did Sumner draw hasty conclusions from this "count," but he implied that changes in the seals' observed behavior from one year to the next demonstrated increased hunting pressure. Sumner made similarly cavalier judgments when he inspected glaucous-winged gull rookeries on North Marble Island. "Great crowds of gulls stood at empty nests," he wrote afterwards, "displaying the listlessness that characteristically settles upon a bird colony a few days after it has been robbed." Noting that he had observed not one mountain goat where goats had been conspicuous in past years, he wrote: "it is likely that some seal-hunting natives, knowing themselves to be completely unsupervised, are in the habit of adding the mountain goats of Mt. Wright, which borders Muir Inlet, to their meat supply."[67] This judgment ignored the fact that wolf predation on mountain goats was known to have increased in the area.[68]

Sumner did not limit himself to biological assessments, but reserved his strongest opinions for the section of his report on "Aboriginal Hunting Territory and Customs of the Natives." Sumner reached two conclusions. In the first place, he maintained that the Indians' aboriginal claims to the present seal hunting grounds in Tarr, Johns Hopkins, and Muir Inlets were fallacious, because these areas had been glacier-covered and inaccessible "to the remote ancestors of the Hoonah Indians."[69] Sumner recognized, of course, that seals congregated on icebergs at the fronts of glaciers, and that seal hunting grounds of one hundred or two hundred years earlier in Glacier Bay now consisted of open water far from the glacier fronts and were therefore now devoid of seals. Nevertheless, he argued that the NPS could legitimately prohibit seal hunting in the critical habitat areas at the upper end of the bay, since these areas were definitely not the same geographic areas where natives had hunted seals in earlier times. This was a completely faulty exercise of logic, yet Tomlinson found the argument persuasive and Drury took it under advisement when Sumner explained it to them both at a regional office staff meeting in July of 1947.[70] Sumner did not address the fact, if he was even aware of it, that Goldschmidt and Haas had indicated that Huna possessory rights ought to extend the full length of Glacier Bay.

Sumner's second conclusion about aboriginal rights in the monument was that their valid exercise ought to depend on the continued use of aboriginal hunting technology. "In aboriginal times," Sumner wrote, "native hunters traveled slowly and with effort in giant war canoes hollowed from spruce tree logs. They hunted with bows and flint or bone-tipped arrows. Today the native hunters travel swiftly and easily over long distances in modern gasoline or diesel-powered fishing boats, and shoot the seals with high-powered rifles." Sumner ignored the historical continuity that underlay Tlingit cultural change and the fact that few Tlingits would have agreed with his argument that they had "forsaken their ancestral way of life."[71]

Sumner also questioned the importance of Glacier Bay seal hunting in the Huna economy. "The natives today," he wrote, "depend neither upon seals nor berries for their living. Fishing and trapping are their principal sources of revenue and these activities are carried on with the same modern equipment, and on the same commercial basis, as is done by the whites." This was a legitimate concern inasmuch as the BIA had argued the case for special hunting rights partly in light of the Huna Tlingits' short-term economic hardships in 1946. However, Sumner failed to acknowledge that this was not a biological but rather a sociological issue, in which the focus shifted from animal populations to the Huna economy. He was quick to jump to conclusions, mistakenly assuming, for example, that the natives' use of glass fruit jars indicated that they no longer preserved wild berries in seal oil.[72]

Sumner's report was influential within NPS circles. In Washington, D.C., NPS officials consulted the FWS and the Alaska Section of the Division of Territories and Island Possessions on a way to rescind the agreement. The following January, Assistant Director Hillory A. Tolson informed Tomlinson that the NPS would recommend to the secretary of the interior that the agreement be rescinded on two grounds. "We would cite the depletion of hair seals as observed by National Park Service employees during the summer of 1947 and we would also point out that the natives have been observed in the act of infringing on the privileges which have been extended to them in the Monument." One of these infractions was the possession of traps, for which three Huna Tlingits were arrested back in March 1946; the other was the bearing of a nonregulation .22 caliber rifle by a native, reportedly identified by Sumner on June 25, 1947, as the native boarded his boat in North Sandy Cove and sped away.[73]

The sad lesson in all of this was that NPS officials framed their analysis of the problem so narrowly that the natives' seal hunting privilege was soon reduced to a matter of law enforcement. No one in the NPS even touched on the possibility that by eliminating the indigenous people from Glacier Bay, the NPS was itself altering the natural conditions. They merely assumed that the land would be better off if the wildlife was afforded full protection from hunting. This assumption harkened back to the early years of the NPS, when predators were shot in order to make the deer and the mountain goats thrive. By the late 1920s, biologists figured out that this was a short-sighted policy because predators actually played a vital role in controlling the populations of prey species, preventing them from overrunning their food supply. In 1931, NPS Director Horace M. Albright announced that the NPS would no longer eliminate predators in national parks; henceforth the NPS would protect all wildlife.[74] Now a similar shift of thinking was needed for Glacier Bay. NPS officials needed to consider how the land might be affected if the government drove out the human inhabitants in one area and forced them to make so-called "reasonable adjustments" of their traplines and fishing places in another. But to pose that question would require a shake-down of some of the basic premises of national park management.

The NPS's nine-day field study of the ecological consequences of native hunting in Glacier Bay might have been compared with its excellent two-year field study of the wolf in Mount McKinley National Park by Adolph Murie in 1939–41. In that study, Murie sought to situate the effects of wolf

predation on Dall mountain sheep within a complex web of other predator-
prey relationships and historical and environmental factors influencing
the park's fauna.[75] The marked contrast between these two investigations,
which NPS officials studiously ignored at the time, shows the bias with
which NPS officials approached native hunting — even from a supposedly
objective biological perspective. The comparison also suggests that the
inadequacy of the Glacier Bay study could not be attributed solely to bud-
getary constraints.

Drury highlighted the need for wildlife protection and law enforcement
in Glacier Bay National Monument in his annual report of the NPS for
1949. In the spring of 1950, he suggested to Tomlinson that a wildlife
investigation of the monument was "long overdue," and asked whether
Murie, who was again working in Mount McKinley, could be assigned to it.
Tomlinson answered that Murie was unavailable until perhaps the following
summer, but a seasonal ranger could provide valuable information in the
interim. Consequently, the western region scrounged together $8,000 with
which to reassign one seasonal ranger from Yosemite to Glacier Bay for the
summer of 1950.[76] Ranger Duane Jacobs's sojourn in Bartlett Cove that
summer represented the first on-site administration of Glacier Bay National
Monument. With this assignment, the NPS's approach to native hunting
definitely shifted from biological investigation to law enforcement.[77]

Ranger Jacobs's report at the end of the season presented much evidence
of poaching. With the assistance of FWS warden Lynn Crosby and an
FWS boat, Jacobs spent approximately half his working days patrolling
monument waters and investigating trapper cabins around Excursion Inlet
and Dundas Bay, where deer heads, goat feet, and other scattered refuse
showed that the cabins had been recently occupied for hunting and trapping. On one occasion while patrolling Dundas Bay, Jacobs and Crosby
heard rifle shots and tried to intercept eight natives in an outboard as they
returned to their fishing boat from the shore. The natives reached the boat
first and as Jacobs and Crosby pulled alongside, one of the natives planted
himself squarely on top of the pilot house. Jacobs spied a seal hide and a gun
before they had been fully stowed, but he was too unsure of his authority to
try to board the boat without a search warrant.[78]

Jacobs consulted the office of the Federal Bureau of Investigation in Juneau regarding jurisdiction for natives charged with a felony and the likelihood of obtaining convictions for natives charged with a misdemeanor. "It
was generally agreed that violators should be prosecuted in Juneau if possible," Jacobs reported, "in order to keep them away from the native officials
in Hoonah, where our chances of securing convictions and penalties would

be greatly lessened." To protect the monument adequately, Jacobs concluded, the NPS would need either a float plane or a small force of rangers working in pairs and equipped with fast boats, and the rangers would need authority to board boats without search warrants, because it was generally necessary to seize items for evidence in order to prosecute Game Law violators.[79]

However, senior NPS officials had no intention of staffing the national monument with a force of rangers when there were, as yet, no tourists in the place. Nor did they seek a four-year review of the agreement with the BIA in 1950. Instead, in the absence of a better idea, NPS "policy" was to establish a token administrative presence in the monument in the hope that native use of the area would just fade away. Following the short tour of duty by Jacobs in 1950, Ranger Oscar T. Dick drew the first permanent ranger assignment in Glacier Bay in 1951. It was an unusual post: one man, half a million acres. Duty-stationed in Sitka, Dick made six patrols of monument waters on the NPS boat, M/V *Nunatak*, between June and October. In the course of the summer, he issued warnings to two Huna crab fishermen who were using seal carcasses for bait. In the second incident Dick told the man, Ed Metjay, that it was now illegal for Huna Tlingits to take seals within the monument. Metjay reportedly responded, "You pay me, I no shoot." When Dick went to Hoonah for supplies a few days later he found "the entire town up in arms." People told him that they thought "the permit allowed them to hunt for all time." Dick's supervisor, Ben C. Miller of Sitka National Monument, figured that the Huna Tlingits were "aware of the expiration date of the permit," and that this assertion was "one of the many alibis" they would use when caught.[80] Nine days after Dick sent his report to the regional office in San Francisco, word came back from Washington, D.C., that the natives' privileges had not expired at the end of 1950 after all — they were only awaiting review.[81]

NPS officials would later infer that native use of Glacier Bay waned in the 1950s, that the NPS administrative presence was an effective deterrent to poaching, and that the NPS had time on its side because the younger natives showed less desire for seal meat and seal oil. Their best evidence was the shrinking number of permits that Huna Tlingits requested after the NPS instituted a permit system in 1954. But the shrinking number of permits could just as easily indicate a declining spirit of cooperation on the part of the natives. As one exasperated superintendent wrote in 1953, "The old axiom that 'no law is worthy of a place in the statutes unless it can be enforced' applies very well in this instance."[82] Putting rangers in the natives' way only tended to make the natives' use of the area clandestine. The natives hunted seals in the fall and spring when the rangers were not on patrol. They ceased stopping at the ranger station in Bartlett Cove to register for a permit. By the time Glacier Bay National Monument finally began to attract a few adventuresome tourists at the end of the 1950s, the NPS had only created a worse problem for itself. The natives of Hoonah still had their special privilege to hunt seals and gather food in the monument, but the NPS had no idea of the dimensions of that use. Instead, there was mutual suspicion and resentment on both sides.[83]

THREE

Fallen Indians

✣

In early March of 1964, Chief Ranger David B. Butts set out with his assistant on the first patrol of the new year up bay. The ranger staff's single patrol boat was a seventeen-foot outboarder; its modest size restricted routine patrols to fair-weather conditions and a maximum range of about thirty miles from the monument headquarters at Bartlett Cove. On this occasion the rangers headed for Muir Inlet, curious to see what remained of a camp on Garforth Island that had been occupied by two native hunters from May through October of the previous year.

Approaching the edge of the pan ice near the entrance to Muir Inlet, the rangers watched as numerous hair seals scrambled off the ice at the sound of their engine. Still nearly a mile away, the seals appeared as so many black specks on the white ice. Butts had never before observed such wariness on the part of the seals and assumed it was because the animals had been hunted from a boat the previous year. When the two men drew closer to the shoreline, they caught the stench of partially decomposed carcasses wafting on the chill breeze. Once ashore, they inspected the refuse left by the past season's hunt: backbones and rib cages picked clean by shore birds, rotting entrails twisted and scattered by the tides, skinned seals lying pink and glassy-eyed on the rocks. Butts stood amidst this animal wreckage and stared grimly into the camera as his partner snapped pictures of the devastation. According to a photo caption, the scene extended along a stretch of beach for nearly two miles.[1]

Altogether, 243 seals were reported killed by the native hunters. Butts and others on the staff at Bartlett Cove reacted to the large hunt of 1963 with dismay. Many felt a visceral response to the slaughter that was proba-

66

bly akin to the emotions that coursed through John Muir when, back in 1879, the famous naturalist rocked the Tlingit canoe and spoiled the aim of his native companions as they tried to shoot deer along the shoreline. Killing animals in such a place was sacrilege. "This type of shooting has no place in a National Monument," Butts declared.[2] "The stench from decomposed carcasses is somehow not fitting for this fine wilderness," wrote another of the staff.[3] "Somehow" is the key word here. Intuitively, they knew this was wrong.

A number of new circumstances converged in the 1960s to make NPS officials treat this longstanding issue with greater urgency than before. First, the NPS as a whole acquired what historian Alfred Runte has described as "a new seriousness" in the 1960s.[4] As public concern over the world's environmental problems burgeoned, national parks acquired new significance as laboratories for the study of relatively undisturbed ecosystems. Secretary of the Interior Stewart Udall set the new tone in his keynote address to the First World Conference on National Parks, held at the Seattle World's Fair in 1962, when he likened national parks to "nature islands for the world" in a latter-day Great Flood. National park managers, said Udall, might well "become the Noahs of the 20th century."[5] Glacier Bay National Monument was one of the few "nature islands" in the national park system whose establishing act explicitly mandated ecological research as one of its purposes.[6] It seemed unconscionable to continue to permit seal hunting in such a time and place.

Second, with the achievement of Alaska statehood in 1959 and the establishment of the state ferry system four years later, Glacier Bay National Monument finally began to assume its long-intended function as a wilderness haven for tourists. The advent of tourists increased the NPS's discomfort with the native seal hunting privilege, since tourists were apt to be perplexed by this exception to the well-known prohibition of hunting in national parks. Native seal hunting threatened to become a public issue. Specifically, NPS officials insisted that no legislative proposal to upgrade Glacier Bay from a national monument to a national park would find support in Congress as long as the native seal hunting privilege remained in effect.

Third, the problem of native possessory rights in Glacier Bay ground toward a resolution in the case of *Tlingit and Haida Indians of Alaska v. United States.* The U.S. Court of Claims handed down a preliminary judgment on October 7, 1959. The court ruled in favor of the Indians, finding that their aboriginal title was valid and that they were entitled to recover for the uncompensated taking of their land and property. This included some

18 million acres embraced by the Tongass National Forest and Glacier Bay National Monument. When the court reached its final judgment on January 19, 1968, recommending that Congress compensate the plaintiffs $7,546,053.80, it seemed to NPS officials that the legal basis for the Huna Tlingits' possessory rights in Glacier Bay had at last been removed.

Fourth, and finally, NPS officials perceived a change in the character of native use of Glacier Bay. They maintained that the native hunters were now motivated by the commercial value of seal hides rather than the meat and oil obtained from the animal. They believed that the rising market for hides was drawing young natives into seal hunting who had otherwise shown declining interest in it. This revelation undermined their earlier feeling that native use of the area would fade with time.

The NPS's "new seriousness" derived from many sources, but none was more influential than a report on wildlife management commissioned by Secretary of the Interior Stewart Udall in 1963. The report, titled "Wildlife Management in the National Parks," was prepared by an advisory board of five biologists chaired by A. Starker Leopold, the son of Aldo Leopold and a professor of zoology at the University of California. The impetus for the report was the demand by some sportsmen's groups that the NPS use sport hunting as a tool for controlling wildlife populations in national parks. The advisory board used the opportunity to address the larger question of nature preservation and the meaning of national parks. Conservationists embraced the report's broad-ranging conclusions, and Secretary Udall directed the NPS to adopt the report's findings as policy. The landmark document became known in national park circles as the "Leopold Report."[7]

The Leopold Report recommended as a primary goal for national park management that plant and animal communities in each park "be maintained, or where necessary recreated, as nearly as possible in the condition that prevailed when the area was first visited by the white men." The purpose of such management was to make each national park "represent a vignette of primitive America."[8] The idea was not new — it had been stated in nearly so many words by another University of California zoologist, Dr. Joseph Grinnell, in 1916, and by a team of NPS biologists in 1931. But the old idea had never before been harnessed to such an ambitious plan of ecological research. The committee itself acknowledged, "The implications of this seemingly simple aspiration are stupendous."[9]

The goal seemed more ambitious because the models that ecologists used to understand ecological succession had grown more complicated. In the 1920s and 1930s, the ruling concept in ecology had been the "climax community." It was thought that ecological successions proceeded in an orderly and predictable way toward a mature stage of development, or climax. The climax community was likened to a superorganism; after each natural or man-made disturbance, nature would begin to heal its wound through ecological succession. In light of this model, it was not unrealistic to conceive of national parks as places where the climax community was relatively intact or could be more or less restored. But as ecological research grew in sophistication, the concept of the climax community did not hold up. Ecologists began to think in terms of smaller, more varied, and much less predictable units called "ecosystems." By the 1960s, ecologists were no longer assuming that when nature renewed itself, ecological successions led back to the same assemblage of plants and animals that had been present in the first place. As a model for preserving nature, the ecosystem was decidedly more problematic than the older concept of the climax community. For national park managers, it was abundantly clear that park boundaries seldom conformed to natural ecosystems and that they were dealing, in any case, with biotic communities that had been altered by past logging, livestock grazing, hunting, and other land uses.

Undaunted by the new thinking in ecology, the advisory board proposed manipulations of the existing plant and animal assemblages in national parks in such ways to set up the preconditions that would cause natural ecological successions to restore the so-called primitive scene. Prescribed burning, reintroduction of extirpated plant and animal species, control of animal populations — these were just some of the management methods that would be required. "In essence," the advisory board boldly stated, "we are calling for a set of ecologic skills unknown in this country today." The work would begin with historical research of the natural conditions that had once prevailed in each area, and would end with each park providing the public with "a reasonable illusion of primitive America."[10] Paradoxically, the Leopold Report seemed to stress the instability and flux in nature, yet returned to the idea of some kind of imagined pre-Columbian landscape whose defining quality was that it was timeless and unchanging.

Glacier Bay National Monument posed some problems for the Leopold Report policy. First, there was the fact that the monument embraced not a primitive landscape but a strikingly new one. At the time of its earliest sighting by a white man — the benchmark suggested by the Leopold Report for defining a pristine state of nature — it was covered by ice. During the entire period of European and American expansion in North America, Glacier Bay was undergoing its own invasion of colonizing plant and animal species. There was no climax community to restore; indeed, scientific interest in the ecological succession taking place in Glacier Bay was one of

the reasons for the monument's existence. "Clearly," wrote park biologist
Gregory P. Streveler and park naturalist Bruce Paige, "the biotic flux that
contributes so importantly to the essence of the Monument should not be
disturbed." They proposed a variation on the directive contained in the
Leopold Report, redefining the goal of biological management in Glacier
Bay: "that the natural processes and systems operative during the period of
discovery by white man be allowed (and, perhaps, in some cases, helped) to
continue as if civilized man did not exist."[11] Streveler and Paige accepted
the Leopold Report's premise that humankind disturbed the natural order,
and that biological management must not only minimize such disturbances
but actively compensate for them, but the goal must be to preserve the
evolution of the primitive scene, rather than to try to restore it.

To preserve a natural evolution, to protect the primary ecological succession in Glacier Bay from unnatural disturbances, park managers often had
to substitute hunches for historical data. In a place where one colonizing
species constantly succeeded another, biologists had little way of determining whether the increase or decrease of a species was natural or the result of
human action. Did the influx of coyotes in the 1920s and 1930s relate to a
decline in the brown bear population, itself a result of cattle grazing and
homesteading on the small plain near the entrance to Glacier Bay? Or had
the coyotes come into the area in the tracks of the Sitka deer? Was a potential salmon stream empty of salmon because it had been fished out or because it had never been colonized? What was the hair seal's role in the evolving marine ecosystem, and what effect did native seal hunting produce?[12]

This led to the second problem that the monument posed for the Leopold Report policy: was the natives' take of seals natural or unnatural? By
insisting that national parks should reflect the way North America once
looked to the first white men who appeared on the scene, the Leopold
Report implied that Europeans, not Native Americans, were the intruders
in nature. By the same token, it implied that Native Americans had once
lived in harmony with nature. Whatever changes in the environment they
had wrought through burning or hunting were entirely natural. What to
do, then, with a modern native presence that had roots in this primitive
scene? Streveler and Paige again provided an answer. In their adaptation of
the Leopold Report's basic directive, "white man" became "civilized man."
Thus, the native seal hunters were separated from nature by virtue of being
acculturated.

Ironically, the NPS knew even less about the ecology of the hair seal in
Glacier Bay in the early 1960s than it did about native seal hunting. The
monument staff observed numerous seals in the lower bay in the winter and

early spring, and recorded large congregations of seals near the fronts of the glaciers in late spring and summer. It was thought that the seals migrated up bay in the spring in order to feed on crustaceans and give birth on the icebergs, then returned to the lower bay in the summer to resume their main diet of fishes. The NPS had not yet made a reliable census, but it was safe to say that the seal was the most abundant large mammal in the monument and an important part of the marine ecology.[13]

After the big hunt of 1963, Ranger Butts became concerned about numbers. Not knowing how many seals were in the monument, he was understandably wary that the population might be overhunted or even exterminated. In May 1964, a native from Haines stopped at Bartlett Cove and informed Butts that a friend in Juneau had recently taken 300 seals from Glacier Bay without a permit. Butts had already issued permits to twenty Huna Tlingits since the start of the year — including the two hunters who had slaughtered over 200 seals in Muir Inlet the year before. He guessed the total number of seals in Glacier Bay might be 800 to 1,000. "There are no bag limits, no closed season, and no closed area to protect this population," Butts wrote the superintendent. "Under present agreement this entire herd could be wiped out if the natives so desire."[14]

Numbers assumed even greater significance when the NPS tried to get Secretary Udall to revoke the natives' seal hunting privilege. The NPS's central office in Washington, D.C., instructed Superintendent Leone J. Mitchell to compile statistics on the numbers of permits issued, kills reported, bounties paid, and various other indices of hunting pressure on the seal population over the preceding several years. Ranger Charles V. Janda, who transferred to Glacier Bay from Yellowstone National Park in May 1964, found these statistics disturbingly difficult to piece together. For example, the permit system required hunters to report kills within thirty days to the chief ranger, but the level of compliance was very low. Janda conceded, "there is absolutely nothing in our files which indicates any attempts on our part to enforce the regulation or at least remind the hunters of their responsibility." Determining the amount of hunting pressure on the population was a matter of guesswork. In the summer of 1965, Janda estimated that the total kill in Glacier Bay for the first half of the year had already reached 1,200. This was more than four times the reported kill of 291, and exceeded Butts' total population estimate by 200 to 400 animals. Janda arrived at this estimate by extrapolating from state bounty records held in Juneau, which showed significant increases of seal harvests in 1963, 1964, and the first quarter of 1965. But the bounty records did not indicate where the seals had been taken.[15]

Meanwhile, on the basis of further rough counts of the hair seals, Janda raised the earlier population estimate more than eight-fold to 7,000 or 8,000.[16] Strictly in terms of a biological assessment, the higher population estimate significantly altered the picture of seal hunting. It now seemed doubtful that the annual harvest by Huna Tlingits exceeded the number of surviving pups each year. Present hunting pressure, one staff report stated, was not "sufficiently intense to cause a noticeable change in the seal population."[17] But that only laid bare the fact that the NPS objected to the native seal hunting privilege on more than biological grounds. NPS officials opposed it because it seemed morally and aesthetically wrong to them.

In June 1966, the long-awaited park lodge opened at Bartlett Cove and a tour boat began providing day-trips up bay. The new superintendent, Robert E. Howe, worried about the impression that native seal hunting made on tourists. He stated in a report of that year that the passengers on the tour boat expressed great interest and pleasure in viewing the seals. The tourists were "visibly shaken" when they learned that natives were allowed to shoot seals within the monument boundaries. Howe gave no thought to interpreting the native seal hunting privilege to tourists in a sympathetic light. Instead, he pointed out to his superiors that hunting made the seals elusive and difficult for the tourists to observe at close range.[18]

Like Ranger Janda, Howe had transferred to Glacier Bay from Yellowstone, where he had been chief wildlife biologist. Superintendent Howe and his chief ranger agreed that Glacier Bay had the potential to join Yellowstone as one of the nation's premier wildlife parks. They were frank to point out that the outstanding wildlife viewing opportunities in Yellowstone resulted from the national park policy of wildlife protection, which allowed wild animals to become habituated to the presence of park visitors.[19] Yet, inadvertently perhaps, they turned the tables on the hunter. They equated tame animals with natural conditions and hunters with unnatural conditions. This may have been a minor point to NPS officials concerned with preserving nature for the enjoyment of the American public, but it was a bitter irony for the area's indigenous people. In effect, it created the illusion that native hunters were intruders in the Glacier Bay ecosystem.[20]

Ranger Butts had done the same thing in 1964. He reported that the presence of hunters made the seals "much more wary of approaching boats." As the seals were spooked off the ice whenever a boat came within earshot of them, it deprived "the bona fide visitor of the opportunity to observe the seal under natural conditions." Of course, if Glacier Bay's seals were any less wary than seals outside of the monument, that was hardly natural. Butts missed the irony. "Everywhere in the state," he continued, "the seal is shot at and withdraws from the approaching boats and people. Glacier Bay should be the one place where it is protected as a member of the ecological community and enjoyed in its natural state."[21]

The ranger's comments went to the nub of the NPS's concept of nature. Like John Muir in 1879 and William S. Cooper in 1916, NPS officials saw nature in Glacier Bay as the intricate interplay of all living things in the absence of civilized humankind. To preserve nature, national parks had to insulate these delicate ecological relationships from human disturbance. Human beings might be present in national parks as visitors, but their influence was benign. Well-managed visitors did not introduce anything into, or take anything out of, the food chain; their use of the national park was "non-consumptive."[22] In contrast to the benign tour boat passenger, the native hunter was extracting something from the environment. Hunting was by definition a consumptive use. Therefore, it was an unnatural intrusion upon the environment.

The NPS was unable to persuade the secretary of the interior that the native hunting privilege was impairing the wildlife. Even if the logic of its argument was convincing, the biological data assembled to back that up was not, and more than a year of agitation by the NPS to have the native seal hunting privilege revoked finally came to nothing. The NPS therefore turned from biological and aesthetic considerations to a third line of argument — one that was reminiscent of its agonizing over this issue twenty years earlier. NPS officials shifted the focus from the safety and behavior of the seals to the native hunters themselves, arguing that the hunters were now motivated by the commercial market in hides rather than by traditional needs.

This line of argument caused some bitterness. That bitterness was compounded by fundamental differences of opinion between NPS officials and Huna Tlingits over the legal and historical background to the present situation. In the first place, they did not agree as to whether the Huna Tlingits' privileges were transitional or permanent. The NPS's 1957 master plan for the monument commented that the privileges would be "reduced and eliminated within a reasonable period of time."[23] Superintendent Howe repeatedly stated that the hunting privilege had outlived its original intent, which in his view was to help the village of Hoonah through a period of economic adjustment at the end of World War II.[24] Huna Tlingits, on the other hand, viewed the negotiated terms of their continued use of the area as being "for all time."[25] Their interest in the area not only involved food resources, but *origin* myths and ancestral burial grounds too.

There was also a profound difference of opinion as to the extent of the use that Huna Tlingits actually made of Glacier Bay in the 1950s and 1960s. NPS officials assumed that the use was very light and of negligible importance to Hoonah's economy.[26] They based this assessment mainly on the trifling number of seal hunters who requested permits at Bartlett Cove each year in the 1960s. When approximately 10 percent of the population of Hoonah petitioned against the NPS's threatened termination of the agreement in 1964, NPS officials construed this as the full extent of Huna interest in the area.[27] But according to a 1986 survey of Huna households by the Alaska Department of Fish and Game (ADFG), respondents estimated that 55 percent of their household's annual subsistence take had come from the monument area when they had access to it. Based on its survey data, the ADFG calculated that nearly 70 percent of "active users" in the village of Hoonah took subsistence resources from upper Glacier Bay at least once in 1950, while just under 40 percent did so in 1965. The ADFG study indicated even higher percentages, with the same downward trend, for lower Glacier Bay and Dundas Bay.[28]

But the most contentious difference of opinion related to the nature of seal hunting itself. When an upturn in the hide market in 1963–65 led a handful of Huna Tlingits to start taking a hundred or more seals apiece each season, NPS officials assumed that these individuals represented a new class of native seal hunter because they were oriented to the market rather than the village subsistence economy. The NPS perceived a discontinuity between this kind of seal hunting and the aboriginal seal hunting practices of the hunters' forebears. This discontinuity, NPS officials alleged, ought to disqualify the market hunters from hunting in the monument. They saw the market hunter as a sort of fallen Indian. Park biologist Gregory P. Streveler concluded that the native seal hunters were trying to "outdo the whites in their resource-rape."[29] Chief Ranger Butts wrote, "If they [the seals] were used for domestic purposes such as hide for clothing and meat for food I might feel differently."[30] Ranger Janda, filling out an incident report on a native by the name of Kenneth Schoonover who had taken 210 hair seal from the monument out of season in February 1969, entered Schoonover's race as "Caucasian claims Tlingit Lineage."[31] Superintendent Howe maintained that the hide hunters who came into the bay in large fishing boats with skiffs in tow "were not real Indians."[32] These NPS officials overlooked the fact that natives had been market hunting as well as subsistence hunting for generations.

The NPS showed that it was little better informed about the cultural meaning of seal hunting to Huna Tlingits than biologist Lowell Sumner had been in 1947. Like Sumner, NPS officials in the 1960s operated on the assumption that increased material wealth and cash income for Tlingits was equatable with decreased need for native foods and animal hides, as if there were a reciprocal relationship between the two. The familiar idea was advanced anew in 1964: "The natives involved are no longer dependent on these animals for food and clothing. They are employed in industry and are commercial fishermen with the most modern boats and gear."[33] Howe reiterated this idea in subsequent memoranda when he reported a decline in the number of permits issued after 1966: "Our people at Bartlett Cove cannot offer a concrete explanation [for the decline] except that it is generally recognized that the Hoonah natives do not rely on the seal as a principal source of food and clothing. In fact, there is only one family who consistently hunts in Glacier Bay."[34] There was a predilection by the monument staff to see all that was modern in Hoonah and to interpret subsistence use as a vanishing way of life.

This was misleading. A 1970 study of employment opportunities for Tlingit and Haida Indians found that while 56 percent of the male labor force was employed in the commercial fishing industry, about one in ten of these men was a year-round commercial fisherman. While 43 percent of the female labor force was employed in the canneries, this work was seasonal. Only one in four men and women in the labor force held year-round jobs of any kind. One in three men and a somewhat higher proportion of women in the labor force were unemployed at least six months of the year. As for the natives' "modern boats and gear" to which the NPS alluded, this probably referred to some 130 seiners (about one vessel per six Tlingit and Haida families) that had been purchased on credit from the IRA's revolving loan fund during the late 1930s and early 1940s. Few fishermen had completely paid off their mortgages on these boats. The 1970 study recommended to the Tlingit-Haida Central Council that the cost of refinancing most of these vessels was unjustified given their poor condition.[35]

This kind of information was not readily available in 1965 when the NPS looked to the BIA for economic data on the Huna community, yet NPS officials contented themselves with glib assurances from the BIA that Hoonah was better off than 90 percent of other Alaska native villages. Rather than conduct a hearing in Hoonah on this issue as the natives requested, NPS staffers went to Juneau and assembled data on bounty payments and market prices for seal skins to prove their point that modern seal hunting was now disembodied from traditional native subsistence use.[36]

Their investigation disclosed that seal skins were selling for $10 to $12 apiece on average, compared with prices of $1 to $4 only three or four years earlier. The market price had not been that high for ten to twenty years.[37] The NPS presented these figures as evidence that the seal hunters were making large profits; as Butts told Superintendent Mitchell, "This is big business."[38] Butts was correct in that the market was now international, with Canadian buyers accounting for most of the local purchases and a large proportion of the skins from Southeast Alaska eventually being shipped to Europe to be turned into high-fashion apparel, but he exaggerated that market's importance to the Hoonah economy. The cash value of seal skins in this period was only about double what the value of the $3 bounty had been in the 1940s; and total harvest levels in Alaska in the 1960s were below what they had been in the 1930s and 1940s when bounty payments were the most significant cash incentive. Meanwhile, the state of Alaska had frozen the bounty at $3 and ended it altogether in 1967. Unless seal hunting was conducted from a factory ship equipped with compressed-air skinning devices, hunting seals for their skins was about as marginal to the cash economy of Southeast Alaska as hunting them for the bounty had been during the 1940s.[39] Its marginality ensured that some, though not all, of the seals taken in Glacier Bay were consumed as meat and oil in the subsistence economy.

That no credible moral distinction really existed between subsistence and market hunters is confirmed by the fact that the first two native hunters to exploit the higher prices paid for hides in 1963 were George Dalton and James Austin, two longtime hunters whom the NPS would later describe as the only remaining true subsistence hunters using monument waters.[40] These two hunters acquired permits at Bartlett Cove on May 3, 1963, and proceeded up bay to Garforth Island, near the entrance of Muir Inlet. They killed more than 200 seals that season before taking out their camp in November. According to a writer for *Alaska Sportsman*, who invited the two seal hunters aboard his cruiser one day, Austin and Dalton were saving some of the hair seal hides to make moccasins and selling others to a fur dealer. They distributed seal oil to friends and kin in Hoonah and sold some of the carcasses to crab fishermen for crab bait.[41] By the end of the season they had also collected $729 in bounty payments.[42]

Dalton and Austin harvested these seals in the usual manner. They hunted the seals from a skiff and from the shore, shooting them in the back of the head in such a way that their jaws stayed shut; otherwise, a shot seal had a tendency to open its mouth, inhale a lot of water, and sink before the hunter could get to it. They skinned the seals on the beach, and what carcasses they could not use they left to rot. When Butts found the putrefying remains of their work the following spring, he was appalled by the waste, the gore, and the stench. He was even more dismayed when another seal hunter, Jimmy Martin, told him that he had shot 161 seals and lost 40 percent to sinking. To Butts, it was a travesty to kill so many animals without being able to retrieve them all; to Martin, it was a test of the hunter's efficiency and skill to secure as large a percentage of his kills as possible.[43]

Just as the purpose and intensity of seal hunting disturbed NPS officials, so too did the technology that was now at the seal hunter's disposal. In early April 1964, a converted 110-foot submarine chaser came into Bartlett Cove to wait out a storm. The white crew was seal hunting and inquired about the monument boundaries along the outer coast. The next day, after the submarine chaser had left, four Huna Tlingits docked in Bartlett Cove to obtain permits. Asked what they knew about the submarine chaser, they said that the crew had been trying to hire "sharpshooters" in Hoonah. While it was unclear whether the crew's intent was to gain access to Glacier Bay seals, Butts thought the NPS had no legal recourse to stop such a plan. "So long as they are natives and have a permit they can operate under any subsidy they can work up," he wrote to Superintendent Mitchell. "One boat such as this 110 foot one could keep a sizable crew of hunters in the Monument and really slaughter the seal."[44] Two years later in 1966, Superintendent Howe again raised this specter of a "mother ship" employing Huna Tlingits with hunting permits: "Why no one has taken advantage of this loophole is surprising to all of us," he wrote.[45]

Some time later (no record of the incident is contained in the park's files) some Huna Tlingits entered Glacier Bay on Willie Marks's fishing boat *New Annie* with more than a dozen skiffs in tow. This was not quite the factory ship that the monument staff feared, but the enterprise struck the superintendent as morally wrong and illegal. NPS rangers intercepted the boat, boarded it, and confiscated the natives' rifles for evidence. The incident became something of a symbol for both points of view: one of native avarice to the NPS, and one of NPS belligerence to the natives. Huna Tlingits were outraged but also cowed by the incident. Most of them would not concede that the mission of the *New Annie* was an aberration from subsistence seal hunting.[46]

While the *New Annie* incident formed a de facto turning point for the Huna Tlingits' position in Glacier Bay, an actual legal resolution of Huna possessory rights in the monument still remained in the offing. As is so often the case in national park administration, the NPS's difficulties with this issue were compounded by the fact that it was not strictly local, but embraced a wider geographic area and various other government entities.

Each attempt by the NPS to terminate the Huna Tlingits' privileges in Glacier Bay involved a number of political entities directly or indirectly, from the Tlingit-Haida Central Council and the BIA to the state of Alaska and the ADFG. How the NPS maneuvered through this political minefield in the late 1960s and early 1970s had important implications not only for Glacier Bay but for the future Alaskan national parks as well.

Somewhat apart from the problem of native privileges in the monument was the dispute between the NPS and the state of Alaska over ownership of Glacier Bay. The dispute arose out of the Alaska Statehood Act of 1958, which conferred all navigable waters and submerged lands of the public domain to the state of Alaska. The state claimed that the two presidential proclamations of 1925 and 1939 that established and enlarged Glacier Bay National Monument covered the land area only, leaving the bays and coastal waters in the public domain; thus, they now belonged to the state of Alaska. The NPS held otherwise. The jurisdictional dispute simmered, neither the state nor the NPS wanting to take the matter to court yet each of them being leery of any action by the other that would prejudice either's case. Tacitly, the NPS allowed the ADFG to regulate the small-scale commercial fishery in Glacier Bay. It also assumed that native seal hunters would respect the ADFG's closed season on seal hunting while operating under NPS permits in the monument. For its part, the ADFG informed Huna Tlingits that they did not need permits to hunt seals in Glacier Bay below the tide line, because the state controlled the waters.[47]

The legal muddle posed a problem for enforcement of seal hunting restrictions: NPS officials were unsure of their authority to board vessels or make arrests on the open water; the U.S. commissioner in Juneau informed Howe that he would not hear any federal cases where jurisdiction was in dispute between the federal agency and the state.[48] While this situation was troubling in itself, NPS officials did not want a confrontation with native seal hunters to force the issue of jurisdiction. If taking a hard line toward native seal hunting resulted in an arrest, followed by the filing of charges in federal district court, then the unwanted legal contest with the state over jurisdiction would likely ensue.

The jurisdictional dispute seems to have been an important factor in muffling the issue of native seal hunting after 1966, although evidence of this is only circumstantial. Late in that year, NPS Director George B. Hartzog, Jr. tried unavailingly to interest state officials in "concurrent jurisdiction" of Glacier Bay.[49] Some time later—the communication was undated—NPS officials in Washington, D.C., informed Superintendent Howe by telephone that the seal hunting agreement would be continued, with the thought that it would "die a natural death when the few old timers still participating [can] no longer hunt."[50] In other words, the NPS no longer wanted to resolve this issue with either the BIA or the Huna Tlingits themselves. Ostensibly, the change of tack was in response to a drop in the hide market and an easing of pressure on the seal population. There was little further communication out of the monument on this subject until 1970.

There may have been another political consideration weighing in this decision. The growing Alaska native rights movement, together with the U.S. Court of Claims's decisions in *Tlingit and Haida Indians of Alaska v. United States* (1959, 1968), may have persuaded NPS officials to wait and see how these developments affected the Huna Tlingits' position in Glacier Bay — as well as indigenous people's rights in other Alaska national parklands — before moving too aggressively against them. Howe alluded to these political considerations in 1969 when he recalled his unrecorded telephone communications with the Washington, D.C., office in which he had been told to let the seal hunting controversy subside.[51]

The Alaska native rights movement developed in reaction to state land selections and state wildlife laws that encroached on native subsistence resources in the early 1960s. The Alaska Statehood Act had entitled Alaska to select 103 million acres of land from the public domain for state ownership. This was a greater proportion of the total public lands than any other new state had ever received, the idea being that a viable government of this far northern state would need a hefty income from oil and mineral leases in order to compensate for the state's scant population and minuscule agricultural and manufacturing base. The Statehood Act acknowledged that Indian title to this land would have to be settled at a later time. As the patenting of state lands went forward in the early and mid-1960s, Eskimos, Aleuts, and Athapaskan Indians formed several native regional associations, and these came together with Southeast Alaska's Tlingit-Haida Central Council to form the Alaska Federation of Natives in 1966. With the notable exception of the Tlingits and Haidas, who had organized the Alaska Native Brotherhood in 1912, all of these native groups were organizing politically on a regional basis for the first time in their history. Nevertheless, the fledgling Alaska native rights movement was already sharply focused on land.[52]

With these developments in the background, the NPS could no longer afford to address Huna Tlingit privileges within a strictly local context. In effect, the problem of native seal hunting was swept out of Glacier Bay on a tide of legal and political maneuverings that turned not on seals but on state land selections, native land claims, and nearly a billion dollars' worth of

North Slope oil leases. In the summer of 1966, the BIA began its first halt-
ing efforts toward drafting a comprehensive solution to the aboriginal land
claims of all Alaska natives, and in the fall of that year Secretary Udall issued
a controversial land order that prohibited further patenting of state lands
(as allowed under the Statehood Act) until native claims were settled.[53]

With so much attention focused on Alaska's anticipated oil riches lying
somewhere beneath the North Slope — verified in the spring of 1968 by oil
strikes at Prudhoe Bay — the Southeast Alaska region and the Tlingit and
Haida Indians would have played a relatively minor part in the process of
settling native land claims except for the long history of Tlingit and Haida
claims. Now the case of *Tlingit and Haida Indians of Alaska v. United States*
was seen as precedent-setting.

The U.S. Court of Claims had handed down a preliminary judgment in
the case on October 7, 1959. The court had ruled in favor of the Indians,
finding that their aboriginal title was valid and that they were entitled to
recover for the uncompensated taking of their land and property. This
included some 16 million acres that had been set apart as Tongass National
Forest by presidential proclamations on August 20, 1902, September 10,
1907, and February 16, 1909, and some 2,297,598 acres embraced by the
original 1925 boundaries of Glacier Bay National Monument. (The addition to the monument in 1939 was immaterial to this case since it amounted
to a transfer of land from Tongass National Forest, or from one federal
agency to another.) The amount of the settlement was to be established by a
subsequent proceeding.[54]

On January 19, 1968, the U.S. Court of Claims concluded its second
and final proceeding in this case with a judgment for the plaintiffs, but it
was a Pyrrhic victory for the Tlingits and Haidas. Their attorneys had
sought an $80 million settlement; the trial commissioner had calculated the
fair market value of the total land claim, including fishing grounds, at
$15,934,368.80; the judges, however, ruled that no awards in respect to
fishing grounds should be made, and arrived at the figure of $7,546,053.80.
Especially significant was the court's finding that aboriginal title did not
extend to submerged lands or fisheries.[55]

The decision in *Tlingit and Haida Indians of Alaska v. United States*, coming
in the midst of the Alaska native rights movement, provided an important
impetus toward a legislative settlement of native land claims throughout the
rest of Alaska, not least because the judgment of the court convinced native
leaders that an act of Congress would be preferable to another judicial
settlement based on monetary compensation alone.[56]

The Alaska Native Claim Settlement Act (ANCSA) was enacted on December 18, 1971. The act extinguished all aboriginal title to lands and submerged lands and all aboriginal hunting and fishing rights. It granted the natives $925,500,000 as compensation apportioned between twelve regional corporations and as many native villages as would choose to incorporate under the terms of the act. All natives born on or before the date of the act became shareholders in their respective regional corporations, with the option of joining their village corporations as well. These corporations were to oversee native land selections amounting to 40 million acres, development of these lands, and other capital investment. ANCSA provided for the same corporate structure in Southeast Alaska, but granted onefourth as much land to each of the ten Tlingit and Haida villages, including Hoonah, as other native villages were entitled to, and declared that the funds appropriated to pay the judgment of the U.S. Court of Claims in *Tlingit and Haida Indians of Alaska v. United States* were in lieu of additional lands. The main intent of this complicated legislation was to provide a vehicle with which Alaska natives could determine their own path into the corporate economy.[57]

At the same time, ANCSA laid the foundation for modern legal protections of native subsistence use in Alaska. At an early stage in the development of this legislation, namely in the Federal Field Committee's preparation of its report, *Alaska Natives and the Land* (1968), it became apparent that Alaska natives were dependent on far more land for their subsistence needs than Congress would be willing to allow them to retain. The Federal Field Committee estimated that Alaska natives required a minimum of 60 million acres to support their subsistence take. Not only was this acreage unacceptably high as a share of the total land area of the state, but the regional corporations that ANCSA established were expected to select native lands on the basis of development potential rather than subsistence resources, and often the two did not coincide. Therefore, lawmakers recognized that the extinguishment of aboriginal title would have to be accompanied by legal protections of the natives' continued subsistence use of the public lands.[58]

The Senate version of the Alaska native land claims bill provided for this protection, but the House version did not. When the two houses of Congress went to conference on the bill in December 1971, the conference committee decided to exclude explicit language on subsistence protection, despite two last-minute appeals by the Alaska Federation of Natives.[59] The reason for the omission appears to be the conferees inability to reach agreement on how such protection would be implemented — under a permit system or a land classification system.[60] However, the conference report on the bill stated that the committee "expects both the Secretary and the State to take any action necessary to protect the subsistence needs of the Natives."[61]

It would have been reasonable to assume that Congress's deliberations over native subsistence protections pertained to the Huna Tlingits' position in Glacier Bay, but the NPS did not see it this way. In 1972, Superintendent Howe began once again to press his superiors for an end to the natives' seal hunting privilege, maintaining that the U.S. Court of Claims's judgment in 1968 had now compensated the Tlingits for any aboriginal rights they had once enjoyed in Glacier Bay.[62] The NPS informed the people of Hoonah that it had in its possession a department solicitor's opinion that stated that the court's decision in 1959 had terminated any such rights.[63] The NPS did not disclose that this solicitor's opinion was now nine years old. Dated December 15, 1965, it had been written prior to the court's second decision and ANCSA, and was of doubtful worth. At least two significant problems were unaddressed by this nine-year-old opinion: first, did the court's subsequent restriction of its judgment to *land* areas still affect the Huna Tlingits' privileges in Glacier Bay? Second, did the court ruling affect hunting rights, and if so, was it superseded by ANCSA and the intent of Congress to protect native subsistence?[64]

Because ANCSA did not specifically address subsistence, the outlines of the new policy were not well understood in the early 1970s. Important questions, such as who qualified as a subsistence user and how the federal government would implement some kind of prioritization of subsistence over other forms of resource consumption, remained to be worked out. Perhaps the key question with regard to Glacier Bay was this: did subsistence protection assure subsistence users access to all public lands of which they had made traditional use? For purposes of debate, the House and Senate conference committee had framed the subsistence issue in this way: "Should native people's historic use of public lands for subsistence purposes — hunting, fishing, trapping, berry-picking — be protected under the Act, and if so: (1) By a permit system (2) By a land classification system."[65] The conference committee provided no definitive answer to this question.

Less than six months after passing ANCSA, Congress considered subsistence protection for Alaska natives in terms of another bill — which would become the Marine Mammal Protection Act of 1972 (MMPA). While the bill placed a moratorium on the hunting of marine mammals, it allowed Alaska natives to continue to harvest marine mammals for subsistence and limited commercial use. Dozens of Alaska natives testified before congressional hearings in Bethel and Nome, Alaska, on May 11–13, 1972, about the importance of seal, walrus, and whale hunting to their village economies and culture. Robert Willard, a Tlingit representing the Alaska Commission on Human Rights, testified that the sole income for 10,000 natives derived from the manufacture of arts and crafts items, mainly from sea mammals and by-products.[66] George Miller, president of Cook Inlet Regional Association, stated that the harvesting of ocean mammals "for subsistence and commercial purposes . . . is so interwoven into the fabric of traditional Native life that it cannot be altered or terminated without seriously jeopardizing the culture of our people."[67] Conservation groups including Friends of the Earth, the Sierra Club, and the Alaska Conservation Society supported the bill's provision for Alaska native subsistence, though they urged careful limits on the size of the arts and crafts commerce.[68]

The enactment of MMPA on October 21, 1972 introduced four significant refinements of the vague subsistence protections that Congress had mandated in the course of settling the Alaska native land claim. First, there was a notable shift in emphasis from the economic to the cultural significance of subsistence. In the context of ANCSA, most discussion of subsistence protections had an economic bent; lawmakers as well as native leaders had treated subsistence as a safety net or stopgap while the native villages and regional corporations developed the necessary job base to bring their people fully into the cash economy. Although the language in MMPA was neutral on this point, the congressional hearings and debate on the bill clearly laid a new stress on cultural preservation. Second, Congress decided to broaden the natives' subsistence protections in MMPA to include limited commercial use of harvested marine mammals. That is, natives could use animal products to make authentic handicrafts and clothing that could be sold in native villages and towns in Alaska. Third, Congress decided to overlook the protests of some white Alaskans that these subsistence protections were racially discriminatory; in MMPA Congress unequivocally restricted the allowance of marine mammal harvests to "any Indian, Aleut, or Eskimo who dwells on the coast of the North Pacific Ocean or the Arctic Ocean." Fourth, Congress insisted that marine mammal harvests must not be "accomplished in a wasteful manner."[69]

To NPS officials who wanted to end native hunting in Glacier Bay National Monument, MMPA suggested a need for haste in ruling that seal hunting was no longer legal. If the two decisions in *Tlingit and Haida Indians of Alaska v. United States* had strengthened the NPS's case for terminating the privilege, ANCSA's effect was rather ambiguous, and MMPA could potentially work against it. Five days after Congress enacted MMPA, Superintendent Howe wrote to the NPS state director that if native seal hunting in the monument was ever to be stopped, an effort must be made without further delay.[70] Howe finally got the answer he had been looking for when the director of the Alaska field office told him by telephone to arrange a meeting with the people of Hoonah and inform them that their privileges in the monument were terminated.[71]

If a meeting to explain this to the people of Hoonah ever occurred, it is not a part of the official record. Indeed, the record shows that after 1966 the NPS successfully suppressed this issue and eventually settled it quietly and unilaterally. Whereas the record in the 1940s contained interagency communications and meetings with the people of Hoonah, it dwindled to telephone conversations between NPS officials and memoranda to the files in the 1970s. While the mayor of Hoonah's inquiries in the 1940s had been answered by the secretary of the interior, now they were answered by the chief ranger or the superintendent. Chief Ranger Janda informed Mayor Frank See on April 4, 1974 that as of that date all people entering the park were equally subject to the Code of Federal Regulation's prohibition of killing wildlife in national parks. In this letter Janda also noted a telephone conversation with See the previous January in which Janda had informed the mayor that all hunting privileges were terminated. In addition, Janda stated that there had been only one request for a permit over the past two years. Thus, it is not clear exactly when the Huna Tlingits had lost their privileges in Glacier Bay. In recent years, the Huna Tlingits have expressed anger that the NPS did not put the rule making against native hunting in writing or run it through the normal public review process for regulatory changes. The record would seem to justify their anger.

There is some irony in the fact that MMPA forced the NPS's hand. By affirming the new federal policy of subsistence protection in Alaska, it might have provided the kind of enforceable legal definition of the Huna Tlingits' rights in Glacier Bay that had long been sought by both the NPS and the Huna Tlingits. The NPS might have invoked the law on the one hand to answer criticisms that native hunting had no place in the national park system, and on the other hand to prevent native hunters from defiling the shores of Glacier Bay by taking seals only for their skins. The law practically eliminated the market for seal hides. It removed the perceived threat that native hunters could legally exterminate the monument's seals while in the service of a factory ship. Moreover, MMPA provided a way around the problem of jurisdiction in Glacier Bay, because it took marine mammal management away from Alaska (and other states) and assigned it to a new federal agency, the Marine Mammal Commission. NPS management of seal hunting in Glacier Bay would no longer represent a pocket of federal law enforcement in an otherwise state-managed activity.

Unfortunately, this perspective on MMPA was not within the frame of reference of most NPS officials in 1972. Hunting in national park areas, no matter in what form, was anathema to the NPS. It was only in the course of eight years of land use planning in the 1970s, leading up to passage of the Alaska National Interest Lands Conservation Act (ANILCA) in 1980, that the NPS adopted a new stance on subsistence hunting. By then the NPS would maintain that in Alaska, the nation's "last frontier," subsistence hunting could be compatible with wilderness preservation and the national park idea. Even then, however, it insisted that native subsistence use had no place in Glacier Bay.

After passage of ANILCA, Glacier Bay National Park stood apart from most of Alaska's national parklands in its disallowance of subsistence uses — but for how long remained unclear. In 1989, Huna Tlingits reopened the issue by successfully petitioning the State of Alaska Board of Fisheries for permits to subsistence fish in Glacier Bay. Three years later, with the defeat of two bills introduced in Congress that would have allowed subsistence use in Glacier Bay National Park, and the subsequent arrest and trial of a Huna fisherman for shooting a seal in the park, the longstanding conflict of interests between the NPS and the indigenous people of Glacier Bay showed no sign of an imminent resolution.

The story of the Hunas' displacement from Glacier Bay is an illustration of what could occur when a national park was created on the traditional model from lands that were claimed and occupied by an indigenous people. The NPS and the Hunas were unable to reach an accommodation on the core problem of seal hunting in Glacier Bay even though both parties were in agreement that the area should remain wild and undeveloped. Instead, they feuded with each other over their basic difference of perspective on the native hunter's place in nature. Both parties had additional cause to be intransigent in this case: park officials believed that they had an especially strong mandate to protect ecological processes from being disturbed in Glacier Bay, while the Hunas believed that they had a strong territorial claim to the area based on their clan legends and aboriginal use. Though the negotiation remained deadlocked, it underscored the need for a more constructive dialogue between preservationists and native peoples elsewhere in Alaska.

But the issues that were raised in Glacier Bay illuminated only some of the paradoxes and dilemmas that confronted environmentalists, NPS planners, and subsistence users in the 1970s. Another dimension to the problem involved white Alaskans who had adopted "subsistence lifestyles" and resided in areas that were being recommended for national park status. These rural whites, or "bush Alaskans" as they were sometimes called, claimed that they had as much right in the land as Alaska natives. Generally, they received strong support from the urban populace in Alaska, who insisted that the hardy existence led by these people was an essential quality of Alaskan life. To most whites who lived in the forty-ninth state, Alaska wilderness was not their "bread basket," as Glacier Bay was to the Hunas, much less their ancestral homeland, yet the wilderness was something more than a place to recreate; it possessed tangible cultural significance to them. There was a historical precedent for their arguments, and it could be found in the making of Alaska's first national park.

FOUR

"A Game Country Without Rival in America"

✣

The Alaska Range extends across south-central Alaska in an east-west arc, forming a great rampart between Alaska's wet, coastal section and the drier, colder, interior plateau. At its northernmost point the Alaska Range is about twenty miles wide; its serrated crest rises 6,000 to 8,000 feet above sea level and holds innumerable small glaciers. As the mountain range begins to curve southwestwardly toward the Alaska Peninsula, it broadens into the huge massif of Mount McKinley, whose summit reaches 20,320 feet above sea level, the highest point in North America.[1]

At a latitude of sixty-three degrees north, Mount McKinley is the coldest, snowiest mountain on earth. No forest mantles its lower slopes. In summertime, the rolling tundra laps at the mountain's base, sending splashes of delicate velvet green a few hundred feet up the talus slopes. Talus and solid rock, dry and brown in the summer, extend a few thousand feet higher to the permanent snow line at approximately 7,000 feet.[2] Above this swath of bare brown scree, which appears from a distance as a dark stain around the foot of the mountain, nearly three vertical miles of permanent snow, ice, and windswept rock loom against the sky. The iceclad mountain creates its own weather. On most clear summer days it is veiled in clouds by mid-morning, as if slowly exhaling its frosty breath into the atmosphere.

Numerous glaciers plunge down the mountain's slopes and deploy onto the surrounding tundra. The vast concentration of snow and ice gives rise to a number of large rivers on the north and south flanks of Mount McKinley and the Alaska Range. Nearest their glacier sources, these rivers are characterized by wide, gravelly beds of alluvium, or river-born sediment, carried out of the glacier snouts and deposited where the river gradients

87

begin to lessen. Through these broad expanses of sand and gravel bars the rivers form many branching channels. The volume of glacial meltwater surges on hot summer days, falls off to a trickle on cold summer nights, and ceases altogether during the deep "freeze-up" of winter.[3]

So rugged and forbidding is this country that it is difficult at first to conceive of it as a landscape defined by cultural values and the myth of the frontier, yet it was this landscape that originally inspired the idea of preserving a portion of Alaska as inhabited wilderness. The idea originated with sportsmen-conservationists, while the inhabitants whom they had in mind were prospectors and miners. The sportsmen found the foothills and tundra plain north of Mount McKinley to have a spectacular abundance of game, and they sought to preserve the game together with a small population of frontiersmen in a kind of frontier national park. Although the original scheme for this park was modified under the NPS's aegis in the 1920s, the sportsmen's idea of including frontiersmen in the national park anticipated the modern conception of Alaska wilderness. The establishment of Mount McKinley National Park cannot be understood apart from the myth of the frontier. This chapter seeks to define the frontier myth as it relates to Alaska and the making of Alaska's first national park.

The Mount McKinley region's aboriginal people, the Tanana-speaking Athapaskan Indians, made use of the area for generations before the coming of white men. They called the mountain "Denali" (The High One). The Tanana Indians' territory centered on the Tanana River drainage of east-central Alaska, with the Alaska Range forming the southern limit. Most of this region is covered by spruce forest and "muskeg," a bog common in the northern latitudes where fallen timber decomposes slowly. Woodland caribou, moose, and various smaller mammals formed the bulk of the Tananas' subsistence base. In this boreal forest country, animals were too scarce to support a large population of hunters. Population estimates for the Tanana in the nineteenth century ranged from a mere 400 to 800 people.[4] Groups of one or two families formed the basic unit of social organization for most of the Tananas' seasonal rounds, though several groups usually associated as a band, claiming a distinct hunting territory and coming together for caribou drives, potlatches, and trade.[5] By the end of the nineteenth century, the various Athapaskan peoples had formed into village units along the navigable rivers, and individual hunters probably spent less time in the vicinity of the Alaska Range than they had in the past.[6] Although Tanana Indians continued to hunt occasionally in the Mount McKinley area in the early twentieth century, their presence would be relatively inconsequential to the creation of the national park.[7]

Nineteenth-century explorers made even less of an impression on this part of Alaska. The mountain was a familiar landmark to Russians, British, and Americans in the nineteenth century, appearing as a white dome on the horizon from as far away as Cook Inlet on the southern coast and the Yukon River to the north. Yet viewing the mountain from these great distances, across such vast expanses of unmapped country, it was impossible to appreciate the mountain's enormous scale. Consequently, the mountain went by various names and remained virtually unknown outside of Alaska until 1896–97.[8]

The discovery and naming of North America's highest mountain in 1896–97 coincided with the beginning of the Alaska gold rush, and constituted the first link between Mount McKinley and the Alaskan frontier myth. In 1896, a party of prospectors journeyed up the Susitna River from Cook Inlet and approached near enough to the great mountain to discover its true geographical significance. One member of the party, William Dickey, sent an announcement of the party's discovery to the *New York Sun*, which published it in January 1897. Dickey wrote that the party had estimated the mountain's summit to be more than 20,000 feet above sea level, making it the highest peak on the continent. The prospectors named the mountain after Senator William McKinley of Ohio, who, as the newly nominated Republican Party candidate for president, was the most visible champion of the gold standard in the land. Dickey later explained that they had chosen the name somewhat facetiously, as their answer to the free-silver rhetoric they had been hearing in the mining camps.[9] Early mountaineers, who picked up on Dickey's story with great interest, would soon try to change the mountain's name to the more romantic Athapaskan name of Denali, but the goldbuggish "Mount McKinley" had its own historical logic, for the same year that Dickey and his companions decided to make the mountain into a political statement prospectors struck gold in Klondike Creek in the Yukon, precipitating the Alaska gold rush.[10]

The gold rush experience in Alaska was unlike any other. It was the defining event on the Alaskan frontier. Thousands of Americans took passage for Alaska as much for the sake of adventure as for the chance of striking it rich.[11] Writers and photographers rushed to Alaska and the Klondike because they thought their experiences would make great copy. National magazines and newspapers followed the story avidly. Frontier towns, raw and "wide open," sprang up in the northern wilderness at Nome, Fairbanks, Skagway, and Dawson City.[12] The Alaskan wilderness setting was mythologized as the nation's "last frontier," and the Alaskan prospector, or "sourdough," fittingly took his place at the center of this myth — just as the cowboy had captured the role of mythic hero in the Far West a generation earlier, and the hunter-pathfinder had been made into the romantic hero of the old frontier a generation before that. Alaska's mythic identity as the nation's last frontier would have a large bearing on the original conception of Alaska's first national park and, indeed, on the making of Alaska's other national parks a half-century later.

But the mythic last frontier was distinctive in another way. Nature wore a harsher countenance in the Far North; the environment was more perilous on this frontier. First, there was the killing cold, "the white silence" of Jack London's popular Alaskan story, which quickly became a cliché in London's other works of fiction on Alaska. Second, there was Alaska's wildlife. Wild animals had formed a part of Americans' image of Alaska since the heyday of sealing and the maritime fur trade; but now Alaska's big, dangerous, game animals became a part of the mythic Far North. Even more than the killing cold, wild animals became an enduring symbol of Alaska; they formed a companion image to that of the prospector. While the sourdough with his pick and pan personified the go-getter on the last frontier, wild animals just as surely symbolized the Alaskan wilderness. For this reason the wolfish sled dog came to be one of the most popular images of Alaska; the sled dog unified these two separate worlds of the miner and wild animals in a colorful and appealing way.[13] It was no accident that Jack London, who contributed more than any other individual to the Alaskan frontier myth, named the young hero of his first collection of short stories the Malemute Kid, chose to write about the frontier from the perspective of a dog named Buck in *Call of the Wild* (1903), and created a wolf-dog hero to mediate between civilization and nature in *White Fang* (1906). London well understood that his readers connected the Alaskan frontier with wild animals as much as they did with the Klondike gold rush, and he knew how to capitalize on this popular demand.[14]

Sportsmen-writers helped to weave the image of Alaska's wild animals into its frontier mythology, too. The big-game hunting literature of the early twentieth century reflected popular Darwinian ideas about competition and natural selection. The harshness of Alaska's northern environment was thought to have produced "arctic" animal types of mythic superiority. It was commonly observed that the moose of Alaska was the largest animal in the deer family, the brown bear of Alaska's southern coast was the largest bear in the world, and Alaska's wolves were the largest members of the canine family.

This was an influential group of people. They came from the elite in American society; they were members of an upper-class, "old stock," eastern establishment. As historian John F. Reiger has shown, their attention to the conservation of game at the end of the nineteenth century in many ways prefigured the Progressive conservation movement. The Boone and Crockett Club, which would lead the campaign for Mount McKinley National Park, set the standard for turning sportsmen into conservationists: founded by Theodore Roosevelt in the 1880s as a gentlemen's hunting club, the club stood at the forefront of wildlife conservation after 1900. As conservation became a central part of United States economic policy under the first Roosevelt administration, sportsmen-conservationists enjoyed considerable influence with agency chiefs and committees of Congress. Their books on big-game hunting and wilderness travel attracted a wide readership — popularized in part by the sportsmen-president himself.[15] Thus, sportsmen were able to influence contemporary thinking about the Alaskan frontier in a way that had not been possible twenty or thirty years earlier.

Some sportsmen-writers suggested that animal speciation paralleled human racialism. Therefore, these writers assumed, the superiority of arctic animal forms underscored the racial superiority of Nordic peoples. Sportsman-conservationist Madison Grant, who dabbled in nineteenth-century racial theory in his book *The Passing of the Great Race* (1916), argued that the many large species of game in Alaska appeared "to be the very culmination of their respective genera."[16] Grant's fellow wildlife conservationist, George Bird Grinnell, warned against allowing introduced reindeer to mingle with the native caribou, a larger and more robust animal, "and forming a mongrel race."[17] Many sportsmen prized the Dall mountain sheep over the Rocky Mountain bighorn because of its snow-white coat and more graceful, slender horns. For many sportsmen-conservationists of the era, the scientific classification of animal species bore a close relationship to the identification of racial differences in the human species.[18]

Another idea which sportsmen contributed to Alaska's frontier myth related directly to their own conception of the frontier process. The wilderness, in the sportsmen's view, was always teeming with game before the coming of the white man. Each advance of the frontier entailed a bloody assault upon the wildlife. The classic episode in this process was the near-extermination of the buffalo in the 1870s and early 1880s. George Bird Grinnell was the acknowledged expert on this event.[19] The story of the great buffalo hunt was all the more poignant because Grinnell and his fellow sportsmen could condemn the stupendous waste that had occurred and lament the buffalo's disappearance, but they could not argue with the outcome — the settlement of the land by stockmen and farmers. It had been "a necessary part of the development of the country."[20] Thus, sportsmen harbored deep misgivings at the very heart of their conception of the frontier process. Visions of wildlife abundance held mixed associations of nostalgia and backwardness; visions of wildlife slaughter held mixed associations of terrible waste and progress. Without necessarily confronting this problem, they invoked scenes of buffalo — either remembered or imagined — whenever they wanted to describe their wilderness ideal.

At the turn of the century, the closest thing left to that wilderness ideal in North America was the Far North where the caribou still roamed. An example of how sportsmen constructed the myth of the last frontier may be found in the introduction to *The Arctic Prairies* (1911) by Ernest Thompson Seton. Seton began his account of a hunting expedition by asking his readers, "what young man of our race" would not gladly give a year of his life "to see the Wild West" with its herds of buffalo, teeming big game, and roaming Indians? Seton had discovered that this "miracle" was still possible when he arranged an expedition in 1907 to the Peace and Mackenzie Rivers of northwest Canada. There he had found a virgin "prairie" land that would "some day be an empire peopled with white men."[21] Seton used all the standard elements of the myth of the last frontier in framing his tale: the nostalgia and romance of the Old West, the centrality of big game to the frontier imagery, the implication that this was last opportunity to experience the frontier before it was too late, the whiff of social Darwinism in the references to race and empire. Significantly, it was sportsmen like Seton who were the first to revel in the myth that they themselves were helping to create. The sportsmen were among the original consumers of what a later era would call "an Alaska wilderness experience."

While sportsmen were inventing and experiencing the myth, they were thinking about how to preserve this new hunting ground from destruction so that future generations could enjoy it too. When they considered how to preserve the game, their analysis of the problem began with their own take. The sport hunter had certainly not been blameless in the slaughter of the buffalo, and in any new hunting field one was sure to find the latter-day Buffalo Bill, or "game hog." Ideally, the sport hunter was constrained from taking an excessive amount of game by his loyalty to the sportsman's code. According to the code, the true sport hunter measured his success by the quality of the hunt, not the quantity of his take. He derived all his satisfaction from the skill that he exercised in hunting his quarry. The sport hunter disdained a sure kill. He accepted limitations on his own weaponry while affording his quarry the benefit of a "fair chase." He did not waste his kills, but took the meat, hide, head, and whatever else the animal carcass would yield. By following this code, the sportsman not only did his part to conserve the supply of wildlife for his fellow hunters, but he gained a deeper aesthetic appreciation of nature, too.[22]

American sportsmen liked to identify their exploits with the American frontier. Ironically, the idea of sportsmanship in hunting was not a part of the American frontier heritage; it had been introduced by a group of English immigrants in the 1830s. The sportsman's code slowly took root in the United States among the upper class in the cities of the Northeast in the 1840s, but it failed to get very much further in the United States for another generation. It was the irreversible destruction and great wastage of the buffalo during the 1870s that first awakened a large segment of the American public to the need for a new wildlife conservation ethic. In that decade, scores of game clubs and sport hunting magazines were launched; and in the following two decades, several states passed game laws with the object of preserving a continuous supply of game for sport hunting. Yet most state game laws remained ineffectual at the turn of the century, and in many parts of the country the sportsman's code had barely made inroads on the old pioneer ethic of hunting, in which animals were slain for practical uses as efficiently as possible and with no thought for the future.[23]

Sportsmen-conservationists generally believed that the so-called "pot hunter" who did not obey the game laws was not incorrigible; he was simply backward. He would be converted to the new wildlife ethic in time. It was the professional, or market, hunter whom they despised. All of the attributes of the true sport hunter were practically the opposites of those of this loathsome character. The market hunter sought efficiency. He looked for the easy slaughter, the prodigious kill, the most effective weaponry — in short, the most profitable use of his time. If the market hunter made large profits on heads, then heads might be all that he took. The market hunter usually moved from place to place, showing little concern for the long-term prospects of the local animal population; he therefore did not discriminate between old and young or male and female of a given species. In the southern part of Alaska, the market hunter hired Indians to increase his take; the Indians themselves then became market hunters. Thus, the sportsman conceived of the problem of wildlife depletion in terms of a hierarchy of offenders: "The destruction of game is far more often effected by local residents than it is by visiting sportsmen, but the chief evil doer, and the public enemy of all classes is the professional hunter, either Indian or white, who kills for the market."[24] This conceptual framework underpinned the sportsman's basic program of wildlife conservation. It informed the game laws that limited bags, seasons, and methods for the hunt, set up game commissions, and authorized the appointment of game wardens.

The sportsmen achieved their first major victory for conservation in Alaska with the enactment by Congress of an Alaska Game Law in 1902. This was followed by the passage of a slightly more stringent code in 1908. Still, despite the law's federal jurisdiction, there was so little enforcement that it was practically useless. Members of the Boone and Crockett Club agreed that stronger measures were required to protect the game, and they looked to the creation of game preserves as their most important objective in Alaska. Such preserves would need to be patrolled by federal game wardens. The preserves would have to be "as thoroughly controlled as the Yellowstone Park."[25] Indeed, to obtain national park designation for an area was the surest way to protect the game supply. "The Club could successfully influence the Federal Government to preserve game under its jurisdiction," one Boone and Crockett Club publication stated, "and once the government had been committed to it, police power could be obtained for the purpose."[26] Another club book averred, "In such areas . . . the game will then retain its native habits and breed freely, while the overflow would populate the adjoining districts."[27] The members of the Boone and Crockett Club knew nothing of population ecology or natural cycles of abundance and scarcity. They imagined that a game population, if relieved of hunting pressure, would grow in much the same way as a herd of domestic livestock. The game sanctuary would effectively "stock" the range with game animals. Though the animals within a national park could not be shot by hunters, they would still benefit hunters by forming a source of breeding stock for the surrounding country. Herein lay the main reason for their enthusiastic support of national parks.[28]

Ironically, it was the sportsmen's naive, anthropocentric understanding of wildlife abundance and scarcity that originally made the Mount McKinley region famous as a game country. Early accounts of the Mount McKinley region interpreted the extraordinary abundance of game strictly in terms of the region's remoteness from civilization. Alfred H. Brooks of the USGS, who led the first official exploration of the Mount McKinley region in 1902, reported that he had never seen such an abundance of bear, sheep, moose, and caribou anywhere else in Alaska, and that the area must rank as "one of the finest hunting grounds in North America."[29] It would be an attractive new field to the big-game hunter, Brooks wrote, "but the very reason of this abundance lies in the inaccessibility of the field, which must deter most sportsmen."[30] Charles Sheldon, a wealthy sportsman from New York, eagerly accepted the challenge described by Brooks and made the first sport hunting expeditions to the Mount McKinley region in 1906 and 1907–8. Even though he entered the country on the heels of a gold stampede in 1905–6, Sheldon painted a romantic portrait of a virgin land in *The Wilderness of Denali*.[31] The following year, Sheldon's packer and guide, Harry Karstens, told an interviewer for *Alaska-Yukon Magazine* that even in a frontier land where virtually the whole territory was "a vast hunting ground," the area around the base of Mount McKinley was still the best to be found anywhere.[32] To the USGS geologist Stephen R. Capps, who described the area for *National Geographic Magazine* while the national park bill was before Congress, the Mount McKinley region was "a game country without rival in America."[33]

Twenty years after the area was made a national park, a new generation of scientifically trained wildlife experts would provide insight into the ecological reasons for the profusion of animal life on the north slope of the Alaska Range — reasons that had more to do with climate than its remoteness on the Alaskan frontier. The experts would point out that Mount McKinley and the Alaska Range influence the region's climate profoundly, forming a rain shadow across the plain that lies north of Mount McKinley. In this area, annual precipitation is a mere twenty inches; temperatures are marked by extremes, particularly in the winter; the soil is poor and the vegetation is sparse. Nowhere does timberline extend higher than 3,000 feet and in many areas it is much lower, while most of the plain supports only a thin covering of bunch grasses and vetch. The abundance of large fauna, the experts explained, was due to the fact that snow depths were not too great to prevent caribou, moose, and Dall sheep from reaching their winter browse. The limiting factor for all hoofed mammals in the Subarctic tended to be the availability of winter range, the experts pointed out, and snow depth was crucial to the animals' ability to survive. In hard winters when the snow cover became deeper or lingered longer, precipitous population decreases, or die-offs, could result. Thus, the general abundance of animals in this region, and indeed throughout the Subarctic, was subject to wide fluctuation.[34] At the time when biological experts were explaining this, in 1932, Mount McKinley's Dall sheep population had just crashed and numbered perhaps a tenth of what it had been when Sheldon or Capps saw it. These ecological insights did not negate the threat to the game from market hunters, but they did suggest that there was an element of unreality, or naivete, in the sportsmen's dream of preserving the landscape just as they had encountered it.

The Boone and Crockett Club agreed with Sheldon's suggestion, upon his return from Mount McKinley in 1908, that the region should be made a national park, but its members disagreed as to whether the club should proceed immediately or wait several years to make the proposal. Sheldon's

feeling was that Alaskans were not yet ready for a national park; if their
abuse of the Game Law was any indication, Alaskans would not give a
national park much credence, either.[35] Sheldon believed that the development of local support for wildlife conservation must precede the national
park proposal. This required time and patience.[36] Madison Grant took
the opposite view, arguing that the federal government should act sooner
rather than later to establish game preserves in Alaska. In the same vein,
Grant opposed any reform of the Alaska Game Law that would allow Alaskans regulatory control over bag limits and closed seasons, and he regarded
the creation of an Alaskan territorial government in 1912 as a grave setback
for the conservation of Alaska's big game.[37]

This was more than a difference of strategy. It reflected two different
views of the way the Alaskan frontier was developing — two versions of the
Alaskan frontier myth. In Grant's view, Alaska's geographic position in the
Far North would keep the territory from developing into a state as other
western territories had. Its white population would remain small and transient. Miners, who made up most of the white population in 1912, had no
permanent interest in the country in the sense that farmers who were
attached to the soil did. Miners were accustomed to living off the land with
little regard for its future. It would be impossible to sow a new wildlife ethic
in such a population. Alaska must remain a ward of the federal government.
Congress, not the residents of Alaska, must retain responsibility for the
enactment and enforcement of wise laws. Grant's vision for Alaskan big
game was both romantic and apocalyptic: Alaska represented "the last great
opportunity to preserve our native fauna on a large scale," but if Alaskans
were given a hand in setting bag limits and closed seasons, it would be "the
death knell of many species of game."[38]

Sheldon, meanwhile, saw the Alaskan frontier as a continuation of the
western frontier. He took a more sympathetic view of the white miner or
Indian who killed game out of season in order to feed himself. In the
interior, where Alaskans were practically sealed off from the outside from
freeze-up till break-up, they depended on the supply of game around their
camps for food. No wonder that they still regarded the game as a subsistence resource. Sheldon recalled that there was a single beef distributor in
Fairbanks who purchased a quantity of livestock each summer after it was
driven north from Skagway or Valdez. By winter the beef would be rancid.
Local residents preferred to eat wild meat; they would shoot game while
prospecting, cache it, and let it spoil with the next thaw. Officers of the law
simply turned their backs. "When I was up there," Sheldon told a congressional committee, "if they hauled a breaker of the game laws into Fair-

banks they could not get judge or jury to convict him."[39] His point was that Congress should not pass game laws that were so contrary to local opinion as to be mocked by the local populace. Instead, Congress should adapt the law to Alaska's frontier conditions. In the interior of Alaska, Sheldon believed, the white miners and Indians should be allowed to hunt for their own subsistence but not for the market.[40] If local opinion could only be turned against the market hunter the wildlife would be preserved.

There were signs that such a shift in local opinion was indeed occurring. Faint glimmers of a new, wildlife conservation ethic were reflected in the *Fairbanks Daily News-Miner,* which gently chided its readers for many of the hunting excesses that took place. The worst case of excess was the frenzied slaughter that occurred in 1905 when the fall caribou migration brought thousands of caribou practically within gunshot distance of the Fairbanks gold diggings. For a period of a few weeks, the flats around town were turned into a killing field as prospectors slaughtered hundreds of caribou with appalling ease. For years afterwards, each September, the people of Fairbanks braced themselves for a recurrence of this savage spectacle. Rumors about the gathering herd's size and whereabouts received large play in the town's newspaper as prospectors tried to decide "whether to sit tight and wait for their winter supply of meat to come to them, or whether to get out after it."[41]

Alaskans began to infer that the "legitimate prospector" had a greater claim than the market hunter to the local game supply. The sportsmen's claims that the market hunter was greedy and shortsighted and would deplete the game supply if left unchecked began to hit home. In the fall of 1907, the *Fairbanks Daily News-Miner* reported that the "mighty nimrod," Tom Gibson, was making his second large shipment of caribou meat from his hunting camp to Fairbanks, over the protests of local prospectors who thought a good portion of this meat should be consumed by "the creek people."[42] Even though the people of Fairbanks were the recipients of this meat shipment, the newspaper was sympathetic toward the prospectors who inhabited the drainage where Gibson had his main camp. In 1909, the newspaper reported that a prospector named J. P. Sherman had been appointed field deputy to the U.S. marshal in Fairbanks to assist with game protection in outlying areas. According to Sherman, market hunters had carried out their work in his district the previous year "to a shameful extent." The hunters had taken moose and sheep to sell in the Fairbanks market and "as a result the legitimate prospector suffered for lack of meat."[43] Three years later, even the amateur market hunter came in for abuse, as the *Fairbanks Daily News-Miner* poked fun at eight Fairbanks miners who had reached the "real limit in hunting expeditions" with their plans to set out for the caribou herd twenty or thirty miles from town. The newspaper satirically described their "elaborate preparations by study of natural histories and kindred works, such as those telling of Bwana Tumbo's expedition."[44] To equate the market hunter with the stereotype African big-game hunter would have appalled most sportsmen, but for readers of the *Fairbanks Daily News-Miner* it made perfect sense. Sport hunters were notorious in Alaska for collecting scientific specimens in order to get around the bag limits of the Game Law. In the minds of some Alaskans, all visiting sportsmen who supposedly killed game in the name of science were hypocrites and game hogs.[45]

What these accounts reflect is the origin of a distinctively Alaskan, wildlife conservation ethic. Alaskan whites accepted the sportsmen's admonition against waste, but according to their own terms. Different groups of hunters had a prior claim upon the limited supply of game. Local inhabitants — Indian and white — had first priority. Transient hunters, whether they were hunting for sport or profit, had a lesser claim. This legitimation of subsistence hunting (or "pot hunting," as the sportsmen called it) and its prioritization ahead of sport hunting would finally become law in Alaska in 1976, but its origin can be found in the early twentieth century. Significantly, as the white resident population came to embrace the idea that each mining camp had a prior claim to the game in its particular drainage, it put the miners in the position of defending what were essentially traditional Athapaskan hunting territories. Even though the pattern may have been undeliberate and had no basis in law, it did serve to reduce tension between Indian and white subsistence hunters in the interior of Alaska and gave the two races common cause to oppose the most flagrant market hunters as well as the visiting sport hunters.

It is doubtful that Charles Sheldon perceived the emergence of a distinctively Alaskan, wildlife conservation ethic. His universal model for game conservation continued to be the diffusion of a sportsman's code among the general populace. According to this model, western territories developed into states, pioneer communities matured into towns and cities like those in the eastern United States, and sportsmen's clubs took root and spread the sportsman's code.[46] He expected the same historical development would take place in Alaska. If this had been the controlling idea for his national park proposal, he might have waited indefinitely to begin his campaign for a national park. When Sheldon finally did act, it was not the maturation of Alaskans' conservation ethic that prompted him to go forward, but fears of what would happen with the coming of the railroad.

In 1914, Congress chartered the Alaska Engineering Commission (AEC) to oversee construction and operation of a railroad from Seward to Fairbanks. The railroad line would go up the valley of the Susitna River and cross the Alaska Range at Broad Pass, then down the valley of the Nenana River and up the Tanana and Chena valleys to Fairbanks. For approximately forty miles, the line would flank the exceptional game country north of the Alaska Range. In the next several years, the AEC hired thousands of workers and laid out several construction camps at intervals along the line. Camps for railroad section crews spawned permanent settlements in or near the Alaska Range at Cantwell, Healy, and Nenana. For the first time, the caribou and Dall sheep in the Mount McKinley region began to attract the market hunter. These were only the most immediate consequences of the coming of the railroad for the Mount McKinley region.[47]

Just as it did in so many other parts of the country, the coming of the railroad on the Alaskan frontier raised a complicated set of expectations, hopes, and fears well in advance of its actual arrival. The anticipation of the railroad deserves analysis because it propelled the movement for the national park, from October 10, 1915 when Sheldon announced his intention to begin the campaign, through the congressional committee hearings in 1916 when the railroad–national park connection was explored as a basis for developing Alaska's tourist industry, to February 19, 1917 when Congress passed the Mount McKinley National Park Act as an "emergency measure" to forestall the destruction of game by market hunters employed by the railroad camps. It must be emphasized that the Alaska Railroad did not actually reach the area of the park until 1917, and that it was not completed until six years after the creation of the park, in February 1923. It was mainly the *idea* of the railroad that influenced the national park movement. Prophesies about the changes that the railroad would bring were inconsistent, but this did not lessen their impact. If the coming of the railroad did not overthrow Alaska's basic mythology — that the last frontier was a wilderness peopled by miners and wild animals — it did introduce new contradictions and ambiguities.

Alaska's governors had been recommending that the federal government build a trunk railroad in Alaska for many years, but it was the Wilson administration that finally committed itself to the idea. The Wilson administration hoped that the federally commissioned railroad would become an engine of progress for the territory of Alaska, linking coastal shipping lanes with Yukon River commerce and spurring the development of coal lands and farming communities along its route. The Alaska Railroad was the centerpiece of the Wilson administration's plan to develop the Alaskan frontier. Congress approved the plan and appropriated $35 million for construction and operation with the expectation that the railroad would eventually become self-supporting.[48] That Congress and the Wilson administration should have such expectations was hardly surprising, for the railroad had long been seen as a remarkable agent of industrialization and progress. According to the frontier myth, the railroad was what bound the nation together after the Civil War — tying north to south, east to west, backwater to booming city, and wilderness to civilization. The railroad was a modern circulatory system for distributing the nation's enterprising spirit and resource abundance. By more evenly distributing these twin national assets, the railroad turned prairies into cropland, farms into towns, and towns into industrial cities. Why should the Alaskan frontier be different?

The railroad was also a potent symbol of industrial America's domination over nature. Cultural historian Richard Slotkin has written that the building of railroads appeared to allow men to evade the limitations of nature, penetrate mountains, span rivers, and cross empty spaces as never before. In the myth of the frontier the railroad represented the might of industry loosed upon the natural landscape, and it always took the form of humankind establishing control over nature.[49]

The railroad's symbolism was quickly assimilated into the myth of the last frontier. Just as railroads on the western frontier had brought hope and prosperity to isolated settlements as railroad builders succeeded in breaching one mountain barrier after another, so too railroads on the Alaskan frontier would open up settlements in the interior, which had previously faced isolation during the long winter freeze-up. Alaskan writer Rex Beach concluded his novel *The Iron Trail* (1913), about the construction of Alaska's first railroad, with the spectacle of spring break-up on the "Salmon" (Copper) River and tons upon tons of ice straining against the untried abutments of the new railroad bridge. In this climactic scene, the hero of the allegorical tale, railroad builder Murray O'Neil, wins the heart of the conservation-minded newspaperwoman, Eliza V. Appleton, as they watch his railroad bridge withstand this ultimate test of nature in the Far North.[50] Beach's message is obvious: the railroad will triumph over the wilderness and unlock Alaska's natural riches, and civilization will go forward in spite of all the nay-saying and obstructionism by conservationists. The coming of the railroad greatly encouraged those who believed that Alaska would develop in the same way as the western states, its northern climate notwithstanding.

In this era, the railroad also conjured up images of scenic landscapes and resort hotels. National parks were conspicuous in the western railroads' extensive advertising literature.[51] Western railroads promoted the parks because the parks stimulated demand for passenger service on the western railroads.[52] Historian Alfred Runte has observed that "among all the publicists of the region, the railroads were without rivals in their ability to bring the West into the living rooms of the American people."[53] Railroads also provided much of the capital investment for tourist hotels and transportation services in the parks. The Northern Pacific owned and operated the hotels and stage lines in Yellowstone, the Great Northern built the hotels in Glacier, and the Santa Fe developed the South Rim of the Grand Canyon, to name just three prominent examples.[54] The proposal to establish a national park near the Alaska Railroad raised the question of whether a similar connection could be forged in Alaska. Before considering how the national park movement responded to this issue, however, it will be helpful to consider one other set of images that the railroad evoked.

For Americans of a primitivist bent, the railroad was a powerful symbol of destruction. The railroad was the "Iron Horse" disrupting the Indian way of life. It was the industrial age bearing down on the farmer. It was America's technological intrusion into nature. It was the slaughter of the buffalo. The last image was particularly important to Charles Sheldon and other supporters of the Mount McKinley national park idea. As Sheldon's friend George B. Grinnell continually reminded him and other associates, the coming of the railroad had been the key event in the "dismal story" of the great buffalo hunt.[55] Grinnell related the story in *The Last of the Buffalo* (1892), and again in his essay on bison in *Musk-Ox, Bison, Sheep and Goat* (1904). Certainly the aboriginal Indians had been wasteful in their buffalo hunts, and the pioneers and hide hunters had taken a heavy toll in the mid-nineteenth century, but the construction of the transcontinentals in the 1870s and 1880s had suddenly made it cheap and profitable to ship buffalo hides to the East.[56] The market hunter who slaughtered the buffalo in the 1870s and 1880s was merely the poison at the tip of the spear; it was industrialization that had plunged the spear into the buffalo's heart. Grinnell's *The Last of the Buffalo* was an allegory for the passing of the Great West. In his story, the coming of the railroad prophesied the end of the frontier.

There is no question that this latter, dark vision of the railroad strongly influenced the original conception of Mount McKinley National Park. Sheldon announced his intention "to inaugurate a plan" for the establishment of a "Denali National Park" in a letter to the chief of the Biological Survey, Dr. E. W. Nelson, on October 10, 1915. Sheldon opened and closed his letter with references to the railroad, which, he said, made the

park "absolutely necessary as a reserve for the game."[57] Sheldon described
boundaries to Nelson that would leave a thirty-mile-wide buffer between
the park and the railroad — just enough distance to inhibit market hunters if
the area were patrolled by park rangers. Clearly his first thought was for the
preservation of wildlife, not the development of tourism by and for the
railroad.

Ironically, Sheldon himself was a former railroad builder. At the pinnacle
of his fourteen-year career in business, from 1898 to 1903, Sheldon had
served as a general manager of the Chihuahua and Pacific Railroad and of
the Chihuahua and Pacific Exploration Company. He had made a fortune
on investments in a Mexican silver mine, and retired from this work in 1903
in order to dedicate all his energy to his three avocations of big-game hunting, writing, and wildlife conservation.[58] Sheldon's feelings about the Alaska
Railroad were complex. He believed that economic and political progress
went hand in hand. He was sympathetic to the desire of white Alaskans to
develop their territory's resources and acquire more self-government. The
way that Sheldon resolved these conflicting values was to insist that a relatively large national park in interior Alaska would suffice to preserve a
representative portion of the last frontier, while the territory as a whole
would undergo the normal course of development from frontier territory to
prosperity and statehood. For these reasons, Sheldon consistently argued
that Alaskans themselves must be convinced that the national park would
assist in the development of the territory and that they must participate in
the political process leading to the park's establishment.[59]

This imperative led Sheldon to take a compromising, even illusory, stand
on mining in the park. Alaska's territorial delegate to Congress, Judge
James B. Wickersham, who was practically the first person after Nelson to
be brought into Sheldon's campaign, insisted that the national park allow
mining and prospecting.[60] As Sheldon and Wickersham drafted the bill
early in 1916, there was never any serious discussion that mining should be
prohibited. Wickersham's support of the park was viewed as essential, and,
moreover, various administration officials, from Commissioner Thomas B.
Riggs of the AEC to the USGS's Alaska expert, Alfred H. Brooks, agreed
with him that local mining interests should be protected.[61]

As antithetical as the mining provision might seem to the purposes of
a national park, it was not an unusual feature of early national park establishing acts. The legislation creating Yosemite, Mount Rainier, Crater
Lake, and Glacier National Parks all carried provisions for mining. But the
Mount McKinley National Park bill was the only one to go a step further
and grant miners and prospectors a special privilege to hunt game in the

park. Wickersham insisted on this unique provision as well, because he and Sheldon, try as they might, could not agree on adequate boundaries for the national park that would take in enough game country while cutting out the resident miners' hunting ground.

The park boundaries as finally drawn described a nearly rectangular area along the northeast–southwest axis of the Alaska Range. The southern boundary was high up on the unexplored south slope of the range and was unlikely to raise any objections. The northern boundary was the difficult one, for here Sheldon's aim was to take in all the Dall sheep's winter range in the outlying hills north of the Alaska Range, as well as a significant portion of moose and caribou range on the "piedmont plateau" north of Mount McKinley and Mount Foraker, while leaving out most of the gold diggings and all of the miners' cabins at the foot of the Kantishna Hills. The eastern boundary, meanwhile, would leave a margin of rough country between the park and the railroad line. The proposed park boundaries would encompass nearly 3,000 square miles — more than any national park except Yellowstone.[62]

The Kantishna mining district had been formed more than ten years earlier in 1905, when prospectors Joe Quigley and Jack Horn discovered gold in paying quantities along Glacier Creek in the Kantishna Hills. A stampede had ensued as several thousand gold seekers traveled up the Kantishna River by boat, with late arrivals coming by dog sled. The towns of Glacier City, Diamond, Roosevelt, and Square Deal sprouted in the spruce forest north and west of the Kantishna Hills. By the early part of 1906, however, disappointment was sweeping through the camps. When Sheldon and his guide, Harry Karstens, came upon these towns in July 1906, they were already practically deserted. Only about thirty to fifty miners stayed behind to work the claims, prospect, and supplement their income by trapping in the winter. The history of this community is significant because it lent itself to wishful thinking by those both for and against mining development in the area. To men like Wickersham, it indicated that the Mount McKinley region held promise for future mining development and must remain open; to men like Sheldon, it indicated that mining would not seriously endanger the park because it would never amount to much.[63]

Wickersham introduced the Mount McKinley bill in the House in April. Senator Key Pittman of Nevada introduced the same bill in the Senate six days later.[64] On May 5, 1916, the Senate Committee on Public Lands held a hearing on the Mount McKinley bill and invited Sheldon, Wickersham, and two members of the Camp Fire Club of America, William B. Greeley and Belmore Browne, to testify. The committee members passed over the matter of boundaries and the provision for mining and focused on two other issues: the national park's potential to attract passenger traffic on the government railroad, and the bill's peculiar provision that allowed miners and prospectors a special privilege to hunt game in the park.

Sheldon, Browne, and Greeley all testified that the national park would be a boon to the Alaska Railroad. The park would attract publicity and thereby generate passenger traffic on the line. Senator Wesley Jones of Washington State pressed Sheldon on how the national park could be expected to draw passenger traffic when it still lay thirty miles from the railroad and was inaccessible by stage coach or automobile. The senator drew Sheldon into a discussion of the feasibility of constructing a wagon road or narrow-gauge line into the park. When Sheldon allowed that something of that kind would need to be done, Senator Jones asked how this could be reconciled with earlier testimony that the park would cost very little to administer — only enough to field a ranger or two for game protection? The senator's questions aimed at a cost-benefit analysis of the park — whether the cost of developing and administering the park would outweigh its benefit as a game refuge and public playground. But the questions also got at something deeper by suggesting the paradoxical nature of the railroad's relationship to the park. The park's supporters wanted to preserve the wilderness from the destructive influence of the railroad, yet they hailed the railroad as the means of bringing pleasure-seekers to the wilderness. Despite the senator's effort to trip him up, however, Sheldon seemed to satisfy the committee that the national park would work in conjunction with the Alaska Railroad to increase the Alaskan tourist trade.[65]

On the second critical issue of miners in the park, the committee focused on Section 6 of the bill, which concerned the miners' and prospectors' privilege to hunt game. The committee wanted to know what was the point of protecting the game if the only people in the area would be allowed to kill it anyway. The club men's answer was that the national park would protect the game from the market hunter. Section 6 read:

> That the said park shall be, and is hereby, established as a game refuge, and no person shall kill any game in said park except under an order from the Secretary of the Interior for the protection of persons or to protect or prevent the extermination of other animals or birds; Provided, that prospectors and miners engaged in prospecting and mining in said park may take and kill therein so much game or birds as may be needed for their actual necessities when short of food; but in no case

shall animals or birds be killed in said park for sale or removal there-from, or wantonly.[66]

However, it remained for the club men to convince the senators that prospectors and market hunters could really be distinguished from one another, and that the distinction would be enforceable.

Belmore Browne, an artist, sportsman, mountaineer, and author of *The Conquest of Mount McKinley* (1913), about his nearly successful climbing expedition in 1912, told the Senate committee that there was no peril from the prospector. "All peril would be from the poachers and hunters of meat to sell. There is no peril in allowing the bona fide prospector to secure such meat as he wants; he could never deplete the supply."[67] In one sense, the difference between the two kinds of hunting could be laid down to numbers — miners and prospectors hunted for their own subsistence only, while market hunters slaughtered animals for hundreds or even thousands of consumers in Nenana, Fairbanks, and other towns on the railroad. But explaining this provision of the bill narrowly in terms of numbers satisfied neither the club men nor the senators. Instead, they wanted to cast the special hunting privilege in terms of cultural values and a selective perception of the American frontier experience. Browne drew a sharp, moral distinction between the prospector and the market hunter. "The American prospector is a sensible man, and he looks out for and guards jealously the wild life about him, because he knows his life depends on the game," Browne stated. "With the opening of the railroad, you are going to get a class in there that is not going to protect the game as the prospector has, and you are going to have repeated over again the slaughter of the big game animals that has followed our march westward."[68] Thus, the issue was not solely numbers, but also which kind of hunter was morally superior to the other.

The Alaskan prospector deserved the privilege because he symbolized the myth of the last frontier. Like the hunter-pathfinder of the old frontier and the cowboy of the Old West, the Alaskan prospector possessed the right qualities to be the latest hero of the frontier myth: humble origins; a solitary, adventuring spirit; and the skill to survive in a wild, uncivilized landscape. When Browne and Sheldon praised the Alaskan prospector, they were echoing the sentiment of most white Alaskans themselves.[69]

Sheldon and Browne both suggested that the creation of Mount McKinley National Park would tend to preserve the prospector as well as the game. Browne told the committee that Mount McKinley National Park's greatest value would be as "a breeding ground and refuge," which would "insure a supply of meat in the years to come." There was no other place in the United States where the citizens were so dependent on the game supply, Browne declared. The development of Alaska depended on its game resources; consequently, the park was "an economic necessity to the citizens of Alaska."[70] Sheldon testified, "I know the Alaskans well enough to know that they themselves want to protect their game. . . . They want a reservoir of game for a game supply."[71] It is tempting to assume that the sportsmen-conservationists were acknowledging the emergence of an Alaskan, wildlife conservation ethic based on the prior claim of local subsistence hunters, but there is no direct evidence to support that assumption. Rather, they seem to have countenanced hunting in the park partly in the belief that it would be so minimal as to cause no harm, partly to win the support of Alaskans for the national park, and partly to honor their romantic conception of the Kantishna miner as frontiersman.

The committee reported back favorably on the bill and it was passed by the Senate at the end of that session, but in the House the bill died in the Committee on Public Lands, the traditional burial ground for national park bills. That fall the Mount McKinley National Park proposal received critical support from the first director of the new NPS, Stephen T. Mather.[72] Mather had had little to say about it when Sheldon first approached him nearly a year earlier; he was too busy getting Congress to enact the landmark National Park Service Act of August 25, 1916. With that first imperative achieved, Mather got behind the Mount McKinley proposal with all of his characteristic enthusiasm.[73] Mather decided to make this national park bill his top priority in the next session of Congress. During the fall and winter of 1916–17, he gathered information through other bureaus in the Department of the Interior, which would give more weight to the sportsmen's entreaties of an emergency need for game protection.

The two most important reports that Mather received came from Alaska Governor J. A. Strong and a USGS geologist named Stephen R. Capps. Governor Strong ordered his game warden in Fairbanks to investigate where the railroad camps were getting their meat supply, and in February 1917 he confirmed for Mather that the AEC had purchased more than 5,000 pounds of Dall sheep meat from market hunters since 1914. The AEC fed its workforce on sheep meat by exploiting what it claimed to be a loophole in the Alaska Game Law. It furnished meal tickets to its employees as part of their compensation and banned nonemployees from taking meals at any of the camp messes. These meals were valued at thirty-three cents each, nineteen cents below the cost to the government. By insisting that it provided the meals below cost, the AEC narrowly circumvented the law's prohibition against "dealers" of wild meat, but it was a highly questionable interpretation of the law.[74]

Stephen R. Capps had been dispatched to the Kantishna mining district by the USGS in the summer of 1916 as the national park bill was pending. Sheldon had asked Capps to canvas miners on their views of the need for game protection. Capps reported to Mather in December 1916 that the total sheep kill by market hunters in the Mount McKinley region came to perhaps 1,500 to 2,000 each year. About half of this kill was sold in the new railroad town of Nenana, whose population of 4,000 rivaled that of Fairbanks and was much closer to the proposed park. The other half of this meat was consumed by the hunters' sled dogs. Capps was certain that without protection the game would soon be depleted. He was less sanguine about the miners' sympathies. The three market hunters who were known to work in the Mount McKinley region during the winter were themselves miners during the summer. If this revelation gave Mather any qualms about the special provision that would allow miners and prospectors to hunt game in the park, he did not let on.[75]

At Mather's urging, Capps hastily rewrote his report for Mather's friend, Gilbert H. Grosvenor, the editor of *National Geographic* and a loyal supporter of national parks. Grosvenor slipped the Capps article into the magazine's January 1917 issue just weeks before the Mount McKinley National Park bill was due on the House and Senate calendars, with the news-headline title, "A Game Country Without Rival in America: The Proposed Mount McKinley National Park." File photographs depicted sled dogs, trapper cabins, Alaskan sourdoughs, and Athapaskan Indians, while Capps' text brimmed with enthusiasm about the abundance of wildlife in the proposed national park. "The mountains at the head of Toklat and Teklanika Rivers literally swarm with the magnificent white bighorn sheep," Capps wrote. "I have counted over 300 in a single day's journey of 10 miles along the river bars, and doubtless as many more were unobserved in the tributary valleys beyond my view. From a single point at my tent door one evening I counted nine bands of sheep, containing in all 171 animals." But unless the area received protection, he warned, the great herds of game could be destroyed in a matter of a few years.[76] This timely article added to the sense of urgency that surrounded the bill when it was brought up for a vote the next month.

The House finally considered the bill at the end of the session, on February 19, 1917. An amendment was offered to limit park appropriations to $10,000 annually, following the pattern of the two national park bills passed in the previous session. Such an arbitrary measure was aimed at preventing the new NPS from growing too quickly and was further justified on the grounds that parklands could be set aside immediately and developed for tourism at some later time. Delegate Wickersham objected that this park bill was an emergency measure and required immediate expenditures to protect the game. However, the House passed the amendment, then passed another amendment clarifying that nothing in the bill would affect the mineral laws in Alaska, and then passed the bill.[77] The Senate took it up as an emergency measure and passed it the same day. Sheldon delivered the bill to President Woodrow Wilson personally, and the president signed it into law on February 26, 1917.[78] Mount McKinley had the distinction of being the first park added to the national park system after the passage of the National Park Service Act of 1916.

Mount McKinley National Park was the original frontier national park. Its founders aimed to preserve not only a wilderness, but a way of life. Here, according to their ideal, the Alaskan frontier would remain in its primitive phase: wild and undeveloped, thinly populated by prospectors, and rich in game resources. But NPS officials soon learned that an inhabited wilderness was a very different beast to administer.

VIEW OF MOUNT MCKINLEY LOOKING ACROSS THE THOROFARE BAR

(Photograph courtesy Denali National Park Archives.)

CHARLES SHELDON, 1906

The big game hunter and naturalist led the campaign to establish Mount Rainier National Park.

(Photograph courtesy Hartley H. T. Jackson Collection, 84–4674, Smithsonian Institution.)

RILEY CREEK CAMP DURING CONSTRUCTION OF THE ALASKA RAILROAD,
CA. 1921

The camps consumed large quantities of wild meat. The coming of the railroad posed a threat to the game resource and precipitated the establishment of Mount McKinley National Park.

(Photograph courtesy Alaska Railroad Collection, PCA 108–24B, Alaska State Library. Juneau.)

MINERS IN THE KANTISHNA DISTRICT, CA. 1918

The small buildings on stilts are caches for keeping meat out of reach of bears and other scavengers. These residents were permitted to hunt for their subsistence in the national park.

(Photograph courtesy Stephen Foster Collection, 69–92–295, Alaska and Polar Regions Department, University of Alaska, Fairbanks.)

DALL SHEEP, ALASKA RANGE

The Dall sheep is more northern in range and smaller than the Rocky Mountain bighorn sheep. Trophy hunters prized the animal for its distinctive white coat and slender, dull amber horns.

(Photograph courtesy National Park Service, 102587–2149–24, Washington Office.)

A SPORT HUNTER AND HIS BAG

The abundance of Dall sheep and other game animals north of Mount
McKinley inspired the campaign to establish Alaska's first national park.
(Photograph courtesy Robert Marshall Collection, University of California, Berkeley.)

BUSES AND CARS READY FOR TOURISTS AT VALDEZ
This was the point of entry for many Alaska tours in the 1920s.
(Photograph courtesy A. L. Washburn Collection, 82–58–106, Alaska and Polar Regions Department, University of Alaska, Fairbanks.)

SAVAGE RIVER CAMP

This camp was the center for tourist accommodations in Mount McKinley
National Park until the construction of the park hotel.

(Photograph courtesy Denali National Park Archives.)

FIVE

The Saga of the Seventy-Mile Kid

↓

The NPS's tribulations in administering the frontier national park were twofold, and basically paralleled the new agency's dual responsibility to provide for the public use and preserve the natural conditions in national parks. In the matter of preservation the NPS found that the special privilege accorded exclusively to miners and prospectors to hunt game in the park was practically unenforceable; market hunters claimed to be prospectors while legitimate prospectors killed game as wantonly as the market hunters. The preservation of frontier conditions and wildlife abundance proved to be incompatible aims. Within a few years park officials recommended that the law be changed to prohibit miners and prospectors from living off the land inside the park.

In the matter of visitor use, meanwhile, officials discovered that to provide a frontier experience for tourists was problematical as well. Tourists demanded better and better accommodations, services, and access to the park—or at least the NPS assumed that they did. Rather than risk discouraging or disappointing park visitors by maintaining the area in a primitive condition, the NPS aimed to develop the area much as it did other national parks. It would construct basic hotel, road, and campground facilities. Meanwhile, to preserve the feel of the frontier, park staff would work and reside in rustic buildings, and tourists would ride stage coaches in and out of the park from the railroad depot at McKinley Station. The tourists' desire to experience the frontier would be met by creating a kind of frontier ambiance in the national park, with hardy rangers taking the place of frontiersmen. However, even this arrangement could not be maintained indefinitely. By the end of the 1920s, Mount McKinley National Park was becoming, like other United States national parks, more and more oriented to the automobilist.

The central figure in this transitional era was Harry Karstens, who served as the park's first superintendent from 1921 to 1928. Sourdough, entrepreneur, mountaineer, and conservationist, Karstens's varied interests personified the paradoxes that lay at the root of Mount McKinley National Park. Karstens left his native Illinois for the Klondike at the age of seventeen. After trying his luck in the Klondike, he went down the Yukon to the Seventy-Mile River, where he worked a small claim for a short time and then turned to packing supplies and mail for the other miners in the area. The miners nicknamed him the "Seventy-Mile Kid" for all the solitary traveling that he did around the country with his bulky, moosehide bedroll lashed to his dog sled. Later, he joined a small party of miners who laid out the townsite of Eagle.[1] In 1903, following a new gold strike in Alaska's interior, Karstens moved to the boomtown of Fairbanks and, with Charley McGonogall, established a two-man mail service on the long trail between Fairbanks and Valdez. Karstens and McGonogall led pack trains in the summer and drove dog teams in the winter. After the Kantishna mining district was organized in 1905, Karstens added that area to his rounds. Still known among locals as the Seventy-Mile Kid, Karstens grew into a savvy businessman, a first-class dog handler, and a man of legendary stamina on the trail.

Karstens's association with Mount McKinley began in 1906, when Charles Sheldon employed him as a packer and guide on his hunting trip to the Mount McKinley region. Sheldon, who was ten years older than Karstens, and, like him, in the prime of his life physically, admired his guide's energy and enthusiasm. When Sheldon returned to Fairbanks the following year, he hired Karstens to help him build a cabin, take out his horses in the fall, and bring in sled dogs after freeze-up.[2] Karstens, with his flair for self-promotion, made the most of his important client. He told the *Fairbanks Daily News-Miner* in 1907 of the "millionaire big-game hunter" whom he had left on the upper Toklat. He baited a reporter for *Alaska-Yukon Magazine* one year later by telling him that he could not reveal too much about his exploits with Sheldon, the "well-known sportsman of New York" and "representative of the Smithsonian Institution," lest his employer intended to use the information for his book. Largely on the strength of his association with Sheldon, Karstens developed a reputation as "one of the best-known guides in Alaska."[3]

Sheldon, for his part, thought Karstens was just the kind of man the territory needed to promote the idea of game conservation among the resident population. Sheldon very likely discussed with Karstens his idea of a "Denali National Park" before leaving Alaska in 1908.[4] In 1915, Sheldon wrote to Karstens on the subject, promising him that he would do all that he could to get Karstens the job of park superintendent in return for the Alaskan guide's public support.[5] Karstens evidently liked the idea. He applied for the post in 1918, reminding the NPS's assistant director, Horace M. Albright, of Sheldon's role as the park's founding father and of the park's essential purpose as a game preserve, and listing his own qualifications for the job. (By then, Karstens had added one more impressive and unusual credential to his job candidacy, having accompanied Archdeacon Hudson Stuck on the first successful ascent of Mount McKinley in 1913.) "One thing which brings it home to me," Karstens added, "is [that] Sheldon promised to assist me to get the Wardenship if it went through."[6]

NPS Director Stephen Mather was not inclined to put local men in charge of the western national parks; rather, he preferred to appoint ex-military men or civil-service professionals from other agencies such as the USGS to these positions. This was one way in which Mather sought to put the national parks on a new administrative footing after the creation of the NPS in 1916. But in the case of Mount McKinley National Park, Mather and Albright accepted Sheldon's advice that a local man would be more effective than some unknown official who was new to the territory. The key to the situation was to win over the local people to the idea of a game refuge, and protecting the game was the NPS's immediate goal, as Albright made clear in a letter to the Senate Appropriations Committee shortly after the park bill was passed. "There is no intention of immediately improving this park or making it accessible to the public," Albright wrote. "Our deep concern is for the preservation of the wild animals."[7] As it turned out, Congress did not appropriate funds for the administration of the park until 1921, so Karstens had to wait four years to take up his duties.

Karstens, like Sheldon, perceived that the main task of wildlife protection would be to cultivate local support for the principle of a national park. Public opinion was critical, because if and when a poacher was brought to trial, the park superintendent would need the cooperation of a jury to get a conviction. Everyone knew that no game warden in Alaska had ever secured a conviction for a violation of the unpopular Game Law. Karstens's experience as a mail and freight carrier gave him some sense of local attitudes from Fairbanks to the Kantishna, but he overestimated the moral authority that he would wield as park superintendent. There were a few men he would be watching closely, he informed Sheldon in 1920, while awaiting his appointment to the job. "First time will be a warning second time there will

be a happening for I know I will have the backing of the people in there."
The men he suspected of past infractions he would soon bring to justice.
"They got away from the local warden and marshall but they will not give
me the slip for I have their number and methods."[8] Karstens conceived of
the superintendent's role partly in terms of bringing order to a lawless
frontier. In a national park that had been established with the intent of
preserving frontier conditions, this was the first of Karstens's paradoxical
roles.

Next to the task of gaining local support for the national park so that
market hunters would be deterred from breaking the law, the greatest challenge of administration would be to prevent resident miners and prospectors from abusing their special hunting privilege. Mather indicated in his
letter of instruction to Karstens that this was a matter of much concern to
him. For example, there was the issue of whether the miners would be
permitted to feed game meat to their sled dogs. Despite the large number
of caribou, this was not a trifling matter. During the winter, a single team of
dogs could consume a whole caribou per week, and the Kantishna miners
kept dozens of dog teams in or just outside the park.[9] But Karstens advised
Mather that to prohibit the use of game meat for dog food would cause the
miners a considerable hardship, for the alternative of dried salmon was too
bulky to haul into the Kantishna without great expense. Mather compromised with the new superintendent. As the park regulations were finally
drawn, they prohibited miners from killing animals in the park specifically
for dog food, but permitted them to feed scraps to their dogs. This was
hardly an enforceable distinction.[10]

The park regulations also required miners and prospectors who intended
to prospect or hunt in the park to register with the superintendent. The
object of this requirement was to prevent poachers, if caught, from simply
claiming that they were legitimate prospectors, for anyone with a pick and
pan in his outfit could match that description. The regulation was supposed
to be innocuous from the standpoint of the resident miner or prospector.
Whether the resident prospectors were suspicious or simply could not be
bothered with the arduous trip to park headquarters, most of them did not
comply with the regulation. Karstens wanted every miner and prospector
to come to him for a permit so that he could inform them about keeping a
clean camp, limiting their consumption of firewood, and so on. When they
did not cooperate he became petulant, traveled out to their cabins, and
threatened them with eviction. Instead of having the local miners' support
as he had anticipated, he quickly alienated nearly everyone in the area.[11]

Alaska's fur warden, Olaus J. Murie, commented on the superintendent's problems to the chief of the Biological Survey in August 1921, just two months after Karstens had assumed his duties. Karstens had told Murie that he would fight the park's opponents and enforce the law strictly. "I believe he should subdue his personal feelings and not make too much a show of his authority," Murie confided. "This is what rankles in the minds of the people in that vicinity. Roosevelt's famous saying comes to mind — 'Speak softly and carry a big stick.' Some of Karsten's [*sic*] friends here have spoken to me about Karsten's [*sic*] methods and fear that it will not do him much good."[12] Murie agreed with his boss, Dr. E. W. Nelson, and with Charles Sheldon, that the conservation of Alaskan big game depended on changing Alaskans' attitudes, and this would be accomplished through patient persuasion. Here lay another paradox: it was fast becoming evident that the frontier national park was premised on the idea of remaking the prospector into a responsible conservationist at the same time that it romanticized him as a cultural relic of the frontier.

The lawbreakers were harder to catch than Karstens had anticipated. Karstens had only two rangers, both local men like himself, for patrolling the nation's second largest national park. The rangers mostly patrolled the eastern boundary of the park, nearest the railroad, where they thought they would be most apt to apprehend market hunters entering or leaving the park. Karstens believed that market hunting was going on nearly unabated in the more distant sections of the park; he reported a noticeable decline in the number of sheep observed from year to year between 1921 and 1924. While tracking poachers, his rangers often came upon piles of sheep hides and skulls.[13]

Early in 1924, one of Karstens's rangers finally caught a man named Jack Donnelly illegally removing game from the park. Karstens thought he had a very good case against Donnelly. As Ranger E. R. McFarland explained to the six-man jury in Healy a few days later, he had encountered Donnelly leaving the park by dog sled with a large load covered with canvas. Since Donnelly was outside the park and refused to let McFarland inspect his load, McFarland returned to the site the next morning and followed Donnelly's track through the snow back into the park. About three or four miles inside the park he found a place where the dogs had rested and where a broad trough-like trail with traces of blood in it branched off the sled trail. Backtracking up this trail, McFarland came upon the fresh entrails of a caribou. McFarland testified to the jury that there were no other tracks and only one conclusion could be drawn from the evidence.

Donnelly then took the stand and told the jury that he had been prospecting when his sled broke down and that while repairing the sled one of his dogs had gotten loose and led him to a dead caribou "which had been killed by someone or something." Not wanting the meat to go to waste, he had dragged the carcass back to his sled and hauled it out. Karstens then took the stand and testified that he had tracked Donnelly the previous year, that the tracks had shown evidence of hunting rather than prospecting, and that he had warned Donnelly to cease hunting in the park. He read to the jury Section 6 of the park's establishing act. The jury was out for a perfunctory few minutes and returned a verdict of not guilty. "The prosecution failed," Karstens reported dejectedly to Mather, "because of the reluctance of the people, as represented by an average jury in this instance, to convict anyone for illegal hunting. . . . Our only hope for adequate conservation lies in the obtaining of whole-hearted support by the people."[14]

A second attempt to make a public example of poachers revealed another dimension of the problem: a reluctance to apply the law with equal force to natives. On November 15, 1924 two rangers named Nyberg and Degen caught two Indians named Enos John and Titus Bettis handling four sheep carcasses in the northeast corner of the park. Right after they caught them the rangers heard several gunshots farther inside the park, so they told the Indians to leave the sheep and go down to Healy while they tracked the third poacher. They finally picked up a third set of tracks the next day, this poacher having cunningly used the Indians' sled trail into the park to conceal his own tracks as far as a creek crossing, where the third set of tracks turned off up a long, exposed gravel bar and led several miles up to an old cabin. The rangers found this poacher above the cabin with two Dall sheep in his possession. An old timer named J. P. Sherman, he produced a 1919 map of the park and claimed to be ignorant of the 1922 boundary extension.

Meanwhile, Karstens received a phone call from Enos John of Healy, who said that he and his friend Titus Bettis were in trouble and needed the superintendent's help. Enos John lived in Healy with his wife and three small children. Arriving in town, Karstens found the man in poor health, nearly blind, and Karstens observed that the family had very little food in the cabin. Titus Bettis had come from Nenana to assist Enos John in getting some meat for himself and his family. The two men claimed that they had been told by whites that there was sheep range outside the park, and Karstens guessed that they might have misunderstood this to be true of the north side of the park as well as the east side.

Karstens decided that in Sherman's case he would have him sign a statement acknowledging the act but would not press charges. The misleading map was one factor in his defense; he was also the first white who had killed game in the park who had not claimed to be a prospector — "and to that title," Karstens wrote, "he has more claim than most of those who have killed game in the park under that designation." In the two Indians' case, Karstens also declined to charge the men "seeing it was their first offense and that it would be almost impossible to get the conviction of a hungry Indian with a family who pleaded ignorance." Karstens informed Mather that he hoped his leniency would in this instance win some local respect for the park laws. Acting Director Arno B. Cammerer praised the superintendent for his handling of the cases.[15]

The NPS's handling of a fourth poaching incident, this time involving a New York sportsman, demonstrated how clubbish the national park's core constituency still was. William N. Beach was on an expedition through the park to film wild animals when he was caught with three dead sheep in his possession. He claimed in his defense that the animals were for food rather than trophies, although this made no difference under the law because he was not prospecting. Karstens felt no sympathy for him, having resented Beach's arrogance when the sportsman first arrived. (Beach had demanded an escort and a loan of government hay and oats from the NPS, and had ranted and raved, according to Karstens, when he was told he could not hunt in the park.)[16] Mather's assistant, Arno B. Cammerer, eventually disposed of the case by accepting a $500 donation from Beach for trail work in the park — an amount equal to the maximum allowable fine under the law. The NPS decided that the publicity of a trial would not be constructive, particularly since Beach, a member of the Camp Fire Club of America, had "already been subjected to considerable mental anguish in the knowledge that he transgressed the law."[17] In short, the NPS did not want to make a public example of a sportsman who belonged to one of the very clubs that had facilitated in the park's establishment. Rather, it wanted to bring attention to a perceived pattern of abuse of the hunting privilege by resident Alaskans.

NPS officials argued that the legal distinction between market hunters and legitimate subsistence hunters was untenable. According to reports from Karstens, more prospectors were coming into the park following the discovery of copper-bearing ore east of the Muldrow Glacier in 1923. The new arrivals, Karstens alleged, were abusing the regulation against killing game to feed their dogs.[18] Moreover, there was now a mining company interested in developing the copper mine. NPS officials agreed that neither the company nor the wage-earning miners whom it brought in deserved the same hunting privilege that self-employed miners and prospectors enjoyed.

The company should provide its employees with beef from Fairbanks; it should not be given the opportunity to buy wild meat from hunters as the Alaska Engineering Commission had done.[19]

Fortunately the flurry of interest in Mount McKinley National Park's copper soon passed — the ore being too low-grade for the company to attract investors — but the concerns that it raised were enough to turn NPS officials against the subsistence hunting privilege. "This privilege has been abused," Mather declared in his annual report for 1924, "and unless the residents of that section can be appealed to for a fuller observance of the law there is no satisfactory solution except by amendment of the organic act creating that park so as to provide complete game protection, as is done in the other parks."[20] The NPS finally had its way in 1928, when Congress passed a law that prohibited all hunting in the park and lifted the $10,000 limitation on the park's annual appropriations.[21]

Certainly it was no coincidence that by the time their hunting privilege was taken away, the prospectors and miners in the Kantishna bore less resemblance to the heroes of the frontier myth than they had only a dozen years earlier. Not only were some of the residents leaving each winter for places like Seattle in order to locate capital investors for their mining prospects, but they were now able to get in and out of the Kantishna by airplane and would soon be able to come and go by automobile on the park road.[22] There was no longer any romantic impulse to treat these residents, as a Senate report had once referred to them, as "the advance guard of civilization."[23] Karstens himself ceased to draw any distinction between transient and resident hunters in his wildlife reports; they were all to blame for what he and his staff perceived to be a diminishing game supply.[24] If the park's founders had once insisted that a game refuge would preserve the miner in this country as well as the game itself, the miner had now become a source of irritation. Far from preserving this section of Alaska as a representative piece of the last frontier, the creation of a wildlife preserve and the development of the park for tourism actually undermined the miner's and prospector's status as cultural icons in the Mount McKinley region.

Meanwhile, the evolving tourist experience in Mount McKinley National Park demonstrated in another way how the idea of a frontier national park posed a unique set of problems for park administration. Just as Karstens was placed in an impossible position by having to police the way the frontier population of miners lived on the land, so too was he put in a predicament by having to make the frontier park the flagship for Alaska's tourist industry. It has been said that effective management of national parks is bedeviled by the competition between two fundamentally different concepts of what national parks are for—one treating national parks respectfully as "artifacts of culture," and the other treating national parks exploitatively as "commodity resources."[25] In the early years of the NPS, these two conflicting impulses were closely intertwined. Stephen Mather enthused that the national parks were the New West's "scenic lodestones," which served to draw "future settlers and investors" out West on their vacations. In this way, national parks contributed "their vital share in the prosperity of the institutions, scenic resorts, and general business of the country."[26] Clearly, Mather saw the national parks as both artifacts of culture and commodity resources. Mount McKinley National Park was intended to preserve an authentic sample of the Alaskan frontier at the same time that it would benefit the Alaska Railroad, Alaska's tourist industry, and the whole development of Alaska's economy. Because this was an inhabited wilderness, prone to cultural as well as ecological change, the original idea of the national park quickly unraveled.

Karstens himself had a typical frontier outlook on tourism. He reckoned the value of tourism not only in terms of the money that tourists spent on services—this, after all, was a minuscule sector of the frontier economy. More than that, Karstens valued tourists as potential investors and boosters in a place where capital and advertising were always in short supply.[27] "To my way of thinking the park is going to be a great asset to Alaska," Karstens told Sheldon. "Many who will come to visit the park, will take in the towns and mining districts, some may stay[,] others may invest[,] and a great many will boost." Karstens believed that he knew Alaskan tourists well, and understood better than his fellow citizens how many would want to visit the national park. "Alaskan's *[sic]* as a rule don't think much of the park, but that is because they don't know," Karstens wrote. "I have every confidence that it is going to be a big thing." His one urgent request would be to get a road built from the railroad line into the park, over the Toklat and Teklanika Mountains to the base of Mount McKinley.[28]

On Karstens's recommendation, Mather agreed to a proposal by the Board of Road Commissioners of Alaska in 1922 for a road from the east boundary of the park to the Kantishna mining camp. The road would be for the mutual benefit of miners and tourists. The Alaska Road Commission would survey and build the road and the Park Service would fund it.[29] Though the road was not completed until 1938, the ninety-mile route was soon staked and cleared of brush for the whole distance, and began almost immediately to serve as a single, long arterial through the park for the development of tourist camps and ranger stations.

Karstens awarded the first park concession to outfitter Dan T. Kennedy in 1923. The concession contract permitted Kennedy to use from sixteen to thirty horses in the park, to maintain a permanent summer camp at Savage River, and to erect spike camps at Igloo Creek and Sable Pass. For two summers Kennedy led a few large horse parties into the park. These hardy tourists gained what was, according to the standards of the day, a primitive national park experience, but in Karstens's view, this was not what the park visitors wanted. They wanted more comforts. Over Kennedy's bitter protests, he recommended a change of concessionaires in 1925. Rather than renew Kennedy's permit, the NPS contracted with the Mt. McKinley Tourist and Transportation Company.[30]

Karstens may have been correct in his assessment that most park visitors now expected better accommodations. Improvements in transportation were rapidly opening up the interior of Alaska to the mass tourist. While few tourists brought their own automobiles to Alaska in this era, they increasingly patronized auto tours over the territory's rough and embryonic system of highways. A popular package tour in the mid-1920s was the so-called Golden Belt Line, which started in Cordova, on Alaska's southern coast, and proceeded via the Copper River and Northwestern Railroad to Chitina, then by touring car over the Richardson Highway to Fairbanks, and then back south via the Alaska Railroad to Seward.[31] When the Alaska Railroad commenced passenger service between Seward and Fairbanks in 1924, its advertising brochures billed the railroad as the "Mount McKinley Route," and ticketing agents were advised to boost the national park as often as they could. The following year, the first length of road from Mc-Kinley Station to the park boundary was improved to make the road passable to automobile traffic.[32] These changes in transportation resulted in a marked increase in the number of visitors to Mount McKinley National Park, and probably a change in visitor expectations as well.

Within the national park, Savage River Camp remained the center of tourist activity into the 1930s. By national park standards the accommodations remained fairly primitive; the camp consisted of tent cabins without plumbing, a mess hall, and a large community house where dances were held. But improvements in transportation changed the tourist's experience. By 1928, all tours began with an automobile trip from McKinley Station to Savage River Camp. From there tourists chose from a number of round-trips to the Company's subsidiary camps at Igloo Creek, Sable Pass, Toklat River, Copper Mountain, and Clearwater Creek. The trips varied in cost depending on distance, duration, and mode of transportation. The Company charged lower rates for automobile trips than it did for the same trips by stage coach or saddle horse simply because they required fewer days.

There was no rate incentive for the tourist to experience the frontier national park by the more primitive means. Nor did the Company's automobiles have to stay on the completed roadway, but jostled up gravel bars and mountain trails as well. The Company's trip offerings and rate structure, approved by the secretary of the interior, did much to shape the visitors' experience. Karstens agreed with the head of the Mt. McKinley Tourist and Transportation Company, Robert Sheldon, that their joint purpose was to respond to visitor demand, yet they certainly had it in their power to channel that visitor demand in different ways.[33]

If Karstens could be faulted for putting the national park on a course toward overdevelopment — making it impossible to administer as an inhabited wilderness — it would be on the grounds that he and his superiors failed to appreciate that the frontier national park required a nontraditional, minimalist approach to tourist accommodations so as to minimize the tourists' social and economic impact on the wilderness inhabitants. However, Karstens's whole frame of reference as a frontiersman went against this idea. His desire was to develop tourist accommodations that would attract as many tourists as possible.

By trying to develop Mount McKinley National Park along the same lines as national parks outside Alaska, Karstens and his superiors reduced the idea of a frontier national park from a living reality to a collection of stage props that would preserve the park's frontier ambiance. One of the most dramatic (and pathetic) stage props was the use of stage coaches by the Mt. McKinley Tourist and Transportation Company to convey visitors from the railroad station to the Savage River Camp. The four-horse stage coaches were brought from Yellowstone National Park.[34] Though they might have been reminiscent of the Old West, the stage coaches were entirely out of context in Alaska. In any case, the Company retired them after a few years of service and replaced them with diesel-powered buses.

Another significant and more lasting effort at creating a frontier ambiance was the use of a rustic style of architecture in the park headquarters complex, which was built between 1925 and 1929. The complex consisted of a number of gable-roofed log buildings, set out in two neat rows amongst the spruce trees. The site admirably projected an image of frontier living combined with spit-and-polish government efficiency. While the NPS's use of the rustic was by no means unique to Mount McKinley in this era, few park administrative sites attracted as much interest as did Mount McKinley's, owing in large part to the novelty of the dog kennels.[35] Tourists enjoyed a close-up look at the wolfish, Alaskan work dogs, and the unique dog barn where harnesses dangled on the walls and the smell of dried fish wafted down from the loft. These were picturesque symbols of the last frontier. Even if tourists now traveled through the park by automobile, they could appreciate that rangers still patrolled the park in the winter by dog sled. In time, dog sled demonstrations became an essential part of the park's interpretive program.[36]

In a sense the rangers themselves became stage props for the frontier national park. From the NPS's standpoint they were the ideal wilderness inhabitants: tough, seasoned, authentic Alaskan frontiersmen, yet dedicated to conservation. "Patrolling this park is a man's job," Mather wrote in one of his annual reports, and any visitor to the park could see how true that was.[37] Tracking poachers and hunting varmints through the winter cold, the park ranger would seem to have made a suitable reincarnation of the fabled hunter-tracker of the frontier myth. That the ranger did not grab the popular imagination in the same way as the Alaskan prospector was not surprising, however. The hero of the frontier myth always lived just beyond the reach of the law; "frontier justice" was an essential part of his code. The ranger *was* the law.

In presiding over the domestication, rather than preservation, of a piece of the Alaskan frontier, Karstens eventually brought about his own obsolescence as park superintendent. For years, Mather and Albright were willing to overlook this frontiersman's tough, brawling style as an administrator. Karstens feuded with the first park concessioner, Dan T. Kennedy, who accused him of wanting to get control of the tour guide business for himself. He quarreled with all the chief officials of the Alaska Engineering Commission. He tried to evict a McKinley Station roadhouse proprietor, Maurice Moreno, from his 160-acre homestead claim, and when that failed he bullied Moreno into relinquishing 64 acres where he wanted to locate his headquarters. Karstens fired one ranger after another for petty causes. Once he assaulted a ranger and nearly beat him to death for some rude remarks that the ranger made to two ladies — an offense for which the court in Healy fined Karstens $20.[38] Mather and Albright put up with all of this because they appreciated Karstens's dedication to the job. For all of his faults, Karstens never tired of getting out to remote sections of the park and taking care of business, even in the most adverse conditions. But following a lengthy investigation of his competency following the beating incident, Karstens felt that he no longer had the confidence of his superiors in Washington, D.C. He resigned in October 1928 and moved to Fairbanks, where he went back into the transportation business. The days when a hard-fisted Alaskan sourdough could administer the national park had drawn to a close.

In his place, Mather appointed a NPS professional from Yellowstone, Harry J. Liek.

If there was any remaining doubt about the NPS's intentions to develop the park for mass tourism, it was dispelled the following summer after a visit by the agency's chief landscape architect, Thomas C. Vint. As requested by Mather, Vint drew up a blueprint, or master plan, for the park's development. His plan included the completion of the ninety-mile road, the construction of hotels at McKinley Station and at a site deep inside the park overlooking Mount McKinley, and the maintenance of the Savage River Camp. In line with other national park master plans of this era, Vint's plan aimed to provide tourists with a choice of long-term or short-term visits, rustic or sophisticated accommodations, and automobile-oriented or backcountry experiences. These proposed developments might succeed in getting tourists close to nature, but they would tend to insulate the tourist from the Alaskan frontier. In a territory where the roadhouse was still the predominant type of overnight accommodation, the two government-built park hotels would be among a mere handful of large hotels in Alaska. Vint commented without irony, "We find ourselves in one park where we are pioneering in a pioneer country."[39] His point was that the NPS must take special care to coordinate its development plans with territorial officials, the railroads, and the steamship companies, but he might just as well have pointed out that the NPS was doing its part to bury the last frontier rather than preserve it.

It would be too harsh a judgment to say that the NPS botched the idea of a frontier national park when, in reality, it never fully embraced it in this era. Mather favored the establishment of Mount McKinley National Park because of the mountains, glaciers, and abundant wildlife that it contained, and he agreed to the continued presence of miners in the park only because it was politically expedient. Even the park's principal architect, Charles Sheldon, had only a vague idea of how frontiersmen would figure in the national park over the long run. It is fairer to conclude that the frontier national park idea did not succeed here because it was too far ahead of its time. Sheldon and the other sportsmen who conceived the idea of a frontier national park were too steeped in the era's commitment to progress to contemplate what would really be required for such a thing to succeed. Mather and Albright, even if they did sympathize with the idea of a frontier national park, were too intent on opening up national parks with roads and hotels, thereby securing their place in American life, to consider holding one park apart from this pattern.

The frontier national park idea materialized and faded away in Mount McKinley National Park because it was too inchoate to succeed. Its significance lies in the fact that it provided a historical antecedent to the modern concept of Alaska's wildlands as inhabited wilderness. It took another wilderness traveler and philosopher to turn Sheldon's idea into a guiding vision. That individual was a young forester by the name of Bob Marshall.

SIX

Bob Marshall's Alaska

✧

Three hundred miles north of Mount McKinley the Brooks Range stretches east and west across the full breadth of the Alaskan Arctic. In the central portion of this long range the Middle Fork and South Fork of the Koyukuk River converge with the Alatna River to form the Koyukuk. The Alatna comes down from the northwest, the Middle Fork from the northeast. In this broad wedge of mountain country, stretching longitudinally from the Arctic Circle north to the Arctic Divide, Bob Marshall made six extended backpacking trips in the 1930s. He mapped and named dozens of mountains, rivers, and creeks that had never before been charted, or in some cases seen, by whites. Near the northern limit of the boreal forest he found two peaks of surpassing beauty, which he named Mount Boreal and Frigid Crags. Since these mountains rose majestically on either side of a northward-trending valley, he named the place Gates of the Arctic.

Bob Marshall was a forester by training, a wilderness explorer and preservationist by avocation. Founder of the Wilderness Society and author of two books on the Brooks Range, Marshall perceived these mountains to be the last refuge for people like him who were seeking wild country so primitive and vast that their wilderness experiences would call to mind the experiences of nineteenth-century explorers. He himself had chosen to explore the Brooks Range because it was one of only two "blank spaces" left on the map of Alaska.[1] Near the end of his short life, Marshall staked out an uncompromising position in support of preserving this last great wilderness. In a congressionally commissioned study, *Alaska — Its Resources and Development* (1938), Marshall proposed that the federal government establish a vast area — in fact, all of Alaska north of the Yukon River excepting a small area around Nome — where frontier conditions would be preserved. Since this was all public domain, Marshall reasoned, the federal government need only refuse to authorize road construction, mineral applications, and other kinds of industrial development to keep it wild. The area's inhabitants, native and white, could continue their meager yet untrammeled existence on the nation's last frontier. This would constitute a singularly great wilderness, a national treasure.[2]

Marshall's bold vision for Alaska wilderness raises three thematic problems for this study. First, what were the special qualities of the Brooks Range that made it stand as the ultimate wilderness for Marshall and so many preservationists who came after him? Second, did Marshall's vision embrace the needs of the area's inhabitants sincerely and realistically? Third, to what extent were Marshall's ideas carried into NPS planning in the 1940s, 1950s, and 1960s? This chapter addresses these questions and makes the overall argument that Bob Marshall had a significant though delayed influence on the making of Alaska's national parks.

Marshall's influence cannot be separated from the memory of his charming personality and poignant death by heart attack at the age of thirty-eight, both of which contributed to his legendary status in the wilderness movement. He was a man of infectious spirit, amusing eccentricities, habitual self-analysis, and eclectic tastes and accomplishments. Millionaire, socialist, scholar, inveterate backpacker, lover of fine music, and host of many a social gathering of New Deal bureaucrats and conservationists at his Washington, D.C., apartment, Marshall was widely respected by people both inside and outside the government as a bright young man with a future. In addition to his work for the Wilderness Society, he held two important public posts — chief of forestry in the BIA from 1933 to 1937, and head of recreation management in the Forest Service from 1937 to 1939. In the former position he created sixteen wilderness areas on Indian reservations; in the latter he obtained administrative protections for 14 million acres of national forest land.[3] Though he chafed at the rigmarole of government work and was continually unburdening himself in saucy letters and rhymes sent to his superiors, Marshall nevertheless enjoyed the power that he wielded as an insider in the reformist New Deal administration. As one friend eulogized, Marshall was "a lively and insistent cross-current in the Washington scene," continually provoking his associates to think deeply about what they were doing. "Bob had the nerve systematically to get all kinds of people together — congressmen, prima donna bureaucrats, professional civil servants, promoters of this or that — hand them a dubious drink, and then insist that they debate seriously and exhaustively on some such topic as Public Ownership of Resources, Soviet Russia, or Refugee Policy."[4]

Born into a wealthy, prominent Jewish family in New York City in 1901, he was fairly bred to appreciate wilderness and outdoor recreation. His father Louis Marshall, a constitutional lawyer, conservationist, and civil rights activist, instilled in Robert his basic outlook that conservation was good social policy. In the course of innumerable family excursions to the Adirondack Mountains of upstate New York when he was a teenager, Robert developed an abiding love for high country and endurance hiking. While on summer break from the New York State College of Forestry in 1921, young Bob, with his brother George, succeeded in climbing all forty-two Adirondack peaks with summits over 4,000 feet above sea level — a peculiar feat that aptly combined his love of physical challenges and his lifelong obsession with keeping statistics and lists. (He developed an even more esoteric list of hikes over the course of his adult life, consisting of those states in which he had made at least one thirty-mile day hike. The list was not limited to mountain states, but came to include the likes of Iowa and Rhode Island as well.) In 1924, he went to work for the Forest Service, continuing his education with a two-year stint at the Northern Rockies Forest Experiment Station in Montana.

Marshall was twenty-eight years old and less than a year away from completing a Ph.D. in plant physiology at Johns Hopkins University in Baltimore when he made his first trip to the upper Koyukuk and the central Brooks Range in 1929. In Fairbanks he teamed up with a prospector and part-time college student named Al Retzlaf and chartered an airplane to the mining town of Wiseman in the upper reaches of the Middle Fork of the Koyukuk, where the two men set out with pack horses on a 25-day trip into mountain country that had scarcely before been visited by whites.[5] The scientific object of the trip was to study tree growth at the northern timberline near the Arctic Divide, but Marshall was quick to acknowledge that his primary interest was the aesthetic call of the wilderness — a motivation that he had already begun to submit to rigorous self-analysis. While Retzlaf prospected and hunted moose and mountain sheep, Marshall scrambled up numerous peaks, reveling in the expanse of serrated ridges and glacier-hewn valleys and indulging in the conceit that he was standing atop these windy summits as no man had ever done before him.

Marshall began to hone his ideas about wilderness in an important essay, "The Problem of the Wilderness," published in 1930. His experience in the Brooks Range clearly influenced his thinking as he worked toward a definition of wilderness and a philosophically sound argument for the value of outdoor recreation in American life. Defining his subject as something more nuanced than an uninhabited, uncultivated tract, he conceived of wilderness as "a region which contains no permanent inhabitants, possesses no possibility of conveyance by any mechanical means and is sufficiently spacious that a person in crossing it must have the experience of sleeping out."[6] It was the feeling of primitiveness that mattered above all. Marshall characterized essential wilderness values in terms of the wilderness traveler's experiences. "The dominant attributes of such an area are: first, that it requires any one who exists in it to depend exclusively on his own effort for survival; and second, that it preserves as nearly as possible the primitive environment. This means that all roads, power transportation and settlements are barred. But trails and temporary shelters, which were common long before the advent of the white race, are entirely permissible." These criteria were distinctly anthropocentric; that is, they evaluated the natural environment in terms of human perceptions and preferences.

More than that, however, Marshall's criteria were ethnocentric. He assumed a white man's perspective in proposing that the essence of wilderness was the kinship of experience created between the Euroamerican explorer of the past and the modern (white) recreationist. "When Columbus effected his immortal debarkation, he touched upon a wilderness which embraced virtually a hemisphere," Marshall wrote. In the Brooks Range he was Columbus. Better yet, he was Meriwether Lewis, the hero of his youth. On his second visit to Alaska, less than a year after writing this essay, Marshall described to friends and family how often he had wished, on past visits to national parks, "egotistically enough," that he "might have had the joy of being the first person to discover this grandeur." As a boy, he explained, the journals of Captain Lewis had stirred in him the feeling that he had been "born a century too late," and that though he might have some good times, he would never enjoy "anything as glorious as I would have known had I lived in the days of Lewis and Clark." But to his surprise, he discovered just such a glorious experience while exploring the Brooks Range, "at a place where only three other human beings aside from [him]-self had ever been and with dozens of never visited valleys, hundreds of unscaled summits still as virgin as during their paleozoic creation."[7] Marshall felt that his experience was deeply enriched by his sense of discovery, of being the first white man — the first human for all he knew — to lay eyes on this land.

Marshall elaborated on this theme in his essays on backpacking in the Brooks Range, which were published posthumously in 1956 as *Arctic Wil-*

derness. The fundamental difference between figures like Columbus or Lewis and the twentieth-century wilderness explorer was that the earlier explorers were significantly advancing the frontiers of knowledge. By contrast, exploration in the twentieth century was little more than a self-indulgence, a form of recreation. In his own case, he declared that his study of the northern treeline had been a mere rationalization, a sop to his old-fashioned sense of social obligation, and he no longer pretended that his exploration of the central Brooks Range would produce any significant benefit for society.[8] He went even further in a letter to a friend, intimating that his mapping of unmapped rivers and scaling of unscaled peaks was consuming a nonrenewable resource. "I have developed a particular prejudice against airplane exploration," he wrote. "The area left in the world where people can get the explorer's thrill is very limited and the slower such areas are used up, the better it will be."[9] If this observation seemed somehow inverted, it was precisely what Marshall was aiming at: just as the explorer had evolved from a producer of knowledge into a consumer of the last remaining virgin wildernesses, so too the myriad adventurers who followed in the explorer's footsteps had evolved from wealth-producing pioneers in the nineteenth century into scenery-consuming recreationists in the twentieth. In recasting the wilderness traveler as a consumer of scenery — a shopper, so to speak, of quality wilderness experiences — Marshall was pioneering the anthropocentric approach to wilderness preservation and management.

Marshall obviously did not want to limit his defense of wilderness to those few remaining "blank spaces" on the map. Insofar as wilderness recreation could be characterized as playing the role of the nineteenth-century explorer or pioneer, it was the feeling of primitiveness that made a tract of land succeed as wilderness. By Marshall's time, most remaining wild country had been traversed, mapped, and prospected, and now qualified as wilderness by virtue of its roadless condition. On these "shrunken remnants of an undefiled continent," Marshall maintained, the recreationist could see the land essentially as it had looked to the first white explorer, but even these areas were endangered by the pressure for road development, summer cottages, logging, grazing, and mining.[10]

Marshall constructed a defense of these remaining wilderness areas based on utilitarian principles. He proposed to measure the "extraordinary benefits of wilderness" and to weigh them against the costs of leaving these same areas undeveloped, and to perform a kind of calculus in order to arrive at a public policy that would achieve the greatest good for society. He defined the benefits as "extraordinary," because in his view wilderness values could not be quantified. Wilderness provided a unique setting for inspiration, contemplation, repose, and physical exercise. It was indispensable to the physical and mental health of an increasingly urban populace. Even if a majority of the citizenry did not use wilderness directly, it was a balm to an "overcivilized" people simply to know that wilderness still existed. Wilderness was a place in everyone's imagination where dangers lurked and adventures abounded.[11]

Marshall contended that it was facile to argue, as so many automobile clubs did, that wilderness areas should be opened up by roads and campgrounds so that more people could enjoy them. This was a corruption of the utilitarian principle of achieving the greatest good for the greatest number, for it overlooked the intensity of the aesthetic experience. Scenic roads provided mild enjoyment for the many but despoiled the wilderness for the few. If this deceptively simple measure were applied to all forms of aesthetic experience, Marshall suggested, "we would be forced to change our metropolitan art galleries into metropolitan bowling alleys. . . . The Library of Congress would become a national hot dog stand, and the new Supreme Court building would be converted into a gigantic garage where it could house a thousand people's autos instead of Nine Gentlemen of the Law."[12] Society was enriched when it demonstrated a spirit of tolerance toward a variety of forms of aesthetic experience. Society gained by respecting the interests of that small minority who cherished wild country above all else.

These ideas lay behind Marshall's recommendation to Congress in 1938 to preserve virtually all of Alaska north of the Yukon River in its wilderness state. The superlative quality of this wilderness had to be considered. None other presented as much physical challenge or such a panoply of dangers including extreme climate, rushing rivers, wild animals, lack of maps, and distance from help. Above all, Alaska wilderness provided a unique sense of discovery, or at least pioneering. "When Alaska recreation is viewed from a national standpoint it becomes at once obvious that its highest value lies in the pioneer conditions yet prevailing throughout most of the territory," Marshall advised. "These pioneer values have been largely destroyed in the continental United States. In Alaska alone can the emotional values of the frontier be preserved." Marshall pleaded for that spirit of tolerance which governs a truly liberal society. Though the number of people who would directly benefit from such a supreme wilderness would be small, he wanted an approach that would fit Alaska's recreational resources "into the whole picture of United States recreation so that there [would] be a reasonable balance in the types of outdoor recreation obtainable on United States lands."[13] Marshall rested his case on the superlative quality of Alaska wilderness. He argued that the most important attribute of wilderness was neither its scenic grandeur nor its biological interest, but rather the feeling of primitiveness that it inspired in the wilderness recreationist. It followed that the wilderness of the Brooks Range, indeed the wilderness of all northern Alaska, was without peer in the United States. Marshall's thought was a long way from the monumentalism of nineteenth-century excursionists in Glacier Bay or even the carefully delimited frontier national park idea of Charles Sheldon. Here lay the seed of the idea that Alaska's wildlands should be preserved in a wilderness condition on an unprecedented scale.

Marshall unwittingly created in the minds of a later generation of wilderness advocates the impression that wilderness and resident peoples were incompatible. Marshall's descriptions of his backpacking trips in *Arctic Wilderness* depicted the central Brooks Range as a place so forbidding it had never been inhabited, a place in which the wilderness explorer could feel as if nothing had changed since the "paleozoic creation." It became part of the Marshall legend that he had traveled a mountain country where no humans had gone before. Together with Marshall's practical definition of wilderness as an uninhabited tract, this memory of the founder of the Wilderness Society reinforced the traditional preservationist idea that humankind and nature were separate and juxtaposed. However, a closer reading of Marshall shows that he thought deeply on how to preserve northern Alaska as an inhabited wilderness.

Like the campaigners for Mount McKinley National Park earlier, Marshall insisted that the inhabitants of this great wilderness would neither oppose nor detract from the government's purpose if the government preserved the land in a wilderness condition. Unlike Charles Sheldon, Belmore Browne, and the other club men of a half-generation earlier, however, Marshall went to some lengths to understand the wilderness values of the whites and natives who lived there. In the fall of 1930, he returned to Wiseman with the purpose of making a sociological study of the people — "of painting a complete picture of the civilization of whites and Eskimos which flourishes in the upper reaches of the Koyukuk, 200 miles beyond the edge of the Twentieth Century."[14] Also in contrast with Sheldon, Browne, and their fellow wildlife conservationists, Marshall was less concerned about the inhabitants' effect on the wilderness than he was with the wilderness's effect on the inhabitants. This was consistent with his anthropocentric vision of wilderness.

For his fifteen-month sojourn in Wiseman, Marshall rented a one-room cabin next to the village's single roadhouse. He furnished the cabin with books, records, phonograph player, and writing desk, the latter placed so that he could sit by the cabin's single window and admire the view of the Koyukuk River and a range of steep, snow-covered mountains beyond. After a preliminary four-week jaunt to the Arctic Divide, Marshall settled in and proceeded to befriend a considerable number of the region's inhabitants.[15] He filled his days with writing, reading, visiting, and attending all eleven dances held at the Pioneer Hall in the course of the year. He logged thousands of hours of conversation — his favorite indoor recreation — and after each conversation he meticulously recorded all subjects discussed and the number of minutes devoted to each. He persuaded a number of Wisemanites to take intelligence tests. He developed statistics on all aspects of the Wisemanites' lives, from their financial resources to their diets to their sexual promiscuity.[16]

The book that came from these experiences was acclaimed as an important work of sociology. *Arctic Village* was arranged in seven parts, with sections on the setting, people, economic life, communal life, sexual life, recreational life, and philosophy of the Koyukuk. Most of the inhabitants were single white males, the majority of whom had come into the country between fifteen and thirty years earlier. Even the several native families, who constituted slightly less than half the total population on the Koyukuk north of the Arctic Circle, were nearly all transplants to the area since the gold rush era. An extremely lopsided sex ratio and a shortage of children gave the community an air of impermanence, yet the community's long-range prospects were not really of concern to Marshall; he was fundamentally interested in assessing the people's happiness. For this reason, *Arctic Village* was a book about lifestyle, a wilderness lifestyle, even though the term "lifestyle" was not yet in usage at the time when Marshall was writing.

Marshall argued that wilderness invigorated the Wisemanites' lives in three distinct ways. First, the primitiveness of this society, the simplicity of its economic system and class structure, permitted its members a feeling of independence and self-reliance which they all treasured. Subsistence hunting and fishing held the intrinsic value of yielding immediate, tangible necessities of life. Even the work of mining, which occupied most of the whites most of the time, required ingenuity and continual planning and was not routinized. Perhaps most importantly for the whites, there was "no horror of unemployment" as there was in the Depression-ridden society outside.[17]

Second, wilderness magnified the individual on the upper Koyukuk. Men who were separated in space by a two-day journey were neighbors, and each member of the society was appreciated for his or her own talents. "Every person can really feel that he is a vital element in the world in which he lives, not merely one infinitesimal soul among millions of his fellowmen," Marshall wrote. "Every individual in the Koyukuk is important just because he is alive, and thus there is eliminated from his life all the nerve-racking striving which accompanies any effort to be distinguishable among the overwhelming numbers of the outside world."[18]

Third, and finally, wilderness provided adventure. The hazards of wilderness travel — exposure to the elements, river crossings, wild animals — were shared by all, practically from infancy. Everyone in the Arctic possessed tales that would be the envy of the "thrill-starved citizens of the United States." These adventures added "tone, vitality, and color to the entire functioning of life."[19]

Despite its honest, unexaggerated prose style, *Arctic Village* had a Panglossian tone. The book gave a particularly optimistic view of race relations. Marshall reported that whites and natives mingled at social functions, helped each other out, and intermarried, and he judged that nearly a third of the whites and a larger number of Eskimos truly believed in racial equality. The key figures in Wiseman's race relations were the single white males and the young Eskimo females, or "chickens" as the Eskimos called them. Marshall, who was thirty years old and unattached during his sojourn in Wiseman, responded well to this community dynamic. He devoted a chapter of *Arctic Village* to "chickens," and clearly acquired much of his information about the Eskimos from his young female friends. While Marshall found a couple of the Eskimo men very companionable, he had considerably less to say about them than the white men. As for the seven white females in Wiseman (all married), they received very little mention in *Arctic Village*, and virtually none of it was flattering.

Much of what Marshall admired about life on the upper Koyukuk sprang from his growing antipathy for modern industrial society, an antipathy shared by many of the white miners whom he befriended. He appreciated, for example, the often-repeated claim that each person in the upper Koyukuk was his own boss. He found the white people surprisingly well-read and the people as a whole quite intelligent for their overall level of education, qualities which he attributed to the amount of leisure time that they had and their habit of taking care of so many problems for themselves. There was dignity in the work they performed — an old-fashioned pride of workmanship, and no social stigma attached to wage work. Mine owners and their hired hands worked shoulder to shoulder, and the man who hit a rich pay streak and hired help one year might work for the man he had hired the next. "As a result we discover that the capitalist and the working class have become thoroughly merged in the Koyukuk," Marshall wrote pointedly.[20] The contrast between Wiseman's independent and egalitarian frontier values and the painful dysfunctions of industrial capitalism in the rest of the United States sharpened in the time that elapsed between Marshall's stay in Wiseman during 1930–31 and the publication of *Arctic Village* in 1933. Certainly the Great Depression influenced the way the book was written and contributed to its critical and commercial success, for Marshall's description of life on the arctic frontier became an oblique commentary on mainstream America.

Marshall's socialism created an interesting tension in *Arctic Village*. Was *Arctic Village* a serious critique of modern life or a fanciful escape from it? The tension reflected deeper contradictions in Marshall's evolving thought. His love of wilderness was grounded in a primitivist view of America's wilderness heritage, which bore little relation to an imagined socialist future. In his youth, he had imbibed the nineteenth-century nature writing of James Fenimore Cooper — hardly the stuff of working-class dissent.[21] His defense of wilderness demanded tolerance for the aesthetic needs of a refined minority, yet his socialist convictions pushed him to think in terms of the common interest and the material needs of the underprivileged. Marshall found a partial resolution of this conflict in the way the white miners of the upper Koyukuk described themselves as "failures." They were failures in the sense that they had not made their fortune and gone back to the States, as each of them had once imagined that he would, and in the sense that the outside world would scorn their poverty. More importantly, however, they used the term "failures" ironically to explain their expatriation from the outside world's materialism and conventionality. To boast of themselves as "failures" was as close as these fiercely independent miners came to acknowledging a kind of brotherhood with one another. These were people who expressed their lifestyle both in terms of their opposition to the capitalist-oriented mainstream and in terms of the happiness that wilderness-living gave them.[22] And yet Marshall seemed unsure in his own mind as to whether the wilderness-dependent lifestyle he was describing was really a viable alternative to the modern world. Were these men and women relics of the pioneer era, or were they ahead of their time in making self-conscious statements about lifestyle?

Marshall seemed to have resolved this question four years later when he made his plea to Congress to establish a great wilderness in northern Alaska. The Alaskan frontier was best understood as a preferred way of life, rather than a stage of economic development that Alaskans were trying to get beyond. This made the Alaskan frontier different; it was uniquely modern because it was self-consciously juxtaposed to modernity. Certainly the Alaskan frontier had its boosters, and the development of Alaskan recreation would benefit those few residents who owned hotels, resorts, and real estate, but it would injure the much larger number of Alaskans who cherished the territory's frontier character and their way of living close to the land. It was in the best interests of these people — white and native — to discourage an influx of tourists and migrants to Alaska. A horde of new people would undermine the high-wage structure presently enjoyed by the sparse population. It would disrupt the residents' subsistence base by increasing the take of game for sport as well as the number of human-caused forest fires.[23]

It was also in the best interests of the nation to preserve Alaska's frontier character, Marshall insisted. "Sound national planning should strive to preserve as many different types of good life within the United States as is possible in order that the immensely varied desires and ideals of the human race may have opportunity of fulfillment," he wrote. "In Alaska alone it is yet possible for those who crave the good life of the frontier to lead such a life. We should not destroy this opportunity, unless there is some compelling necessity."[24] In his references to the good life and the varied desires of the human race, Marshall was anticipating the intense debate over lifestyle choices and the preservation of native cultures that preceded the enactment of ANILCA more than forty years later.

The fact that Alaska's frontier was a way of life rather than a stage of economic development, Marshall argued, made it uniquely possible to preserve frontier conditions there. "Economically, the population is so scattered that airplane transportation is the only feasible means of mechanical conveyance, and auto roads could not possibly justify their great cost. At the same time, the country is too remote from markets for successful industry. Sociologically, the country of northern Alaska is inhabited by native populations which would be much happier, if United States experience is any criterion, without either roads or industries."[25] Marshall no doubt had the miners of the upper Koyukuk in mind as he thought about the resident white population. It is not so clear whether he was thinking of the Eskimos whom he had known in Wiseman when he referred to "native populations." In *Arctic Village*, Marshall observed that the upper Koyukuk's natives were "immigrants," being comprised of Kobuk, Selawik, and Arctic-coast Eskimos, and one Athapaskan Indian family.[26] The adults had all moved to Wiseman since the turn of the century, and he did not think the children who had been born in Wiseman were developing any great attachment to the area. Moreover, these transplanted natives showed varying degrees of acculturation, with about half of those under forty-five years of age being "closer to the white culture than the original Eskimo culture."[27] Probably Marshall was not generalizing about Alaska natives from his experience in Wiseman. Rather, he was thinking primarily of the more typical native communities where few or no whites were present. He saw an opportunity in Alaska to avoid some of the problems that beset American Indians in the United States.

As chief forester in the BIA from 1933 to 1937, Marshall had much opportunity to ponder the relationship of Native Americans to the past North American environment, the conservation movement, and wilderness. The BIA's program of forestry faced constant pressure from Indian tribes and individuals to allow more cutting and grazing on Indian lands that the federal government still held in trust.[28] It was ironic, in view of the American Indians' record of living "in balance with nature," that many modern Indian groups now confronted severe ecological problems on their reservations. This sad state of affairs, Marshall explained in an article titled "Ecology and the Indians," stemmed from the inadequacy of their land base. The reservations were simply too small to support the tribes. It was a twentieth-century consequence of the nineteenth-century legacy of Indian defeat.[29] Clearly this held lessons for the future development of Alaska.

One of Marshall's last initiatives as chief of Indian forestry was to recommend 4.8 million acres of Indian lands for management as either "roadless" or "wild" areas. Commissioner of Indian Affairs John Collier signed the order shortly after Marshall left office. To opponents of this ruling who succeeded in having it mostly undone some twenty years later, it seemed that Marshall had acted mainly in the interests of the wilderness movement, but Marshall claimed to have the Indians' interests at heart. He believed that the Indians' forest resources possessed cultural as well as economic value, and to conserve portions of the Indians' forested heritage in a primitive condition was to promote the cultural revitalization of these Indian groups. If Indian tribes possessed their own wilderness areas, the tribal members would always have a place to "escape from constant contact with white men." This was vital to their cultural autonomy, since "almost everywhere they go the Indians encounter the competition and disturbances of the white race."[30] Moreover, the wilderness areas would accrue economic value to the tribes, attracting recreationists and creating a market for Indian-owned and -operated wilderness guide services. Considering how few reservation Indians actually secured jobs with the timber companies that logged off their lands, the economic argument was not far-fetched. Again, Marshall's primary frame of reference was the reservation Indians of the contiguous United States, but the ideas were equally, if not more, applicable to conditions in Alaska.

It is clear that Marshall conceived of Alaska wilderness as fundamentally an inhabited wilderness. Marshall wanted above all to define it as the nation's only permanent frontier — a distinctly cultural environment. Alaska's primitive infrastructure and economy and the "good life" led by its people were its preeminent qualities, surpassing even its superb scenery. Recreational use of this wilderness should remain oriented to the hardy and committed few and should not impose on the resident peoples. Marshall's interest in the welfare of the inhabitants was sincere. His estimation that northern Alaska's inhabitants would accommodate themselves to the preservation of wilderness conditions and gladly accept limitations on economic development may seem unrealistic with hindsight. Social change raced on, even in the isolated villages of interior Alaska. Social change inevitably entailed a desire for economic betterment, no matter how much that desire might be tempered by nonmaterialistic considerations. Nevertheless, it should be remembered that for thirty years after Marshall made his recommendation — that is, until the discovery of oil on the North Slope — the entire Brooks Range did remain roadless, a de facto wilderness. This was not because of any deliberate policy, but simply because the area was, as Marshall said, too remote from markets to support any industry.

Marshall's concept of Alaska wilderness would eventually inform the Alaska wilderness preservation movement in the 1970s. To understand how this was so, it is necessary to examine the evolution of national park planning in Alaska through the 1940s, 1950s, and 1960s. Although no Alaskan lands were added to the national park system in these decades, the NPS made a number of reconnaissances and recreational-planning studies that looked to the day when Alaska's level of development and tourism would justify a larger NPS presence. Eventually the NPS came to champion Marshall's idea that Alaska wilderness constituted a singularly grand national treasure.

Initially, the NPS responded indifferently to Marshall's proposal for Alaska wilderness preservation. It did not perceive Alaska wilderness to be a cultural environment that the nation should preserve on an unprecedented scale. Marshall's proposal to zone virtually all of Alaska north of the Yukon River as wilderness contrasted with the traditional national park idea in three vital aspects. First, the purpose of national parks was to preserve nature, not the frontier. The NPS was the trustee of the nation's cultural heritage, but not its cultural diversity. Preserving wilderness for the purpose of preserving a way of life was not in the national park tradition.[31]

Second, national parks were intended for the public's enjoyment. It was the NPS's responsibility to develop the parks for public use. The NPS took this to mean the development of carefully landscaped roads and appropriately designed accommodations. In its search for the proper balance between preservation and use, the NPS assumed that its mandate referred principally to the preservation of a park's scenic beauty, not its primitive feeling.[32] In the 1930s, the NPS started setting aside portions of national parks as "primitive areas" where no further road development would take place, but it was not until the NPS first proposed Gates of the Arctic National Park in 1969 that it considered managing an entire national park as a primitive area. Third, and finally, national parks were relatively small. Even Glacier Bay and Katmai, the two largest units in the system, looked small when compared on a map to all of northern Alaska.

In the long run none of these conceptual problems was insurmountable and in the 1970s the emergent new Alaskan park system would embody Marshall's main ideas. Thirty-four years after Marshall's death the NPS proposed its first "national wilderness park" in the Brooks Range, together with a Nunamiut National Wildlands specifically directed at preserving a native group's way of life.[33] With passage of ANILCA in 1980, the NPS assumed jurisdiction over 44 million acres of Alaska wilderness, more than doubling the size of the NPS system. A recent NPS brochure featuring these several new areas summed up the agency's concept of Alaska wilderness by its title, "Our Lasting Frontier."[34]

There was some irony in the fact that NPS officials were the only ones left in the field to pick up the banner of Alaska wilderness preservation after Marshall died in 1939. Marshall had not particularly admired the NPS. While leading the Wilderness Society in myriad campaigns against road-building projects in national parks, Marshall came to the conclusion that the NPS had been captured by automobile clubs, park concessions, and all the local boosters who wanted the parks to be turned into resorts for attracting tourist dollars. He believed that Director Arno B. Cammerer was a weak administrator and that the agency as a whole could no longer be trusted to protect wilderness.[35] The NPS's program of widening, grading, and oiling its backcountry trails epitomized its overweening approach toward backcountry management.[36] In working on the Alaska recreation report to Congress, Marshall had tried and failed to collaborate with the NPS's John Cameron and the Alaska Railroad's Paul W. Gordon. He had objected to his colleagues' emphasis on development, noting sardonically that Cameron had used the word "develop" thirty-eight times in twenty-two pages.[37] Marshall had submitted his own unadulterated ideas as a minority report, and this was preserved in the final congressional document as "Appendix B. Comments on the Report on Alaska's Recreational Resources and Facilities by Robert Marshall, U.S. Forest Service."[38]

The majority report by Cameron and Gordon suggested just how much the NPS had distanced itself from Charles Sheldon's original idea of an Alaskan frontier national park—and how far it had to go to return to that conception in the 1960s. The report explored how the NPS could assist in developing a tourist industry that would contribute to the territory's struggling economy. It advocated a virtual cloning of the automobile-oriented national parks and recreation areas in the forty-eight states, proposing new access roads, tourist hotels, and wayside developments along an anticipated Alaskan Highway. The highway would go through Canada and tie Alaska to the rest of the nation's highway system. The majority report practically ignored Alaska's frontier character, and when it did finally touch on that topic — in the last paragraph — the authors immediately downplayed its significance by saying that it should only be preserved when it was consistent with development.[39]

The international highway came sooner than expected, as the outbreak of World War II and the Japanese invasion of the Aleutian Islands prompted the U.S. Army to push the Alaska-Canada or Alcan Highway project forward with all possible haste, advancing it through diplomatic, planning, and construction phases within a few years at a cost of about $140 million. In 1944, the NPS received a small slice of this funding with which to update its recreational planning proposals. In the resulting study it reiterated its enthusiasm for developing Alaska's recreational resources around the automobile.[40]

The 1944 report would have been no less anathema to Bob Marshall than the earlier one had he still been alive to comment on it. It recommended twenty-three sites along the Alaskan portion of the highway for the development of overnight lodging, food service, and filling stations, each new complex to be attractively landscaped and set back from the road not less than three hundred feet "to protect the scenic attractiveness of Alaska roads."[41] The plan only required funding by Congress, cooperation by the General Land Office, and the dedication of a single concessioner, who would operate the wayside developments under NPS oversight. In this way, by 1950, the government would open up the last frontier for a projected swarm of 6,000 summer automobile tourists each day.[42]

Even the architectural and landscaping details of the NPS plan had a modern, homogenizing quality that Marshall would certainly have found objectionable. The heart of the NPS proposal was its conception of orderly, controlled communities designed especially for the tourist business flowing through them. The authors of the report stressed that the new wayside buildings would be aesthetically superior to the existing roadhouses, and built to last. "Too many structures in the Territory have been closely akin to 'Topsy,'" the report observed. "The 'Topsy' is razed far sooner than its neighbor of professional design, not always because of structural instability, often because of more expensive operation or maintenance, sometimes because it fails to attract deserved business to occupant tenants."[43] With this single pejorative, "Topsy," the NPS planners summed up their dim view of Alaska's frontier character. If Alaskan towns were accurate specimens of the vaunted northern frontier, then the frontier was disorderly, unattractive, run-down, and ultimately uncompetitive. The report had the same tenor as Cameron and Gordon's report in 1938. It did not support the preservation of a frontier in the sense that Marshall wanted it preserved; rather, it sought to make Alaskan travel comfortable where it had been rough, routine where it had been unpredictable.

This continued to be the touchstone of NPS aims in Alaska in the early postwar period. The agency focused narrowly on obtaining appropriations with which to develop hotel accommodations in Glacier Bay, Mount McKinley, Katmai, and now along the Alaskan Highway, with the object of promoting increased travel to Alaska to make these hotels operational. Officials argued that the national park hotels would be catalysts for the development of an Alaskan tourist industry. Associate Director Arthur E. Demaray, lobbying for a $2.5 million appropriation for wayside tourist facilities on the Alaskan Highway, explained that the purpose of these facilities was "to get the ball rolling."[44] Director Drury confided to Governor Gruening, "I have long felt that if the national parks in Alaska could be developed properly and adequately, the resulting flow of tourist business to the territory would not only stimulate present business activities there but would induce the investment of new capital in Alaska, perhaps to a very considerable degree."[45] Such comments reflected the service's conception of Alaska as a backwater area in the national park system. Acting primarily to bring a few choice beauty spots within reach of American tourists, the NPS refused to break out of its traditional mold and consider Alaska wilderness as something unique in the nation, as Marshall had urged.

In 1950 the NPS appointed George Collins and Lowell Sumner, both from the NPS regional office in San Francisco, to survey all of Alaska's scenic, scientific, historic, and recreational resources; recommend the development of recreational facilities for residents of Alaska; and propose the development of tourist facilities for visitors to Alaska. The NPS funded the survey on Collins's advice that the NPS had a responsibility under the Park, Parkway and Recreation Act of 1936 to inventory the territory's recreational resources. The multi-year survey marked the first milestone on the NPS's road to a greatly expanded presence in Alaska.[46] It ranged across the full breadth of Alaska in what Collins later described as a "dragnet sort of reconnaissance and inventory."[47]

The most important phase of the survey came in 1952–53 when Collins and Sumner explored the eastern Brooks Range and North Slope. This was the first time the NPS had been in the Arctic. From the standpoint of the wilderness movement, it was as if the Brooks Range had been rediscovered. The two men sowed interest among Wilderness Society and Sierra Club members and generated enthusiastic support from scientists attached to the Arctic Research Laboratory in Barrow. For the latter group, Collins recalled, the question was never what were they doing way up there, but "Where have you been all these years? Why haven't you been in here a long time ago?"[48] Their first report on their rambles about the Brooks Range, written in Barrow, launched a campaign that would culminate eight years later in the proclamation of a 9-million-acre Arctic National Wildlife Range extending from the Canning River to the Canadian border and from the Brooks Range to the Arctic coast. This would be the most significant gain for Alaska wilderness preservation in the whole period from the establishment of Mount McKinley, Katmai, and Glacier Bay to the passage of ANILCA some fifty-five years later.

Two questions arise in connection with Bob Marshall's legacy: why did attention shift from the central to the eastern portion of the Brooks Range, and why did the NPS push for a wildlife range (which came under the jurisdiction of the FWS) instead of a national park or monument? Collins and Sumner were thinking in terms of the area's biological interest. They wanted an area that would take in the whole continuum of arctic wildlife habitat from the mountains to the coast. Sumner, an NPS biologist, wanted a "wilderness reserve" large enough to provide sanctuary for the migrating caribou, as well as wolves, polar bears, Dall sheep, and other arctic fauna. He and Collins envisioned a reserve that would enclose enough habitat to be "permanently self-maintaining."[49] Collins chose to concentrate on the eastern portion of the Brooks Range after consultation with the USGS's John Reed, a geologist associated with the Arctic Research Laboratory in Barrow. Reed was familiar with oil exploration on the U.S. Navy's Petroleum Reserve Four (now the National Petroleum Reserve in Alaska) and elsewhere along the North Slope. "Stay east of Pet Four and you'll have one of the greatest national park possibilities," Reed told Collins. "You'll be out of our hair; and that's where the finest relief, the highest mountains in the Alaskan Arctic, and the greatest landscapes are."[50] Collins decided from the outset to heed Reed's and other geologists' advice in the hope of locating an area that would not conflict with future oil development. Thus, the area that Bob Marshall had explored in the central Brooks Range hardly entered into the picture at this time.

Collins and Sumner were intrigued by the possibility of a national park in the Arctic. To their knowledge no national park existed anywhere in the whole circumpolar Arctic and here was the possibility for a great international park extending into Canada. Collins found the scenery "enthralling ... stupendous ... absolutely magnificent." The wildlife-viewing possibilities were tremendous.[51] Sumner contended that such a park, though austere and remote, might some day fit the traditional mold. "Provided safe, comfortable, reasonably-priced accommodations were available, thousands, eventually even millions, of tourists surely would buy a visit, if only to gratify their curiosity and to experience a new kind of adventure in this last of all the frontiers."[52] However, once they had enlisted wide support for the reserve — from wildlife biologists Olaus and Adolph Murie, Starker Leopold, and Fraser Darling among others — Collins and Sumner began to reconsider whether national park status was the proper objective. The decision by the NPS to play a supporting role in this campaign crystallized in a meeting at the Wilderness Conference in San Francisco in 1957, arranged by Collins and attended by Wilderness Society president Olaus Murie and his wife Margaret, FWS Regional Director Clarence Rhode, and representatives of other federal agencies in Alaska.

The decision revealed much about the NPS's evolving position on Alaska wilderness. In the first place, everyone agreed that the area possessed scenic, scientific, and recreational values of national significance. This provoked discussion as to whether the NPS had a responsibility to include in the national park system "representative types of all the landforms, the landscapes, the history, the earth and life science interests that are outstanding in the nation."[53] If such a responsibility indeed existed, it obliged the NPS to seek and administer new units in places such as the North Slope that would attract very few park visitors. This pushed NPS officials toward a more expansive concept of public use. In addition to fulfilling its traditional role of administering public parks (or "pleasuring grounds" as they were termed in early national park establishing acts) for the people's enjoyment, it now seemed that the public's enjoyment extended to scientific and recreational uses that would perhaps never appeal to the mass tourist. For the first time, NPS officials contemplated the possibility of national parks that would remain virtually undeveloped, yet in the final analysis they still preferred to yield such an area to another agency.[54]

The problem of hunting proved to be the crucial factor militating against a national park. If NPS officials seemed willing to consider the idea of a national park without tourist accommodations, they had more difficulty with the idea of a national park in which indigenous people hunted for their subsistence. No one wanted to prevent the natives in the area from hunting and trapping, but no one wanted to sanction these activities in a national park either. Everyone agreed that a less restrictive type of land-use designation was required, and a consensus formed in favor of a wildlife range administered by the FWS.[55]

Still another factor in this decision was the personality of Olaus Murie. In 1956, Murie headed a small expedition to the eastern Brooks Range to gather data and publicize the need for action. Sponsored by the Conservation Foundation and the New York Zoological Society, the expedition was much more successful than Collins and Sumner's had been in attracting attention to the area. Supreme Court Justice William O. Douglas joined the expedition in its final week, thus assuring it of media coverage. Olaus and Margaret Murie, who were well known and liked by Alaskans, spoke in several Alaskan towns after the expedition, advancing the idea of a great wilderness and wildlife reserve where sport and subsistence hunting would be permitted.[56] Their breakthrough came in Fairbanks, where Olaus addressed the Tanana Valley Sportsmen's Association. Preservationists outside Alaska were doubtful that Alaskans would ever support such a large federal reservation, so when the Tanana Valley Sportsmen's Association endorsed the proposal many preservationists reacted as though Murie had pulled a rabbit out of a hat. Consequently, when the strategy meeting took place in San Francisco one year later, Collins was inclined to let Murie take charge of the campaign.[57]

Although the NPS had little more to do with the eastern Brooks Range after 1957, the establishment of the Arctic National Wildlife Range three years later still formed something of a watershed in the service's developing position in Alaska. Nine million acres of wilderness stood as an impressive gain in 1960, and the NPS could not help but look upstaged when the American public learned of the new reserve's vast extent and its marvelous assemblage of wildlife.[58] More importantly, the campaign for the wildlife range acted as a weather vane for Alaskans' attitudes about wilderness, and NPS officials were surprised by what they saw. Several other Alaskan gun clubs followed the Tanana Valley Sportsmen's Association's lead and endorsed the wilderness proposal. Alaskans testified before congressional hearings in favor of federal administration of hunting and against permitting mineral exploration on the wildlife range. The University of Alaska advocated leaving the wildlife range undeveloped and pristine for educational and scientific use.[59] Alaskan newspapers and magazines editorialized about the importance of wilderness for maintaining the quality of life in the forty-ninth state. "We must accept the fact that the great Alaskan wilderness itself is our dominant resource," stated the *Alaskan Sportsman*. "All who love Alaska have one basic conviction in common. They like Alaska because it is tremendously big and beautiful, our last real wilderness frontier."[60]

There were other encouraging signs that Alaskans were making lifestyle choices that would favor wilderness preservation. In Fairbanks, citizens formed the Alaska Conservation Society. In Anchorage, Alaskans organized a chapter of the Izaak Walton League. Celia Hunter and Ginny Hill Woods started a wilderness retreat called Camp Denali, near the ghost town of Kantishna on the edge of Mount McKinley National Park, which aimed at attracting guests who wanted to experience "the essence of Alaskan living — the sincere, informal hospitality of the 'bush country.'" Their camp featured minimal accommodations and an emphasis on activities that would enable guests to enjoy and learn about the subarctic tundra environment. "Just as dude ranches have preserved the spirit of the Old West, Camp Denali offers activities in a setting that is typical of the North," read their brochure.[61] Hunter, born and bred in Alaska, became a leader in Alaska's homegrown wilderness movement. In 1963, Camp Denali hosted the annual council of the Wilderness Society, at which time the Society officially committed itself to the goal of establishing wilderness areas and new national parks in Alaska.[62]

These developments formed the background to the most significant reappraisal of the NPS's role in Alaska since it had undertaken the Alaska Recreation Survey in the early 1950s. Once again, George Collins headed the effort. Appointed chairman of an Alaska Task Force in November 1964, Collins largely wrote the task force report, *Operation Great Land*.[63] The 76-page report was noteworthy less for what it accomplished in the short term than for the vision it provided for NPS officials a few years later as Alaska wilderness preservation moved onto the national agenda. Commissioned by the new director of the NPS, George B. Hartzog, Jr., *Operation Great Land* redefined the NPS's goals at a crucial time in the developing contest over the disposition of Alaska lands.[64]

What was most impressive about *Operation Great Land* was its sense of urgency — an urgency that echoed Marshall's plea thirty years earlier to consider the quality of Alaska wilderness from a national standpoint. Just as

Marshall had, the authors stressed Alaska's unique frontier character. Alaska's population had grown from approximately 60,000 in the 1930s to more than four times that number in 1965, yet Alaska still remained a "rugged pioneer land."

> As important as scenery perhaps, or hunting and fishing, [or sites of] archeological and historic interest[,] is the nebulous aura of romance which still lives on wherever one goes. Starting with the Gold-Rush at the turn of the century and epitomized by Robert Service, still quoted fondly by Alaskans, Rex Beach, and Jack London, the feeling is there, at Skagway and White Pass, at Chilkoot, the headwaters of the famous Yukon and on the beaches of Nome. Everyone wants to see Alaska and catch even fleetingly this sense of the old frontier but as one recent observer said, "They want to see it before it is too late, before it loses the character it still has."[65]

The way to preserve this quality of Alaska, the authors urged, was to make recreation the engine of Alaska's economy. This would reduce the pressure for other kinds of economic development that would degrade the environment. Frontier peoples usually overlooked the economic potential of wilderness and scenery in their rush to exploit minerals, timber, and other raw materials, but Alaskans were different; they were awakening to the value of recreational resources in their state. It was the NPS's responsibility and opportunity to nurture this outlook and to help Alaskans realize their goal of a recreation-based economy.[66]

> What the National Park Service is concerned with is the total environment of the nation. Alaska has a part of this environment which has a quality and character that must be preserved at all costs. Alaska must not succumb to the modern or it will lose much. What it has must be known and made available while still maintaining its integrity. The Service with its long experience can make a real contribution not only in preserving the areas themselves but the character and flavor of a land which is still the frontier.[67]

Alaska's wildlands constituted a distinctly cultural environment, an inhabited wilderness. The delicate mission of making this landscape "available" to visitors while maintaining its "integrity" mirrored the NPS's longstanding balancing act between preservation and use. It increased the scope and complexity of the problem by including humankind in nature.

The important difference between *Operation Great Land* and Marshall's minority report to Congress of 1938 was the role that the federal government would play. Marshall had recommended a policy of restraint that would essentially institute inaction by zoning an area in which the federal government would fund no road construction, lease no mineral lands, and patent no mining claims. *Operation Great Land* called for bold action by the federal government. Superficially, this resembled the report by Cameron and Gordon that Marshall had mocked by counting the number of times the authors used the word "development." Collins suggested that the program he was calling for would cost $150 million over a ten-year period, just for the development of existing parks. He included the familiar refrain, "Every dollar invested will be returned many times over as the business of parks and recreation progresses."[68]

This time the real thrust of federal action would be in the area of public education. Visitor or cultural centers would be established in Anchorage and Fairbanks, and lesser information stations would be located in several Alaskan towns. NPS interpreters would direct their message to Alaskans as much as to visitors. The mission of "Operation Great Land" would be nothing short of "realistically, methodically, determinedly and effectively selling cultural Alaska to Alaskans."[69] The service's top administrator in Alaska would be the "chief diplomat of the organization in selling Alaskans and all others on the northland." The message would be: "that Alaska is our finest, most extensive, recreation resource — our greatest reservoir of latent natural cultural values."[70] The difference between Marshall's proposal and "Operation Great Land" was one of means rather than ends. Perhaps Marshall would have ridiculed this plan just as he had criticized Cameron and Gordon's report for its odd promotional quality. Perhaps, on the other hand, thirty years of population growth and improvement in living standards demanded this different approach.

But the NPS still had not proposed a national park in which it contemplated no development whatsoever. It was fitting that the first such proposal should be made with regard to the central Brooks Range and that the necessary prod should come from Bob Marshall's Wilderness Society. At the Wilderness Society council meeting in Camp Denali in 1963, a resolution was passed calling for discussion with the secretary of the interior of a suitable wilderness-type designation for the area featured in Bob Marshall's *Arctic Wilderness*. In 1968, an NPS team made an airborne reconnaissance of the headwaters of the Koyukuk, Alatna, and Kobuk Rivers and the north slope of the divide as far as Chandler Lake. They proposed a 4-million-acre national park, comprised of two units, one on either side of an anticipated transportation corridor through Anaktuvuk Pass. The team proposed that the national park "would be preserved primarily as a status quo wilderness area." Moreover, the team suggested that "national park status should not invalidate subsistence hunting and fishing rights by natives or limited fishing by others." These statements honored the basic tenets for Alaska wilderness preservation advanced by Marshall, and they showed how far official thinking in the NPS had come since 1938. The team tossed around several possible names for the park, but "Gates of the Arctic," Marshall's name for the geologic feature at the head of the North Fork, "gripped the imagination of all concerned."[71]

The fate of this original NPS proposal may be briefly related. In the summer of 1968, Secretary of the Interior Stewart Udall suggested to President Johnson that he make a "parting gift" to the nation by adding a number of areas to the national park system under the Antiquities Act of 1906. The Antiquities Act authorized the president to proclaim areas of outstanding scientific or historical interest as national monuments; history showed that several presidents had taken similar action during their final days in office. Johnson directed Udall to prepare a list of proposed areas, which he would consider in the fall. On the advice of NPS Director Hartzog, Udall's list focused on seven areas in Alaska and the Southwest. The 4-million-acre Gates of the Arctic together with a 2-million-acre addition to Mount McKinley topped the list and comprised more than three-quarters of the total land area; a smaller addition to Katmai plus four areas in Utah and Arizona made up the rest. Udall submitted his report to the president in September, and made a thirty-minute presentation to the president and a large assembly of his aides on December 11. The president kept postponing his decision, however, and finally disappointed Udall and conservationists by paring the three Alaskan areas from the list and proclaiming just four new national monuments in the Southwest. Historian John P. Crevelli has made a close study of this episode and concluded that the leading factor in Johnson's decision was his concern that this action might be perceived as an abuse of his authority under the Antiquities Act. It was the opinion of Johnson's close advisor, W. DeVier Pierson, that the Southwest tracts had genuine scientific and historical significance but that the Alaskan areas were "a closer question because their real importance [was] of scenic value."[72]

As if the president's eleventh-hour change of heart was not disappointment enough, it was during the winter of 1968–69 that Governor Walter J.

Hickel ordered his Alaska Department of Highways to bulldoze a temporary winter haul road from Fairbanks through the Brooks Range to the oil strike at Prudhoe Bay. Working in winter darkness, the bulldozer crews sometimes got ahead of the road-staking crews, blading up blind canyons and back out again. The bulldozers ripped into the permafrost, with the result that the road dissolved into an impassable, muddy trench as soon as the sun rose above the horizon in the spring. Enraged conservationists called this fiasco the "Hickel Canal." It provided a vivid symbol of the greed that the oil rush had spawned and the frailty of the great Alaskan Arctic. Sadly, it awakened many Americans to the beauty of the Brooks Range at the very moment when Marshall's dream of a virtually roadless Alaskan Arctic was ended.[73]

President Johnson's rejection of a Gates of the Arctic National Monument, together with Governor Hickel's roughshod action in punching a haul road through the Brooks Range, galvanized Alaskan conservationists during the winter of 1968–69. If Alaskans failed to act, it seemed to them, outside oil companies would soon control the state's future. Dr. Robert Weeden, research coordinator for the ADFG's Division of Game in Fairbanks and president of the Alaska Conservation Society, warned that the petroleum industry was "terra incognita" to most biologists, and that oil companies were being secretive about their expanding interests in Alaska. He was disturbed by the complacency of the state government. "Resource managers scribble plans in the wake of bulldozers," he wrote to his superior in the ADFG.[74] That winter, Weeden initiated the first state-wide gathering of Alaska conservationists. Organized by Glacier Bay Superintendent Robert E. Howe, Regional Forester Howard Johnson, and the Southeast Alaska Conservation Council's Richard J. Gordon, and held in Juneau on February 15–16, 1969, the Wilderness Workshop was attended by more than seventy representatives from Alaska's conservation groups and public agencies. The workshop focused on strategies for fulfilling the goals of the Wilderness Act of 1964 in Alaska, and voted to establish an Alaska Wilderness Council. It marked the coming of age of Alaska's homegrown wilderness preservation movement.[75]

The Alaska Wilderness Council agreed on four main principles to guide its efforts. First, echoing Marshall's advice, the council recommended that the public domain in Alaska must be evaluated not only for national park potential (based on the traditional criteria of outstanding scenic and scientific resources) but for its sheer wilderness value too, for here was America's last opportunity to preserve "a wild and largely unaltered environment."

Second, the traditional small-area approach in the establishment of national parks would not work in Alaska because wildlife populations migrated over such large areas. Third, much of Alaska's wilderness would be better preserved as state parks or wilderness areas with hunting a permitted use. Fourth, in view of the oil rush, certain key areas required immediate attention.[76]

One such key area, of course, was the central Brooks Range. The Wilderness Council's Rich Gordon developed a new Gates of the Arctic proposal, with input from Bob Marshall's brother George, which took in the two units east and west of the envisioned transportation corridor and went over the Arctic Divide to include several large lakes. The area would be closed to sport hunting and trapping but would permit subsistence hunting by natives. Gordon submitted the plan to Secretary of the Interior Hickel in April 1970, but it went nowhere.[77]

Ironically the failure of this and the earlier park proposal was fortuitous, because it placed wilderness advocates in a much stronger position to demand that new parklands and wildlife refuges receive due consideration in the approaching native land claim settlement. Conservationists would succeed in getting the native land claim bill amended such that Congress would have an opportunity to establish national parks and wildlife refuges before state and native land selections could proceed. This was a brilliant stroke. Had conservationists succeeded in getting the relatively small additions to the national park system that they sought in 1968–70, it is possible that Congress would not have seen to the interest of conservation in the Alaska Native Claim Settlement Act of 1971. Instead of the ten new national park areas and additional wildlife refuges that were established nine years later under ANILCA, conservationists might have obtained little more than these two modest rectangles of mountain terrain in the central Brooks Range and the smaller additions to Mount McKinley and Katmai.[78]

Bob Marshall's vision of Alaska wilderness eventually reached far beyond the central Brooks Range and even northern Alaska to touch all of Alaska's national parklands and wilderness areas. As wilderness preservationists prepared for the crucial debate over the future of Alaska public lands — a debate that would occupy Congress for the whole of the 1970s — Marshall's cogent ideas about Alaska wilderness were more influential than ever. Yet wilderness preservationists still wrestled with the contradictory nature of Marshall's legacy as symbolized by his two books on the Brooks Range, *Alaska Wilderness* and *Arctic Village*. *Alaska Wilderness* was the record of Marshall's own superlative wilderness experiences. It served as an inspirational compass for a later generation of wilderness explorers who went, like Marshall, in search of that lonely dream of going where no man had ever gone before. *Arctic Village* was Marshall's ode to the bush people. It romanticized the last frontier at the same time that it laid the conceptual groundwork for his subsequent proposal for the preservation of a singularly great wilderness, a wilderness that would somehow embrace the area's inhabitants.

BOB MARSHALL ON THE SUMMIT OF MOUNT DOONERAK,
CENTRAL BROOKS RANGE

Marshall's writings on his Alaska wilderness explorations helped establish
the Central Brooks Range's reputation as the ultimate wilderness.

(Photograph courtesy Robert Marshall Collection, University of California, Berkeley.)

MARGARET AND OLAUS MURIE AT THE ANNUAL MEETING OF THE
WILDERNESS SOCIETY IN 1953

Olaus Murie's campaign for the establishment of the Arctic National Wildlife Range in the late 1950s resulted in the biggest gain for Alaska wilderness preservation between 1925 and 1978.

(Photograph courtesy The Wilderness Society.)

In *Arctic Village*, Marshall described the sociology of wilderness living.
(Photograph courtesy Robert Marshall Collection, University of California, Berkeley.)

ARRIGETCH PEAKS, CENTRAL BROOKS RANGE
This area was first proposed as a national monument in 1968.
(Photograph by Stephen C. Porter courtesy National Park Service, Anchorage.)

SOD HOUSE AND DRYING RACKS AT ANAKTUVUK PASS, 1959
(Photograph courtesy Stephen C. Porter.)

SUMMER AND WINTER DWELLINGS, ANAKTUVUK PASS, 1971
Note the snow machine, oil drums, and radio antenna.
(Photograph courtesy T. Weber Greiser.)

ANAKTUVUK PASS, CA. 1974

(Photograph by John Kauffmann courtesy National Park Service Alaska Regional Office.)

In the 1970s, NPS planners envisioned that the NPS would restrict visitor numbers in order to preserve the area's outstanding wilderness values of grand scenery and spaciousness.

(Photograph by John Kauffmann courtesy National Park Service Alaska Regional Office.)

SEVEN

The Lost Tribe

↓

One day in the late spring of 1943 Sig Wien, Alaska's best-known bush pilot, made his regular run from Fairbanks to Barrow. The flight path took him north by northwest out across the dark, wooded hills of interior Alaska; over the mighty Yukon River whose blue-grey coils turned to liquid silver as they looped away toward the horizon; then over the headwaters of the Koyukuk where broken, spruce-covered uplands soon gave way to treeless ridges that stretched east and west, one after another, grey and bleak, the protuberant ribs of a gaunt and hungry land. These were the mountains of the Brooks Range, sculpted here and there by past glaciation into shining granite walls and needle-sharp spires, the half-way point on the 500-mile flight from Fairbanks to Barrow. Wien's single-engine Bellanca could not make the whole distance on one tank of gas, so Wien normally put down in Wiseman to refuel. When Wiseman was weathered in, the pilot would land at a fuel cache at Chandler Lake on the north slope of the Brooks Range. The large lake lay north of the Arctic Circle and the treeline and usually remained frozen until early summer. On that spring day in 1943 Wien found the snow on Chandler Lake considerably melted down but the ice solid enough for a landing on skis.

Wien was pouring gasoline from his cached jerry cans into the fuel tank of his airplane when he spotted a dark speck moving across the lake's surface to the north of him. At first he thought it was a caribou, but as it came closer he recognized the speck as a human being. As this person trotted purposefully down the eight-mile length of the lake toward his airplane, Wien grew faintly apprehensive. "Finally," Wien later recalled, "here comes

somebody with a big smile on his face. That reassured me that contact with
the person would be agreeable."[1] He was an Eskimo dressed in hides and
furs. Wien was surprised when the man greeted him in English. His name
was Simon Paneak.

Paneak explained to Wien that he had just flown over his camp at the
north end of the lake, that his people were out of several items, and that
they had credit at the Northern Commercial Company store in Fairbanks.
He wanted Wien to bring them some ammunition, salt, flour, tea, and
coffee. A few days later Wien returned to Chandler Lake, this time landing
at the other end, where he found about six families numbering thirty to
forty people living in caribou-skin tents. In return for the requested goods,
Paneak and the other family heads plied Wien with furs with which to
replenish their accounts at the Northern Commercial Company store.
Amidst much smiling and waving and good feeling about return trips in the
future, Wien taxied away from the lakeshore and took off into the sky.

A mere thirty years later Paneak and his people would witness airplanes
arriving almost daily in their village of Anaktuvuk Pass, off-loading parties
of brightly dressed backpackers into the pale arctic sunlight. The Nunamiuts' village then numbered more than 100 residents and featured a
school, church, post office, coffee shop, and modern, ranch-style, oil-heated
homes. Oil-industry dividends enabled the Nunamiuts to acquire snow-
machines and some minimal modern appliances.[2] It was a long way from the
1940s to the 1970s for the Nunamiut people and this remote section of
Alaska. In 1980, with the creation of Gates of the Arctic National Park,
Anaktuvuk Pass gained the distinction of being the only village in Alaska
enclosed within a national park.

Paneak kept a journal in which he sought to record his people's remarkable twentieth-century cultural evolution. Ethel Ross Oliver, a census taker
who struck up a long correspondence with Paneak after her first visit to
Anaktuvuk Pass in 1950, preserved Paneak's leatherbound journal and letters in her private papers and later deposited them with the Rasmuson
Library at the University of Alaska, Fairbanks. Paneak's writings provide us
with an indigenous view of Nunamiut affairs and a point of reference for the
descriptions left by anthropologists and other visitors. If one theme may be
distilled from Paneak's writings, it is that there was no shame in his people
wanting to shuck off some of the hardness in their lives and acquire com-
modities — from modern education and medicine to snowmachines and oil-
heated homes. At the same time, Paneak wanted to maintain the cohesive-
ness of the families and the group and pass down the traditional knowledge

and skills that were basic to his people's identity. It was this latter thought that inspired Paneak one day to begin setting down in painstaking English what his father had taught him orally in family gatherings after the main meal of the day:

I wanted first from my life beginning remember.
First. An old man like to telling old story and recent times story so youngerpeoples should learn or remembering on all kind of old peoples living and how to make a living or learning.
An old peoples of Nunamiut like to tell in Happy house or larger of family hunts before lunch time and after.
That why among Eskimos learn an implement such things like a how to make Bow & Arrows and many other items. Snow shoes and netting and netting make fish net and sled and skin boat frame — Umiak & Kayak frame work and spear head of flint and learned how to chipping all kind of tools. Very thin sharp flint chip was moose — caribou mountain sheep horn cutters and also very fine for cutting for mammoth and walrus tusk.[3]

Although the Nunamiut homeland embraced only a part of the huge national park, these people were central to the creation of Gates of the Arctic. The Nunamiuts attracted not only Sig Wien, but anthropologists, wildlife biologists, wilderness explorers, and ultimately the NPS planners who formulated legislative proposals and conceptual plans for Gates of the Arctic National Park in the late 1960s and 1970s. These observers constantly referred to the Nunamiuts' hunting way of life as "ancient," "Stone Age," and "timeless." They found the Nunamiuts' lifestyle as hauntingly beautiful as the mountain country in which they lived. A young USGS surveyor named Charles Metzger, who witnessed a caribou hunt at Chandler Lake in 1945, carried the image in his head for nearly forty years before putting it down in vivid detail in his book *Silent River*.[4] For Metzger and many others, the quiet strivings of this lost tribe so far removed from the world's problems reinforced their own sense of escape. The survival of the Nunamiuts' hunting way of life in the second half of the twentieth century seemed to authenticate claims that the Brooks Range was the "ultimate" or "last great wilderness."

The Nunamiuts sought refuge in this white man's wilderness. They addressed themselves directly to the romantic primitivism of their white admirers. Initially they used their primitive image to protect their cultural

autonomy. Later they used it to defend their hunting way of life. By the
1970s they went so far as to propose to Congress that they be preserved in
their homeland in a Nunamiut National Park. As Robert F. Berkhofer, Jr.,
and other scholars have shown, the white man's image of the Indian has
exerted a powerful influence on Indian cultures and Indian-white relations
from earliest contact to the present day.[5] The white man's image of the
Nunamiuts largely took form in the context of Alaska wilderness appreciation. The Nunamiuts understood this and cultivated their white man's
image as a tribe so removed from civilization as to be virtually a people of
nature.

Unfortunately the Nunamiuts' hunting way of life lost much of its pic-
turesqueness as the group adopted new technology. Like the Tlingit seal
hunters who had traded canoes for outboards a few generations earlier, the
Nunamiut caribou hunters who traded dog teams for snowmachines became less sympathetic in the white mind. The changes in the Nunamiuts'
hunting way of life in the 1960s and 1970s jeopardized their haven in the
wilderness movement. It was at this stage that the Nunamiuts and the NPS
began working together to develop some kind of land-management system
that would satisfy both the practical needs of indigenous hunters and the
primitivist ideals of wilderness users. Discussion of this problem in the
1970s laid the foundation for so-called "cooperative management" of
the area by the NPS and the Nunamiuts after passage of ANILCA. In
theory, co-management meant that the NPS and the Nunamiuts would
endeavor to respect one another's conflicting land values, that through the
synergy of co-management there would be an evolution toward greater and
greater compatibility of land values.[6] In practice, the partnership was so
unequal and the NPS so firmly committed to traditional mandates that the
dialogue broke down. The Nunamiuts eventually found themselves, much
as the Huna Tlingits had earlier, being treated as intruders in their own
homeland.[7]

That these people had an ancestral claim to the area was never in dispute.
Anthropologists have determined that the Nunamiuts of the central Brooks
Range represent a remnant population of an inland Eskimo culture, which
numbered perhaps 1,000 people in the nineteenth century. There are other
inland groups of Eskimos in the western Brooks Range, who live at salmon
fishing locations on the Kobuk and Noatak Rivers, but anthropologists
debate whether these riverine groups are culturally distinct from the mountain Eskimos of the central Brooks Range.[8] Anthropologists believe that the
ancestors of the Nunamiuts occupied the Brooks Range for the first time

only some 500–600 years ago, and that they did not move into the central Brooks Range until the arrival of European trade goods in northern Alaska, probably early in the nineteenth century.[9] Stone tools recovered from numerous archeological sites attest to seasonal occupation of the central Brooks Range by other big-game hunting cultures as long ago as 6,000 years.[10]

The twentieth-century Nunamiuts' place in nature was more complicated. Nunamiut subsistence traditionally revolved around the caribou. This animal provided skins for clothing and shelter, sinew for sewing, bone and antler for tools, and up to 90 percent of the Nunamiuts' diet during certain times of the year. The caribou migrated in spring and fall through the mountain passes of the Brooks Range, plodding hundreds of miles between calving grounds on the North Slope and winter range on the far side of the mountains. Like most herding animals the caribou was relatively easy to kill — once it was found. The only consistent feature of the caribou migration was its unpredictability. One year the herd might sweep through the country in a long and sprawling procession; the next, it might dribble through in small bands. One year it might take one route; the next, another or multiple routes. One year the southward migration would come in October; the next, not until December.[11] The caribou traveled too swiftly to be pursued; rather, it had to be intercepted. To miss the migration entirely was to court disaster. It was chiefly for the hunter's skill in locating the caribou that each Nunamiut band picked its *umialik*, or headman.

The mountain Eskimos adapted to the uncertainty of the caribou migration by placing rows of rock cairns or piles of sod at strategic points along the migration trails. On top of these mounds the Eskimos mounted willows with strips of rawhide — or in the twentieth century, streamers of toilet paper — to wave in the wind. These "surrounds" had the effect of deflecting the movement of caribou in a desired direction or corralling a portion of the herd as it moved through the area. The Eskimos also learned which passes the caribou used most frequently and where the hunter could most effectively stand sentinel during the season of migration. The many surviving rock structures built by these caribou hunters — cairns for deflecting the caribou's movement, wind breaks and blinds for the waiting hunter, caches built into the scree slopes for protecting the hunter's kill from scavengers — provide clues to the prehistory and history of the area. Tulugak Lake, a favored camp of Simon Paneak's band in the 1940s, has many such sites surrounding it. On one occasion in 1945, probably in an effort to conserve precious ammunition, the Eskimos drove caribou into the lake where they speared them from kayaks in the manner of their nineteenth-century forebears.[12]

The caribou migration was one ecological factor that dominated the lives of the Nunamiut; another was the caribou's population. When the caribou migration came later in the season or largely passed them by, the Nunamiuts were able to subsist on alternative sources of food: Dall sheep, grizzly bear, wolverine, ptarmigan, and other animals of the tundra. But when the arctic caribou herd's population crashed around the turn of the century, the effect on the Nunamiuts was more drastic. Most bands either emigrated to the coast or starved to death in the attempt. The human population of the central Brooks Range fell to no more than a few families in the early twentieth century. Around 1920, the mountains were probably completely deserted.[13] Was this a disruption of aboriginal conditions or part of a cycle for the caribou hunters?

Some anthropologists pointed to the decline of the caribou herd as the one inescapable condition that made the Brooks Range virtually uninhabitable after the turn of the century, but others maintained that the depopulation of the Brooks Range was not purely a function of ecology.[14] The attractions of whaling ships, mission schools, and trading posts along the Arctic coast were significant factors, too. Anthropologist Norman A. Chance went so far as to suggest that the Brooks Range was depopulated mainly because of a disruption of trade between inland and coastal Eskimos. When American whalers initiated trade with the coastal Eskimos, Chance maintains, these groups no longer traveled inland to trade, and inland Eskimos were subsequently forced to travel to the coast to obtain needed items.[15] However, Chance's argument fails to explain why the inland Eskimos who came annually to trade fairs on the coast and still spent most of the year in the mountains eventually left the mountains altogether.

Anthropologist Ernest S. Burch, Jr., presented a more balanced view of social and ecological change, but placed no less emphasis on the general theme of disruption. Based on archeological evidence and interviews with Eskimos of northwestern Alaska whose parents and grandparents had once lived in the Brooks Range, Burch pieced together a story of social disintegration in the face of white contact and ecological disaster. Burch believed that prior to about 1850 northwestern Eskimos were divided into numerous distinct societies. Each society had its own internal ties of kinship, Inupiat dialect, seasonal rounds, and traditional location at the time of fall freeze-up. Beginning around 1850, these societies were all beset with difficulties as New England whalers introduced liquor and diseases on the

Arctic coast at the same time that the caribou population began to decline inland. There followed a gradual out-migration of Eskimos who inhabited inland areas. Burch estimated that the Eskimo population of northwestern Alaska dropped by half, while the caribou population plummeted from a high of perhaps 300,000 to a low of perhaps 10,000 between 1850 and 1890. Under the combined pressures of demographic decline and geographic dislocation, the traditional Eskimo societies ceased to exist. "The traditional kinship system continued to exist in the minds of the people," Burch postulated, "but their ability to realize the ancient ideals in practice was seriously impaired." Many Eskimos adapted one way or another to non-kinship-oriented social relations in the whaling industry as crew members, cooks, sewers, and prostitutes. Eskimo women married and produced children on board the whaling ships, only to be put ashore and abandoned when their husbands returned to the United States.[16] In Burch's interpretation, the turn of the century found the Eskimos of northwestern Alaska at a cultural nadir as they adjusted to European influence. The problem with Burch's representation was that he had no proof that the traditional kinship system had ever in fact been more than an ideal. His assumption that the Eskimos enjoyed a period of social equilibrium prior to 1850 was purely theoretical.

Anthropologists were able to trace the Nunamiuts' story after 1890 with greater confidence, as this period fell within the life spans of many of their Nunamiut informants in the 1950s and 1960s. Moreover, for the period around the turn of the century anthropologists had the descriptions of inland Eskimo villages and cultural life left by a handful of explorers, notably Lieutenant George M. Stoney's account of the small villages he encountered on the upper Noatak and Colville Rivers in 1886 and Vilhaljmar Stefansson's description of a Nunamiut band living near the mouth of the Colville in 1908–9.[17] The story that anthropologists recovered from these sources was that the Nunamiut people had left the mountains for the coast over a span of years. Each spring more and more families made the long trip by skin boat down the Colville River to the annual trade fair at Nigalik on the delta to exchange caribou skins and sinew for white man's goods and the products of the sea, each summer more and more families prolonged their stay on the coast after the fair was over, and each fall perhaps one or two more families chose not to return to the mountains at all.[18]

Gradually the Nunamiut left the familiar delta region and spread east and west along the Arctic coast seeking the trade goods and wage-earning jobs that could be had at Point Barrow, Herschel Island, and elsewhere.[19]

Around 1910 fur trapping replaced whaling as the main source of cash
income for Eskimos on the Arctic coast. Fortuitously, several trading posts
opened along the coast to capitalize on the high market value of arctic fox
furs about the same time that the whalers departed. The Nunamiuts traded
furs for guns, ammunition, coffee, tea, flour, tobacco, and other goods
while obtaining most of their food from the sea. Most lived in sod houses,
adopted Christianity, and allowed their children to attend mission schools.
Occasionally they hunted for caribou and Dall sheep in the foothills. The
pattern of their lives basically merged with that of the Tareumiuts, or
people of the sea.

> According to my parent telling me all about old peoples living . . . said
> Nunamiut is large number peoples all along in Colville river before
> beginning move out of this country to everywhere. More peoples
> move up to east when whalers usually stay around Herscel Island hav-
> ing winter among whalers . . . in that times caribou meat is valuable to
> whaler. In that times Eskimos killing many — many caribous. Whalers
> have plenty meat in ship to go outside load of meat. . . . Eskimos have a
> happy times to get white mens grubs and lots of whiskey to drink. . . .
> That main thing to Eskimo and everything is so easy for Eskimos and
> some Eskimo come down to Niglik in summer time from Herscel
> Island and bring all kind of news to Nunamiut and some Nunamiut
> follow them back and more and more finally almost no more Nuna-
> miut only few family left and some Nunamiut family move over to
> Barrow and some few family move over to Kobuk & Noatak because
> gold seekers or white men prospectors bring supplies more easy to
> Eskimos bringing white men outfit.[20]

With the coming of the Great Depression a small number of Nunamiut
families embarked on a new course that joined their cultural evolution to
wilderness like that of no other native group in Alaska. As the fur market fell
and the trading posts closed, these Nunamiut families decided to extend
their hunting forays into the mountains, making them at first the most
obscure native group in Alaska and later perhaps its best known. Reversing
the pattern by which they had moved to the coast, these Nunamiut families
spent longer and longer amounts of time in their mountain locations — one
band of eight families at Chandler Lake and another band of five families on
the Killik River. After 1939 they gave up the trips to the coast altogether.
For four years their only contact with the outside was an occasional journey

by dog sled southward to one of the trading posts on the Koyukuk or Kobuk Rivers; for another four years their only contact was with the bush pilot Wien every few months.[21] In 1947 Paneak suggested to Wien that his people might favor a permanent settlement in a place where they could have a school, church, and airstrip, such as at Anaktuvuk Pass. Thus, the Nunamiuts quietly reclaimed their homeland high up in the Killik, Chandler, and Anaktuvuk river drainages at the same time that Bob Marshall discovered extraordinary wilderness values in the Brooks Range south of the Arctic Divide and NPS officials Lowell Sumner and George Collins reconnoitered the Brooks Range east of the Canning River.

Anaktuvuk Pass was so broad it was really a plateau a little over 2,000 feet above sea level. It was bordered on the east and west by high, craggy limestone cliffs where sheep could be found, and it lay on the path of the caribou migration. It was also favored by an abundance of willows, which the Nunamiuts used for cooking and heating fuel. At Paneak's request, Wien discussed the plan with BIA officials in Fairbanks and airdropped a message to the second Nunamiut band on the Killik River stating that the new settlement would likely acquire a school teacher. When Wien flew over the Killik River camp again a few days later he saw the band on the move, struggling across swollen rivers in its haste to get to Anaktuvuk Pass.[22]

The move was an epochal event in the cultural evolution of the Nunamiut people. It stood for more than the end of eight years of nomadism. For the first time, the outside world learned of the existence of these primitive caribou hunters. Henceforward, the Nunamiuts could not escape an awareness of their peculiarity in the eyes of the rest of the world. Nor could outsiders who observed Nunamiut culture resist seeing the moment of their discovery as a bittersweet turning point. Not long after the Nunamiuts had pitched their round, caribou-skin tents in two camps located sixteen miles apart at either end of the pass, they began to see a succession of visitors. Norwegian anthropologist Helge Ingstad arrived in September 1949 and lived with Paneak's band through the winter. Laurence Irving, an ornithologist from the Arctic Research Laboratory at Point Barrow, and Robert Rausch, a parasitologist from the Arctic Health Research Center in Anchorage, flew in together a few weeks later. A trader named Pat O'Connell built a trading post at the smaller of the two camps that same summer. On July 29, 1950 Ethel Ross Oliver arrived to record the number of people living in the two camps (twelve men, eleven women, and thirty-nine children) for the U.S. Census.

Anaktuvuk Pass Alaska
22 August, 1950
Mrs. Simeon Oliver
P.O. Box 1845
Anchorage Alaska

Dear Her:

   Mrs. May Kakena finished parka for you and she said big Hello to
you and Susie my wife finished parka for you also. You will see by tag
which was made by and Mrs. Frank Rulland hasn't finished yet but
will be send in little later.
   My wife said if any one like a parka and she said better send a
money or check sometime.
   My wife will make a man jacket size like I am with mountain sheep
lamb skin and I collect all good skin in this village and Susie said it
will cost $75.00. If you can get childrens shoe pack size you know our
childrens Robert — Raymond — Mabel — Roosevelt. If can get those
please let us know how much of price and please get 1 good wolverine
skin also to us. That all about what she had saying. If she did not busy
on her childrens foot wear she would make more clothing for sell.
   The peoples get short of meat during this summer no caribou.
   We will going up to Contact Cr. pretty soon now.
   Abraham Kakena still in Bethel Hospital. He getting better we
hear.
   Everybody is all OK.

                    With best wishes,

                    Simon Paneak

P.S. Oh yes. I say big Hello Okwak.[23]

   The Nunamiuts' early visitors came to Anaktuvuk Pass expecting to find
the Eskimos as pristine as the wilderness that they inhabited. Parasitologist
Robert Rausch, coming to investigate animal-borne disease in what was
"biologically one of the least-known regions in North America," attributed
the same quality of innocence to the human inhabitants of the Brooks
Range. He reported erroneously that the Nunamiuts encamped at Anaktuvuk Pass "knew no English and existed almost exclusively by hunting."

With the exception of their use of firearms, "these people apparently lived as they had done for centuries."[24] Pat O'Connell, the trader, assumed that the Nunamiuts knew nothing of timber framing or sod house construction when he settled in their midst. He told visitors to Anaktuvuk Pass that the Nunamiuts followed his example as they gradually replaced their caribou-skin tents with sod houses in the 1950s.[25] But the Nunamiuts were familiar with timber and sod construction from their years on the Arctic coast; their slowness to build such homes at Anaktuvuk Pass stemmed not from ignorance but from the fact that logs had to be sledded laboriously from the nearest forest some forty miles south of Anaktuvuk Pass (rather than scavenged from the beach), and because the sod houses were uncomfortable in summer. For each new sod house that appeared at Anaktuvuk Pass a canvas tent over a wooden frame appeared alongside it for summer use.

The wilderness framed Ingstad's impressions of the Nunamiuts too. He recalled how the "wilderness lay on every side" as one of Wien's pilots flew him toward the Brooks Range. Marveling over this country, he wrote, "No town defaces it, no soot soils it. Only here and there are traces of man: a lonely trapper's hut beside a lake, a gold mining camp with heaps of sand, a river-borne canoe." Naturally the Nunamiuts ensconced in this wilderness homeland had "little knowledge of the outside." Their way of life took essentially "the same shape as that of their ancestors." Ingstad was impressed especially by the Nunamiuts' primitiveness. "It is curious to find a community so utterly primitive in structure. There is no social organization, no chief or other head, no criminal law. The one stable feature is the family. . . . The society is not communistic, for as a rule every man hunts on his own account, and his bag is his own. . . . But at the same time a sense of social responsibility runs through the community; there are unwritten laws for the common good."[26] Ingstad assumed that the culture he was describing in 1949 provided a unique window on the Eskimo past.

Ingstad found the Nunamiuts' world view to be essentially unchanged. Despite the fact that Christianity had "found its way into the mountains" at about the turn of the century, it had affected the Nunamiuts later than any other native group in Alaska; and although the Nunamiuts had easily accepted the idea of a supreme deity that could assure good hunting, protect against misfortune, and bring happiness in the afterlife, Ingstad had doubts as to "whether Christianity had gradually acquired a deeper significance." Meanwhile, the Nunamiuts continued to live by their traditional beliefs that everything in nature had a spirit, that both men and animals had a soul that lived on after death, and that physical beings shared the earth with many invisible demons. The Nunamiuts preserved their ancient religion through a "mass of legends and myths which have been handed down from the Stone Age."[27]

Ingstad was most impressed by how close the Nunamiuts were to their earlier material culture. They had used bows and arrows as recently as the turn of the century. The Nunamiuts' return to the mountains in the 1930s had caused them to leave behind most of the material culture that they had acquired on the coast. "The tribe's old hunting grounds in the mountains called, and so the people came back," Ingstad wrote romantically. "Now they live year after year quite by themselves." Although they used rifles and ammunition for hunting, cotton material for summer clothing, knives and pots for preparing and cooking meat, and tobacco, coffee, flour, and salt to supplement their provisions, these items represented no more than a "dash of civilization." The Nunamiuts purchased these items with credit obtained from sales of furs, especially wolf skins. Wolf skins paid a bounty of $50 apiece in addition to the value of the fur. These contacts with the outside were so sporadic, Ingstad suggested, as to be insignificant.[28]

Tolugak L. 16 air miles north of Pass
2 May, 1956

Dear Ethel:

It is nice to have your nice letter and the $10.00.

I am sorry that the peoples cannot coming down to our camp because our country is almost break up now not much times to driven dog teams by now.

Everybody do not like early spring but nobody could stop. We can't hauling logs for fuel, and we had another epidemic flu again lasting 2 weeks and now everybody seems to be OK except Homer Mekiana is in Hospital in Fairbanks. We did not hear since he left.

I only hope you bring some Blazo for Coleman cook stove. I have new Coleman cook stove here cost too much to for you to carry but you will need it. If I have logs or willow wood for fuel and I would not bother you to bring some white gas.

No more snow and are not good for driving sled.

Your personal friend and from Susie & Simon Paneak.[29]

The Nunamiuts were featured in a number of books and articles between 1949 and 1971. Ingstad's book, *Nunamiut*, which the Norwegian anthropologist wrote for a popular audience and published in an English-language edition in 1954, laid the groundwork for several more anthropological studies of the Nunamiuts over the next twenty years. All of these started with the premise that the people of Anaktuvuk Pass were one of the least acculturated native groups in Alaska.[30] With anthropologists taking so much interest in their people, the two *umialiks* of the village, Homer Mekiana and Simon Paneak, each tried his own hand at defining what made the Nunamiuts a distinctive people. Mekiana wrote a column for the *Fairbanks Daily News-Miner* entitled "Anaktuvuk Passages." In addition, Mekiana's family allowed the Naval Arctic Research Laboratory to publish his diary from the 1950s, *This is the Story of Anaktuvuk Pass Village*. Simon Paneak, with the encouragement of his friend Ethel Ross Oliver, sent his story, "We Hunt to Live," to the *Alaska Sportsman*.[31] Also in this period, two wilderness enthusiasts contributed their impressions of the Nunamiuts: Dallas sportsman F. Wallace Taber described his experience for *American Rifleman* in "Hunting with Alaska's Nunamiute," and California sociologist Sam Wright wrote an account of Anaktuvuk Pass for *Living Wilderness* in "Eskimo Village." The fullest account by a wilderness enthusiast, though not published until 1983, was Charles Metzger's *Silent River: a pastoral elegy in the form of a recollection of an Arctic adventure*, based on his encounters with the Nunamiut while exploring for oil in 1945.[32] Most of these accounts recited a similar series of firsts for the village that had come remarkably late in time and close on the heels of one another: first year-round habitations in 1949; first visiting school teacher in 1950; first mail service in 1951; first chapel in 1958; first schoolhouse in 1961.

Taken altogether the literature on the development of Anaktuvuk Pass presented a kaleidoscopic picture. One incongruous feature was radio. Metzger, in 1945, was struck by the sight of a Zenith radio perched in the back of Paneak's tent, a long line of insulated copper wire strung overhead for reception. Paneak told Metzger that he liked to listen to Voice of America, G.I. Jill, and Tokyo Rose.[33] Twenty years later, Sam Wright sat in Noah Ahgook's tent, noted a similar thin wire overhead, and felt saddened and perplexed by the strains of rock and roll music and consumer advertisements coming over the air waves from one of the stations in Fairbanks.[34] Mekiana's diary referred often to radio reports and included numerous details of the Korean War. Mekiana's family sometimes listened to church services on KFAR.[35]

Visitors to Anaktuvuk Pass were sometimes surprised by the Nunamiuts' Christianity as much as they were by their interest in radio. Metzger related how Elijah Kakena told him and his companions that he had once attended a mission school on the Koyukuk River and that he still sang some hymns. Kekinya then led Metzger and his companions in a group sing. "As it turned out," Metzger wrote, "he knew both the tunes and the words a good deal better than we did. We could fake the tunes after a fashion, but the words escaped us; we were in effect led by Elijah to reveal that we had never learned them. Although we tried to respond to Elijah's attempts at establishing rapport with us on Christian missionary terms, we failed him miserably. He was, at least in Christian missionary terms, a much better Christian than we were."[36] What was happening in the encounter between Metzger and Kakena was precisely what was happening in all the literature that accumulated on Anaktuvuk Pass in this period: while the Nunamiuts tried to define themselves as a distinctive though essentially American people, those who visited and wrote about their village insisted on making the Nunamiuts an exotic people, a people of nature.

Sam Wright was a professor of social ecology at the Starr King School for the Ministry in Oakland, California. One summer while Wright was on sabbatical leave, he and his wife backpacked 100 miles to Anaktuvuk Pass. His purpose was to study "value formation" among a people who were still far removed from urban life. Wright's hypothesis was that the Nunamiuts enjoyed a relationship to their environment that involved a finite set of discrete, identifiable, social and ecological variables. He supposed that each facet of the Nunamiuts' relationship to the environment could be isolated, analyzed, and understood in relation to the whole. What Wright had in mind by "value formation" was to study at the village level how land-use values changed through time — a formula that was subsequently applied to numerous Alaska native village studies, including a study of Anaktuvuk Pass in the late 1970s. But instead of attempting to delineate values in a village undergoing rapid social change, the Wrights overthrew their own value system, quitting their California jobs and moving into an old miner's cabin deep in the wilds of the Brooks Range. From this adopted home, Wright sent occasional writings to *Living Wilderness* and became an apostle for an Alaskan wilderness lifestyle. Wright claimed that he and his wife had chosen a subsistence lifestyle "much like that of the caribou-hunting Nunamiut Eskimo."[37]

Wright's description of the Nunamiuts' land wisdom was particularly romantic. The Nunamiuts possessed a spiritual quality of "at-homeness" which his informants described as *koviashuktok*. The term could be loosely translated as joy, but *koviashuktok* was an action rather than a thing. Language was the key to understanding the way that Eskimos conceptualized their relationship to the environment, Wright explained. All Eskimo words were, in effect, forms of the verb "to be." The Eskimos' words for snow were so numerous because snow never existed in itself but took form from the action in which it participated. Snow was falling, blowing, clinging to one's clothes, and so on. Whatever existed, the Eskimo himself shared in bringing it into being. "With each act and statement his world is created, brought into existence, and each act accomplished is as quickly lost. His ecological relationship to the world is not passive. Man is the force that reveals form. With man creation becomes."[38] Through the use of language the Nunamiut so embedded himself in his environment that his consciousness or self-identity almost merged with his surroundings. For the romantically inclined observer like Wright, this suggested a pervading spiritualism or self-evident meaning in life.

I go by myself on my traplines, pick few marmots from my stone deadfalls and I saw more marmots but I cannot shoot them. When I come near to our home camp pretty soon I see grizzly bear on my caribou meat. I took my telescope and see great big grizzly bear sleep on caribou meat. After he buried it with ground and dirt he sleep on top of it. He laying like a man laying on top his back. Distance about two miles.

I know I only have six shells before but I counted them again and never different. It was only six shells. I was thinking and sit down and smoke and bear was sleep on top of caribou carcasses. Finally I think I have enough shells to kill the bear and I walk right up to him but I did not went very close, one hundred yards away close enough for little .22 Hornet. And I hollered to him and wake him up before I took a shots. But at first holler he do not wake at all just stretching out his forearm. Almost wake up. And I hollered once more and then he wake and head up he look at me while I aimed in his neck and after I almost pull my trigger the bear beginning to get up. I pull my trigger anyway and hit the bear in his ear and he almost drop dead, rolled and roaring hollering and shooking his head. Little 46 grain .22 Hornet bullets make him mad. Just soon rolled and roaring were finished he begin to run after me and I fired another little bullet while he was running toward me and little bullet drop him again, but he got up again and running sideway. I aimed in shoulder blade while bear running and shoot. Bear fall down and can not get up any more. Dead there. And I only have three shot left and the grizzly bear was pretty good size bear.[39]

It is impossible to know precisely what the Nunamiuts thought about
Wright or Ingstad or any of the other primitivists with whom they became
acquainted in the 1950s and 1960s. For the most part these people came
to Anaktuvuk Pass to learn rather than to instruct. They encouraged the
Nunamiuts to value their primitiveness. Ethel Ross Oliver, Paneak's faithful
correspondent, encouraged Paneak to write the Nunamiuts' story and send
it to her friend, the editor of *Alaska Sportsman*. "Lots of people wrote me
from all over in States. Everybody like it," Paneak wrote to her appre-
ciatively afterwards.[40] Even the scientist Robert Rausch showed great respect for the Nunamiuts' practical knowledge of the animals they hunted—
particularly the caribou—since there was probably no white man living
who knew the animal as well.[41] Certainly the Nunamiuts must have found
their contacts with these people to be benign.

This becomes more obvious when one considers the alternatives they
were faced with in the 1950s and 1960s. At the same time that Wright,
Metzger, Ingstad, and Rausch were eulogizing the Nunamiuts as the keepers of an ancient land wisdom, wildlife conservationists were constructing a
very different image of this hunting and gathering culture. They advanced
the more traditional view that the Nunamiuts were a benighted people
whose use of modern technology made them more destructive of the game
than they had been in the past. Wildlife conservationists alleged that Eskimos all across northern Alaska were slaughtering more game because they
had acquired large numbers of rifles along with ammunition through the
National Guard during World War II.[42] They suggested that Eskimo communities such as that at Anaktuvuk Pass lacked any means for preventing
members of the group from killing animals in excess of what they could use.
"The natives now kill many more animals than formerly," a past director of
the FWS told readers of *Audubon Magazine*. "The fact that the natives will
be the ones who suffer the most if the herds are gone is no deterrent to the
individual who is killing for profit or for the joy of killing."[43] Two reputable
scientists, Starker Leopold and Fraser Darling, offered their thoughts on
Alaska natives and wildlife conservation in their influential essay, *Wildlife in
Alaska: An Ecological Reconnaissance* (1953). It was not the Eskimo's fault that
he seemed to have no understanding of the concept. "His extremely un-
abstract, practical philosophy, and ability to live in the present have not
fitted him in his own culture to indulge in reflection on the dynamics of
animal populations or to consider questions of conservation from a developed point of view." They drove their point home by citing recent reports
on the Nunamiuts of Anaktuvuk Pass, who appeared to hunt caribou with
no thought of conservation but only an immediate view to procuring food

for themselves and their dogs, and the hides, tents, blankets, clothing, and harnesses that made up such a substantial part of their material culture.[44] In short, wildlife conservationists put little stock in the idea that primitive peoples knew instinctively how to live within the limits of their environment. If they had possessed such a capability in the past, it had been purely a function of their small numbers and simple technology.

These were familiar arguments that had been applied to many Native American groups before.[45] However, once again the Nunamiuts' wilderness setting framed the debate in a different way. Wildlife conservationists found the establishment of a new Eskimo village in the heart of the Brooks Range vaguely disturbing.[46] Sportsmen found it unsporting. F. Walter Taber's article in *American Rifleman* featured a photograph of an old Nunamiut hunter seated against his tent handloading his ammunition, captioned: "Jesse Ahguk, who, according to the author, probably has killed more caribou than any other man on the entire North American continent."[47] In the course of the 1950s and 1960s the Nunamiuts could not fail to see the contradiction in these two white man's images: one so friendly and admiring, the other so critical.

The most significant thing about the wildlife conservationists' critique of the Nunamiuts and the Nunamiuts' response to it was that it occurred in a law-enforcement context. The FWS, faced with dwindling big-game populations, growing numbers of resident sportsmen, and rumors of excess harvests of game in the Arctic by Eskimo villages such as Anaktuvuk Pass, decided in 1950 to begin enforcing the Alaska Game Law in the Arctic. That is, it decided to cease construing large annual harvests of game by Eskimo villages in northern Alaska as essential to meet "emergency" needs as allowed under the law. The effect of this change of policy was to thrust the Alaska Game Law into the center of the Nunamiuts' efforts to interpret their culture for outsiders. The people of Anaktuvuk Pass together with other Eskimo groups in northern Alaska found themselves defending their way of life against charges that they were breaking the law. They described their diet, their methods of hunting and gathering and food storage, their transportation and commerce, and even their ties to other Eskimo groups and the rest of American society, all in relation to the Game Law.[48]

This process was intrinsically adversarial. The Nunamiuts had to match their version of events against what wildlife officials said about them. For example, in 1952 FWS Regional Director Clarence J. Rhode flew into Anaktuvuk Pass and queried the village council about the village's yearly harvest of caribou. Soon afterwards a newspaper reported an anonymous FWS official's estimate (presumably Rhode's) that the people of Anaktuvuk

Pass killed as many as 4,000 caribou each year. *Elks Magazine* reprinted the newspaper article in December 1952. In January the Anaktuvuk Pass Council protested Rhode's investigation to the Alaska Native Service (BIA) in Juneau. "We surely never reached even 1,000 caribou a year," the council objected. "How did the game warden know us by only landing here and stop one or 1½ hours and know that we always kill 4,000 a year while the group of Anaktuvuk Pass have not much anything to eat in camp at that time and [FWS Regional Director] Clarence [Rhode] told us we can go to Kobuk where there is fish and to Fairbanks where there is place to work and earn money." The council went on to explain that the people had no money for transportation to these places, and that if they observed a bag limit of one bull caribou per person per season they would all starve. The council also rejected the idea that the village dogs were consuming excessive quantities of wild meat. The dogs were essential for travel—pulling sleds in winter and packing saddle bags in summer. "We always feed our dogs with caribou blood, lungs, intestine and anything that is not good to eat for human being also cut the caribou hide in pieces mixing into dog soup. No money to buy corn meal or tallow to cook with for dog food."[49] As was true of similar protests by other Eskimo groups, the Nunamiuts were constructing an image of themselves in direct response to the wildlife conservationists. This image built on two main themes: that their culture did not waste game, and that they were persecuted by the law.

The threatening posture taken by wildlife law enforcement officials in the early 1950s provided the initial spark for north Alaskan Eskimo involvement in the native land claim movement. This movement, viewed later against a backdrop of state land selections and leases of land to oil exploration companies in the mid- to late 1960s, would appear to be narrowly focused on real estate, but the origins of the movement can be found in the Eskimos' dependence on fish and game resources. This was the first time in their experience that outsiders had tried to interfere in that relationship. It was not long before the many groups saw their common interest in resisting the federal government's intrusion. Word spread quickly from village to village after each new investigation like Rhode's in Anaktuvuk Pass.[50] In the process of coming to one another's defense the Eskimos of the North Slope began thinking of themselves as one people, the Inupiat, based on their common language and their common interest in maintaining the privileges that they had formerly enjoyed under the Alaska Game Law.

A second crackdown by the FWS some ten years later threatened the resource base of both the Inupiat and Yup'ik Eskimos of western Alaska. The flat, water-logged tundra of the North Slope and western Alaska were the summer range for millions of waterfowl and other migratory birds. Ducks formed an important part of the Eskimos' diet when they arrived in late spring, as this was a time of year when the winter store of caribou meat ran low or began to spoil. During 1960–61 FWS officials and Eskimos traded charges over alleged violations of the Migratory Bird Treaty Act. This set the stage for an incident that has often been described as the beginning of the Alaska native claim movement.[51] On a summer day in 1961 FWS wardens booked two Eskimo men in Barrow for illegal possession of ducks. The next morning 138 Barrow Eskimos appeared outside the hotel where the wardens were staying, each one holding a dead duck in his hand and demanding to be arrested as well. This act of civil disobedience and community solidarity galvanized Alaskan Eskimos in much the same way that Rosa Parks's famous act of defiance and the subsequent boycott of Montgomery, Alabama's segregated buses had inspired black Americans six years earlier. In the following months the Association of American Indian Affairs corresponded with Eskimo village leaders and helped finance a meeting in Barrow in November 1961.[52] Simon Paneak flew to Barrow to represent Anaktuvuk Pass.[53] One of the main proposals put forward at the meeting was to recommend setting aside most of the North Slope as a hunting preserve for the Eskimos.[54]

Ironically, federal officials had entertained the idea of a large reservation for the north Alaskan Eskimos in 1944–48. Commissioner of Indian Affairs John Collier proposed a reservation of some 750 square miles of land and fifty square miles of water. At a hearing in Barrow in 1946 the Eskimos favored the idea but thought the proposed reservation too small to meet their needs. Their counterproposal for an arctic game reserve of 30,000 square miles in which natives would have an exclusive right to hunt and trap was approved by the BIA, FWS, and NPS, and submitted to Secretary of the Interior Krug in 1948. Probably Krug rejected the plan for the same reasons that he opposed Indian reservations in Southeast Alaska, believing they would be racially divisive.[55] In any case, the political situation had changed decisively by 1961. Now that Alaska was a state and its Department of Fish and Game was empowered to manage Alaska's wildlife resources, the time had passed when federal officials could realistically promote such a large reservation for Alaska natives.[56] Belatedly, the duck controversy alerted federal officials to the need for some kind of federal oversight of Alaska natives' subsistence needs. Apart from a few remaining areas of federal jurisdiction, such as enforcement of the Migratory Bird Treaty Act, any federal policy regarding native subsistence uses would require the cooperation of the state of Alaska.

This became clear when a special task force on Alaska native affairs, appointed early in 1962, traveled around Alaska in June visiting thirty-two villages and taking testimony from representatives of more than a hundred native communities.[57] Subsistence hunting and fishing issues dominated the hearings even though the task force's overall directive was to outline an economic development plan for Alaska's native villages. At the hearing in Barrow the Eskimos expressed concern that the FWS intended to step up its enforcement of the Migratory Bird Treaty Act. The natives were either unsatisfied with or uninformed about recent assurances from Secretary of the Interior Udall that the law would not be rigorously enforced in northern and western Alaska.

The task force recommended that the Department of the Interior reexamine the Migratory Bird Treaty Act to determine whether relief for the natives could be obtained administratively or the treaty would have to be amended. In addition the task force proposed two significant changes for Alaska game management: first, that the state of Alaska establish special licensing procedures, seasons, and bag limits for subsistence hunters — in effect creating two separate management regimes for subsistence and sport hunting; and second, that the federal government ensure that natives were represented on the Alaska State Board of Fish and Game and on the local advisory boards in each game-management unit. The task force reported that state officials were already moving on the former recommendation in response to informal discussions with task force members.[58] These proposals anticipated the federal subsistence protections that evolved in the 1970s. Most significantly, however, the task force did not endorse the Eskimos' idea of an exclusive hunting preserve.

The native land claim movement crystallized in the mid-1960s. Responding to the state's action in selecting lands under the Statehood Act, and to the federal government's action in opening the North Slope and other parts of the state to mineral leases by the petroleum industry, Alaska natives formed one regional native association after another and filed protest claims based upon their "aboriginal use and occupancy." The Arctic Slope Native Association filed a "native protest" for 58,017,300 acres, while the village of Anaktuvuk Pass filed its protest claim for 422,500 acres.[59] As these native protests proliferated, it became evident that Congress's decision to ignore the problem of aboriginal title in the Alaska Statehood Act of 1959 would not stand.

The village council's action was a consciousness-raising event. Like the native land claim movement itself, it was intended simultaneously to engage the larger society and to change the way its own people thought about land values. As native leaders saw the problem, the land claim would serve two purposes. First, native leaders looked to a large cash settlement of the claim, which would provide their people with capital to develop their own industries. Inevitably, such industries would be based primarily on extraction of raw materials, particularly on the North Slope where there was a likelihood of large oil reserves. Thus, the movement aimed to teach natives that their land claim had enormous monetary value, both in terms of a one-time real-estate transaction for whatever portion they ceded to the United States government, and in terms of the potential oil, mineral, and timber production on lands that the natives selected to own.[60] Second, native leaders wanted to protect the subsistence bases of more than 200 native villages like Anaktuvuk Pass. They wanted to retain enough of the land claim in native ownership to be able to influence land-use decisions and preserve wildlife populations that were threatened by development. Native leaders viewed the protection of their people's subsistence base as vital to the preservation of their cultural autonomy as well as their economic well-being.[61] In short, the native land claim movement sought to inculcate the idea that land was both a commodity and a heritage.

The leaders of the native land claim movement faced a different task in educating the American people and Congress, on whom they ultimately depended for success. The natives based their claim on the fact that the United States had never extinguished aboriginal title in Alaska. Therefore, the movement stressed the Alaska natives' status as an indigenous people with a distinctive way of life and an unusual dependence on the land. But in doing so, the movement tended to reinforce the white image of Alaska natives as an impoverished people. The roots of this image could be traced far back, for as historian Robert F. Berkhofer, Jr. has shown, whites had been characterizing Native Americans as indigent, or "deficient," for as long as the two races had been in contact.[62] What was distinctive about this situation was the way whites were forming an image of Alaska natives in the context of the nation's War on Poverty in the mid-1960s. The Alaska native land claim movement did not hesitate to exploit the new context. Willie Hensley, a native leader from Kotzebue, expressed the movement's goals: "We are seeking an alternative to wardship. We seek to offer alternatives to Eskimo and Indian people rather than a one way ticket into the confused mainstream. We feel our people cannot convert to a cash economy overnight and will continue to fish and hunt for many years. On the other hand, we see that the young Natives seek education and new places. These should be available. We want to be able to live longer and more decently without having to stoop in indignity because of a degrading welfare system. We feel this is possible if we can secure the kind of land settlement we are proposing."[63]

Unfortunately, by defining itself in relation to the anti-poverty crusade the movement distracted attention from the core issue of aboriginal rights and allowed white Americans to perceive the problem in terms that they could more easily understand. Whites focused on the material conditions found in the villages. The most significant thing about the natives' land claim to whites was that the land did not support a rising standard of living in the villages. Indeed, whites saw places of habitation like Anaktuvuk Pass as an underlying cause of the natives' impoverishment.[64]

The white conception of the native claim issue found fullest expression in a congressionally mandated study, *Alaska Natives and the Land*, produced by the Federal Field Committee for Development Planning in Alaska and published in October 1968.[65] The committee's 600-page, large-format report replete with maps, pie charts, and photographs aimed to establish the natives' economic, cultural, and ecological relationship to the land, but its principal effect was to focus attention more narrowly on native villages and to define the government's responsibility in terms of raising the natives' living standards. It profiled the many rural native communities, or what it termed "village Alaska." Health and education were poor; housing was "the most primitive, dilapidated, and substandard of any occupied by Eskimos or Indians anywhere in the U.S." Most villages still lacked basic utilities like water systems, electricity, and adequate sewage disposal. Some lacked health clinics and schools. Virtually all the communities lacked natural resources for development, yet none was likely to vacate the land on which it was located. The committee predicted that social and economic progress in the villages would be slow. If the condition of the villages elicited compassion from outsiders in the short term, the committee warned, it would likely provoke impatience over the long term.[66]

Media coverage of the Alaska native claim movement generally bore this out. *Life* and *National Geographic* introduced Americans to color photographs of the spare, hard life of Alaska's Eskimos, the former magazine posing the question to its readers whether Eskimos now joining the twentieth century would be a productive part of the economy or a millstone around the neck of the forty-ninth state. *Time* chided Senator Ted Kennedy for his grandstanding tour of village Alaska in the spring of 1969, while *Business Week* and *Esquire* each ran stories about the Eskimos' poverty, the former accompanied by a photograph of an Eskimo girl standing over an open sewer, the latter endorsing an anonymous government official's comment that "sooner or later the villages will have to go."[67]

This kind of jaded outlook on the poverty of village Alaska came to trouble Alaska natives nearly as much as the wildlife conservationists' unceasing accusations of their wastefulness with fish and game. To some whites, the grim appearance of most native villages appeared to signal the "death of a culture."[68] Why should native aboriginal rights be protected, the logic seemed to be, when the natives' culture had disintegrated and their values had become debased? Or, why should environmentalists be concerned about native hunting and trapping privileges if the natives themselves were so desperate to escape poverty through oil, timber, and mining development? These were spurious arguments to the natives, of course, but they held a certain attraction for many whites. They also made the vision of an inhabited wilderness much more problematic for the primitivist.[69]

From the preservationists' standpoint, even the remote little village of Anaktuvuk Pass, seated high up on the spine of the central Brooks Range, did not escape this shroud of poverty. Something had changed. The place that had been so exotic and picturesque to the outside world was now just another impoverished native village. In 1967, the Nunamiuts asked the BIA for assistance in moving to an abandoned oil exploration camp called Umiat after they had exhausted their supply of willow fuel around Anaktuvuk Pass. The BIA investigated both Umiat and Anaktuvuk Pass and determined that Umiat showed even less promise for economic development than Anaktuvuk Pass, where the villagers presently earned a modest cash income by turning animal products into handmade clothing and masks. The BIA offered the Nunamiuts material inducements to stay. After two months of debate within the community and correspondence and meetings — both in Anaktuvuk Pass and Fairbanks — between BIA officials and village council members, BIA officials finally prevailed on the Nunamiuts not to relocate.[70]

While the village council and the BIA saw the resulting government grants of home-heating oil and other housing improvements as signs of progress, preservationists regarded the advent of fuel assistance as a sad and symbolic passage. No longer would this collection of sod huts and tents in the central Brooks Range present the picture of a pristine, aboriginal people, for what could be more ruinous to such an image than the sight of dozens of oil drums parked alongside a landing field? To the NPS's Merrill Matthes, who visited the place in June 1968, Anaktuvuk Pass was "not exactly Shangri-la."[71] To two members of the Advisory Board on National

Parks who visited the Nunamiuts a few years later, "the modern village of
Anaktuvuk" was no asset to the potential national park. "The denuding of
the area of all the willows for fuel has seriously impaired the natural landscape. The village itself could not exist without the paternalism of the
government."[72] These were aesthetic responses to the physical appearance
of the village. In both cases, preservationists found that the village did not
project the primitive feeling or sense of harmony with nature that they
wanted to see.

However, not all preservationists saw poverty and cultural ruin in the
village. Some preservationists looked past the changes in the Nunamiuts'
material life and insisted there were other, indispensable cultural values still
in evidence. Each native culture contained a unique fund of knowledge
about the environment. Each had its own distinct ethos toward the land.
The surviving traditions in these cultures could, in the future, teach humanity vital truths. "These cultures should be taken seriously and considered as rational alternative life-styles instead of as inferior dead ends to be
eliminated as quickly as possible," wrote freelance journalist Jane Pender.
"Not much time is left in Alaska. The accelerating rate of destruction of the
native, land-based cultures is not encouraging."[73] Preservationists such as
Pender had begun to think of native cultures like endangered species. Like
gene pools, they had to be shielded from the outside world.

It was with a sense of anguish, therefore, that these preservationists followed the progress of the Alaska Department of Highways as it bulldozed a
temporary winter haul road north from the Yukon River through Anaktuvuk Pass to the Prudhoe Bay oil field in the winter of 1968–69. Not only
did they mourn the long, thin scar across the delicate face of the Arctic, but
they dreaded the effect of the road on the Nunamiuts' culture as well. A
handful of preservationists flew to Anaktuvuk Pass and filed reports to try to
bring this village to the nation's attention.[74] Sam Wright was speaking for
them all when he wrote, "the arrival of the road at Anaktuvuk Pass signals
not only the end of a way of life for the Nunamiut but for the wilderness
itself."[75]

For the six weeks that the road was in operation, the Nunamiuts were
exposed to a rough, hard-drinking class of truckers. Twelve thousand dollars in cash went through the village like a flash flood. The Nunamiuts were
sickened by the sight of animals being hunted from helicopters and animals' carcasses mutilated and displayed alongside the road for no explicable
reason.[76] When the possibility arose of reopening the road for a short time
five years later, in 1974, the Nunamiuts went to court to try to keep it
closed — and lost.[77]

Anaktuvuk Pass Alaska
19 March, 1974

Dear Okwak Ethel:

Thank you very much for your most welcomed letter again and we learned you & Mary are fine that is most important.

The box of puzzles are arrive and I have a fun with them and Susie was say hi! We are doing well. We are watch truckers in one after another in every day lots of them big heavy duty equipment. May Kakinya [*sic*] is in hospital in Fairbanks and she has been surgery on her knee and she will be home soon. Elijah is doing fine also.

I was home in 16 Feb so far not bad. Your check is spending by Susie.

The village going to have electricity beginning 23 March. Every house are hooked, wire & ready to light.

U.S. Public Health workers are in yesterday and said try a drill hole to make well and have water running.

Weather has been pretty cold in 3 months but now warmer and longer day.

The village has gas for snowgoes for this season and have enough fuel oil for house warm.

My son Allan was guiding truckers from Bettle [*sic*] to here. And from here Raymond & Roosevelt are guiding to Tootlik lake located in east of Itkilik R.

The village is no worried about meat after big caribou herd are come thru the valley in last Sept. Oct. Nov. had stored up plenty of meat until caribous come back to north or move this way from Killik Valley all way to upper Kobuk Valley.

Sorry to hear Mr. Bob Matsen were surgery on his both eye but hoping he be alright by now.

I was up in Pt. Barrow in shortly after I came home because North Slope Regional Corporation was inviting me and stayed up there only a day because meeting about truckers which is decide gone right by here. And the Village has benefit from oil company.

Sincerely
Your Sakigak

Simon & Susie

For more than twenty years the Nunamiuts of Anaktuvuk Pass struck observers and commentators as one of the best examples in Alaska of natives living close to the land. These preservationists were strongly attracted to the primitiveness of the people, the village, and the austere mountain setting in the Brooks Range. For their part the Nunamiuts found the admiring stance of the preservationists on their hunting way of life vastly preferable to the critical stance taken by wildlife conservationists. As the Nunamiuts' material culture changed, as they traded dog teams for snow-machines and sod huts for oil-heated homes, they alienated a significant portion of their preservationist admirers. Nevertheless, when the Alaska wilderness preservation movement finally claimed the attention of Congress in the 1970s, the Nunamiuts cast their lot with the preservationists. In 1974 they would make the unprecedented request that their homeland in the central Brooks Range be encompassed within a great, new national park.

EIGHT

"We Eskimos Would Like to Join the Sierra Club"

↓

If the Nunamiuts defined their place in nature largely in opposition to wildlife law enforcement in the 1950s and early 1960s, increasingly they aligned themselves with wilderness preservationists in the late 1960s and 1970s. As the orientation and substance of their dialogue with outsiders changed, so too did the political context of their relations with the larger society. Like native groups throughout Alaska, the Nunamiuts became enmeshed in the prolonged national debate over the just and rational division of Alaska's 375 million acres into state and native lands, wildlife refuges, national parks, and national forests.

Two landmark laws framed this debate: the Alaska Native Claim Settlement Act of 1971 (ANCSA) and the Alaska National Interest Lands Conservation Act of 1980 (ANILCA). While ANCSA focused on Alaska natives, and ANILCA focused on the division of Alaska lands, both laws were part of a whole process that addressed the relationship of Alaska natives to the land.

There was a historical logic to the fact that the most encompassing conservation act ever passed by the United States Congress should grow out of the most significant piece of federal Indian legislation in Alaskan history. Inasmuch as conservation laws were about the control and exploitation of natural resources, conservation of Alaskan resources had never ceased being tied to Alaskan native affairs. Resources that were basic to the native subsistence economy — fish, furs, big game, marine mammals — were also basic to the export economy that the Americans developed in Alaska in the nineteenth century. Even the addition of twentieth-century exports such as gold, pulpwood, and oil did not undo the basic similarity that existed between Alaska's market economy and the native subsistence economy. Indeed, in certain instances the two economies were increasingly interwoven, as in the case of the Southeast Alaskan salmon fishery.

There was another underlying connection between native policy and conservation in Alaska. Since the United States government had never removed Alaska's native population or concentrated it on reservations as it had done with the Indians in the lower forty-eight states, the land was never "widowed" of its aboriginal inhabitants. Except for a few small executive-order reservations established in the 1940s, there were no Indian trust lands in Alaska. With most of the white population centered in the cities and towns, natives continued to be by far the most numerous inhabitants of the public domain. The FWS, the Forest Service, and the NPS all had to take native subsistence uses into account in their respective jurisdictions. The BIA, for its part, saw to natives' interests throughout Alaska. BIA and conservation officials were used to working together on areas of mutual concern. Lawmakers usually tried to coordinate conservation with native policy, too, and the legal mess brought about by the Tongass Timber Act of 1947 pointed out the consequence of failing to do so.[1]

Thus, the connection between ANCSA and ANILCA was to be expected. ANCSA mandated that the federal government secure the natives' place on the land by forging a comprehensive legislative settlement of the conflict between development and conservation of public lands. Nine years later, ANILCA harkened back to the earlier law by recognizing the native right to subsistence uses on virtually all of the natural reserves created by the passage of ANILCA. The right to hunt and fish on these lands, the law stated, was "essential to Native physical, economic, traditional, and cultural existence."[2] The passage of these two acts bracketed the most formative period in the history of Alaska's national parks. In these years conservationists, natives, and lawmakers all grappled with the problem of designating and administering inhabited wilderness.

The politics that led to ANCSA and ANILCA must be viewed against the backdrop of Alaska's oil rush. No doubt there would have been some kind of native claim settlement with or without an oil boom, and very likely there would have been additions to the national park system in Alaska, too. But as it happened, both the native claim settlement and the dramatic additions to the national park system were wedded to Alaska's oil boom. When oil companies discovered, in 1969, that the Prudhoe Bay oil field was the largest known deposit in North America, it seemed to the Nixon administration and the majority of Congress that it was in the national interest to put this new source of fossil fuel into "production." Many Alaskans believed that it was their state's destiny to develop the oil reserve. However, without a resolution of the native land claim issue, oil companies could not construct a pipeline from Prudhoe Bay to the Gulf of Alaska. Without a pipeline there was no feasible way to get the oil to market. North Slope oil suddenly pushed the native land claim issue into the national consciousness. Alaska natives found themselves in an unusually strong bargaining position. The promise of lower oil prices contributed mightily to Congress's and the Nixon administration's spirit of generosity in the $925 million settlement with Alaska natives.[3]

Wilderness advocates also found themselves in a strong bargaining position at the end of the 1960s. The timing of Alaska's oil rush could not have been more fortuitous from the standpoint of wilderness preservation. This was a time of growing environmental concern among the American public. An increasing number of Americans was dismayed by the nation's addiction to cheap oil prices and large, gas-guzzling automobiles. Some saw an Alaskan oil pipeline as the moral equivalent of a national drug fix. Passage of the National Environmental Policy Act of 1969 (NEPA) handed environmentalists precisely the legal weapon they needed. The law required that every potential disturbance of the public lands receive an environmental-impact study beforehand. Everyone recognized that a hot-oil pipeline across the arctic and subarctic tundra posed enormous engineering challenges. There were complicated questions about the environmental impact of such a project. If environmentalists could not rely on NEPA to block construction of the pipeline altogether, they could at least use the law to hold it up in the courts for a long time. Most important of all, wilderness advocates recognized that the promise of a huge windfall for the state of Alaska in the form of oil royalties now made it politically and economically feasible for the federal government to set aside a large portion of Alaska's total land area in national parks and wildlife refuges — more than was ever thought possible only a few years earlier when Alaska's economy appeared to be barely able to support a state government.[4] In a sense, Alaska wilderness was purchased with Alaska oil.

This is not to say that the discovery of Prudhoe Bay oil was a boon for Alaska natives or wilderness preservationists. Perhaps Alaska native cultural life would have been more enriching in the absence of Alaska's oil boom, and perhaps Alaska's de facto wilderness would have fared just as well or better without all the publicity it received in the 1970s. Moreover, the ultimate environmental costs of North Slope oil development have yet to be tallied. How many more disasters like the 1989 *Exxon Valdez* oil spill can Alaska sustain before the American people judge that the entire project was unwise?[5] The movements that culminated in ANCSA and ANILCA were not opportunistic so much as they were efforts to cope with the completely new situation brought about by the discovery of oil.

Though Inupiat Eskimos were quick to grasp the significance of the oil discovery, their reactions were decidedly mixed. Some thought they would be better off if the oil stayed in the ground. Others argued that oil would aid in the natives' pursuit of capital for economic development. The native regional associations and the Alaska Federation of Natives (AFN) climbed a slippery slope as they tried to exploit this extraordinary economic and political opportunity to the natives' best advantage without bringing about their environmental ruin. The more that native leadership mingled with oil corporation executives and politicians and the more time they spent in Anchorage and Washington, D.C., the more susceptible they felt to the charge that they had lost touch with the cultural and economic life of village Alaska. Their critics said that they had lost sight of their constituents' overriding concern with the preservation of healthy fish and wildlife populations. They responded by saying that they were being realistic and wise in leading their people toward a settlement that would best help them cope with the future. In any event, no one polled the native villagers to determine their sentiment toward oil development. What the majority of them thought was altogether a matter of speculation.[6]

After the discovery of oil on the North Slope, Eskimo leaders and environmentalists began to consider one another as potential allies. Although their interests far from coincided, each saw the other as a useful countervailing force against the state of Alaska and the oil industry. Eskimos had to overcome their historical mistrust of wildlife officials. They had to stop grumbling out loud, for example, that more land was reserved for wildlife in Alaska than for the native people. They also had to cope with those environmentalists who presumed that all the lands that the natives received in a claim settlement would be preserved in a pristine condition. The natives insisted that they had as much right as anyone else to benefit from mineral and oil wealth.[7] These problems aside, the natives shared with environmentalists a deep concern that oil companies, backed by the state of Alaska, would show a callous disregard for the arctic environment. The proposed pipeline could spill oil into the freshwater lakes and ponds where the Inupiat Eskimos got their fish and where the migratory waterfowl bred. It might also disrupt the migration routes of arctic caribou herds.[8] Alternatively, if oil tankers tried to negotiate the Beaufort Sea beyond Prudhoe Bay, an oil spill could cause even more damage to marine life. "We eskimos would like to join the Sierra Club," wrote William Willoya of the AFN in

January 1969. "We have no money but lots of thoughts and collective action (28,000). First thing we would like is testing of tankers coming to load oil through Northwest passage with water first so our Billions of dollars worth of God given seafood will not be polluted."[9] Willoya's comments went to the heart of the Eskimos' concerns: they feared that the development of the Arctic would be undertaken rashly and without due regard for the native people's food supply.

Environmentalists, for their part, saw the native claim movement as a growing power with which to be reckoned. The movement had come a long way since 1961. The regional native associations had successfully forged a united front in their creation of the AFN in 1966. The native claim issue provided environmentalists with a first line of defense against an all-out onslaught on Alaska's resources. In the long term, assuming that Alaska natives acquired control of a large amount of land, environmentalists hoped that they might be able to influence the natives' land stewardship. The natives' desire to preserve their traditional way of life augured well for the environment.[10]

As Congress and the Nixon administration took up the native claim question in 1969, a number of individuals in the Wilderness Society and the Sierra Club advanced the idea of linking new national parks and wildlife refuges to the actual native claim settlement. They argued that the national interest in Alaska wilderness demanded consideration along with the national interest in Alaska energy development and the native interest in an aboriginal claim. Just as the impending major oil development had persuaded Congress and the Nixon administration to cut a deal with the natives, so too, they argued, there should be a quid pro quo between the proponents of industrial growth and the advocates of wilderness preservation.[11]

It was David Hickok, a member of the Federal Field Committee for Development Planning in Alaska and coauthor of *Alaska Natives and the Land*, who first suggested adding a provision to the native claim settlement bill that would see to the interests of conservation. Hickok proposed the amendment to Senate Interior Committee Staff Counsel William Van-Ness, who saw that the provision was inserted in a native claim settlement bill that the Senate passed in 1970. This bill died in the House Interior Committee, but when the Ninety-second Congress took up the native claim issue again in 1971, an ad hoc coalition of national environmental groups, the Alaska Coalition, was ready to lobby for specific language to protect Alaska's national interest lands.[12]

The Alaska Coalition received warm support for their desired amendment from Representatives John Saylor of Pennsylvania and Morris Udall of Arizona in the House Interior Committee, but it was now the Senate Interior Committee that proved recalcitrant. The key figure in the Senate was Alan Bible of Nevada, chairman of the Senate Subcommittee on National Parks and Recreation. The key advocate for the environmentalists was now NPS Director George B. Hartzog, Jr. To Hartzog, it seemed that this was the time for the NPS to push for an unprecedented role in Alaska — something like what George Collins's team had sketched for him in *Operation Great Land*. Hartzog persuaded Senator Bible to accompany him on a trip to Alaska that summer. Their itinerary included the proposed Gates of the Arctic National Park, additions to Mount McKinley and Katmai, an area of national park potential on the Kenai Peninsula, and the historic town of Skagway. By all accounts the trip was crucial in securing Bible's support. In his memoirs, Hartzog claimed credit for the amendment and insisted that its original intent was to earmark most of the Alaska national interest lands for inclusion in the national park system.[13] However, NPS historian Frank Williss, in his fine legislative history of ANILCA, was unable to find any evidence of this. Bible, for his part, would only disclose that he had received additional advice on his amendment from the Wilderness Society and Sierra Club, Representatives John Saylor and John Dingell of Michigan, and Senators Henry M. Jackson of Washington State and Gaylord Nelson of Wisconsin, who co-sponsored the amendment.[14]

The Bible amendment became the famous Section 17(d)(2) of ANCSA, which President Nixon signed into law on December 18, 1971. The section of the law directed the secretary of the interior to withdraw up to 80 million acres of the public domain for possible addition to the national park, forest, wildlife refuge, and wild and scenic rivers systems, gave the secretary two years to perfect these withdrawals, and gave Congress a limit of five years after the end of the current two-year period to act on the secretary's proposals. For the entire period of seven years these lands would be ineligible for selection by the state of Alaska or the native regional corporations. The national interest lands became known as "D-2 lands" after Section 17(d)(2) of the law during the seven years that they were held in limbo.[15]

The first signs of strain in the newly formed alliance of natives and environmentalists were evident immediately after passage of ANCSA. Environmentalists were accused of seizing onto the coattails of the native claim movement almost as an afterthought. This was inaccurate. Environmental groups had been busy for the past three years preparing recommendations for the Department of the Interior on suitable areas for inclusion in the national park and wildlife refuge systems. The Alaska Coalition, with help from the NPS and the FWS, showed itself to be well prepared as it plied members of Congress with maps and acreages in the weeks leading up to the vote on ANCSA.[16] Moreover, the Federal Field Committee had been involved in the legislative process of ANCSA from the beginning. As early as 1966, the chairman of the Federal Field Committee, Joseph Fitzgerald, had suggested that conservation concerns be linked to the native claim settlement.[17] Indeed, it was originally the committee's idea to fashion the native claim settlement around native regional and village corporations.

The use of corporations was ANCSA's most enduring and controversial feature and bore directly on the question that most concerned environmentalists: what kind of land stewards would the natives turn out to be? In theory, the native corporations would be communal, making land selections and investing the settlement money as their shareholders saw fit. Hickok stated afterwards that the Federal Field Committee originally saw the native regional and village corporations as institutional structures that would be essentially communal; they visualized nonprofit corporations run by common input from their shareholders. An AFN task force proposed that the corporations be profit organizations. The leader of this task force, Willie Hensley, maintained that the idea of profit-driven corporations was seen as an alternative to the trust approach. "A lot of native people saw the trust approach as a throwback to the days the feds ran the Indian reservations as though they were concentration camps," Hensley later recalled. Lawmakers wanted to accommodate native demands for self-determination, but the profit orientation of the native corporations would prove to be unwieldy for the native cultures and unrealistic in the Alaskan environmental setting, and would cause environmentalists no little amount of concern about their allies.[18]

On the other hand many environmentalists in their jubilation over Section 17(d)(2) of the law lost sight of ANCSA's overall intent, which was to foster native economic development while clearing the way for greater development of the state's natural resources. Many natives soon came to believe that Section 17(d)(2) had skewed the law's purpose, diverting attention away from their need to get their land selections approved in order to secure a land base for their regional and village corporations. "The Natives were practically abandoned," Hickok later admitted. "When the bill was passed, the Department of Interior sent everybody out into the field to look at the national interest [D-2] lands. I never thought that was right."[19] At the various hearings that were held in the 1970s on the D-2 lands, the natives frequently complained of how slowly their land selections were being acted upon.[20]

In Anaktuvuk Pass and elsewhere on the North Slope, the Eskimos had been considering land selections for months before ANCSA became law. With passage of the act, the Arctic Slope Native Association became the Arctic Slope Regional Corporation (ASRC), and the village associations became village corporations. The first order of business of the Nunamiut Corporation of Anaktuvuk was to select a village land chief. That person then involved all the villagers in putting down on maps the collective experience of the village — the hunting areas for various animal species, the favored places for fishing, berry picking, willow gathering, and tree cutting, and what they knew of oil seeps, coal outcrops, springs, and gravel sources. The Nunamiut Corporation also reached an understanding with the ASRC soon after passage of ANCSA concerning land selections. In the Anaktuvuk Pass area, both the regional and village corporation would give first priority to lands that would support the local people's subsistence economy and second priority to lands with potential for mineral development.[21] ANCSA provided that the native corporations could begin filing land selections ninety days after passage of the act — on any public-domain lands that the secretary of the interior did not withdraw under Section 17.

Secretary of the Interior Rogers C. B. Morton announced his preliminary withdrawal of national interest lands on March 15, 1972. The preliminary D-2 withdrawals included 11,323,118 acres for Gates of the Arctic National Park. (This was nearly three times the amount proposed by Secretary Udall to President Johnson in 1968, but considerably less than the singularly huge area suggested by Director Hartzog after his tour with Senator Bible in 1971; it eliminated the transportation corridor up the John River through Anaktuvuk Pass, but it left out the coastal plain.)[22] The NPS had until the following September to refine the boundaries of all thirteen of its D-2 areas, and it was an indication of the priority that Hartzog still gave to Gates of the Arctic that the NPS fielded its crack team of land planners in the central Brooks Range in May 1972. The team captain, John M. Kauffmann, had many years of Alaskan experience. He had worked with George Collins seven years earlier on *Operation Great Land*.[23]

It was the state of Alaska that drove the next wedge into the native-environmentalist alliance. In April, the state of Alaska filed suit against Secretary Morton for his initial D-2 withdrawals, alleging that they intruded on 42 million acres of "preselected" state lands. Justice Department attorneys advised the secretary that the state of Alaska could not win its case but could probably hold up native land selections for years by litigation. Clearly, under the circumstances, an uncompromising stand on the D-2 lands would thwart another major purpose of ANCSA. Compromise was the price of effecting wilderness preservation through a piece of Indian legislation. After months of negotiation with Governor William Egan, Secretary Morton agreed to an out-of-court settlement on September 5. Among the D-2 lands that were sacrificed in order to get the state of Alaska to drop its claim were two key areas in the central Brooks Range: the lower sections of the Alatna and John Rivers.[24] Between these changes and some boundary revisions recommended by Kauffmann's planning team, the final D-2 withdrawals that the secretary announced on September 13 lopped some 2 million acres off of Gates of the Arctic.[25]

The Nunamiuts began to consider the possibility that they might forge some kind of dual-ownership arrangement with the federal government on a permanent basis. As the ASRC and the Nunamiut Corporation proceeded to make their respective land selections, they began warming to the idea of a national park. If the proposed national park would adequately protect the Anaktuvuk Pass villagers' subsistence base, the Eskimos reasoned, then the ASRC could use its allotment of land selections to obtain mineral lands elsewhere. On April 23, 1973, ASRC president Joseph Upicksoun testified before the Joint Federal-State Land Use Planning Commission that the Inupiat Eskimos were in favor of a Nunamiut National Park. The park would embrace the central Brooks Range, including Anaktuvuk Pass. It would be cooperatively managed by the NPS and the Eskimos. The proposal's bold premise was that national and native interests would coincide within the national park area.[26] This was the first proposal of its kind in Alaska.

In view of the ASRC's extraordinary proposal, Kauffmann was authorized to discuss with the Nunamiuts how the NPS would manage the Gates of the Arctic, including the area around the village of Anaktuvuk Pass, if it were part of a national park. Out of these discussions a somewhat different proposal emerged. The national park was once again divided into east and west units and was designated "Gates of the Arctic National Wilderness Park." The area in between was designated "Nunamiut National Wildlands." In the wilderness park, subsistence hunting by natives would be permitted. "Fair-chase hunting" by sportsmen would also be permitted, Kauffmann reckoned, provided it was done on foot without assistance by air-sightings and radio communications, and involved a minimum of ten days in the wilderness. Visitors would be permitted to enter the park by charter flight, landing at designated lakes only. Backcountry users would need to make reservations and obtain permits. There would be no development of visitor accommodations. Management of the Nunamiut National Wildlands would be substantially the same, except that subsistence hunting would take priority over sport hunting and the area would be cooperatively managed by the NPS, the Nunamiut Corporation, and the ASRC. Back-country users would have "wandering rights" to traverse native-owned lands within the national wildlands. Modest visitor accommodations were envisioned at Anaktuvuk Pass.[27]

Kauffmann took the negotiations with the Eskimos as far as he could, but a measure of doubt about cooperative management crept into the final NPS proposal. On the last day before the secretary of the interior's deadline for submitting all the national interest lands proposals to Congress, the Office of Management and Budget (OMB) rejected the Nunamiut National Wild-lands designation. OMB officials explained that the national park system should not be encumbered with new area designations, and that the OMB would not accept a proposal in which the federal government yielded some of its management authority to outside parties. To the chagrin of NPS officials, the proposal for Gates of the Arctic was sent to Congress with an errata sheet clipped inside the cover indicating that the wildlands concept was not the administration's preferred alternative. Of all the park proposals, it was the only one so marked.[28]

The central issue of whether native interests were compatible with a national park received further attention when the ASRC and the Nunamiut Corporation developed their own national park proposal early in 1974. Senator Henry Jackson introduced the bill in Congress, but like a number of other Alaska lands bills that were introduced in 1974 without administra-tion support, it was allowed to die in committee. Nevertheless, the Nuna-miut National Park proposal was significant because it was the clearest statement yet of the Eskimos' position. The Nunamiut National Park would have comprised a patchwork of federal, village corporation, regional corporation, state, and private lands, divided as before into wildlands and wilderness park, but in this proposal the wildlands, rather than bridging the two wilderness park units as in the NPS proposal, encompassed an addi-tional 5 million acres. The wildlands included a large amount of native-owned land. The whole park covered more than 16 million acres and would have been cooperatively managed by federal, state, and native entities. A Board of Nunamiut Commissioners, appointed by all parties, was to over-see park administration. The Nunamiut National Park bill carried two other provisions that the NPS proposal had not addressed. One section provided for oil and gas development inside the park; another detailed plans for health, water, and sanitation facilities as well as park facilities in Anaktuvuk Pass and provided for easements across the wildlands for an oil pipeline that would serve the village.[29]

Environmentalists generally played down the Eskimos' interest in oil and gas developments while emphasizing their common interest in preserving healthy wildlife populations. Jim Kowalsky, Alaskan representative for Friends of the Earth, praised the bill as a demonstration of the Eskimos' concern for protection of natural conditions and traditional lands.[30] David Hickok of the Federal Field Committee made an even more telling appraisal. Addressing a conference on subsistence held in Juneau in February 1974, Hickok laid out the terms of the Nunamiut National Park proposal and then commended the people of Anaktuvuk Pass for standing up to the oil companies when Alyeska, the huge consortium that was building the Trans-Alaska Pipeline System, sought to reopen the Hickel Highway through the pass that spring. (At the time when Hickok was speaking, the Eskimos had filed suit against Alyeska; a few weeks later the court ruled that Alyeska must post $50,000 bond, but that the village could not block its use of the haul road in view of the "national interest" at stake.)[31] Hickok seemed to suggest that the Nunamiuts' action against Alyeska ought to assure environmentalists that the Nunamiuts' interest in progress and development would be modulated so as not to undermine their subsistence way of life.[32] In other words, the Nunamiuts still had a basic compatibility of interests with environmentalists. Hickok glossed over the hard-headedness displayed by the Nunamiuts in challenging the state's right of way for hauling pipe through Anaktuvuk Pass at the same time that they were proposing a pipeline easement of their own through the national park. The Nunamiuts' action could just as easily have been viewed as a warning that issues of sovereignty and land ownership were now taking precedence over mutual environmental concerns.

That was precisely the conclusion that NPS planner John Kauffmann drew from the bill. Enthusiastic about the cooperative management concept in 1973, Kauffmann subsequently backed away from the idea. He warned that the Nunamiut Wildlands "would drive an ominous wedge between the two park units, a wedge where management could well become more permissive, allowing developments and uses that could change the primitive character of the central Brooks Range." Writing in 1977 when the transportation corridor through Anaktuvuk Pass seemed moot, Kauffmann suggested that cooperative management of the central area could tempt the oil companies to reopen the issue. "Even without that spectre," Kauffmann wrote, "the central area could be vulnerable to mining, mechanical vehicles, inappropriate developments and other influences erosive of the wild values of the central Brooks Range."[33]

The more troubled he became by the complications of inhabited wilderness, the more Kauffmann emphasized the anthropocentric and ethnocentric wilderness qualities of the Brooks Range that had so impressed Bob Marshall. Kauffmann and other NPS planners increasingly came to view the Gates of the Arctic as the "ultimate wilderness." In their view, this was to be a national park that would challenge the wilderness traveler's endurance and resourcefulness. The Gates of the Arctic would reward the wilderness traveler's longing for a sense of discovery and exploration like no other place in the United States could. It would be the purpose of the national park to preserve that experience. There would be no trails, foot bridges, signs, shelters or any other trappings of the typical national park's backcountry. Nor would there be any roads or accommodations. Not for the faint-hearted, Gates of the Arctic would be at the ascetic end of a spectrum of national park experiences in Alaska that ranged from luxury cruises and comfortable stays in park lodges to basic wilderness survival.[34]

The park planners based their assessment on personal experience — not just reconnoitering the area by air but getting on the ground and backpacking through it to get the feel of the place. Kauffmann took a couple weeks leave to hire a hunting guide and experience for himself the feel of "fair-chase" sport hunting in the Brooks Range.[35] Kauffmann's planning team also drew upon a welter of writings about the Brooks Range by contemporary wilderness advocates. Ecologist John P. Milton described his south-to-north traverse of the Brooks Range in *Nameless Valleys, Shining Mountains* (1969). George Marshall brought out a timely second edition of his brother's *Alaska Wilderness: Exploring the Central Brooks Range* (1970). Friends of the Earth founder David Brower published his son Kenneth Brower's *Earth and the Great Weather: The Brooks Range* (1971). The Wilderness Society's magazine *Living Wilderness* published a number of articles on the subject. These were only the most important publications in a growing literature on the Brooks Range. Virtually all writings on the Brooks Range emphasized that the arctic and subarctic environments were unusually fragile and susceptible to degradation, especially in the face of Alaska's oil boom, but they just as surely reiterated Bob Marshall's message that this was America's last great wilderness.[36]

Thus, the park planners viewed Gates of the Arctic as the ultimate wilderness in the sense that it was the last of a kind, too. They saw the Brooks Range as a tremendous opportunity and a weighty responsibility. They were driven by a deep conviction that here, as nowhere else, they must uphold the highest standards of wilderness preservation. "If we screw it up here," said the NPS's Ray Bane, "we can all stop arguing, because there won't be anything left to argue about it!"[37] The park planners kept two Bob Marshall corollaries firmly in mind: in Alaska alone can the emotional values of the frontier be preserved; in the name of a balanced use of American resources, let's keep northern Alaska largely a wilderness. "Somehow," wrote Kauffmann, "the nation would have to make this last remnant do, forever, what the whole American wilderness had done to challenge and mold and temper and inspire us as a people and nation."[38] If Glacier Bay held exceptional interest to science, and Mount McKinley was famous for its wildlife, Gates of the Arctic derived its national significance most of all from its wilderness qualities.

To preserve this ultimate wilderness the park's boundaries would have to be generously drawn, for sheer spaciousness was perhaps the park's greatest resource. The NPS would have to assume at first that the carrying capacity of the wilderness was very low. A reservation and permit system would be required for monitoring and dispersing backcountry use and for keeping parties of backpackers small, for it was known that large groups had much more impact on the ground cover than did small ones. Though the reservation and permit system would raise the hackles of many wilderness users, it would be an essential management tool for accomplishing the park's fundamental purpose — to ensure that visitors a century hence would find the same quality of environment and enjoy the same wilderness experiences as their counterparts in the present day.[39]

The hope was that the overall management scheme for wilderness preservation and use would suit the indigenous people's interests as well. Points of conflict would be identified early and resolved mutually. To this end, the NPS contracted with anthropologists Richard K. Nelson, Kathleen H. Mautner and Ray Bane to make a close field study of the way the Koyukon Indians and the Nunamiut Eskimos related to the environment in the central Brooks Range. The authors took up residence in the Koyukon villages of Huslia and Hughes from September 1975 to June 1976 and spent the balance of the year in the mountains with Nunamiut and Koyukon hunters. Their report, prepared for the NPS in 1978, was published four years later as *Tracks in the Wildland: A Portrayal of Koyukon and Nunamiut Subsistence.*[40] The project also spawned Nelson's *Make Prayers to the Raven: A Koyukon View of the Northern Forest* (1983).

Nelson, Mautner, and Bane placed contemporary changes in native land use on a historical continuum of change, emphasizing continuity over discontinuity. They argued that contemporary land-use patterns of the Koyukon Indians and Nunamiut Eskimos in the central Brooks Range bore fundamental similarities to earlier patterns of land use. Contemporary native hunters possessed environmental knowledge and skills that had been accumulated and honed over countless generations. "Many Natives continue to acquire a substantial portion of their livelihood directly from the environment, and virtually all express an affinity to their natural surroundings," Bane wrote. "Thus many skills and much of the accumulated environmental knowledge of the past continue to survive and function."[41] The natives' environmental knowledge was spiritual as well as practical. "Traditional Koyukon people live in a world that watches, in a forest of eyes," wrote Nelson. "A person moving through nature—however wild, remote, even desolate the place may be—is never truly alone. The surroundings are aware, sensate, personified. They feel. They can be offended. And they must, at every moment, be treated with proper respect."[42] Where previous observers had pointed out disruption in the passing down of knowledge from generation to generation and signs of breakdown in native relations with the environment, Nelson, Mautner, and Bane painted a much more positive picture.

Nelson contended that the Koyukon hunters of the central Brooks Range were natural conservationists. They had an intimate grasp of local variations in the resource base due to such subtle factors as wind exposure and snow depth, and they had a personal knowledge of plant succession and animal population fluctuations—all fundamental characteristics of boreal forest ecology. Though their explanations for these variations in the environment were unscientific, their knowledge of them was profound. Moreover, they had a conservation ethic. This was manifested in their concepts of territory, attitudes toward competitors for subsistence resources, methods of avoiding waste, and use of sustained-yield practices. These patterns of land use seemed to be of twentieth-century origin and related chiefly to the regulation of traplines and the conservation of fur-bearing animals, but they were underpinned by the traditional Koyukon view of nature as a community of spirit beings.[43]

Tracks in the Wildland was an idealized portrait of native subsistence. *Make Prayers to the Raven,* Nelson's interpretation of the Koyukon view of nature, went even further in attempting to reconstruct the traditional culture based on the ethnographic present. Yet these studies provided a valuable counterbalance to the insidious idea that subsistence was no more than a transitional mode of living between the traditional and the modern and that it would soon pass out of existence. As the D-2 process wore on during the 1970s, Alaska natives came to see this latter idea as a grave threat to their economic base and their cultural survival. They resisted it at every turn. The report by Nelson, Mautner, and Bane was an important document because it eloquently stated the natives' position that the NPS must recognize subsistence to be a legitimate, desirable, and enduring value within the new national parks in Alaska.

The Nunamiut National Park proposal was one of several events that forced the subsistence issue into the limelight in the mid-1970s. Alaska natives also focused attention on their need for subsistence protections in their testimony in numerous hearings during the 1970s, beginning with those of the Joint Federal-State Land Use Planning Commission in 1973. This ten-member body, created by ANCSA, learned from the natives that subsistence ranged across a broad spectrum of activities. Subsistence ranged from direct use of the resource by the family of the provider, to certain commercial activities such as trapping, to the taking of resources for ceremonial purposes. The commission reported to Congress in 1974 that subsistence was "deeper than physical need. The native particularly feels these activities are integral to his culture."[44]

The commission's report was followed shortly by another, *A Report on Subsistence and the Conservation of the Yupik Lifestyle* by Yupiktak Bista, a nonprofit organization of the Yup'ik Eskimos of the Kuskokwim-Yukon delta region. The report went much further in redefining subsistence as a cultural rather than an economic issue. Yupiktak Bista declared that subsistence was the native people's answer to assimilation. Most natives did not want to assimilate fully into the larger society. They were coming to equate subsistence with cultural survival. Subsistence, the report declared, was "directly related to and affected by everything that is happening within this region in the way of education, land use, economic development, wildlife management and other areas of public policy. Subsistence is really an entire way of life." Too many federal and state officials wrongly equated subsistence with poverty, Yupiktak Bista insisted. Too many mistook subsistence as a temporary phenomenon that would wither in the face of modern economic development. The report sought to jolt federal and state officials out of their complacency. It accused the federal and state governments of recognizing only two cultural alternatives: aboriginal life and Western civilization. "Does it have to be one or the other?" Yupiktak Bista demanded. "Does one way of life have to die, so that another can live?"[45] The report was like a thunderclap in bringing attention to the problem of federal protections for native subsistence on national interest lands.

The key resource for Alaska natives was game, Yupiktak Bista explained. Unlike members of an industrial society, who could afford to exhaust a vital resource in one area only to import it from somewhere else, Alaska natives had only what the land provided. When the game was depleted, their culture would be extinct. If the federal and state governments were really interested in sustaining village Alaska, they would be devoting far more effort to subsistence-resource planning: gathering harvest data, monitoring wildlife populations, restricting the take of sport hunters more effectively. Instead, they were allowing explosive growth of Alaska's population and economy in a manner that would be ruinous to the native peoples. They were blandly pursuing policies that would ultimately lead to the native people's "cultural extermination."[46] These were strong words. The report was reissued under the provocative title *Does One Way of Life Have to Die, So That Another Can Live?* It was entered in the record of the congressional hearings in 1977.

As this dialogue continued into the mid-1970s, it became apparent to natives and environmentalists alike that land-use planning in Alaska required some new models, drawn from other regions of the world. Alaska natives looked increasingly to Canadian and Scandinavian land-use patterns, where arctic and subarctic indigenous peoples still possessed cultures and economies that revolved around fur trapping, fishing, or reindeer herding. These patterns coexisted with the modern capitalist order, according to some economists, in a form of "economic dualism." In theory, the cultural integrity of such societies could be buffered by carefully calibrating the central government's social and economic development programs to serve these mixed economies.[47] Native organizations like the Association of Village Council Presidents and the Subsistence Resources Council looked to these models as they developed their own proposals for a system of local subsistence boards that would mediate between the central authority and local user groups. Their ideas would eventually be codified in ANILCA's Title VIII on subsistence.

Similarly, environmentalists pondered various negative examples in Africa, South America, and Australasia as they looked for new ways of accommodating national parks and indigenous peoples in Alaska. Members of the Joint Federal-State Land Use Commission found the contemporary writings of ecologist Raymond F. Dasmann particularly pertinent.[48] A senior ecologist on the faculty of the International Union for Conservation of Nature and Natural Resources in Switzerland, Dasmann strongly favored the view that the local needs of indigenous peoples were of vital importance, and that global environmental problems demanded local problem solving. He postulated that human societies could be divided into two categories, with some societies in transition from one category to the other. These two categories he called "ecosystem people" and "biosphere people."[49] The former embraced all of the members of indigenous, traditional cultures, while the latter included everyone who was tied to the global technological civilization. Ecosystem people lived within one or perhaps two or three closely related ecosystems. They had to live simply within the carrying capacity of their own ecosystem, or face the consequences of over-shooting their own limited resource base. Biosphere people had access to the resources of the entire biosphere. Biosphere people could exploit the resources of one ecosystem to the point of causing great devastation — something that would be impossible or unthinkable for people who were dependent upon that particular ecosystem. Conversely, biosphere people could afford to create national parks in which, according to the traditional model, nature was set apart from human consumptive uses. In most of the world today, Dasmann observed, areas that biosphere people saw as poten-tial national parklands were the very lands still inhabited by ecosystem people. Dasmann cited examples in Africa and South America where bio-sphere people had created national parks and forcibly removed the eco-system people — to the great cost of the people affected.

It was Dasmann's view that this must not continue. "National parks must not serve as a means for displacing the members of traditional societies who have always cared for the land and its biota," he wrote. "Nor can national parks survive as islands surrounded by hostile people who have lost the land that was once their home. Parks cannot survive in a natural state if they are surrounded by lands that are degraded or devastated by failure to obey the simplest ecological rules." Dasmann suggested that the proper direction for new national parks was toward what he called a "future primitive" — toward the creation of natural landscapes that included human societies that were permanent, sustainable, and embraced nature conservation as a matter of course.[50]

Dasmann's writings and the report by Yupiktak Bista had much in com-mon. Even the Nunamiut National Park proposal was based on similar assumptions. As had happened so often before, however, it required a natu-ral disaster to bring these ideas the attention that they deserved. This disaster was the sudden decline of the western arctic caribou herd, which fell from an estimated 242,000 in 1971 to 52,000 in 1976. For years after-ward, biologists would debate whether or not this decline was chiefly a function of the natural population cycle. Coinciding as it did with arctic oil development, the herd's decline provoked a great deal of nervousness and consternation.[51] Oddly enough, it also came as a rude surprise to the ADFG. Whereas the ADFG had termed the Eskimos' annual harvests of around 25,000 caribou from this herd "average" and "normal" during the early 1970s, it now called these harvests "excessive" and blamed the Eskimos for the herd's demise. Belatedly, the Alaska State Fish and Game Board adopted regulations that would limit the next year's harvest to 3,000, with permits to be allocated among native villages on the basis of need. Sportsmen's groups challenged this action in court, delaying the issuance of permits until the state supreme court would render a decision. In the meantime, many Eskimos refused to believe the ADFG's population estimates, testifying at public hearings that they had seen as many caribou as they had in past years. They chafed at the hunting regulations — the first that the state of Alaska had ever imposed on caribou hunting in the Arctic.[52] When the permits were finally allocated, Anaktuvuk Pass received 340 — approximately a third of their typical annual harvest. The Koyukon villages of Alatna, Allakaket, Huslia, and Hughes received none, for the Game Board wrongly assumed that the reduced population of moose in the Subarctic could sustain them.[53]

People drew many lessons from this fiasco. From the NPS's point of view the most important lesson was that the ADFG had been mismanaging game populations in the Arctic. It was said that the ADFG had been oblivious to what was happening in northern Alaska because the state biologists were too busy counting moose and caribou in southern Alaska for the benefit of sport hunters. The episode ended the NPS's reticence to get involved in this issue for fear of intruding on the state's jurisdiction.[54]

From the natives' standpoint the most important lesson was that the ADFG did not represent them. It represented sportsmen, whose fees for hunting licenses underwrote the department's budget. This was nowhere more apparent than in the Game Board's ignorant bungling of the permit allocations. The episode spurred native demands for the creation of a subsistence division in the ADFG and a system of local subsistence boards.[55]

Finally, the lesson that state and federal lawmakers took from the caribou disaster was that the subsistence issue led inevitably to questions of constitutionality. If subsistence hunters were to receive priority over sport hunters when the game supply was limited, how was the law to distinguish one from the other without being discriminatory? How was subsistence to be defined in legal terms that would hold up in court?

After the caribou crisis called attention to the subsistence issue, seemingly all parties interested in the Alaska lands bill got involved with it. The NPS assigned two experts, Robert Belous and T. Stell Newman, to develop a subsistence-management policy. The AFN formed a Subsistence Resources Council to advise and draft its own legislative proposal. The Alaska Conservation Society exchanged position papers with other conservation groups and native organizations. Friends of the Earth produced a legal brief on subsistence. The Sierra Club drafted D-2 legislation subsistence provisions and circulated them to all members of the Alaska Coalition. In the fall the Alaska Coalition, buoyed by the election of Jimmy Carter, reconvened in Washington, D.C., to work with congressional staffers in drafting House Report 39 and its Title VII on subsistence (Title VIII in the final version). This was the crucial phase in the working out of the human hunter's relationship to nature in Gates of the Arctic and indeed all of the new national parklands. It was a time for summing up of final arguments on all sides of the issue.[56]

Subsistence had enormous theoretical and practical implications for the NPS mission to preserve national parks in their natural condition. Environmentalists were far from unanimous in their support for subsistence hunting in national parks. The parks had a strong tradition of protecting all wildlife from hunting. Experience had shown that when an exception was made to the no-hunting rule it only led to demands by hunters for further exceptions. For this reason, Devereux Butcher, a prominent member of the National Parks and Conservation Association, vehemently opposed allowing any hunting in national parks in Alaska. He said he would rather see the areas made into wildlife refuges than risk weakening this keystone of national park wildlife policy. Butcher quoted the former NPS chief biologist, Victor H. Cahalane, "Where public hunting is a regularly permitted feature, animals become so wary that they are rarely seen by non-hunting park visitors."[57] Many other environmentalists viewed subsistence hunting as an unwelcome but not ruinous park use. As Kauffmann pointed out, many national parks began with adverse uses, which were phased out over time.[58] Probably the majority of environmentalists who did support subsistence hunting in the proposed national parks in Alaska did so for political rather than philosophical reasons. In the estimation of Alaska Conservation Society president Robert Weeden, "Very few conservationists could truthfully say that they would vigorously support subsistence hunting in parks even if Natives had zero political clout."[59]

Some environmentalists supported subsistence hunting in the new national parks because it gave them more leverage to oppose sport hunting. For various reasons, environmentalists came to regard subsistence hunting as benign compared with sport hunting. Subsistence hunting was less technologically dependent than sport hunting, less of a detraction from the wilderness experience of nonhunters, and less disruptive of natural animal populations. (The subsistence hunter was essentially another predator, whereas the sport hunter culled the "trophy" animals — and their genes — from the population.) Giving ground on subsistence hunting, the reasoning went, gave environmentalists greater moral authority to take a firm stand against sport hunting in the new parklands.[60]

However, political expedience was not the sole reason why environmentalists came to embrace subsistence hunting in the new national park areas. Many believed that subsistence hunting was integral to Alaskan wilderness and a desirable feature in its own right. Wildlife populations in Alaska had adjusted themselves over the centuries to a considerable take by native hunters. To eliminate this form of hunting would, in effect, be to disrupt the natural ecology. Moreover, it was sound public policy to help perpetuate the traditional subsistence way of life of the native peoples. Friends of the Earth took the most strident position of any environmental group in this regard. In studying the subsistence issue, Friends of the Earth had developed a "strong admiration and respect for a culture of great antiquity whose skills to live on the land are still very much in use today." The organization's Alaska representative, Jim Kowalsky, informed a House committee, "We are going to go to the wall on this question. It is extremely important that it be protected."[61] The Wilderness Society's Michael McCloskey also expressed enthusiasm for the continuance of native subsistence hunting in Alaska's new national parks. Pointing out the NPS's long experience in interpreting Native American cultures to the American public, he suggested that in Alaska the NPS had "an opportunity to weave it into the fabric of a number of units."[62] Two new ways of thinking about national parks and indigenous peoples were in evidence here. Friends of the Earth primarily sought to bring man the predator back into nature; the Wilderness Society primarily sought to broaden the primitivist wilderness aesthetic so as to include an appreciation of contemporary native life. One spoke to the NPS's mandate of preserving natural conditions, the other to the service's mandate to provide for the enjoyment of national parks by wilderness users. In most respects the two views were complementary rather than contradictory.

Both points of view were concerned about new technology used by native hunters. Snowmachines were the most recent cultural acquisition. By the mid-1970s, they had practically replaced dog teams as the common method of transportation on the hunt. The effect of this change on the caribou population was unclear. It seemed apparent to some observers that native hunters now harvested fewer caribou than before the advent of snowmachines since they no longer needed to feed so many dogs; other observers believed that snowmachines, by increasing the hunters' mobility, also increased their take. In the final analysis, environmental groups were willing to accept snowmachine use in the new parks. "Good or bad, it is the transportation mode used by rural Alaskans today," Friends of the Earth's Pamela Rich testified. Snowmachine use would not preclude designation of these areas as wilderness, because the Wilderness Act made allowance for specified, preexisting, nonconforming uses.[63]

More problematic was the use of airplanes and all-terrain vehicles (ATVs). ATVs, still a rare item in the Arctic in the 1970s, cruised over the delicate tundra in summertime leaving tracks in the earth where snow-machines only left tracks in the snow. Light aircraft, meanwhile, gave the hunter the ability to search out game and put down close to his quarry. ATVs and airplanes were noisy. They were not much noisier than snow-machines, but they generated noise pollution during the summer tourist season when snowmachines were, from the wilderness user's standpoint, thankfully idle. Each additional technology in evidence to non-native wil-derness users diminished the feeling of primitiveness that they associated with the subsistence way of life. In a sense, it did not matter that subsistence hunting remained a way of life while sport hunting was simply a form of leisure as long as the tools and techniques of each type of hunting came to look more and more alike. How long could subsistence hunting be pro-tected if it became outwardly indistinguishable from sport hunting? There had to be limits on the technology or it would no longer be subsistence hunting, environmentalists insisted.

The legislation that emerged from this debate addressed three basic questions about subsistence: who would be eligible, how it would be de-fined, and where it would be permitted. In the matter of eligibility, the basic criterion would be rural residency rather than racial origin. White Alaskans living in the bush would be included in the system. However, in recognition of the fact that ANCSA had extinguished all aboriginal hunting rights in Alaska with the understanding that native subsistence hunting would be protected, the law made a fine though significant distinction between native and non-native privileges:

> the continuation of the opportunity for subsistence uses by rural resi-dents of Alaska, including both Natives and non-Natives, on the pub-lic lands is essential to Native physical, economic, traditional, and cultural existence and to non-Native physical, economic, traditional, and social existence.[64]

The acknowledgment that native cultural existence depended on subsis-tence was an important concession to the native point of view. Moreover, the law stated that to protect native subsistence use it was "necessary for the

Congress to invoke its constitutional authority over Native affairs." Thus, in order to fulfill the purposes of ANCSA, ANILCA maintained that the federal government still had a trust responsibility toward Alaska natives on all national interest lands.

The Alaska Lands Act defined subsistence according to the tried legal jargon of "customary and traditional use."[65] Subsistence was considered:

> the customary and traditional uses by rural Alaska residents of wild, renewable resources for direct personal or family consumption as food, shelter, fuel, clothing, tools, or transportation; for the making and selling of handicraft articles out of nonedible byproducts of fish and wildlife resources taken for personal or family consumption; for barter, or sharing for personal or family consumption; and for customary trade.[66]

Despite native objections that subsistence could not be defined because it was always changing, there was no practical alternative to creating a legal definition. Apart from its nonracial intent, this definition of subsistence was somewhat more restrictive than the definition of subsistence contained in the Marine Mammal Protection Act of 1972. Still, it left the matter of ATV use open to various interpretations.[67]

The answer to the third question, where subsistence would be permitted, lacked precision as well. In the matter of sport hunting, the authors of ANILCA hit upon the "national preserve" designation as an unambiguous way of containing that use.[68] But they failed to be as clear when it came to subsistence use. According to the NPS's interpretation of the law, subsistence uses by local residents were not permitted within the original boundaries of Mount McKinley National Park, Katmai National Monument, and Glacier Bay National Monument, nor in the national park additions to Katmai and Glacier Bay, nor in the new Kenai Fjords National Park. Subsistence uses were permitted in all other national park areas. The basis for this messy configuration was unexplained, but it revealed how the makers of the law generally regarded subsistence as more of a political compromise than a positive innovation that was applicable to all Alaska wilderness.

While the Title VIII subsistence provisions were practically settled by the beginning of 1977, numerous other features of this complicated law still remained under negotiation. It took the entire four years of the Carter administration to get the bill through Congress. The bill faced determined opposition from Alaska's senators and congressman and a host of powerful lobbyists led by the National Rifle Association and Exxon Corporation.[69] A wide gulf developed between the House and Senate versions of the bill in 1978. When time ran out on the D-2 withdrawals that fall, President Carter invoked the Antiquities Act to proclaim all of the national park system areas as national monuments pending a congressional act. After the House and Senate deadlocked once again in 1980, the long, tortuous history of this legislation reached an ironic denouement with the election of Ronald Reagan, who everyone knew would kill the measure if given the opportunity. Now the champions of the stronger House bill had no choice but to salvage what they could in the Senate version before Carter left office. Carter would later muse that ANILCA was the best piece of lame-duck legislation he could remember, but so much had been lost or compromised that environmentalists could hardly rejoice in their victory.[70]

What was overlooked in this process was how much ground native groups had already yielded in the mid-1970s as the administration, Congress, and the Alaska Department of Fish and Game all backpedaled from the idea of cooperative management. Congressman John Seiberling indicated at a subcommittee hearing in Anaktuvuk Pass in August 1977 that cooperative management would be "optional" and "voluntary." "They could do it for five years — a period of time and see how it works out."[71] This was not much of a guarantee for native interests in the national park. The NPS, for its part, indicated that it did not want the law to declare subsistence to be a park purpose (as the Nunamiut National Park proposal did) but only a permitted use.[72] As far as the Nunamiuts could see, cooperative management bore more and more resemblance to a system of permitting. Informal discussions with the NPS in 1977–78 mostly revolved around questions of access and possible land exchanges.[73] To the Nunamiuts' dismay, the NPS drafted the regulations for ANILCA in 1981 without even consulting them, and afterwards they experienced a great deal of difficulty in obtaining and understanding the regulations. The Nunamiuts balked at the NPS's interpretation of customary and traditional use, which the NPS took as a cue to subdivide the park into hunting and no-hunting zones depending on whether or not the Nunamiuts said they had ever hunted in a particular area before. They also took issue with the NPS interpretation of ANILCA that subsistence was a permitted use rather than a park purpose, and they expressed concern that the regulations would not prevent outsiders who were temporarily domiciled in Anaktuvuk Pass from claiming eligibility to hunt.[74] As the new national park administration got on the ground in the early 1980s, the prospects for cooperative management did not seem bright.

The federal government and the Nunamiuts failed to establish a strong

basis for co-management of Gates of the Arctic National Park because of
mutual fears and suspicions. These qualms were rooted in the uneasy alliance that natives and preservationists had forged with one another in the
1960s and 1970s. With the establishment of the national park in 1980, the
Nunamiuts feared that they would lose access to their own homeland, that
they would be frozen out of the new system of game management, and that
they would lose their privacy as so many permits and questionnaires and
summer backpackers came into their village. NPS officials, meanwhile,
feared that by sharing control with the local people, they would be unable
to fulfill their basic mandate of preserving the resources in a natural condition for the enjoyment of present and future generations. As Gates of the
Arctic Superintendent Jim Pepper would later remark, "Fear is the worst
way to create policy because then you are always thinking about the worst
case alternative."[75] Residual fears and suspicions led both parties to fall back
on land ownership as the arbiter of their differences and land exchanges as
the building blocks to better relations. More than a decade after the park
was created, it remained to be seen whether they would find a better way.

Conclusion:
The Burden of Alaska Wilderness

Charles Sheldon, Bob Marshall, Olaus Murie, and other conservationists who campaigned for the preservation of Alaska wilderness shared one basic idea. That idea was that Alaska wilderness, more than any other wilderness area in the United States, evoked the feeling of a truly virgin land, a wilderness on a continental scale: North America at the time of its discovery by Europeans. This continental wilderness was such a strongly imagined entity in the minds of wilderness preservationists that it constituted a kind of platonic ideal. The quality of contemporary wilderness areas could be measured by their ability to evoke or replicate the continental wilderness ideal. Alaska wilderness areas, because of their magnificent expanse, had more authenticity than the pocket-sized wilderness areas in the rest of the United States. Alaska's Brooks Range, lying north of the Arctic Circle and farthest from settlement of any of Alaska's scenic wildlands, came to stand as the ultimate wilderness.

Most Americans who sought out Alaska wilderness associated their experiences with a heroic age of explorers and frontiersmen. If they did not literally reflect on such cultural icons as Lewis and Clark or Columbus, as did Bob Marshall, or on John Muir, as did William Cooper, or on Daniel Boone, as did Charles Sheldon, they invariably imagined the land as primordial and cast themselves as intruders in an exotic terra incognita. Alaska wilderness presented an unparalleled opportunity to penetrate into those blank spaces on the map, discover new fields of hunting or wildlife viewing, and test oneself against the elements. Even the modern wilderness user, equipped with USGS quads and high-tech backpacking gear, went into the Alaska wilderness carrying this cultural baggage.

By contrast, Alaska natives saw the land as their people's inheritance. They did not share the white wilderness traveler's platonic ideal of a continental wilderness, but rather perceived their place in the land in terms of their clan legends and cultural traditions. For them, the wildlands surrounding their villages were what sustained them as a people. Whether they primarily hunted caribou or caught salmon for their subsistence, the land represented food to them, and their food represented a way of life. The land and the way of life were inseparable. The twentieth century introduced Alaska natives to a great deal of change, but it did not supplant one cultural outlook on the land for another. Even the contemporary Eskimo or Indian who left the comfort of a modern home to go out hunting or fishing did not conceive of the land as "wilderness" in the same sense as the wilderness user. Although Alaska wilderness acquired legal definition and federal protection under ANILCA and the Wilderness Act of 1964, it remained a culturally relative entity.

Alaska natives supported wilderness protections insofar as wilderness protections helped to preserve their way of life. Since their traditional cultures were grounded in hunting and fishing, they needed a continuous supply of fish and game populations for their culture to survive. This in turn required that fish and game habitat be preserved on a large scale, and reciprocally, that industrial, agricultural, and commercial uses of the land be kept to a minimum. Bob Marshall had this commonality of interests in mind when he suggested that the native inhabitants of northern Alaska would be better off if the entire region were left in a wild condition. Olaus Murie also had the natives' interests in mind when he campaigned for the Arctic National Wildlife Range. Alaska natives sided with conservationists when conservationists held up, as their broad objective, the preservation of wildlands: hence the Eskimos' proposal for a Nunamiut National Park in 1974. Alaska natives did not embrace the American concept of wilderness, but they worked with it for their own ends.

Difficulties arose when wilderness preservationists conditioned their support for native peoples on romantic conceptions of native culture. One common illusion was that Alaska native hunters ought to evoke images of the primitive redman in America, just as the expansiveness of Alaska wilderness evoked the feeling of a continental wilderness. Thus, the preservation of a hunting way of life in Alaska would authenticate the wilderness. Unfortunately, this romantic illusion led whites to object to the natives' use of modern technology in the hunt. If Hunas, for example, hunted seals in Glacier Bay from modern fishing boats, they were not real Indians anymore. Alaska wilderness no longer had any use for them.

Another common illusion was that Alaska natives, like all Native Americans, were "natural conservationists." By this it was meant that traditional native peoples were culturally predisposed to shepherd their resources, even to inhabit their environment without actually modifying it. They were nature's stewards. According to this romantic conception of the native peoples, when they did in fact alter their environment, it was evidence of the corrosive effects of Western ideas on their culture. This judgment was usually tinged with sharp, moral censure. Some whites argued, hypocritically and misanthropically, that native cultures had fallen so far in the face of Western influences that they were not worth preserving at all.

These romantic conceptions of Alaska native cultures shared a basic element with the preservationists' wilderness ideal. The primitivist envisioned a time in North America's past, before the advent of whites, when nature and culture were static, when Native Americans inhabited a kind of Arcadia. Certainly there had been migrations, wars, and famines in aboriginal times, but no disturbances on a scale to shake Indian civilization loose from its moorings in the Paleolithic era. Similarly, the natural landscape had experienced drought, forest fire, and other local perturbations, but nothing so severe as to prevent a restoration of the balance of nature after each local event. In this imagined world, humankind and nature existed in harmony.

The romantic impulse to preserve a part of America's past in Alaska, the nation's last frontier, finally gained an irresistible national following in the 1970s, but by then, ironically, the primitivists' critique of humankind and nature had been all but demolished by anthropologists and ecologists. It now seemed that aboriginal societies had never been static, nor had the lands that they inhabited been unaffected by cultural change. What nonnatives had once construed as primordial wilderness was actually a series of socially shaped landscapes. The traditional model of national parks as remnants of a once-continental wilderness, or, in the Leopold Report's phrase, "vignettes of primitive America," was no longer a viable paradigm for the preservation of Alaska's inhabited wilderness. There would have to be some sort of melding of natural and cultural preservation — some sort of formula that would satisfy the wilderness users' quest for the primitive at the same time as it made realistic allowances for ecological and cultural change. It made for a perilously uncertain basis of cooperation between preservationists and resident peoples.

Historically, preservationists had dealt with the problem of resident peoples in Alaskan national parklands in one of two ways: removal or regulation. In Glacier Bay National Monument, the NPS took the traditional approach of relocating the inhabitants elsewhere. White trappers and fox farmers were evicted from the area, while the Huna Tlingits were forced to abandon their seasonal-use cabins, smokehouses, and traplines. NPS officials conceded that the natives of Hoonah had been hunting and fishing in Glacier Bay for a long time, but they stuck by their position that the special privileges accorded to the village natives were only an interim arrangement while the natives completed their adjustment to a new economy based on commercial fishing and cannery work. The Huna Tlingits contested that interpretation, holding that their special privileges were permanent. While the legal basis for native subsistence use in Glacier Bay National Monument was taken away in the early 1970s, illegal hunting and fishing continued at some undetermined level, and Huna Tlingits continued to feel a cultural attachment to the area. Twenty years later, it remained doubtful whether the NPS had succeeded in its goal of eliminating seal hunting and other forms of subsistence use from the park.

For the first eleven years of Mount McKinley National Park's administration, the NPS attempted to control subsistence use through the issuance of permits and regulation. Residents of the area, who were mostly whites in this case, were granted the privilege of killing game for their own consumption. This was an innovative response to the social and environmental conditions then prevailing in interior Alaska, but it proved to be fraught with problems. Residents chafed at the regulations and abused them. Men who were not eligible to hunt under the law killed game for the market. When the poachers were caught and prosecuted in the local courts, juries let them go free. NPS officials were fairly quick to judge this experiment a failure and adopted their traditional, exclusionary approach to resident peoples by the end of the 1920s.

Under ANILCA, the NPS revisited its earlier effort to control subsistence use through permitting and regulation, but with one crucial difference. The new scheme involved input from the resident peoples themselves, and was called co-management. Nine of the ten parks established under ANILCA were organized in such a way as to allow subsistence use and to promote effective co-management by the NPS and resident peoples. The legislative mandate for co-management was not as strong as some proponents of the idea had wished, but it nevertheless set up the new parks on a different basis from the traditional pattern of exclusive federal control. As the NPS moved toward a system of co-management in Gates of the Arctic, champions of the idea of inhabited wilderness had reason to cheer. Until resident peoples were actually drawn into the decision-making process, proponents of the change had insisted, there was little hope that they could be made to support national park purposes and to respect the resource values of the national parks. The three different experiences in Glacier Bay, Mount McKinley, and Gates of the Arctic suggested that national park policy in Alaska was evolving toward a greater sharing of power between the NPS and resident peoples, as well as a more complicated construction of the meaning of Alaska wilderness.

A decade and a half after passage of ANILCA, Alaska's national parks continued to be contested ground. Alaska natives agitated for subsistence rights in the old, pre-ANILCA national parks of Glacier Bay and Katmai as well as in Kenai Fjords, the one national park established in 1980 without provision for subsistence use. Meanwhile, the Sierra Club pushed the NPS to constrict subsistence use in five of the new areas created under ANILCA. Concerned about growing ATV use, the Sierra Club declared in the spring of 1994 that there was now a need "to carve out five new traditional national parks" from Gates of the Arctic, Wrangell–Saint Elias, Lake Clark, Aniakchak, and the large additions to Denali. In these "traditional national parks," all forms of subsistence use would be eliminated.[1] In other words, the Sierra Club believed that co-management was failing in these areas and it wanted to go back to the traditional model of excluding resident peoples and managing the land as though any kind of human resource use was unnatural.

The complexities of the subsistence issue threatened to create a schism within the NPS organization itself. The schism cut many ways. NPS officials in the field, working with and living close to the subsistence users, generally favored a liberal interpretation of ANILCA's Title VIII provisions, while NPS officials in the Alaska regional office in Anchorage, remaining attuned to the NPS's traditional urban constituency, generally favored a more stringent construction of the law's intent. Officials in the agency's cultural resources division sought to maintain a dialogue with resident peoples, while those in the agency's subsistence division insisted on greater clarity in the rules and regulations. Most fractious of all was the rift between the NPS's old Alaska hands and the steady stream of career officials eager to do their tour of duty in one of the Alaska parks. The latter increasingly brought with them a skeptical attitude toward co-management. Within NPS circles, a pejorative distinction between "hard parks" and "soft parks" crept into the dialogue on the inhabited wilderness idea. Traditionalists in the NPS wanted "hard" park boundaries that would provide administrators greater control in managing resources and people within those boundaries. The NPS's old Alaska hands, meanwhile, objected that Alaskans, environmentalists, and the Congress had already been over that ground in the 1970s and had determined a need for innovation.

Fifteen years after the passage of ANILCA, it was unclear in which direction NPS policy would move. What was clear was that the making of Alaska's national parks continued to revolve around the central problem of inhabited wilderness. That problem was to provide for resident peoples' traditional use of lands where those lands were dedicated to the preservation of nature, and to strike the right balance between the inhabitants' desire for freedom and the wilderness users' desire for the primitive.

Notes

INTRODUCTION

1. Isabelle F. Story, *The National Parks and Emergency Conservation* (Washington, D.C.: National Park Service, 1933), 3; Roderick Nash, "The American Invention of National Parks," *American Quarterly* 22, 3 (1970): 726–35.

2. *Congressional Record*, 1980, vol. 126, p. 20887.

3. Quoted in Barry Mackintosh, *The National Parks: Shaping the System* (Washington, D.C.: National Park Service, 1991), 10. Alfred Runte comments on the parallel between Catlin's vision and the concept of humankind and nature in Alaska national parks in *National Parks: The American Experience*, 2d rev. ed. (Lincoln: University of Nebraska Press, 1987), 238–39.

4. David Harmon, "Cultural Diversity, Human Subsistence, and the National Park Ideal," *Environmental Ethics* 9, 2 (1987): 152.

5. Much recent thinking on this problem, which draws upon examples from around the world, has been brought together in Patrick C. West and Steven R. Brechin, eds., *Resident Peoples and National Parks: Social Dilemmas and Strategies in International Conservation* (Tucson: University of Arizona Press, 1991).

CHAPTER 1

1. John Muir, *The Mountains of California* (New York: Century, 1894).

2. Quoted in Linnie Marsh Wolfe, *Son of the Wilderness: The Life of John Muir* (New York: Alfred A. Knopf, 1945), 133.

3. John Muir, *Letters from Alaska*, edited by Robert Engberg and Bruce Merrell (Madison: University of Wisconsin Press, 1993), xxv, and *John Muir Summering in the Sierra*, edited by Robert Engberg (Madison: University of Wisconsin Press, 1984), 10.

4. Muir, *Letters from Alaska*, 11, 44–47.

5. Muir accepted the credit, describing the trip in an article titled "The Discovery

of Glacier Bay," in *The Century Magazine* 50, 2 (1895): 234–37. He was the first individual to make the bay's existence known to the outside world, but he and Young were not the first non-Indians to visit it. In 1868 the U.S. Revenue Steamer *Wayanda*, under the command of John W. White, navigated Glacier Bay and Icy Strait with the guidance of a Russian pilot, Cadin. Chief Engineer J. A. Doyle detailed the trip thirty-five years later for the Alaskan Boundary Tribunal (Senate, *Proceedings of the Alaskan Boundary Tribunal*, vol. 2, 58th Cong., 2d sess., Doc.162, 1904, 474–75). In 1877, Lieutenant C. E. S. Wood, on leave from his ship at Sitka, went goat hunting in the Saint Elias Mountains, crossed into the Glacier Bay basin, and hired some native seal hunters to transport him back to Sitka by canoe ("Among the Thlinkits in Alaska," *The Century Magazine* 24, 3 [1882]: 323–39).

6. Muir, *Letters from Alaska*, 49.

7. John Muir, *Travels in Alaska* (Boston: Houghton Mifflin Co., 1915), 152. See also Michael P. Cohen, *The Pathless Way: John Muir and American Wilderness* (Madison: University of Wisconsin Press, 1984), 182–90.

8. Walter R. Goldschmidt and Theodore H. Haas, "Possessory Rights of the Natives of Southeastern Alaska," 1946, unpublished file report at Sitka National Historic Park (hereafter cited as SITK), D-4. Until recently, the spelling for the village and the people were the same. Now the village is spelled "Hoonah," and the people are the "Huna."

9. Muir, *Travels in Alaska*, 146, 150; S. Hall Young, *Alaska Days with John Muir* (New York: F. H. Revell Co., 1915), 99.

10. Linnie Marsh Wolfe, ed., *John of the Mountains: The Unpublished Journals of John Muir* (Boston: Houghton Mifflin Co., 1938), 315.

11. Ibid., 273.

12. Muir, *Travels in Alaska*, 142, 146, 263. On Tlingit superstitions, see Wolfe, *John of the Mountains*, 272–73. For the view that Muir's Alaska travels gave him a more sympathetic understanding of Indians, see Jed Dannenbaum, "John Muir and Alaska," *Alaska Journal* 2, 4 (1972): 14–20, and Richard F. Fleck, "John Muir's Evolving Attitudes Toward Native American Cultures," *American Indian Quarterly* 4, 1 (1978): 19–31.

13. Young, *Alaska Days*, 171.

14. Robert E. Ackerman, *The Archeology of the Glacier Bay Region, Southeastern Alaska* (Pullman: Washington State University, Laboratory of Anthropology, 1968), 85–86.

15. Robert F. Schroeder and Matthew Kookesh, *Subsistence Harvest and Use of Fish and Wildlife Resources and the Effects of Forest Management in Hoonah, Alaska*, Technical Paper No. 142 (Juneau: Alaska Department of Fish and Game, 1990), 22–25; William S. Cooper, "The Recent Ecological History of Glacier Bay, Alaska: II. The Present Vegetation Cycle," *Ecology*, 4 (1923): 223–24.

16. George A. Hall, "The Stories of Glacier Bay Collected at Hoonah, Alaska," July 1960, unpublished file report at SITK; Susie James, "Glacier Bay History," in *Haa Shuka, Our Ancestors: Tlingit Oral Narratives*, edited by Nora Marks Dauen-

hauer and Richard Dauenhauer (Seattle: University of Washington Press, 1987), 245–61; Amy Marvin, "Glacier Bay History," in ibid., 261–93 (quotation, 285).

17. Statements by Albert Jackson, George Carteete, Frank O. Williams, Albert Greenewald, Mrs. Lonnie Houston, Mrs. Oscar Williams, and Mrs. Eliza Lawrence, typescript at Alaska Historical Library (hereafter cited as AHL), Curry-Weissbrodt Papers, MS-43, roll 20 (quotation, Mrs. Houston).

18. Julia Averkieva, "The Tlingit Indians," in *North American Indians in Historical Perspective* (New York: Random House, 1971), 319.

19. C. E. S. Wood, "Among the Thlinkits in Alaska," *The Century Magazine* 24, 3 (1882): 328–29. Cultivation of the nonindigenous potato spread among northwest coastal Indian peoples in the eighteenth century.

20. *Tlingit and Haida Indians of Alaska v. United States*, U.S. Court of Claims, Rept. 7900 (1959), 372.

21. Frederica De Laguna, *Under Mount Saint Elias: The History and Culture of the Yakutat Tlingit* (Washington, D.C.: Smithsonian Institution Press, 1972), 824.

22. Tlingit attitudes are discussed in ibid., 374, 824. An example of a conservationist interpretation is Captain L. A. Beardslee's description of Huna seal and sea otter hunting in Senate, *Reports of Captain L. A. Beardslee, U.S. Navy, Relative to Affairs in Alaska, and the Operations of the U.S.S. Jamestown under his command, while in the waters of th. territory*, 47th Cong., 1st sess., S. Ex. Doc. 71, 1882, 174–75. Morgan Sherwood analyzes native hunting in *Big Game in Alaska: A History of Wildlife and People* (New Haven: Yale University Press, 1981), 103–16. Ann Fienup-Riordan addresses a similar hunting ethic among the Yup'ik Eskimo, and white misconceptions of it, in her essay "Original Ecologists?: The Relationship Between Yup'ik Eskimos and Animals," in *Eskimo Essays: Yup'ik Lives and How We See Them* (New Brunswick: Rutgers University Press, 1990), 167, 173–74.

23. Terris Moore, *Mount McKinley: The Pioneer Climbs* (College, Alaska: University of Alaska Press 1967), 15.

24. J. Alden Loring, "Notes on the Destruction of Animal Life in Alaska," *New York Zoological Society Sixth Annual Report* (New York: Office of the Society, 1902), 142.

25. Senate, *Reports of Captain L. A. Beardslee, U.S. Navy, Relative to Affairs in Alaska, and the Operations of the U.S.S. Jamestown under his command, while in the waters of that territory*, 47th Cong., 1st sess., 1882, S. Ex. Doc. No. 71, 185.

26. Calvin Martin, *Keepers of the Game: Indian-Animal Relationships and the Fur Trade* (Berkeley: University of California Press, 1978), 3.

27. Ted C. Hinckley, "The Canoe Rocks—We Do Not Know What Will Become of Us," *Western Historical Quarterly* 1, 3 (1970): 275–76.

28. Frank O. Williams statement, and Albert Greenewald statement, AHL, Curry-Weissbrodt Papers, MS-43, roll 20.

29. John Burroughs et al., *Alaska: The Harriman Expedition, 1899* (New York: Dover Publications, 1986), 158–65.

30. De Laguna, *Under Mount Saint Elias*, 384.

31. Richard A. Cooley, *Politics of Conservation: The Decline of the Alaska Salmon* (New York: Harper and Row Publishers, 1963), 72–73.

32. Senate, *Conditions and Needs of the Natives of Alaska*, report by Lieutenant G. T. Emmons, 58th Cong., 3d sess., S. Doc. 106, 1905, 13.

33. Economic and technological changes in Tlingit commercial fishing from the early 1900s to the 1930s are described in Senate, Subcommittee on Indian Affairs, *Survey of Conditions of the Indians in the United States, Part 36: Alaska*, 74th Cong., 2d sess., 1939, 19739.

34. W. T. Lopp, "Native Labor in the Alaska Fisheries," *Pacific Fisherman* 12, 11 (1914): 16.

35. This term was frequently used. See the Hunas' statements taken by Walter Goldschmidt and Theodore H. Haas in AHL, Curry-Weissbrodt Papers, MS-43, roll 20, and Mayor Harry Douglas's statement to the NPS and the BIA as recorded in Superintendent to Regional Director, March 2, 1954, National Archives — Pacific Sierra Region (hereafter cited as NAPSR), RG 79, Western Region, Central Coded Subject Files (hereafter cited as CSF), file N-16, box 3.

36. Runte, *National Parks*, passim.

37. Ella Higginson, *Alaska: The Great Country* (New York: Macmillan Company, 1908), 219; Maturin M. Ballou, *The New Eldorado: Summer Journey to Alaska* (Boston: Houghton Mifflin Co., 1891), 276; Burroughs et al., *Alaska*, 36, 42.

38. On the history of scientific studies in Glacier Bay, see Dave Bohn, *Glacier Bay: The Land and the Silence* (Seattle: Sierra Club, Pacific Northwest, 1967).

39. Ballou, *New Eldorado*, xiv. Also see Ted C. Hinckley, "The Inside Passage: A Popular Gilded Age Tour," *Pacific Northwest Quarterly* 56, 3 (1965): 65–74.

40. Clinton Hart Merriam, "1899 Alaska Expedition Journal," June 9, 1899, original at Library of Congress, C. Hart Merriam Papers, box 7, vol. 1, p. 48.

41. The theory that the earthquake fractured the Muir Glacier and caused it to recede at a faster rate over the next several years was first spelled out in an article by C. L. Andrews, "Muir Glacier," *National Geographic*, December 1903, 441–45, and in fuller detail by Fremont Morse, "The Recession of the Glaciers of Glacier Bay, Alaska," *National Geographic*, January 1908, 76–78. Due to the inaccessibility of Glacier Bay, Ralph Stockman Tarr and Lawrence Martin passed up the Muir Glacier in favor of glaciers around Yakutat Bay and Prince William Sound in their major work, *Alaskan Glacier Studies* (Washington, D.C.: National Geographic Society, 1914).

42. Donald B. Lawrence, "Memorial to William Skinner Cooper 1884–1978," Glacier Bay National Park and Preserve (hereafter cited as GLBA), Administrative Files, file N1433b.

43. Donald Worster, *Nature's Economy: The Roots of Ecology* (New York: Cambridge University Press, 1985), 207.

44. William S. Cooper, "Remarks at Dedication of Lodge at Bartlett Cove, Glacier Bay, Alaska," June 4, 1966, GLBA, Administrative Files, file N1433b, and "The

Recent Ecological History of Glacier Bay, Alaska: I. The Interglacial Forests of Glacier Bay," *Ecology* 4, 2 (1923): 93–94.

45. William S. Cooper, "A Contribution to the History of the Glacier Bay National Monument," n.d., typescript at GLBA, Library, p. 4.

46. Ibid., 5.

47. Ibid., 7–8.

48. Runte, *National Parks*, passim.

49. Alfred H. Brooks et al., "Mineral Resources of Alaska," *U.S. Geological Survey Bulletin 773* (Washington, D.C.: Government Printing Office, 1925), 63–65.

50. Philip S. Smith, "Mineral Industry of Alaska in 1924 and Administrative Report," *U.S. Geological Survey Bulletin 783-A* (Washington, D.C.: Government Printing Office, 1926), 4–12; A. F. Buddington, "Mineral Investigations in Southeastern Alaska," *U.S. Geological Survey Bulletin 783-B* (Washington, D.C.: Government Printing Office, 1926), 55–56.

51. Quoted in W. C. Mendenhall to Governor John W. Troy, May 16, 1935, National Archives—Alaska Region (hereafter cited as NAAR), National Archives Microfilm Publication M-939, General Correspondence of the Alaskan Territorial Governor 1909–58, roll 246.

52. Buddington, "Mineral Investigations," 55–56.

53. "Glacier Bay, Alaska Temporarily Withdrawn from Entry," *Ecology* 5, 2 (1924): 223; "Council on National Parks, Forests, and Wild Life," *Ecology* 5, 2 (1924): 185; W. Cooper, "Contribution," 9.

54. *Alaska Daily Empire* (Juneau), April 28, 1924.

55. Quoted in John M. Kauffmann, "Glacier Bay National Monument Alaska: A History of its Boundaries," 1954, open-file report at Alaska Regional Office (hereafter cited as ARO), Administrative Files, file H14, p.5.

56. W. Cooper, "Contribution," 16.

57. *Alaska Daily Empire* (Juneau), February 16, 1925.

58. Kauffmann, "Glacier Bay National Monument," 8.

59. Ibid., 10–11.

60. The curious history of this anomalous and unfortunate piece of legislation is covered in Bohn, *Glacier Bay*, 94–106. Congress repealed the law in 1976.

61. Burton E. Livingston to Governor of Alaska, February 7, 1925, NAAR, M-939, roll 124, frame 42.

62. Other statements are contained in W. Cooper, "Contribution."

63. William O. Field, Jr., "Visit to Glacier Bay, 1926," June 1982, typescript at GLBA, Library, p. 3.

64. Joseph S. Dixon field notes, September 6–10, 1932, copy at GLBA, Library; Joseph S. Dixon report, September 29, 1932, quoted in Kauffmann, "Glacier Bay National Monument," n.p. The background to this can be traced in the articles and editorials of A. N. Pack in *Nature Magazine*, Harry McGuire in *Outdoor Life*, John M. Holzworth, *The Wild Grizzlies of Alaska* (New York: G. P. Putnam's Sons,

1930), and Senate, Committee on Conservation of Wildlife Resources, *Hearing Before the Special Committee on Conservation of Wild Life Resources United States Senate on the Protection and Preservation of the Brown and Grizzly Bears of Alaska*, 73d Cong., 2d. sess., January 18, 1932.

65. J. D. Coffman to Director (NPS), September 14, 1938, and Joseph S. Dixon to Regional Director, April 6, 1939, NAPSR, RG 79, Western Region, Central Classified Files (hereafter cited as CCF), box 294, file 602.

66. E. B. Nixon, ed., *Franklin D. Roosevelt and Conservation*, vol. 2 (New York: General Services Administration, National Archives and Records Service, Franklin D. Roosevelt Library, Hyde Park, 1957), 289, 295–96.

67. Mammalogists now consider grizzlies and Alaskan brown bears to be one species. It is unresolved as to whether the glacier bear is a color phase or a subspecies of the American black bear. Limited to the coastal regions of the Saint Elias region, it has been suggested that the glacier bear is a "relict form" or "dying race," which persisted in refugia after the latest glaciation of the Pleistocene, and is now in competition with the dominant form of American black bear (Anonymous memorandum titled "Glacier Bear," n.d., NAAR, RG 79, 79–83-F0007, box 47/51, file LSD Glacier Bay Addition Wildlife Resources). Also see Morgan Sherwood, "Specious Speciation in the Political History of the Alaskan Brown Bear," *Western Historical Quarterly* 10, 1 (1979): 49–60.

68. John D. Coffman and Joseph S. Dixon, "Report on Glacier Bay National Park (Proposed), Alaska," December 20, 1938, NAAR, RG 79, 79–91–0001, box 3/9, file GLBA administrative history, p. ii.

69. Ibid., 2B.

70. Ibid., p. 16.

71. Dixon, field notes, September 6–10, 1932, copy at GLBA, Library.

72. Ibid., 2C.

CHAPTER 2

1. James A. Fall, "The Division of Subsistence of the Alaska Department of Fish and Game: An Overview of its Research Program and Findings 1980–1990," *Arctic Anthropology* 27, 2 (1990): 68–92.

2. Jack Kruse and Rosyland Frazier, "Report to the Community of Hoonah, Tongass Resource Use Cooperative Survey," September 20, 1988, open-file report at ARO, p. 9.

3. "Conditions of Natives in the Juneau District 1935," NAAR, RG 22, Juneau Fisheries Research Data Files 1904–60, box 26, file Native Reports all Districts, 1935.

4. "Conditions of Natives in the Juneau District 1935," NAAR, RG 22, Juneau Fisheries Research Data Files, box 26, file Native Reports all Districts, 1935.

5. Hair seals killed in and near Glacier Bay National Monument from March

1939 to July 1940, National Archives (hereafter cited as NA), RG 79, CCF, box 2228, file 208.06.

6. Hoonah Census, October 1, 1938, NAAR, RG 75, Juneau Area Office, Tribal Census rolls, box 182.

7. Don C. Foster to Francis A. Staten, May 2, 1946, NAAR, RG 75, Juneau Area Office, General Subject Correspondence (hereafter cited as GSC), box 86, file 917 Annual Statistical Report Hoonah.

8. Commissioner of Indian Affairs to Secretary of the Interior, November 1, 1945, NA, RG 75, Alaska Agency, box 117, file 3246–45–931.

9. In 1941, a BIA official made a sample household survey of stored winter food supplies in Hoonah and listed a total supply of 9,336 pounds of preserved food. With sixty-one people "dependent on this supply" (presumably the number who lived in the sample households), this indicated a winter supply of approximately 153.5 pounds of native food per capita in the village. In 1985, a sample household survey in Hoonah by the Alaska Department of Fish and Game found a per capita consumption of native foods of 245 pounds (Survey of Native Food, Summer of 1941, by L. E. Robinson, October 10, 1941, NAAR, RG 75, Alaska Reindeer Service, box 61, file 917 Agricultural, Hunting, and Fishing Statistics; Schroeder and Kookesh, *Subsistence Harvest*, 94).

10. "Annual Statistical Report," 1943, 1945, NAAR, RG 75, Juneau Area Office, GSC, box 86, file 917 Annual Statistical Report Hoonah.

11. Ibid.

12. Goldschmidt and Haas, "Possessory Rights," 25.

13. The report summarizes information recorded in oral interviews and ethnographic source. Transcripts of the oral interviews are in AHL, Curry-Weissbrodt Papers, MS-43, roll 20.

14. Homer W. Jewell to Claude M. Hirst, July 15, 1939, NAAR, RG 75, Alaska Reindeer Service, box 64, file Hunting, Fishing, and Fur Farming.

15. "Number and Location — Hair Seals Killed in and near Glacier Bay National Monument from March 1939 to July 1940," NA, RG 79, CCF, box 2228, file 208.06.

16. Earl A. Trager, "Glacier Bay Expedition, 1939," NAPSR, RG 79, Western Region, CCF, box 292, p. 86; Frank T. Been field notes, July 25, 1940, Denali National Park and Preserve (hereafter cited as DENA), William E. Brown Historical Files; Horace Ibach to Frank T. Been, January 9, 1940, NA, RG 79, CCF, box 2228, file 208.06.

17. "Amounts Expended for Bounty on Hair Seals," NAAR, RG 75, Juneau Area Office, GSC, box 42, file 923.2 Hair Seal No. 1.

18. Been field notes, July 25 and 30, 1940, DENA, William E. Brown Historical Files.

19. Evidence that Huna Tlingits engaged in these subsistence activities at the head of Excursion Inlet comes from the statements taken by Goldschmidt and Haas in 1946. Goldschmidt and Haas listed this area as one of five where Huna Tlingit

resource gathering had been consistent enough to provide the basis for a claim of "possessory rights" to the area.

20. This letter is quoted in a telegram, Hirst to Zimmerman, April 22, 1938, NAAR, RG 75, Alaska Reindeer Service, box 64, file Hunting, Fishing, and Fur Farming; pre– and post–season employment is also described in "Conditions of Natives in the Juneau District 1935," NAAR, RG 22, Juneau Alaska Fisheries Research Data Files 1904–60, box 26, file Native Reports All Districts 1935.

21. Walter V. Woehlke to John Collier, December 6, 1943, NA, RG 75, Alaska Agency, box 112, file 40088–42–930.

22. Frederick E. Hoxie, *A Final Promise: The Campaign to Assimilate the Indians, 1880–1920* (Lincoln: University of Nebraska Press, 1984), x–xii.

23. Philip Drucker, *Native Brotherhoods: Modern Inter-tribal Organizations on the Northwest Coast* (Washington, D.C.: Government Printing Office, 1958), 13; David E. Conrad, "Emmons of Alaska," *Pacific Northwest Quarterly* 69, 2 (1978), 59–60; David S. Case, *Alaska Natives and American Laws* (Fairbanks: University of Alaska, 1984), 6–10.

24. Frederica De Laguna, "Tlingit," in *Handbook of North American Indians*, vol. 7 (Washington, D.C.: Smithsonian Institution Press, 1990), 224–25; Drucker, *Native Brotherhoods*, 18–19.

25. *Alaska Fisherman* (Wrangell), May 1923.

26. Susan H. Koester, " 'By the Words of the Mouth Let Thee Be Judged': The Alaska Native Sisterhood Speaks," *Journal of the West* 27, 2 (1988): 35–44.

27. Drucker, *Native Brotherhoods*, 37.

28. *Alaska Fisherman* (Wrangell), January 1924.

29. Kenneth D. Tollefson, "The Cultural Foundation of Political Revitalization Among the Tlingit" (Ph.D. diss., University of Washington, 1976), 305.

30. *Alaska Fisherman* (Wrangell), January 1924.

31. Senate, Committee on Indian Affairs, *Survey of Conditions of the Indians in the United States, Part 36: Alaska*, 74th Cong., 2d sess., 1939, 19739.

32. Tollefson, "Cultural Foundation," 290.

33. Senate, Committee on Indian Affairs, *Survey of Conditions of the Indians in the United States, Part 36: Alaska*, 74th Cong., 2d sess., 1939, 19917.

34. Some Tlingits argued against fish traps on conservationist grounds, convinced that the traps were reducing the salmon run from year to year and inexorably ruining the industry. This argument dovetailed the other. But there was not unanimity: some Tlingits who worked in canneries did not want fish traps abolished because they feared it would hurt the canneries and eliminate jobs (Senate, Committee on Indian Affairs, *Survey of Conditions of the Indians in the United States, Part 36: Alaska*, 74th Cong., 2d sess., 1939, 19753).

35. William Paul, Jr. to Charles A. Wheeler, July 13, 1942, AHL, Curry-Weissbrodt Papers, MS-43, roll 5.

36. Alaska Fishermen's Cooperative Association charter, May 31, 1940, AHL, Curry-Weissbrodt Papers, MS-43, roll 5.

37. The AFCA and the plant units forged marketing agreements with the cannery operators according to which minimum fish prices were set, nonaffiliated fishermen were to be limited in what they could sell to the cannery, and the company was to deduct $10 from each employee's or fisherman's earnings, with half paid to the AFCA and half to the plant unit (Marketing Agreement [blank], AHL, Curry-Weissbrodt Papers, MS-43, roll 5).

38. Resolution No. 16, November 15, 1941, 28th Annual Convention of the ANB/ANS, University of Washington (hereafter cited as UW), William L. Paul Papers, MS 2076–2, roll 1.

39. Resolution No. 15, November 11, 1943, 30th Annual Convention of the ANB/ANS, and William L. Paul to Executive Committee, February 11, 1944, UW, William L. Paul Papers, MS 2076–2, roll 1.

40. Drucker, *Native Brotherhoods*, 58; Pat Conover, "Alaska's Fishing Industry," *Alaska Life* 10, 2 (1947): 6–7, 28–31; William L. Paul to James Curry, March 10, 1948, AHL, Curry-Weissbrodt Papers, MS-43, roll 5.

41. Charles W. Smythe, "Tlingit and Haida Tribal Status: A Report of the Central Council of the Tlingit and Haida Indian Tribes of Alaska," February 1989, report at ARO, p. 6.

42. A. E. Demaray to John Collier, May 2, 1939, NAPSR, RG 79, Western Region, CCF, box 294, file 602.

43. Frank T. Been to Director, January 4, 1940, NAPSR, RG 79, Western Region, CCF, box 294, file 610.

44. William Zimmerman, Jr. to Claude M. Hirst, July 7, 1939, NAAR, RG 75, Alaska Reindeer Service, box 64, file Hunting, Fishing, and Fur Farming.

45. All these communications are referenced in two letters: Charles W. Hawkesworth to Frank T. Been, November 29, 1939, NAAR, RG 75, Alaska Reindeer Service, box 64, file Hunting, Fishing, and Fur Farming; and Arno B. Cammerer to Frank T. Been, December 1, 1939, NA, RG 79, CCF, box 2228, file 208.06. The latter also referenced a radiogram of October 19, approved by acting Assistant Secretary Finch, which followed the meeting in Zimmerman's office.

46. Arno B. Cammerer to Frank T. Been, December 1, 1939, NA, RG 79, CCF, box 2228, file 208.06.

47. Horace Ibach to Frank T. Been, January 9, 1940, NA, RG 79, CCF, box 2228, file 208.06; William Horsman to Frank T. Been, May 8, 1940, NAPSR, RG 79, Western Region, CCF, box 294, file 610.

48. Memorandum for the Director, April 9, 1940, NAPSR, RG 79, Western Region, CCF, box 293, file 208.

49. William E. Warne to Acting Commissioner (BIA), Director (Division of Territories and Island Possessions), Director (FWS), and Director (NPS), June 11, 1948, and Grant H. Pearson to Regional Director, September 16, 1948, NAPSR, RG 79, Western Region, CCF, box 293, file 208.

50. Goldschmidt and Haas, "Possessory Rights," Section D, 4–7, 16.

51. Statement of Mrs. Lonnie Houston, Mrs. Oscar Williams, and Mrs. Eliza

Lawrence, AHL, Curry-Weissbrodt Papers, MS-43, roll 20. The name Wright was apparently in error. The man was probably Stanley "Buck" Harbeson.

52. William E. Warne to Commissioner of Indian Affairs et al., June 11, 1948, NAPSR, RG 79, Western Region, CCF, box 293, file 208.

53. Quoted in Frank T. Been to Director, January 4, 1940, NAPSR, RG 79, Western Region, CCF, box 294, file 610.

54. C. P. Russell to Director, April 9, 1940, NAPSR, RG 79, Western Region, CCF, box 294, file 610.

55. William Horsman to Frank T. Been, May 8, 1940, NAPSR, RG 79, Western Region, CCF, box 294, file 610. The white community in Dundas Bay consisted of Mr. and Mrs. William Horsman, Mr. and Mrs. Horace Ibach, and Buck Harbeson. The Horsmans lived in a neat cabin and made their living by trapping and prospecting. William Horsman, alias "Doc Silvers," was a World War I veteran and former boxing champion who had settled in Dundas Bay in the late 1920s on a grubstake from a Juneau merchant named Mrs. Gornick. Together they had some thirty-nine claims on the Dundas River. Buck Harbeson lived on the opposite shore of the bay from the Horsmans. He mainly trapped for a living. Formerly a soldier in Horsman's unit during World War I, he came to Dundas Bay in the early 1930s to work on Horsman's mining claims but decided he preferred hunting and trapping. The Ibachs lived in the abandoned cannery at the entrance to Dundas Bay. According to Horace Ibach, he and Harbeson were "partners," but Harbeson denied it. The Ibachs were evicted from the cannery and left Dundas Bay in 1942. The Horsmans left about the same time and later received a $3,000 settlement from the United States government. Harbeson remained until some time after World War II. The best profile of this community is in Earl A. Trager, "Glacier Bay Expedition, 1939," NAPSR, RG 79, Western Region, CCF, box 292.

56. M. L. McSpadden to O. A. Tomlinson, February 19, 1945, NAPSR, RG 79, Western Region, CCF, box 292, file Glacier Bay and Sitka. Ironically, Harbeson does not seem to have been too law-abiding himself. He told Been and Trager in 1939 that he had trapped in the area for several years, yet his name does not appear on a list of trapping permit applicants in the Icy Strait area for 1937–38. Moreover, on Been's return visit in 1940, Harbeson avoided him and Been found evidence at his cabin that he had been poaching bears (Been field notes, July 28, 1940, DENA, William E. Brown Historical Files).

57. Grant Pearson to Regional Director, September 16, 1948, NAPSR, RG 79, Western Region, CCF, box 293, file 208.

58. Don C. Foster to Secretary Ickes, January 29, 1946, and Don C. Foster to William Zimmerman, Jr., January 30, 1946, NAAR, RG 75, Juneau Area Office, GSC, box 37, file 920 Hunting, Fishing, and Fur Farming.

59. Jack O'Connor to O. A. Tomlinson, March 17, 1948, NAPSR, RG 79, Western Region, CCF, box 293, file 208.

60. Don C. Foster to Secretary Ickes, January 29, 1946, NAAR, RG 75, Juneau

Area Office, GSC, box 37, file 920 Hunting, Fishing, and Fur Farming; Statement by Frank Sinclair, September 20, 1946, NA, RG 79, CCF, box 2228, file 208.06.

61. Goldschmidt and Haas, "Possessory Rights," section D, 4.

62. The legal-political context of "possessory rights" in Southeast Alaska may be briefly related. Commissioner of Indian Affairs Collier and Secretary Ickes were concerned about the growing pressure on the Tlingits' and Haidas' salmon fisheries. The Alaska Reorganization Act of 1936 gave the secretary of the interior the authority to establish Indian reservations in Alaska, but Collier and Ickes hesitated to use this authority for fear of white backlash in Southeast Alaska. Then a Supreme Court decision in *United States v. Santa Fe Pacific Railroad Company* in December 1941 conveniently redefined Indian aboriginal rights. The court decided that (1) aboriginal occupancy established rights of possession, (2) possessory rights need not be based on treaty or statute, and (3) extinguishment of possessory rights might not be inferred from general legislation or from administrative action. On the basis of this decision, solicitor Nathan R. Margold of the Department of the Interior issued an opinion on February 13, 1942, which held that Alaska native possessory rights had never been extinguished by the United States, and that regulations permitting control of such areas by non-natives were unauthorized and illegal. The first change in policy to result from the solicitor's opinion was a revision of fishing regulations for the territory, promulgated on March 13, 1942. This prohibited the establishment of any new fish traps where natives had possessory rights and allowed natives to petition for a hearing where non-native fishermen had occupied their aboriginal fishing grounds. The Tlingits and Haidas of Klawock, Kake, and Hydaburg petitioned for hearings in the summer of 1944. As the combined claims of these three villages affected 3,329,000 acres and posed a threat not only to non-native fishermen but also to white Alaskans' hopes for a pulpwood industry on the Tongass National Forest, the case generated wide concern as a harbinger of the disposition of other native claims. The public's interest had already been pricked by the establishment of a large Indian reservation north of the Arctic Circle in 1943 and the disclosure in 1944 of proposals for some twenty-eight smaller reservations that would total 6,581,048 acres. White Alaskans were upset even though (to put the native claims in perspective) one BIA official estimated that a decision in favor of the entire claim would affect no more than 10 percent of Alaska's $50,000,000 fishing industry. Judge Richard H. Hanna presided over the hearings in Klawock, Kake, and Hydaburg on September 15–20, 1944. He ruled in favor of the Tlingit villages but sharply reduced their total claim to 275,000 acres. On June 10, 1946 the Department of the Interior invited more petitions from native villages by promulgating "Rules of Procedure for Hearings upon Possessory Claims to Lands and Waters Used and Occupied by Natives of Alaska." It was in anticipation of more claims that the department commissioned Goldschmidt and Haas to make a study of the possessory rights of Tlingit groups in Southeast Alaska (William Zimmerman, Jr. to William E. Warne, July 21, 1947, NAAR, RG 95, Regional Forester Juneau, Historical Records 1915–

62, box 2, file Alaska Native Reservations; Department of the Interior, *Opinions of the Solicitor of the Department of the Interior Relating to Indian Affairs 1917–1974*, vol.1 [Washington, D.C.: Government Printing Office, n.d.], 1096; "Hearings on Claims of Natives of the Towns of Hydaburg, Klawock, and Kake, Alaska, Pursuant to the Provisions of Section 201.21b of the Regulations for Protection of Commercial Fisheries of Alaska, 1944," UW, Viola Garfield Papers, MS 2027–72–25, box 5, file 16; Robert E. Price, *The Great Father in Alaska: The Case of the Tlingit and Haida Salmon Fishery* [Douglas, Alaska: First Street Press, 1907], 111; Kyle Crichton, "Storm Over Alaska," *Collier's*, March 31, 1945, 75; Case, *Alaska Natives*, 10–12, 101–2).

63. Jackson E. Price to Newton B. Drury and Hillory Tolson, February 6, 1947, NA, RG 79, CCF, box 2229, file 610 Indian Lands—Glacier Bay.

64. NAPSR, RG 79, Western Region, CCF, box 293, file 208. Assistant Director Hillory Tolson summarized the agreement for Ruth M. Bronson of the National Congress of American Indians as follows: "For many years, the natives have been permitted to hunt hair seals while in the waters of the national monument, and from vantage points on land within 100 feet of the water. Permission was also granted on January 7, 1947, for the natives to carry rifles having a bore not smaller than .30 caliber for the purpose of self-protection while engaged in picking berries within appropriate localities in the Monument *[sic]*" (Letter dated March 14, 1947, NAPSR, RG 79, Western Region, CCF, box 293, file 208).

65. O. A. Tomlinson to Newton B. Drury, February 3, 1947, NAPSR, RG 79, Western Region, CCF, box 293, file 208.

66. O. A. Tomlinson to Newton B. Drury, August 13, 1947, NAPSR, RG 79, Western Region, CCF, box 293, file 208.

67. Lowell Sumner, "Special Report on the Hunting Rights of the Hoonah Natives in Glacier Bay National Monument," August 5, 1947, NA, RG 79, CCF, box 2228, file 208.06, pp. 1, 10, 8.

68. Hoonah native Frank Sinclair's statement on wolves is of interest: "The coyotes and wolves have killed all of the foxes and are killing the mountain goats. There are very few mountain goats left. In two cases during the last few years we have seen wolves and coyotes kill twelve mountain goats at one time and two mountain goats at another time. The wolves spot the mountain goats on the ridge and wait for them to come up the ridge and push them over the steep cliffs from the side, and then go down below to feed on their carcasses" (September 20, 1946, NA, RG 79, CCF, box 2228, file 208.06, part 1). Investigation into this unusual ecological relationship in a later period resulted in James L. Fox and Gregory P. Streveler, "Wolf Predation on Mountain Goats in Southeastern Alaska," *Journal of Mammalogy* 67, 1 (1986): 192–95.

69. Sumner, "Special Report," NA, p. 7.

70. Region Four Staff Meeting Minutes, July 8, 1947, NAPSR, RG 79, Western Region, CCF, box 7, file 1-1-46–1-1-48, part 8. The proposed closures were taken up with the FWS in Washington but were not implemented (Hillory A. Tolson to

Regional Director, January 30, 1948, NAPSR, RG 79, Western Region, CCF, Box 293, File 208).

71. Sumner, "Special Report," NA.

72. Ibid.

73. Hillory A. Tolson to Regional Director, January 30, 1948, NAPSR, RG 79, Western Region, CCF, box 293, file 208. To ensure that rifles were carried on shore for the express purpose of seal hunting and protection against bears only, Drury made 30.06 rifles the minimum gauge permitted on January 7, 1947.

74. Victor Cahalane, "The Evolution of Predator Control Policy in the National Parks," *Journal of Wildlife Management* 3, 3 (1939): 235–36.

75. Adolph Murie, *The Wolves of Mount McKinley*, National Park Service Fauna Series No. 5 (Washington, D.C.: National Park Service, 1944).

76. O. A. Tomlinson to Newton B. Drury, April 12, 1950, NAPSR, RG 79, Western Region, CCF, box 293, file 201.

77. Lowell Sumner to O. A. Tomlinson, October 13, 1950, NAPSR, RG 79, Western Region, CCF, box 292, file 207.

78. Duane Jacobs, "Report of Special Assignment at Glacier Bay National Monument 1950 Season," NAPSR, RG 79, Western Region, CCF, box 293, file 201. FWS wardens had authority to search boats for Game Law violations in Alaskan waters without a warrant, but Jacobs was not sure that park rangers had this authority.

79. Ibid., 8–9.

80. Oscar T. Dick to Ben C. Miller, October 30, 1951, NAPSR, RG 79, Western Region, CCF, box 293, file 201; Ben C. Miller to Regional Director, October 2, 1951, NAPSR, RG 79, Western Region, CCF, box 293, file 208.

81. Bruce W. Black to Superintendent, October 15, 1953, NAPSR, RG 79, Western Region, CSF, N-16, box 3. Black cites a memorandum from Conrad L. Wirth of November 9, 1951.

82. Henry G. Schmidt to Regional Director, November 26, 1953, NAPSR, RG 79, Western Region, CSF, N-16, box 3.

83. The details of the new BIA-NPS agreement and the permit system are discussed in Superintendent to Regional Director, March 1, 1954, GLBA, Administrative Files, file N1619.

CHAPTER 3

1. Superintendent to Director, November 5, 1963, and David B. Butts to Superintendent, March 27, 1964, SITK, Superintendent's Monthly Reports; "A Special Report Containing Information Required for Legislation to Redesignate Glacier Bay as a National Park," September 1964, NAAR, RG 79, 79–91–0001, box 3/9, file GLBA Administrative History, 1938–70.

2. Chief Ranger to Superintendent, June 22, 1964, GLBA, Administrative Files, file N1619.

3. "Special Report," NAAR.

4. Runte, *National Parks,* 183.

5. Stewart L. Udall, "Nature Islands for the World," in *First World Conference on National Parks,* edited by Alexander B. Adams (Washington, D.C.: Government Printing Office, 1963), 7.

6. The preamble of the Presidential Proclamation of 26 February 1925 declares in part, "And Whereas, This area presents a unique opportunity for the scientific study of glacial behavior and of resulting movements and developments of flora and fauna and of certain valuable relics of ancient interglacial forests . . . ."

7. Alston Chase, *Playing God in Yellowstone: The Destruction of America's First National Park* (Boston: Atlantic Monthly Press, 1986), 33–34.

8. A. Starker Leopold et al., "Wildlife Management in the National Parks," *The Living Wilderness,* Spring–Summer 1963, 13. The Leopold Report was printed in various conservation magazines with slight editorial variations.

9. Ibid. Earlier statements of this idea can be found in Joseph Grinnell and Tracy L. Storer, "Animal Life as an Asset of National Parks," *Science News Supplement,* September 15, 1916, 376–77; George Wright, Joseph Dixon, and Ben Thompson, *Fauna of the National Parks of the United States,* National Park Service Fauna Series No. 1 (Washington, D.C.: National Park Service, 1932). Grinnell and Storer wrote, "Herein lies the feature of supreme value in national parks: they furnish samples of the earth as it was before the advent of the white man." Wright, Dixon, and Thompson wrote, "The American people intrusted the National Park Service with the preservation of characteristic portions of our country as it was seen by Boone and La Salle, by Coronado, and by Lewis and Clark. This was primitive America, and it was to be kept for the observation of the recreation-seeking public and scientists of to-day, and their descendants in the generations of to-morrow."

10. Leopold et al., "Wildlife Management," 16.

11. Gregory P. Streveler and Bruce Paige, *The Natural History of Glacier Bay National Monument, Alaska* (Report prepared for the National Park Service, 1971), 2.

12. Park Ranger John W. Fisher speculated on possible correlations between the numbers of wolf, coyote, and Sitka deer in his annual wildlife report of 1962. The annual wildlife report for 1967 stated: "The need for a general study of mammal distribution and population is becoming increasingly important. It is not that Glacier Bay species require management but rather that future studies must be based on such information. These basic investigations should be conducted while the Monument is still relatively free of human interference. Also, with Glacier Bay's rapidly changing environment, the comparison of present conditions with those which might be uncovered in future studies would be of incalculable value" (GLBA, Administrative Files, file N2621).

13. Superintendent to Director, August 13, 1962, and June 6, 1963, SITK, Superintendent's Monthly Reports.

14. David B. Butts to Superintendent, March 27, 1964, and June 3, 1964, GLBA, Administrative Files, file N1619.

15. Charles V. Janda to L. J. Mitchell, June 18, 1965, GLBA, Administrative Files, file N1619.

16. Seal Hunting—Glacier Bay, [1966], GLBA, Administrative Files, file N1619.

17. Ibid.

18. Ibid.

19. Ibid.

20. In recent years some NPS officials have raised the same point with reference to current management issues. The effects of hunting versus wildlife viewing on brown bear behavior and ecology in Katmai National Park and their implications for park managers in defining what is natural are discussed in Ted Birkedal, "Ancient Hunters in the Alaskan Wilderness: Human Predators and Their Role and Effect on Wildlife Populations and the Implications for Resource Management" (paper presented at Seventh George Wright Society Meeting, Jacksonville, Florida, 1992).

21. David B. Butts to Superintendent, March 27, 1964, GLBA, Administrative Files, file N1619.

22. Douglas B. Houston, "Ecosystems of National Parks," *Science*, May 14, 1971, 648–51.

23. Master Plan Development Outline, Glacier Bay National Monument, Alaska [1957], GLBA, Administrative Files, file D18.

24. For example, Robert E. Howe to District Director, October 6, 1969, GLBA, Administrative Files, file N1619.

25. Oscar T. Dick to Ben C. Miller, October 30, 1951, NAPSR, RG 79, Western Region, CCF, box 293, file 201.

26. Bruce W. Black, "A History of Glacier Bay National Monument, Alaska," 1957, typescript at GLBA, Library, p. 84.

27. "Hair Seal Hunting by Indians of Hoonah, Alaska in Glacier Bay National Monument," [1966], GLBA, Administrative Files, file N1619, p. 2.

28. Schroeder and Kookesh, *Subsistence Harvest*, 220–21, 226, 257.

29. Gregory P. Streveler, interview with author, tape recording, April 8, 1992.

30. David B. Butts to Superintendent, March 27, 1964, GLBA, Administrative Files, file N1619.

31. Individual Offense Report, February 12, 1969, GLBA, Administrative Files, file N1619. Kenneth Schoonover's name appears on the land claim census roll for Hoonah in AHL, Curry-Weissbrodt Papers, MS-43, roll 17.

32. Robert E. Howe, interview with author, tape recording, April 4, 1992.

33. "Special Report," NAAR.

34. Robert E. Howe to District Director, October 6, 1969, GLBA, Administrative Files, file N1619.

35. Wolf and Company, "A Development Planning Program for the Central Council of the Tlingit and Haida Indians of Alaska," AHL, Curry-Weissbrodt Papers, MS-43, roll 18.

36. The natives' request for a hearing in Hoonah is noted in Commissioner of Indian Affairs to Director, January 12, 1965, GLBA, Administrative Files, file N1619. Acting Director Howard W. Baker informed the commissioner that the NPS was temporarily suspending action to terminate seal hunting and would resume issuance of permits (March 29, 1965, ibid.), but I found no evidence of a hearing.

37. "Hair Seal Hunting," GLBA.

38. David B. Butts to Superintendent, June 3, 1964, GLBA, Administrative Files, file N1619.

39. Two natives of Hoonah whom I interviewed offered conflicting opinions on the subject of native hunting and waste. Mayor Al Dick said that elders normally accompany groups on subsistence fishing and gathering expeditions and guard against overharvesting, but since hunting is unsupervised in this manner, wasteful practices by younger natives are known to occur. Mary Rudolph insisted that no waste occurs — that when young people take more than they and their families can consume they give meat to the elders or to others. Reports to the contrary, she said, come from outsiders who do not understand this. The photographic documentation from the 1963 hunt provides positive proof, however, that in that particular instance many seals were killed for their skins alone.

40. Charles V. Janda to Superintendent, October 3, 1969, and Robert E. Howe to Regional Director, January 26, 1970, GLBA, Administrative Files, file N1619.

41. Jack Calvin, "Two Seal Hunters," *Alaska Sportsman*, May 1964, 30.

42. Hair Seal Bounties Paid to Persons Claiming Residence in Hoonah, Alaska — Calendar Year 1963, GLBA, Administrative Files, file N1619.

43. Superintendent to Director, August 5, 1963, SITK, Superintendent's Monthly Reports; David B. Butts to Superintendent, June 22, 1964, GLBA, Administrative Files, file N1619; photographic documentation of the carcasses was included in "Special Report," NAAR.

44. David B. Butts to Superintendent, April 7, 1964, GLBA, Administrative Files, file N1619.

45. Robert E. Howe to Assistant Director of Operations, July 11, 1966, GLBA, Administrative Files, file N1619.

46. Robert G. Bosworth, "Tlingit Subsistence in Glacier Bay, Alaska: Adapting to Change in Landscape and Bureaucracy" (paper presented at the Alaska Anthropological Association Meeting, Anchorage, Alaska, March 1989; Schroeder and Kookesh, *Subsistence Harvest*, 218; Robert E. Howe, interview with author, tape recording, April 4, 1992; Albert Dick, interview with author, tape recording, April 10, 1992; Amy Marvin and Mary Rudolph, interview with author, tape recording, April 10, 1992. None of these sources could establish a firm date. Bosworth places the incident in the early 1970s; Schroeder and Kookesh, in 1966 or 1967. Nor is it clear on what grounds the NPS confiscated the natives' guns.

47. Individual Offense Report CR 1–69, GLBA, Administrative Files, file N1619.

48. Robert E. Howe to Regional Director, November 9, 1966, GLBA, Administrative Files, file N1619.

49. Raymond O. Mulvany to Director, December 2, 1966, GLBA, Administrative Files, file N1619.

50. Robert E. Howe to District Director, October 6, 1969, GLBA, Administrative Files, file N-1619. The Howe references are undated, unrecorded telephone communications with the Washington, D.C., office based on his memorandum of July 11, 1966.

51. Robert E. Howe to District Director, October 6, 1969, GLBA, Administrative Files, file N1619.

52. John Borbridge, Jr., "Native Organization and Land Rights as Vehicle for Change," in *Change in Alaska: People, Petroleum, and Politics* (College, Alaska: University of Alaska Press, 1970), 197; Alexander M. Erwin, "The Emergence of Native Alaskan Political Capacity, 1959–1971," *The Musk Ox* 19, 2 (1976): 8.

53. *Anchorage Daily News*, March 21, 1969; Mary Clay Berry, *The Alaska Pipeline: The Politics of Oil and Native Land Claims* (Bloomington, Indiana: Indiana University Press, 1975), 49.

54. 177 F. Supp. 452.

55. 389 F. 2d 778 (1968).

56. Thomas R. Berger, *Village Journey: The Report of the Alaska Native Review Commission* (New York: Hill and Wang, 1985), 23.

57. 85 Stat. 688.

58. Wyman Bautzer et al., attorneys for Alaska Federation of Natives, "A Fair Settlement of the Alaska Native Land Claims; the Key Elements," March 11, 1971, UW, Lloyd Meeds Papers, MS 2900–77–023, box 33, file Alaska Native Claims.

59. Don Wright (AFN) to Lloyd Meeds, November 16, 1971, and Don Wright to Congressman Edmondson, [December 1971], UW, Lloyd Meeds Papers, MS 2900–77–023, box 33, file Alaska Native Claims.

60. Memo to Members, House-Senate Conference on Alaska Native Claims from Bill Van Ness, Chief Counsel, Senate Interior and Insular Affairs Committee, December 6, 1971, UW, Lloyd Meeds Papers, MS 2900–77–023, box 33, file Alaska Native Claims.

61. House, Interior and Insular Affairs Committee, *Alaska Native Claims Settlement Act Conference Report*, 92d Cong., 1st sess., December 13, 1971, Committee Print 92–746, 37.

62. Superintendent to Regional Director, February 29, 1972, GLBA, Administrative Files, file N1619.

63. Charles V. Janda to Mayor Frank See, April 2, 1974, GLBA, Administrative Files, file N1619.

64. Bosworth, "Tlingit Subsistence," contains appended "Note Regarding the 1965 Solicitor's Opinion."

65. Memo to Members, House-Senate Conference on Alaska Native Claims from Bill Van Ness, Chief Counsel, Senate Interior and Insular Affairs Committee, December 6, 1971, UW, Lloyd Meeds Papers, MS 2900–77–023, box 33, file Alaska Native Claims.

66. *Congressional Record,* 1972, vol. 118, p. 17613.

67. Ibid., p. 25261.

68. Senate, Committee on Commerce, Subcommittee on Oceans and Atmosphere, *Ocean Mammal Protection, Part 2,* 92d Cong., 2d sess., May 11–13, 1972, passim.

69. 86 Stat. 1031.

70. Superintendent to State Director, October 26, 1972, GLBA, Administrative Files, file N1619.

71. Bob Howe to Files, November 14, 1972, GLBA, Administrative Files, file N1619.

CHAPTER 4

1. Mount McKinley National Park was renamed Denali National Park and Preserve in 1980. The mountain retains the name Mount McKinley. Throughout this and the next chapter, the contemporary name for the park is used.

2. Joseph S. Dixon, *Birds and Mammals of Mount McKinley National Park, Alaska,* National Park Service Fauna Series No. 3 (Washington, D.C.: National Park Service, 1938), 7.

3. Stephen R. Capps, "The Kantishna Region, Alaska," *United States Geological Survey Bulletin 687* (Washington, D.C.: Government Printing Office, 1919), 10–11.

4. Robert A. McKennan, "Tanana," in *Subarctic,* vol. 6 of *Handbook of North American Indians,* edited by June Helm (Washington, D.C.: Smithsonian Institution, 1981), 568.

5. James W. Vanstone, *Athapaskan Adaptations: Hunters and Fishermen of the Subarctic Forests* (Arlington Heights, Ill.: Harlan Davidson, Inc., 1974), 43–50, 121–26.

6. The reasons for the population movement to the rivers included trade incentives and new technology, such as the fish wheel, which led to a greater emphasis on fishing over hunting in the Athapaskan Indians' seasonal rounds. The interior of Alaska was also considerably depopulated by epidemics (James W. Vanstone, "Ingalik Contact Ecology: An Ethnohistory of the Lower-Middle Yukon, 1790–1935," in *Fieldiana: Anthropology,* vol. 71 (Chicago, Field Museum of Natural History, 1979), 168–74.

7. Nenana (Lower Tanana) Indians claimed sheep hunting grounds at the head of the Toklat and Teklanika Rivers, in what would become Mount McKinley National Park, according to a report in the *Fairbanks Daily News-Miner* (March 25, 1908). Also see Dianne Gudgel-Holmes, *Ethnohistory of Four Interior Alaskan Waterbodies,* (Anchorage: State of Alaska Department of Natural Resources, 1979), 92.

8. William E. Brown, *A History of the Denali-Mount McKinley Region, Alaska: Historic Resource Study of Denali National Park and Preserve* (Santa Fe: National Park Service, 1991), 13–16.

9. Ibid., 17.

10. Conservationists generally favored the use or restoration of original Indian

names for landforms because they reinforced the purpose of national parks in preserving a distinctively American heritage. Early advocates of the name change included Hudson Stuck, who made the first successful ascent of Mount McKinley in 1913, and Charles Sheldon, who led the national park campaign.

11. Roderick Nash, "Tourism, Parks, and the Wilderness Idea in the History of Alaska," *Alaska in Perspective* 4, 1 (1981): 11.

12. Charles Sheldon, *The Wilderness of Denali* (New York, Charles Scribner's Sons, 1930), 4.

13. Tappan Adney, "The Sledge Dogs of the North," *Outing* 38, 1 (April 1901): 129–37.

14. Frank E. Buske, "The Wilderness, the Frontier and the Literature of Alaska to 1914: John Muir, Jack London, and Rex Beach" (Ph.D. diss., University of California, Davis, 1976).

15. John F. Reiger, *American Sportsmen and the Origins of Conservation*, rev. ed. (Norman: Oklahoma University Press, 1986). On the Boone and Crockett Club, see James B. Trefethen, *An American Crusade for Wildlife* (New York: Winchester Press, 1975). Thomas R. Dunlap, *Saving America's Wildlife* (Princeton: Princeton University Press, 1988) discusses how changing ideas about animal nature also increased popular interest in wildlife around the turn of the century.

16. Madison Grant, "The Condition of Wild Life in Alaska," in *Smithsonian Report 1909* (Washington, D.C.: Government Printing Office, 1910), 522.

17. George Bird Grinnell to George A. Lawyer, October 17, 1922, NA, RG 22, entry 162, box 21.

18. Stephen Fox, *The American Conservation Movement: John Muir and his Legacy* (Boston: Little, Brown and Company, 1970), 347–48.

19. George Bird Grinnell, *The Last of the Buffalo* (New York: Charles Scribner's Sons, 1892), 281. Also see Caspar Whitney, George Bird Grinnell, and Owen Wister, *Musk-Ox, Bison, Sheep and Goat* (New York: Macmillan Company, 1904).

20. Grinnell, quoted in Dunlap, *Saving America's Wildlife*, 7. Ironically, the anti-conservationist Alaskan writer, Rex Beach, picked up on this theme as well. In his novel about the construction of Alaska's first railroad, *The Iron Trail* (New York: Harper and Brothers, 1913), the railroad builder and hero of the tale, Murray O'Neil, declares that if conservation had been applied in the Midwest as it was now being applied in Alaska, "buffalo would still be king of the plains and Chicago would be a frontier town" (193).

21. Ernest Thompson Seton, *The Arctic Prairies* (New York: Charles Scribner's Sons, 1911), xv.

22. Reiger, *American Sportsmen*, 28–29.

23. Thomas R. Dunlap, "Sport Hunting and Conservation, 1880–1920," *Environmental Review* 12, 1 (Spring 1988): 51–60.

24. Grant, "Condition," 523.

25. Ibid.

26. Charles Sheldon, "Big Game in Chihuahua," in *Hunting and Conservation*,

edited by George Bird Grinnell and Charles Sheldon (New Haven: Yale University Press, 1925), 181.

27. Madison Grant, "The Condition of Wild Life in Alaska," rev. ed., in *Hunting in High Altitudes: The Book of the Boone and Crockett Club*, edited by George Bird Grinnell (New York: Harper and Brothers, 1913), 371–72.

28. Senate, Committee on Territories, *A Bill to Establish Mount McKinley National Park, in the Territory of Alaska*, 64th Cong., 1st sess., 1916, 12.

29. Alfred H. Brooks, "An Exploration of Mount McKinley, America's Highest Mountain," in *Smithsonian Report* (Washington, D.C.: Government Printing Office, 1904), 418.

30. Alfred H. Brooks, "The Mount McKinley Region, Alaska," *U.S. Geological Survey Professional Paper 70* (Washington, D.C.: Government Printing Office, 1911), 213.

31. The book was based on his journals and was published posthumously in 1930.

32. "A Sportsman's Paradise," *Alaska-Yukon Magazine* 7, 4 (January 1909): 285–86 (based on an interview with Harry Karstens).

33. Stephen R. Capps, "A Game Country Without Rival," *National Geographic*, January 1917, 77–82.

34. Dixon, *Birds and Mammals*, 1–4, 10–14.

35. Madison Grant, "The Establishment of Mount McKinley National Park," in *Hunting and Conservation*, edited by George Bird Grinnell and Charles Sheldon (1925; New York: Arno Press, Inc., 1970), 439.

36. Later, Sheldon would make the same argument in favor of reforming the Alaska Game Law. He supported the Alaska Game Law of 1924, which was widely seen as a watershed in Alaska wildlife conservation.

37. Grant, "Condition," rev. ed., 386.

38. Ibid., 375, 386.

39. House, Committee on the Territories, *To Regulate the Killing and Sale of Certain Game Animals in Northern Alaska Hearing on H.R. 7344*, 65th Cong., 2d sess., 1918, 19.

40. Charles Sheldon to Stephen T. Mather, March 26, 1919, NA, RG 79, CCF, box 112, folder Wild Animals.

41. *Fairbanks Daily News-Miner*, October 4, 1912.

42. Ibid., November 26, 1907.

43. Ibid., March 24, 1909.

44. Ibid., October 17, 1912.

45. The Alaska Game Law of 1902, which Alaskans believed had been foisted upon the territory by eastern sportsmen's clubs, baldly stated that nothing in the act was to be construed "to prevent the collection of specimens for scientific purposes, the capture or shipment of live animals and birds for exhibition or propagation, or the export from Alaska of specimens and trophies" (32 Stat. 328). The revised Alaska Game Law of 1908 barely cinched up this loophole, merely dropping trophies from the list of exceptions (35 Stat. 105).

Not without reason, Alaskans came to regard the collecting of biological specimens with much cynicism; in their view it was a subterfuge commonly used by
wealthy sportsmen whose real desire was to bring back Alaskan big-game trophies.

46. Sheldon explained the unfortunate history of wildlife conservation in the
Mexican state of Chihuahua in terms of this model, too. "The game has been
destroyed exclusively by the unrestricted local hunters. No local protests of any kind
against the destruction were made. The fundamental reasons why this game has
been destroyed are that there has been no local sentiment to save it, and no local
Mexican sportsmen to arouse such sentiment. Mexican sportsmen, if such had existed, would have been the only class of men that would have formed this local
sentiment. Sportsmen have been the only class that have ever effectively aroused it
in the United States" (Sheldon, "Big Game," 181).

47. W. Brown, *History*, 102–4.

48. Ibid., 100. Annual reports of the governor of Alaska first discussed the need
for railroads in 1903. The governors typically began their reports by discussing the
inadequacies of Alaska's transportation infrastructure.

49. Richard Slotkin, *The Fatal Environment: The Myth of the Frontier in the Age of
Industrialization, 1800–1890* (New York: Athenaeum, 1985), 214–16.

50. Beach, *Iron Trail*, 280–91.

51. Alfred Runte, *Trains of Discovery: Western Railroads and the National Parks*, rev.
ed. (Niwot, Colo.: Robert Rinehart, 1990), passim.

52. Alfred Runte, "Pragmatic Alliance: Western Railroads and the National
Parks," *National Parks Magazine* 48, 4 (April 1974): 15–21.

53. Runte, quoted in Joan Lynne Specking, "The Alaska Railroad: Its Influence
on the Promotion of Tourism in Alaska" (Master's thesis, University of Washington, 1987), 35.

54. Robert Shankland, *Steve Mather of the National Parks* (New York: Alfred A.
Knopf, 1951), 134–35; Carlos A. Schwantes, "Tourists in Wonderland: Early Railroad Tourism in the Pacific Northwest," *Columbia: The Magazine of Northwest History* 7, 4 (Winter 1993–94): 25.

55. Grinnell, *Last of the Buffalo*, 281.

56. Whitney, Grinnell, and Wister, *Musk-Ox*, 113–14.

57. Charles Sheldon to E. W. Nelson, October 10, 1915, University of Alaska,
Fairbanks (hereafter cited as UAF), Charles Sheldon Papers, box 1, folder 6.

58. E. W. Nelson, "Charles Sheldon," *American Forests* 34 (November 1928): 659.

59. Charles Sheldon to E. W. Nelson, October 10, 1915, UAF, box 1, folder 6.
Sheldon wrote: "I shall try to win over the Alaska people first. . . . I believe that the
creating of a demand for this in Alaska will be the key to the whole problem and
perhaps I can assist in establishing this. . . . I am already [quietly] having some
favorable correspondence in Alaska about it." Besides Alaska's territorial delegate,
Judge James B. Wickersham, Sheldon's closest contact in Alaska at this time appears
to have been with the Fairbanks guide and packer Harry Karstens, whom he would
sponsor as the park's first superintendent a few years later.

60. Wickersham knew the Mount McKinley region first-hand. He had led a party of five in the first attempt to climb Mount McKinley in 1903, and had staked some claims on the Kantishna River on the way back, two years ahead of the Kantishna gold stampede.

61. Thomas Riggs, Jr. to Stephen T. Mather, December 17, 1915, and George O. Smith to Stephen T. Mather, January 6, 1916, NA, RG 79, CCF, box 111, folder Proposed National Parks.

62. Boundary revisions in the 1920s would marginally extend the park to the north and east, increasing its area to just over 3,000 square miles. The Denali National Park additions in 1980 more than doubled the park's total area.

63. Capps, "Kantishna Region," 75–76; L. M. Prindle, "The Bonnifield and Kantishna Regions," *U.S. Geological Survey Bulletin 314* (Washington, D.C.: Government Printing Office, 1907), 213–21.

64. *Congressional Record*, 1916, vol.53, pp. 6410, 6627; Grant, "The Establishment of Mount McKinley National Park," pp. 444, 522; Charles Sheldon to E. W. Nelson, February 26, 1916, UAF, Charles Sheldon Papers, box 3, folder 3.

65. Senate, Committee on Territories, *A Bill to Establish the Mount McKinley National Park, in the Territory of Alaska*, 64th Cong., 1st sess., 1916, 13–16.

66. 39 Stat. 938.

67. Senate, Committee on Territories, *A Bill to Establish the Mount McKinley National Park, in the Territory of Alaska*, 64th Cong., 1st sess., 1916, 6. On Browne, see Michael S. Kennedy, "Belmore Browne and Alaska," *Alaska Journal* 3, 2 (Spring 1973): 96–104.

68. Senate, Committee on Territories, *A Bill to Establish the Mount McKinley National Park, in the Territory of Alaska*, 64th Cong., 1st sess., 1916, 6, 10.

69. See, for example, the Alaska governor's tribute to the Alaskan prospector in Department of the Interior, *Report of the Governor of Alaska, 1916* (Washington, D.C.: Government Printing Office, 1916), 9. A similar and fuller portrait is Walter W. Atgood, "Prospecting in Alaska," *The University of Chicago Magazine* 3, 2 (December 1910): 53–57.

70. Senate, Committee on Territories, *A Bill to Establish the Mount McKinley National Park, in the Territory of Alaska*, 64th Cong., 1st sess., 1916, 9–10.

71. Ibid., 12.

72. Though Mather was the recognized head of the new service, technically he did not become its first director until Congress funded the new bureau in 1917. During the final stages of the campaign for Mount McKinley National Park, Mather's official title was Assistant to the Secretary, while R. B. Marshall continued as Superintendent of National Parks (Shankland, *Steve Mather*, 106).

73. Shankland, *Steve Mather*, 172.

74. Governor J. A. Strong to Secretary of the Interior, February 13, 1917, NA, RG 79, CCF, box 111, folder Proposed National Parks.

75. Stephen R. Capps to Stephen T. Mather, December 22, 1916, NA, RG 79, CCF, box 111, folder Proposed National Parks.

76. Capps, "Game Country," 77–82.

77. *Congressional Record*, 1917, vol. 54, p. 3629.

78. Grant, "Establishment," 444–45.

CHAPTER 5

1. Grant H. Pearson, *My Life of High Adventure* (Englewood Cliffs, New Jersey: Prentice Hall, Inc., 1962), 7.

2. Sheldon, *Wilderness*, 4; Hudson Stuck, *The Ascent of Denali (Mount McKinley): A Narrative of the First Complete Ascent of the Highest Peak in North America* (New York: Charles Scribner's Sons, 1914), 45; *Fairbanks Daily News-Miner*, September 3, 1907.

3. *Fairbanks Daily News-Miner*, September 20, 1907; "Sportsman's Paradise," 285.

4. Sheldon first recorded his idea of a national park in his wilderness journal in January 1908 (*Wilderness*, 272).

5. Charles Sheldon to E. W. Nelson, October 10, 1915, UAF, Charles Sheldon Papers, box 2, folder 2.

6. Harry Karstens to Horace M. Albright, July 25, 1918, NA, RG 79, Central Files, box 382.

7. Senate, *Supplemental Estimate of Appropriation, Mount McKinley National Park*, 64th Cong., 2d sess., S. Doc. 742, 1917, 2.

8. Harry Karstens to Charles Sheldon, April 25, 1920, UAF, Charles Sheldon Papers, box 1, folder 6.

9. Sheldon, *Wilderness*, 151. In 1924, Karstens estimated there were seventy-five dogs kept in the park. The number may have been higher a few years earlier (Harry Karstens to Stephen Mather, January 4, 1924, NA, RG 79, CCF, box 112, file Wild Animals).

10. Stephen T. Mather to Harry Karstens, April 12, 1921, NA, RG 79, CCF, box 110, file Instructions; Harry Karstens to Stephen T. Mather, April 23, 1921, and Mount McKinley National Parks Rules and Regulations, June 21, 1921, NA, RG 79, CCF, box 111, file Rules and Regulations.

11. Harry Karstens to Stephen T. Mather, January 4, 1924, NA, RG 79, CCF, box 112, file Wild Animals; D. E. Stubbs to Director, November 27, 1924, NA, RG 79, CCF, box 110, file Lands — General; C. Riddiford and P. L. Neil to Chief Inspector, June 29, 1925, NA, RG 79, CCF, box 110, file Employment — General.

12. O. J. Murie to E. W. Nelson, October 29, 1922, UAF, Olaus J. Murie Papers, box 4, file E. W. Nelson Correspondence.

13. Harry Karstens to Stephen Mather, January 4, 1924, NA, RG 79, CCF, box 112, file Wild Animals.

14. Extracts from monthly report from Superintendent Karstens for the month of February 1924, April 25, 1924, NA, RG 79, CCF, box 112, file Wild Animals.

15. Henry P. Karstens to the Director, November 18, 1924, and Arno B. Cammerer to Henry P. Karstens, December 23, 1924, NA, RG 79, CCF, box 112, file Wild Animals.

16. Harry Karstens to Scott C. Bone, February 5, 1924, NA, RG 79, CCF, box 112, file Wild Animals; Harry Karstens to Charles Sheldon, February 7, 1923, UAF, Charles Sheldon Papers, box 2, file 2.

17. Arno B. Cammerer to Secretary of the Interior, April 10, 1923, NA, RG 79, CCF, box 112, file Wild Animals.

18. Harry Karstens to Stephen Mather, January 4, 1924, NA, RG 79, CCF, box 112, file Wild Animals.

19. Minutes of National Parks Committee Meeting, April 17, 1923, Arno B. Cammerer to Stephen Mather, June 1, 1923, and Arno B. Cammerer to First Assistant Secretary, June 14, 1923, NA, RG 79, CCF, box 111, file Rules and Regulations; Arno B. Cammerer to the files, February 6, 1924, NA, RG 79, CCF, box 112, file Wild Animals.

20. Department of the Interior, *Report of the Director of the National Park Service* (Washington, D.C.: Government Printing Office, 1924), 11.

21. W. Brown, *History*, 149. Congress would finally close the park to mineral entry in 1976.

22. The history of the Kantishna mining district is covered in W. Brown, *History*. Contemporary accounts of the increased activity in the early 1920s include B. D. Stewart, *Annual Report of the Mine Inspector to the Governor of Alaska, 1922* (Washington, D.C.: Government Printing Office, 1922), 118–19; "Mt. McKinley Mining People in Seattle in the Interest of Big Placer Project," *Alaska and the Northwest Mining Journal* 13, 9 (September 1919): 21–22; Pearson, *My Life*, 48–49, 54–55.

23. Senate, *Mount McKinley National Park, Territory of Alaska*, 64th Cong., 1st sess., S. Rept. 440, 1916, 2.

24. The estimation of the actual effect of the Kantishna miners on Mount McKinley's wildlife populations was largely conjectural, as the NPS did not begin aerial game counts until 1930. At that time, estimates of the number of Dall sheep and caribou in the park were adjusted upward. Even if the park staff were correct in their estimation that the game populations were declining through the effects of excessive hunting in the early 1920s, it must be said that the populations experienced much sharper declines in the 1930s for reasons that had nothing to do with hunting.

25. Joseph Sax, *Mountains Without Handrails: Reflections on the National Parks* (Ann Arbor: University of Michigan Press, 1986), 108.

26. Department of the Interior, *Report of the Director of the National Park Service* (Washington, D.C.: Government Printing Office, 1925), 2.

27. On frontier attitudes toward tourism, see Earl Pomeroy, *In Search of the Golden West: The Tourist in Western America* (New York: Alfred A. Knopf, Inc., 1957), 18.

28. Harry P. Karstens to Charles Sheldon, April 25, 1921, UAF, Charles Sheldon Papers, box 1, folder 6.

29. U.S. Army, *Annual Report of the Chief of Engineers, 1922*, Pt. 1 (Washington, D.C.: Government Printing Office, 1922), 2250; W. Brown, *History*, 110, 141.

30. Harry P. Karstens to Dan T. Kennedy, July 12, 1923, and Dan T. Kennedy to Harry P. Karstens, July 20, 1923, NA, RG 79, CCF, box 111, folder Annual Reports.

31. W. Brown, *History*, 155.

32. Frank Norris, *Gawking at the Midnight Sun: The Tourist in Early Alaska* (Anchorage: Alaska Historical Commission, 1985), 49, 107.

33. Stephen T. Mather to Secretary of the Interior, November 2, 1928, NA, RG 79, Records of Horace M. Albright 1927–33, box 6, folder Mount McKinley National Park. On the general phenomenon of early automobile tourism and the inexorable homogenization of roadside accommodations, see Warren James Belasco, *Americans on the Road: From Autocamp to Motel, 1910–1945* (Cambridge, Mass.: The MIT Press, 1979). Although the improving standards in Mount McKinley might be seen as part of a ubiquitous pattern, this only underscores why the NPS needed to take special care to preserve the national park's frontier qualities.

34. Norris, *Gawking*, 107.

35. Ibid.

36. Conrad L. Wirth to Harold P. Fabian, November 12, 1957, NAPSR, RG 79, Western Region, CSF, N-16, box 3, file Mount McKinley.

37. Department of the Interior, *Report of the Director of the National Park Service*, (Washington, D.C.: Government Printing Office, 1922), 23.

38. Harry P. Karstens to Stephen T. Mather, January 25, 1923, and D. E. Stubbs to Director, November 27, 1924, NA, RG 79, CCF, box 110, folder Lands General; C. Riddiford and P. L. Neil to the Chief Inspector, June 29, 1925, NA, RG 79, CCF, box 110, folder Employment — General.

39. Quoted in W. Brown, *History*, 180.

CHAPTER 6

1. Robert Marshall, *Arctic Village* (New York: Literary Guild, 1933), 3. The other "blank space" was southwest of Mount McKinley on the South Fork of the Kuskokwim River. Marshall chose the central Brooks Range because he was intrigued by the fact that it lay north of the Arctic Circle.

2. House, *Alaska — Its Resources and Development*, 75th Cong., 3d sess., H. Doc. 485, 1938, Appendix B, 213.

3. Fox, *American Conservation Movement*, 209.

4. Catherine Bauer, "Gap in the Front Lines," undated manuscript at Minnesota Historical Society (hereafter cited as MHS), Raphael Zon Papers, P1237, box 10.

5. Robert Marshall, *Alaska Wilderness: Exploring the Central Brooks Range*, 2d ed., edited with introduction by George Marshall (Berkeley: University of California Press, 1970), 7.

6. Robert Marshall, "The Problem of the Wilderness," *The Scientific Monthly* (February 1930): 141.

7. Robert Marshall to Family et al., September 23, 1930, MHS, Raphael Zon Papers, P1237, box 10.

8. R. Marshall, *Alaska Wilderness*, 3. The book was first published as *Arctic Wilderness* and retitled in the second edition.

9. James M. Glover, *A Wilderness Original: The Life of Bob Marshall* (Seattle: The Mountaineers, 1986), 231.

10. R. Marshall, "Problem," 142.

11. Ibid., 144. Roderick Nash points out the influence of Freudian psychology on Marshall's thought in "Tourism," 16.

12. Robert Marshall, "The Universe of the Wilderness is Vanishing," *Nature Magazine* 29, 4 (April 1937): 237–38.

13. House, *Alaska — Its Resources and Development*, 75th Cong., 3d sess., H. Doc. 485, 1938, Appendix B, 213.

14. R. Marshall, *Arctic Village*, 9.

15. Robert Marshall to Family et al., September 23, and October 6, 1930, MHS, Raphael Zon Papers, P1237, box 10; R. Marshall, *Arctic Village*, 5.

16. R. Marshall, *Arctic Village*, 285–96, 305.

17. Ibid., 376.

18. Ibid., 377.

19. Ibid., 378.

20. Ibid., 105.

21. James M. Glover, "Romance, Recreation, and Wilderness: Influences on the Life and Work of Bob Marshall," *Environmental History Review* 14, 4 (Winter 1990): 26–27.

22. R. Marshall, *Arctic Village*, 364–72.

23. Robert Marshall to Paul Gordon, December 8, 1937 and attachment, "The Development of Alaska Resources Should be Retarded," NA, RG 126, CCF, box 418, folder 9–1-60 Development of Resources, Federal Alaska Committee Reports. The four-page attachment was Marshall's working paper for his minority report and presented his ideas in more detail. Also of interest in this file is a two-page list of "Suggested Changes in Alaska Recreational Report" written by Marshall.

24. Marshall, "Development," NA.

25. House, *Alaska — Its Resources and Development*, 75th Cong., 3d sess., H. Doc. 485, 1938, Appendix B, 213.

26. R. Marshall, *Arctic Village*, 73.

27. Ibid., 74.

28. Alan S. Newell, Richmond L. Clow, and Richard N. Ellis, *A Forest in Trust: Three-Quarters of a Century of Indian Forestry, 1910–1985* (Washington, D.C.: Bureau of Indian Affairs, 1985), passim.

29. Robert Marshall, "Ecology and the Indians," *Ecology* 18, 1 (January 1937): 159–61.

30. Glover, *Wilderness Original*, 209–11.

31. One should not forget, however, artist George Catlin's call in 1832 for "a nation's Park" on the Great Plains where the Plains Indian culture and the vast numbers of buffalo could be preserved "in all the wild and freshness of their nature's beauty" (Runte, *National Parks*, 26, 238).

32. Richard West Sellers, "Manipulating Nature's Paradise: National Park Man-

agement under Stephen T. Mather, 1916–1929," *Montana: The Magazine of Western History* 43 (Spring 1992): 5.

33. Department of the Interior, National Park Service, *Gates of the Arctic National Wilderness Park and Nunamiut National Wildlands Alaska: Master Plan* (Washington, D.C.: Government Printing Office, 1973).

34. ANILCA was fundamentally a compromise between preservation and development. It made open several times the amount of area set aside in parks for mineral entry and development, counter to what Marshall had proposed. Still, this does not diminish the main point that the new park areas were seen as cultural landscapes, aimed at preserving native culture and rural white Alaskans' lifestyle preferences as well as the natural environment.

35. Irving M. Clark, "Notes from Conversation with Bob Marshall," July 13, 1937, UW, Irving M. Clark Papers, box 3, file 18.

36. Thomas C. Vint to Director, April 10, 1937, NA, RG 79, Records of Arno B. Cammerer, box 14. Vint's letter justified the NPS trail maintenance policy in the face of Marshall's objections, and enclosed three letters, which Marshall had received and forwarded to the NPS, all regarding the use of oil on trails.

37. Robert Marshall to Paul Gordon, December 8, 1937, NA, RG 126, CCF, box 418, file 9–1–60 Development of Resources, Federal Alaska Committee Reports.

38. House, *Alaska — Its Resources and Development*, 75th Cong., 3d sess., H. Doc. 485, 1938, Appendix B, 213.

39. Robert Marshall to Paul Gordon, December 8, 1937, and "Suggested Changes in Alaska Recreational Report," NA, RG 126, CCF, box 418, file 9–1–60.

40. The Alaska Highway Land Planning Survey Committee comprised Conrad L. Wirth (chairman), J. D. Coffman, Carl P. Russell, Oliver G. Taylor, and Thomas C. Vint. Department of the Interior, National Park Service, *Recreational Resources of the Alaska Highway and other Roads in Alaska* (Washington, D.C.: Government Printing Office, 1944).

41. Ibid., 47.

42. Ibid., 53.

43. Ibid., 48, 58–62, 73–76 (quotation, 73).

44. Associate Director to Dan Wheeler (Office of the Secretary), March 12, 1948, NA, RG 126, Records of the Federal Interagency Alaskan Development Committee, box 6.

45. Newton B. Drury to Ernest Gruening, November 28, 1949, NA, RG 79, Records of Newton B. Drury 1940–51, box 1, folder Alaska Development Committee.

46. G. Frank Williss, *"Do It Right the First Time": The National Park Service and the Alaska National Interest Lands Conservation Act of 1980* (Atlanta: National Park Service, 1985), 29.

47. Ann Lage, *George Collins: The Art and Politics of Park Planning and Preservation, 1920–1979: An Interview Conducted by Ann Lage in 1978 and 1979*, with introduction by Lowell Sumner et al. (Berkeley: University of California Regents, 1980), 180.

48. Lage, *George Collins*, 191, 194; George Collins and Lowell Sumner, "North-

east Alaska: The Last Great Wilderness," *Sierra Club Bulletin* 38 (1953): 13, and "Arctic Wilderness," *The Living Wilderness*, Winter 1953–54, 5–15.

49. Lowell Sumner, "Why an Arctic Wilderness Reserve is Needed," n.d., NAPSR, RG 79, Western Region, CCF, box 23, file 032 Arctic International Wilderness.

50. Lage, *George Collins*, 189.

51. Ibid., 189, 192.

52. Lowell Sumner, "Arctic Alaska: An Air Survey of its Biological Resources," report prepared for the Alaska Recreational Survey, April 1951, NAPSR, RG 79, Western Region, CCF, box 23, file 0.32 Arctic International Wilderness, p. 26.

53. Lage, *George Collins*, 194–97.

54. One year later, in September 1958, Ben Thompson submitted a list of "preserves" that the NPS might acquire. These areas would be managed in their natural state — emphasizing scientific and biological values over scenic and recreational ones. Although nothing further came of the list, it appears to be the first time that the "preserve" concept was advanced and indicates another step in the NPS's evolving sense of its mission (Williss, *Conservation Act*, 166).

55. Ibid., 198–99.

56. Olaus J. Murie, "Nature in the Arctic," *National Parks Magazine* 32, 132 (January–March 1958): 29; George B. Schaller, "New Area for Hunters," *Outdoor Life* 121 (March 1958): 33–37.

57. Lage, *George Collins*, 190, 201.

58. Fred A. Seaton, "America's Largest Wildlife Area," *National Parks Magazine* 32, 134 (July–September 1958): 117–22. Secretary of the Interior Seaton set aside the range provisionally in November 1957 and sought approving legislation. When that failed, he established it by secretarial order on December 6, 1960.

59. Margaret Murie to Sigurd Olson, October 1, 1959, Sigurd Olson to Fred A. Seaton, October 6, 1960, A. W. Boddy (Alaska Sportsmen's Council) to George W. Abbott (Assistant Secretary of the Interior), October 12, 1960, Olaus J. Murie to David L. Spencer, January 6, 1961, MHS, Sigurd Olson Papers, box 52, file Brooks Range.

60. Quoted in George Collins, *Operation Great Land*, report prepared for the Department of the Interior, National Park Service, January 1965.

61. "Camp Denali, in the shadow of Magnificent Mt. McKinley," MHS, Sigurd Olson Papers, box 52, file Alaska Interior Trip.

62. Robert Cahn, *The Fight to Save Wild Alaska* (Washington: National Audubon Society, 1982), 11; Michael Nadel, "Wilderness Council in Alaska," *The Living Wilderness*, Summer–Fall 1963, 47.

63. The Alaska Task Force included Sigurd Olson, vice president of the Wilderness Society, and Robert Luntey of the NPS. Collins had by then retired from the service and had founded Conservation Associates (Collins, *Operation Great Land*, 76).

64. George Hartzog actually suppressed the report out of concern that it would

"be construed as a Service attempt to take over Alaska resource planning." The report's immediate results were limited to a "grand tour" of Alaska by the Advisory Board on Parks, Historic Sites, Buildings and Monuments, and the opening of an NPS Alaska Field Office in Anchorage. Nonetheless, Hartzog called the report a superb effort with impressive scope, depth, and excitement (George B. Hartzog, Jr. to George L. Collins, June 21, 1965, MHS, Sigurd Olson Papers, National Park Service, box 20, file Alaska-65).

65. Collins, *Operation Great Land*, 4.

66. Ibid., 2–4, 75–76.

67. Ibid., 9.

68. Ibid., 69–70.

69. Ibid., 55.

70. Ibid., 63.

71. Merrill J. Mattes, "Special Report on a Reconnaissance of the Kobuk-Koyukuk Headwaters Wilderness Area, Brooks Range, Northern Alaska," Office of Resource Studies, San Francisco Planning and Service Center, National Park Service, Department of the Interior, March 1969, 42–44. The team members were Merrill J. Mattes, Bailey O. Breedlove, Richard Prasil, and Alden Sievers.

72. John P. Crevelli, "The Final Act of the Greatest Conservation President," *Prologue: The Journal of the National Archives* 12, 4 (Winter 1980): 177. Crevelli found that politics and personality conflicts were also important. Udall's opposition to the Vietnam War had strained his relations with Johnson, and the secretary's failure to follow the president's order to consult in person with the chairman of the House Interior and Insular Affairs Committee, Representative Wayne Aspinall of Colorado, was also a key factor. NPS planner Ted Swem was responsible for assembling all the material on the recommended areas during 1968 and was present at Udall's briefing of the president. Swem's recollection of the episode corroborates Crevelli's account, although Swem stated that Clark Clifford was the key dissenting presidential advisor (see Ted Swem, interview with William Schneider, 1991, UAF, Alaska and Polar Regions Department, National Park Service Collection, Audiotape H91–22–25).

73. Jim Rearden, "Our Last Wilderness Revisited," *Outdoor Life* 149 (March 1972): 206. Governor Hickel's impetuosity in ordering this road to be built was all the more disturbing in light of his nomination that January for secretary of the interior. Ostensibly the road was intended to alleviate the high cost and limited volume of air cargo between Fairbanks and Prudhoe Bay, but the cost of trucking materials over the road proved to be about the same as transporting it by air, and the road saw only limited use in the spring of 1969 and again in the spring of 1974. Journalist Tom Brown suggests that Governor Hickel ordered the road to be built to pay off a political debt to the Teamsters Union (Tom Brown, *Oil on Ice: Alaskan Wilderness at the Crossroads* [San Francisco: Sierra Club, 1971], 43–44).

74. Robert B. Weeden to Joseph Greenley, June 25, 1969, UW, Brock Evans

Papers, box 2, folder Alaska—Oil. Weeden expressed his concerns about the winter road in a letter to Governor Hickel, December 9, 1968 (UW, Brock Evans Papers, box 2, folder Alaska—Oil).

75. Unidentified newsclipping, n.d., UW, Brock Evans Papers, box 3, folder Alaska Wilderness Council.

76. Richard J. Gordon to Dr. Edgar Wayburn (Sierra Club) and Mike McCloskey (Wilderness Society), April 1, 1970, UW, Brock Evans Papers, box 3, folder Alaska Wilderness Council.

77. Richard J. Gordon, "Proposal for a Gates of the Arctic National Park," March 12, 1969, Richard J. Gordon to Walter J. Hickel, April 26, 1970, and George Marshall to Richard J. Gordon, May 7, 1970, UAF, Robert Weeden Papers, box 1, folder Gates of the Arctic National Park 1969–71. Gordon's proposal was published in Kenneth Brower, *Earth and the Great Weather: The Brooks Range* (San Francisco: Sierra Club, 1971), 24–28.

78. John M. Kauffmann, *Alaska's Brooks Range: The Ultimate Mountains* (Seattle: The Mountaineers, 1992), 117.

CHAPTER 7

1. Dan Joling, "Nunamiut Eskimos Welcome Return of Pilot Sig Wien," *Fairbanks Daily News-Miner* (Sunday Supplement), June 12, 1988.

2. Vincent Thomas Matthews, "A Case Study of a Homeland and a Wilderness: Gates of the Arctic National Park and the Nunamiut Eskimos" (Master's thesis, University of Alaska, Fairbanks, 1990), 111, 152.

3. "Some story about Nunamiut written by Simon Paneak who was not been educated during his life," Journal of Simon Paneak, n.d., UAF, Ethel Ross Oliver Collection, box 1, file C.

4. Charles Metzger, *The Silent River: a pastoral elegy in the form of a recollection of Arctic adventure* (Los Angeles: Omega Books, 1983).

5. Robert F. Berkhofer, Jr., *The White Man's Indian: Images of the American Indian from Columbus to the Present* (New York: Alfred A. Knopf, Inc., 1978).

6. Jim Pepper, interview, 1991, UAF, Alaska and Polar Regions Department, National Park Service Collection, Audiotape H91–22–33.

7. Statement by Harry Hugo to Alaska Native Review Commission, Anaktuvuk Pass, 1984, University of Alaska, Fairbanks, Alaska and Polar Regions Department, Audiotape H86–62a.

8. Annette McFayden Clark, *Koyukon River Culture* (Ottawa: National Museums of Canada, 1974), 6. Anthropologists also debated the significance of the cultural distinction between inland and coastal groups in northwestern Eskimo culture. For many years anthropologists generally accepted a land/sea dichotomy, with the inland "Nunamiut" Eskimos subsisting predominantly on caribou and freshwater fish, and the coastal "Tareumiut" Eskimos being hunters of the sea. This cultural distinction was overdrawn; the two terms were relative and used by the Eskimos

much like Americans use the terms "Easterner" and "Westerner" (Ernest S. Burch, Jr., "The Nunamiut Concept and the Standardization of Error," in *Contributions to Anthropology: The Interior Peoples of Northern Alaska* [Ottawa: National Museums of Canada, 1976], 88).

9. Edwin S. Hall, Jr., "Interior North Alaska Eskimo," in *Subarctic*, vol. 5 of *Handbook of North American Indians* (Washington, D.C.: Smithsonian Institution, 1984), 339.

10. William E. Brown, *Gaunt Beauty . . . Tenuous Life: Historic Resource Study for Gates of the Arctic National Park and Preserve* (Anchorage, Alaska: National Park Service, 1988), 525.

11. Robert Rausch, "Notes on the Nunamiut Eskimo and Mammals of the Anaktuvuk Pass Region, Brooks Range, Alaska," *Arctic* 4, 3 (December 1951): 187–88.

12. W. Brown, *Gaunt Beauty*, 526–27; Robert F. Spencer, *North Alaskan Eskimo: A Study in Ecology and Society* (Washington, D.C.: Government Printing Office, 1959), 29–31.

13. Nicholas Gubser, *The Nunamiut Eskimos: Hunters of Caribou* (New Haven: Yale University Press, 1965), 55. A harrowing account of one band of "inland Eskimos" (somewhere in Canada) that was literally wiped out by starvation is Captain Thierry Mallet, "When the Caribou Failed," *Atlantic Monthly* 141 (March 1928): 378–83.

14. Helge Ingstad, *Nunamiut: Among Alaska's Inland Eskimos* (New York: W. W. Norton, Co.), 30; Spencer, *North Alaskan Eskimo*, 28; Federal Field Committee for Development Planning in Alaska, *Alaska Natives and the Land* (Washington, D.C.: Government Printing Office, 1968), 129.

15. Norman A. Chance, *The Eskimo of North Alaska* (New York: Holt, Rinehart and Winston, 1966), 13.

16. Ernest S. Burch, Jr., *Eskimo Kinsmen: Changing Family Relationships in Northwestern Alaska* (St. Paul, Minn.: West Publishing Co., 1975), 10, 22, 27–29.

17. George M. Stoney, "Explorations in Alaska," in U.S. Naval Institute, *Proceedings* (Washington, D.C.: Government Printing Office, 1899), 569–70; Ingstad, *Nunamiut*, 35.

18. Hall, "Interior Eskimo," 342.

19. Michael J. Jacobson and Cynthia Wentworth, *Kaktovik Subsistence: Land Use Values Through Time in the Arctic National Wildlife Refuge Area* (Fairbanks: Northern Alaska Ecological Services, 1982), 3; Charles Wynn Amsden, "A Quantitative Analysis of Nunamiut Eskimo Settlement Dynamics" (Ph.D. diss., University of New Mexico, 1977), 289.

20. Journal of Simon Paneak, n.d., UAF, Ethel Ross Oliver Papers, box 1, file C, pp. 24–25.

21. Amsden, "Settlement Dynamics," 309.

22. Joling, "Nunamiut Eskimos," H14.

23. UAF, Ethel Ross Oliver Papers, box 1, file G.

24. Robert Rausch, "Notes," 147, 157.

25. F. Wallace Taber, "Hunting with Alaska's Nunamiute," *The American Rifleman* 108 (February 1960): 24.

26. Ingstad, *Nunamiut*, 15–16, 26–27, 48.

27. Ibid., 49–50.

28. Ibid., 26–27, 35.

29. UAF, Ethel Ross Oliver Papers, box 1, file G.

30. These included Gubser, *Nunamiut Eskimos*; Spencer, *North Alaskan Eskimo*; Amsden, "Settlement Dynamics."

31. Homer Mekiana, *This is the Story of Anaktuvuk Pass Village* (Special report of the Naval Arctic Research Laboratory, Barrow, Alaska, 1972); Simon Paneak, "We Hunt to Live," *Alaska Sportsman*, 26 (March 1960): 12–13, 55. The *Fairbanks Daily News-Miner* ran Mekiana's column during the mid-1960s.

32. Taber, "Hunting," 23–26; Sam Wright, "Eskimo Village," *The Living Wilderness*, Winter 1970–71, 3–6; Metzger, *Silent River*.

33. Metzger, *Silent River*, 54.

34. S. Wright, "Eskimo Village," 6.

35. Mekiana, *Story*, 5–6, 50, 65.

36. Metzger, *Silent River*, 45–46.

37. S. Wright, "Eskimo Village," 3–6.

38. Sam Wright, "Koviashuktok: The Secret of the Eskimo's Wisdom," *American West* 8, 6 (November 1971): 17.

39. Simon Paneak, "We Hunt to Live," *Alaska Sportsman*, March 1960, 12–13, 55.

40. Simon Paneak to Okwak, Ethel and Mary, May 17, 1960, UAF, Ethel Ross Oliver Papers, box 1, folder G.

41. Rausch, "Notes," 192.

42. Clarence J. Rhode to Don C. Foster, May 10, 1949, and Don C. Foster to Commissioner of Indian Affairs, June 17, 1949, NA, RG 75, Alaska Agency, box 114.

43. Ira N. Gabrielson, "Crisis for Alaskan Wildlife," *Audubon Magazine* 53, 6 (November–December 1951): 350–51.

44. A. Starker Leopold and F. Fraser Darling, *Wildlife in Alaska: An Ecological Reconnaissance* (New York: Ronald Press Company, 1953), 42–43.

45. A lively debate would develop among scholars and environmentalists in the 1960s and 1970s over whether primitive hunting cultures had a natural affinity for modern conservation or not. A contemporary summary of this debate is Douglas Hillman Strong, "The Indian and the Environment," *The Journal of Environmental Education* 5, 2 (Winter 1973): 49–51. A historiographical appraisal is Richard White, "Native Americans and the Environment," in *Scholars and the Indian Experience: Critical Reviews of Recent Writing in the Social Sciences*, edited by W. R. Swagerty (Bloomington, Ind.: University of Indiana Press, 1984), 179–204.

46. Regional Director to Director (FWS), April 27, 1950, NAAR, RG 75, Juneau Area Office, GSC 1933–54, box 38, folder 920 Hunting, Fishing, and Trapping 1950.

47. Taber, "Hunting," 23.

48. The FWS policy decision is discussed in Regional Director to Director (FWS), April 27, 1950, NAAR, RG 75, Juneau Area Office, GSC 1933–54, box 38, folder 920 Hunting, Fishing, and Trapping 1950. FWS officials were concerned that Eskimo hunting had become more destructive as a result of the large quantity of army surplus rifles and ammunition they had acquired from participation in the National Guard during World War II (Clarence J. Rhode to Don Foster, May 10, 1949, and Don Foster to Commissioner of Indian Affairs, June 17, 1949, NA, RG 75, Alaska Agency, box 114). At the same time, wildlife biologists were suggesting that population declines for caribou and Dall sheep were due mainly to the vegetational cycle and increased sport hunting, while native consumption of game was a relatively minor factor in wildlife population dynamics (Ian McTaggart Cowan, "Plant Succession and Wildlife Management," *Proceedings Second Alaskan Science Conference* [Fairbanks, Alaska, American Association for the Advancement of Science, 1951], 322–27; James Hatter, "The Status of the Moose in North America," in *Transactions of the Fourteenth North American Wildlife Conference* [Washington, D.C.: Wildlife Management Institute, 1949], 493–94; A. Starker Leopold and F. Fraser Darling, "Effects of Land Use on Moose and Caribou in Alaska," in *Transactions of the Eighteenth North American Wildlife Conference*, edited by James B. Trefethen [Washington, D.C.: Wildlife Management Institute, 1953], 553–58; Frank Dufresne, *Alaska's Animals and Fishes* [New York: A. S. Barnes and Company, 1946], 21).

49. Anaktuvuk Pass Counsil [sic] to Alaska Native Service, January 10, 1953, NAAR, RG 75, Alaska Reindeer Service, box 64, folder Hunting, Fishing, and Fur Farming 1952–53.

50. For example, after a visit by Rhode to Barter Island, the village chief, Andrew Akootchook, conveyed his people's concerns about the Game Law to Barrow's school principal, Fred K. Ipalook, who relayed the information to an Alaska Native Service official in Kotzebue (Fred K. Ipalook to George S. Wilson, July 13, 1949, NAAR, RG 75, Juneau Area Office, GSC 1933–54, box 38, folder 920 Hunting, Fishing, and Trapping 1950). The most widely discussed incident involved two game wardens and some Kobuk Eskimo hunters near Shungnak in 1949. According to the FWS, the incident proved that Eskimos were making large kills and allowing excess carcasses to rot. According to the Eskimos, the hunters had to make two trips to get all the meat to the village and in between trips the carcasses had been visited by FWS wardens and treated with poison (in order to kill wolves). In any case, the Shungnak incident set the tone for relations between Eskimos and wildlife law enforcement officials in the early 1950s (Charles Q. Crabaugh to General Superintendent, May 28, 1949, NAAR, RG 75, Juneau Area Office, GSC 1934–56, box 7, folder 0.32 Fish and Wildlife Service 1949; Regional Director to Director, April 27, 1950, and Percy Ipalook to Ernest Gruening, April 13, 1950, NAAR, RG 75, Juneau Area Office, GSC 1933–54, box 38, folder 920 Hunting, Fishing, and Trapping 1950).

51. Erwin, "Emergence," 7.

52. *Indian Affairs*, newsletter of the Association of American Indian Affairs, No. 42 (July 1961), UW, William L. Paul Papers, MS 1885, box 2.

53. Simon Paneak to Ethel Ross Oliver, December 18, 1961, UAF, Ethel Ross Oliver Papers, box 1, folder G.

54. *Ketchikan Daily News,* July 18, 1962.

55. Anonymous memorandum titled "Chronological Outline of Events Relating to the Proposed Reservation for the Native Village of Barrow Alaska," NAAR, RG 48, Records of the Alaska Field Staff, Director's Subject Files 1948–51, box 12, folder Reservations and Indian Rights. It is noteworthy that this plan did not contemplate the extinguishment of possessory rights or aboriginal title to lands outside the reservation.

56. The FWS had long since become unpopular with non-native Alaskans as well as natives. During the statehood movement in the 1950s, Alaskans had created a Department of Fish and Game before it had any jurisdiction over Alaskan wildlife. Such was the feeling against the FWS that some Alaskans believed that it was deliberately stirring up trouble with the Eskimos in order to justify a continuation of federal control over Alaskan wildlife after statehood was achieved. The FWS did in fact continue to manage Alaskan fish and wildlife for one year after statehood, due to an amendment in the Alaska Statehood Act requiring federal oversight until the secretary of the interior certified to Congress that the Alaska State Legislature had made adequate provision for the management and conservation of those resources "in the broad national interest." This amendment was the idea of the former director of the FWS, Ira N. Gabrielson. As amended, the Alaska Statehood Act gave the FWS a reprieve in Alaska — long enough to make a new place for itself in the enforcement of the Migratory Bird Treaty Act.

57. Department of the Interior, *Report of the Secretary of the Interior by the Task Force on Alaska Native Affairs* (Washington, D.C.: Government Printing Office, 1962), 28–32.

58. Ibid., 34–38.

59. David M. Hickok, "Nunamiut Experience and Current Approaches to Subsistence Harvest Problems by the People of Anaktuvuk" (paper presented before the Federal-State Land Use Planning Commission for Alaska, February 5–6, 1974, on file at Arctic Environment Data Center, Anchorage, 6).

60. AFN president Don Wright insisted "Our case is real estate," and an AFN attorney said of the proposed land claim settlement, "In effect, this is a real estate transaction that is involved here" (quoted in Berry, *Alaska Pipeline*, 171).

61. Borbridge, "Native Organization," 197; Margaret Lantis, "The Current Nativistic Movement in Alaska," in *Circumpolar Problems: Habitat, Economy, and Social Relations in the Arctic,* edited by Gosta Berg (Oxford: Pergamon Press, 1973), 116.

62. Berkhofer, *The White Man's Indian,* 25.

63. William L. Hensley, "Arctic Development and the Future of Eskimo Societies," *Indian Truth* 47, 1 (February 1970): 7–8.

64. Area Field Representative to Area Director, May 13, 1964, NAAR, RG 75, Juneau Area Office, Fairbanks Agency — Credit Operations Files 1971–72, box 1, folder Anaktuvuk Pass 007.

65. Federal Field Committee for Development Planning in Alaska, *Alaska Natives and the Land* (Washington, D.C.: Government Printing Office, 1968).

66. Ibid., 42, 63, 83 (quotation, 71).

67. M. Leatherbee, "Alaska: The Hard Country," *Life*, October 1, 1965, 76–77; T. J. Abercrombie, "Nomads in Alaska's Outback," *National Geographic*, April 1969, 540–67; Anne Barry, "Now That You Own Alaska, Friends, What Are You Going To Do With It?" *Esquire*, April 1969, 119–25 (quotation, 125); "Natives: Even Hope is Scarce," *Business Week*, November 4, 1967, 152; "Ted's Troubles in the Tundra; Investigating Conditions of Alaska's Natives," *Time*, April 18, 1969, 22–23.

68. Bryan Cooper, *Alaska: The Last Frontier* (New York: Morrow, 1973).

69. See, for example, the four-page diatribe against Alaska natives by two members of the Advisory Board on National Parks, Frank Masland, Jr. and Emil W. Haury, September 11, 1972, MHS, Sigurd Olson Papers, box 52, folder Alaska: "Our contacts with Eskimo villages resulted in a sense of hopelessness. Only one word described them — the word, 'mess.' . . . We had never seen such waste, such carelessness, such lack of respect for values. . . . We cite the conditions we encountered since we saw no evidence that contact with the white man had improved the way of life of the indigene and we are extremely fearful that the implementation of the Native Claims Act may further their deterioration and disintegration."

70. Bob Ahgoc to Mr. Morken (BIA), n.d., Acting Area Plant Management Officer to Tribal Operations Officer, February 9, 1967, Acting Area Director to Bob Ahgook, February 16, 1967, Bob Ahgook to Mr. Morken, March 15, 1967, and Bob Ahgook to Mr. Brewer, March 15, 1967, NAAR, RG 75, Juneau Area Office, Fairbanks Agency Credit Operations Files 1971–72, box 15, folder HR Anaktuvuk Pass Proposed Move; Mary Moses to Bob Mandell, April 12, 1967, Tribal Operations Officer to Superintendent, May 1, 1967, and Z. Hugo to Owen D. Morken, June 6, 1967, NAAR, RG 75, Juneau Area Office, Fairbanks Agency — Credit Operations Files 1971–72, box 1, folder HR Anaktuvuk Housing Progress and Cost Data.

71. Department of the Interior, National Park Service, "Special Report on a Reconnaissance of the Kobuk-Koyukuk Headwaters Wilderness Area, Brooks Range, Northern Alaska," open-file report by the Office of Resource Studies, March 1969, 9, 45.

72. Frank E. Masland, Jr. and Emil W. Haury, "Alaska Report," October 10, 1972, MHS, Sigurd Olson Papers, box 52, folder Alaska.

73. Jane Pender, "Alaskan Natives: Time of Crisis," *National Parks and Conservation Magazine* 44, 278 (November 1970): 27.

74. Jane Pender, "Crisis on the North Slope," *Anchorage Daily News*, March 4, 1969; Michael Frome, "Hickel and the Arctic," *Field and Stream* 73, 6 (November 1969): 16; T. Brown, *Oil on Ice*, 43–44.

75. Sam Wright, "Alaska's Wilderness Cries Out for a Plan," *The Living Wilderness*, Spring 1969, 3–6.

76. Michael S. Cline, "Notes on the Observed Effects of a Winter Road Upon the Nunamiut Eskimos of Anaktuvuk Pass, with Predictions for their Future," in *Pro-*

ceedings of the Twentieth Alaska Science Conference, College, Alaska, August 24 to 27, 1969 (College, Alaska: University of Alaska Press, 1970), 397–98.

77. *Fairbanks Daily News-Miner,* March 7, March 21, April 4, 1974; "The Last Treaty," *Harper's Magazine,* January 1975, 38.

CHAPTER 8

1. See Stephen W. Haycox, "Economic Development and Indian Land Rights in Modern Alaska: The 1947 Tongass Timber Act," *Western Historical Quarterly* 21, 1 (February 1990): 21–46.

2. 94 Stat. 2422.

3. David M. Hickok, "Developmental Trends in Arctic Alaska," July 1, 1970, eleven-page manuscript at Arctic Environment Data Center, Anchorage, Alaska.

4. Arlon R. Tussing, "Issues of Land Use Determination in Alaska," speech delivered in Seattle, September 11, 1970, UW, Brock Evans Papers, box 1, folder Alaska Native Claims.

5. See the chapter on Alaskan oil development in Donald Worster, *Under Western Skies: Nature and History in the American West* (New York: Oxford University Press, 1992) for an example of this view.

6. Jane Pender, "Crisis"; "Native Federation: Flat Broke, But Hopeful," *Anchorage Daily News,* March 21, 1969; Borbridge, "Native Organization," 198; Hensley, "Arctic Development," 7–8. The best study of the influence of oil development on Eskimos is Joseph G. Jorgensen, *Oil Age Eskimos* (Berkeley: University of California Press, 1990), based on ethnographic data gathered in the 1980s.

7. Grant McConnell to Conservation Research Committee, February 1968, UW, Brock Evans Papers, box 1, folder Alaska Native Claims.

8. Pender, "Crisis."

9. William Willoya to Sierra Club, January 2, 1969, UW, Brock Evans Papers, box 1, General Correspondence 1967–72.

10. Grant McConnell to Conservation Research Committee, February 1968, UW, Brock Evans Papers, box 1, folder Alaska Native Claims.

11. Cahn, *Fight to Save Alaska,* 11; Hickok, "Developmental Trends," 2.

12. Cahn, *Fight to Save Alaska,* 11.

13. George B. Hartzog, Jr., *Battling for the National Parks* (Mt. Kisko, N.Y.: Moyer Bell, Ltd., 1988), 213.

14. Williss, *Conservation Act,* 75–82. According to Williss, Hartzog was convinced that he had laid the groundwork on this trip for most of the national interest lands to be put into the national park system. Hartzog was bitterly disappointed by the secretary of the interior's subsequent apportionment of D-2 lands between the four conservation systems, as he made clear in *Battling* (212–21). Interestingly, at the time of Hartzog and Bible's visit to Gates of the Arctic, Hartzog was envisioning a huge Gates of the Arctic National Park that would stretch northward to the Arctic coast. Senator Bible specifically mentioned Gates of the Arctic and the additions to

Mount McKinley and Katmai when he discussed the amendment with Senator Ted Stevens of Alaska.

15. 85 Stat. 709.

16. Williss, *Conservation Act*, 71–72.

17. Ibid., 72.

18. Michael Parfit, "Alaska: The Eleventh Hour for America's Wilderness," *The New Times*, September 18, 1978, 48. ANCSA is analyzed in D. Chase, *Alaska Natives*, especially 14–30; Berger, *Village Journey*, passim.

19. Parfit, "Alaska," 48.

20. Congress, *Land Planning and Policy in Alaska: Recommendations Concerning National Interest Lands*, report prepared by the Joint Federal-State Land Use Planning Commission for Alaska, 93d Cong., 2d sess., June 1974, Committee Print, 3.

21. Hickok, "Nunamiut Experience," 7–8.

22. Williss, *Conservation Act*, 105.

23. Kauffmann, *Alaska's Brooks Range*, 124–25.

24. Cahn, *Fight to Save Alaska*, 13.

25. Williss, *Conservation Act*, 124. Coincident with these negotiations, the Interior Department considered Nunamiut concerns about the D-2 status given to ancestral lands along the Killik River and to areas used for hunting on the John River and Hunts Fork south of Anaktuvuk Pass. The secretary finally reached a separate agreement with the Nunamiut Corporation, which placed the Killik River area in a dual status and made the latter areas available for native selection in exchange for the relinquishment of native selections in two areas to the east (Hickok, "Nunamiut Experience," 9).

26. Hickok, "Nunamiut Experience," 12.

27. Kauffmann, *Alaska's Brooks Range*, 135, 138–39; Department of the Interior, National Park Service, *Gates of the Arctic National Wilderness Park and Nunamiut National Wildlands, Alaska: Master Plan*, (Washington, 1973), passim; Jim Pepper, interview, 1991, UAF, National Park Service Collection, H91–22–33.

28. Jim Pepper, interview, 1991, UAF, National Park Service Collection, H91–22–33.

29. S. 3599, "A Bill to Establish the Nunamiut National Park in the State of Alaska," June 7, 1974, UW, Henry M. Jackson Papers, Acc. 3560–5, box 223, folder 51.

30. Jim Kowalsky to Cooperators, Friends of the Brooks Range and Alaska, UAF, Alaska Conservation Society Papers, box 31, folder D-2 NPS General.

31. The state's dubious right-of-way traversed native-selected lands. Anaktuvuk Pass had filed all of its land selections on November 13, 1973, being the first Alaska native village to do so. The village of Anaktuvuk Pass, Nunamiut Corporation, and ASRC jointly filed suit against Alyeska. In the first week of March, Judge James Von der Heydt of the U.S. District Court in Anchorage denied the request for an injunction, ruling "at a time when the long-term national energy problem is beyond definitive resolution, the adverse effect on the public interest is of such obvious

magnitude in itself as to warrant denial of plaintiff's motion" (*Fairbanks Daily News-Miner*, March 21, 1974).

32. Hickok, "Nunamiut Experience," 15.

33. Park Planner (John M. Kauffmann) to Assistant to the Director (Theodor Swem), March 16, 1977, UAF, Alaska Conservation Society Papers, box 31, folder D2 NPS General. By then Kauffmann was referring to a slightly more restrictive agreement for the proposed Nunamiut National Wildlands, which he negotiated with the Nunamiuts in December 1975. See John M. Kauffmann to Project Leader, December 21, 1975, Denver Public Library (hereafter cited as DPL), Theodor Swem Papers, no box number, file Rich Gordon Alaska.

34. Kauffmann, *Alaska's Brooks Range*, 130.

35. Ibid., 138–39.

36. See for example Rearden, "Last Wilderness," 59–61, 202–4; John M. Kauffmann, "Noatak," *The Living Wilderness*, Winter 1974–75, 17–28; Robert Cantwell, "The Ultimate Confrontation," *Sports Illustrated*, March 24, 1969, 67–76; and the entire issue of *National Parks & Conservation Magazine*, November 1970. One should not forget Lois Crisler's *Arctic Wild* (New York: Harper & Brothers, Publishers, 1958), the first book to appear on the Brooks Range since Bob Marshall's books. Lois and her husband Herb Crisler spent several months in the Brooks Range filming wolves for Walt Disney Studios, and her book was an eloquent plea for wilderness that was large enough to preserve the unique arctic fauna.

37. Quoted in Kauffmann, *Alaska's Brooks Range*, 143.

38. Ibid., 129.

39. Ibid., 132–35; Department of the Interior, National Park Service, *Gates of the Arctic National Wilderness Park and Nunamiut National Wildlands, Alaska: Master Plan* (Washington, D.C.: Government Printing Office, 1973), 24–26; Department of the Interior, National Park Service, *Final Environmental Impact Statement: Gates of the Arctic National Park* (Washington, D.C.: Government Printing Office, 1974), passim; John M. Kauffmann to Keymen, November 25, 1975, DPL, Theodor Swem Papers, no box number, file Rich Gordon Alaska.

40. Richard K. Nelson, Kathleen H. Mautner and G. Ray Bane, *Tracks in the Wildland: A Portrayal of Koyukon and Nunamiut Subsistence* (Fairbanks: University of Alaska, Cooperative Park Studies Unit, 1982), 9; W. Brown, *Gaunt Beauty*, 594.

41. Nelson, Mautner, and Bane, *Tracks in the Wildland*, 23.

42. Richard K. Nelson, *Make Prayers to the Raven: A Koyukon View of the Northern Forest* (Chicago: University of Chicago Press, 1983), 14.

43. Ibid., 203–4, 216–17.

44. Congress, *Land Planning*, 12.

45. Yupiktak Bista, *A Report on Subsistence and the Conservation of the Yupik Life-style* (Bethel, Alaska: Yupiktak Bista, 1974), 2, 6.

46. Ibid., 5.

47. Ottar Brox, "'Conservation' and 'Destruction' of Traditional Culture," in *Circumpolar Problems: Habitat, Economy, and Social Relations in the Arctic,* edited by Gosta Berg (Oxford: Oxford University Press, 1973), 41.

48. Celia Hunter, a member of the commission, described Dasmann's influence in an article in the *Fairbanks Daily News-Miner* (August 9, 1990).

49. Raymond F. Dasmann, "Toward a Dynamic Balance of Man and Nature," *The Ecologist* 6, 1 (January 1976): 3.

50. Raymond F. Dasmann, "National Parks, Nature Conservation, and 'Future Primitive,'" *The Ecologist* 6, 5 (June 1976): 164–67 (quotation, 166).

51. A retrospective summary analysis of this episode by a state biologist is David R. Klein, "Caribou, Alaska's Wilderness Nomads," in *Restoring America's Wildlife 1937–1987: The First Fifty Years in the Federal Aid in Wildlife Restoration (Pittman-Robertson) Act* (Department of the Interior, Fish and Wildlife Service, Washington, D.C.: Government Printing Office, 1987), 192–200. Klein states that the herd had recovered to 170,000 and was sustaining an annual harvest of 10,000 animals by 1987. He further contends that no evidence was ever produced to support the claim that the decline was related to oil development. A contemporary analysis of the crisis is David R. Klein and Robert G. White, eds., *Parameters of Caribou Population Ecology in Alaska: Proceedings of a Symposium and Workshop,* Biological Papers of the University of Alaska, Special Report No. 3, June 1978.

52. Department of the Interior, *Native Livelihood and Dependence: A Study of Land Use Values Through Time,* special report prepared by the North Slope Borough Contract Staff for the National Petroleum Reserve in Alaska, 1979, 18.

53. John G. Mitchell, "Where have all the tuttu gone?" *Audubon* 79, 2 (March 1977): 10.

54. Ibid.

55. The Association of Village Council Presidents and the Subsistence Resources Council took the lead in developing and testifying on behalf of this plan in the congressional hearings held in April 1977. A good explication of the localist position is found in Harold Sparck to Lawrence R. Mayo, March 1, 1977, UAF, Alaska Conservation Society Papers, box 3, folder 32 Subsistence Reports.

56. House, Committee on Interior and Insular Affairs, *Inclusion of Alaska Lands in National Park, Forest, Wildlife Refuge, and Wild and Scenic River Systems, Part 1,* 95th Cong., 1st sess., 1977, 186; Herbert R. Melchior, "A Proposal for the Regulation of Fishing, Hunting, and Trapping and Improved Cooperation among Land Management Groups in Alaska with Federal, State, and Private Participation," August 24, 1977, UAF, Robert Weeden Papers, box 3, folder 32 Subsistence Reports; D. D. Kelso, "Legal Issues in Federal Protection for Subsistence on the Proposed National Interest Lands," reprinted in House, Committee on Interior and Insular Affairs, *Inclusion of Alaska Lands in National Park, Forest, Wildlife Refuge, and Wild and Scenic River Systems, Part 1,* 95th Cong., 1st sess., 1977, 273–490; Mike McCloskey to Celia Hunter, with enclosure, October 21, 1976, UAF, Alaska Conservation

Society Papers, box 18, folder National Interest Lands ACS Position on Hunting; Cahn, *Fight to Save Alaska*, 15.

57. Devereux Butcher, "Public Sport Shooting — A National Park Service Responsibility?" n.d., UAF, Alaska Conservation Society, box 14, folder H.R. 39 1977–78.

58. Park Planner (John M. Kauffmann) to Assistant to the Director (Ted Swem), March 16, 1977, UAF, Alaska Conservation Society Papers, box 31, folder D-2 NPS General.

59. Robert B. Weeden to Devereux Butcher, January 16, 1978, UAF, Alaska Conservation Society Papers, box 14, folder H.R. 39 1977–78.

60. Under pressure from natives and environmentalists, the State of Alaska passed a Game Law in 1975 that authorized separate regulations for subsistence hunting and fishing. This new statutory differentiation of subsistence and sport hunting in Alaska also made it easier to differentiate between the two types of hunting in the national interest lands. On this and other issues, I have tried to avoid duplication of Henry P. Huntington, *Wildlife Management and Subsistence Hunting in Alaska* (London: Belhaven Press, 1992).

61. House, Committee on Interior and Insular Affairs, *Inclusion of Alaska Lands in National Park, Forest, Wildlife Refuge, and Wild and Scenic Rivers Systems, Part 1*, 95th Cong., 1st sess., 1977, 168.

62. Ibid., 137.

63. Senate, Committee on Energy and Natural Resources, *Alaska Natural Resource Issues*, 95th Cong., 1st sess., 1977, 201.

64. 94 Stat. 2422.

65. Customary and traditional use covered a range of issues. While technological changes in modes of transportation were the main issue in Gates of the Arctic, the subsistence issue turned on other questions in other localities. These included the problem of containing market pressures, the desire to protect scarce resources from overharvest, and the demand by rural white Alaskans to be given equal consideration with rural natives.

66. 94 Stat. 2423.

67. Huntington, *Wildlife Management*, 68–69.

68. Senate, Committee on Energy and Natural Resources, *Alaska Natural Resource Issues*, 95th Cong., 1st sess., 1977, 136; Cahn, *Fight to Save Alaska*, 16. By contrast, the Nixon administration's Alaska lands bill would have permitted both types of hunting in most new areas and no hunting in others.

69. Williss, *Conservation Act*, 225–26.

70. For a concise legislative history of ANILCA see Runte, *National Parks*, 236–58. A good account by a participant is Robert Cahn, *Fight to Save Alaska*. An authoritative presentation of the Park Service's perspective is Williss, *Conservation Act*. On Carter's assessment, see Debbie S. Miller, "ANILCA was the best piece of lame duck legislation I can think of," *Wilderness* 54, 91 (Winter 1990): 30–31.

71. House, Committee on Interior and Insular Affairs, *Inclusion of Alaska Lands in*

National Park, Forest, Wildlife Refuge, and Wild and Scenic Rivers Systems, Part 13, 95th Cong., 1st sess., 1977, 145–53.

72. Characteristically, ANILCA can be read two ways on this point. Section 201 (4) (a) lists several park purposes for which Gates of the Arctic will be managed, and then adds, "Subsistence uses by local residents shall be permitted in the park, where such uses are traditional, in accordance with the provisions of title VIII." Section 101 declares "It is further the intent and purpose of this Act consistent with management of fish and wildlife in accordance with recognized scientific principles and the purposes for which each conservation system unit is established, designated, or expanded by or pursuant to this Act, to provide the opportunity for rural residents engaged in a subsistence way of life to continue to do so."

73. House, Committee on Merchant Marine and Fisheries, *Alaska National Interest Lands, Part 2,* 96th Cong., 1st sess., 1979, 1875.

74. Matthews, "Case Study," 151–52.

75. Ibid., 96. For a relatively favorable appraisal of co-management by a former superintendent of Cape Krusenstern National Monument, Kobuk Valley National Park, and Noatak National Preserve, see C. Mack Shaver, "Traditional National Park Values and Living Cultural Parks: Seemingly Conflicting Management Demands in Alaska's New National Parklands" (paper submitted to First World Conference on Cultural Parks,

Mesa Verde National Park, September 16–21, 1984, DPL, Theodor Swem Papers, no box number, file Cultural Parks).

CONCLUSION

1. Jack Hession, "Five Latent Traditional National Parks in Alaska — Brief Remarks to the National Park Service Regional Directors Conference," June 23, 1994, copy in my possession.

Bibliography

MANUSCRIPT COLLECTIONS

Alaska Historical Library, Juneau, Alaska.
James Curry and E. Weissbrodt Papers.
Denver Public Library, Denver, Colorado.
Theodor Swem Papers.
Library of Congress, Washington, D.C.
Clinton Hart Merriam Papers.
Minnesota Historical Society, St. Paul, Minnesota.
Sigurd Olson Papers.
Raphael Zon Papers.
Rasmuson Library, University of Alaska, Fairbanks, Alaska.
Alaska Conservation Society Papers.
Olaus Murie Papers.
Ethel Ross Oliver Papers.
Charles Sheldon Papers.
Robert Weeden Papers.
Suzzallo Library, University of Washington, Seattle, Washington.
Irving M. Clark Papers.
Brock Evans Papers.
Viola Garfield Papers.
Henry M. Jackson Papers.
Lloyd Meeds Papers.
William L. Paul Papers.
Walter Library, University of Minnesota, Minneapolis, Minnesota.
William S. Cooper Papers.

UNPUBLISHED GOVERNMENT DOCUMENTS

Denali National Park and Preserve.
William E. Brown Historical Files.
Glacier Bay National Park and Preserve.
Administrative Files.
National Archives, Washington, D.C.
Record Group 22. Records of the Fish and Wildlife Service.
Record Group 75. Records of the Bureau of Indian Affairs.
Record Group 79. Records of the National Park Service.
Record Group 126. Records of the Territories and Island Possessions.
National Archives, Alaska Region, Anchorage, Alaska.
Record Group 22. Records of the Fish and Wildlife Service.
Record Group 48. Records of the Secretary of the Interior.
Record Group 75. Records of the Bureau of Indian Affairs.
Record Group 79. Records of the National Park Service.
National Archives, Pacific Sierra Region, San Bruno, California.
Record Group 79. Records of the National Park Service.
Sitka National Historical Park.
Historical Files.

PUBLISHED GOVERNMENT DOCUMENTS

Congressional Record. 1970–80. Washington, D.C.
Congress. House. *Alaska — Its Resources and Development.* 75th Cong., 3d sess.,
    1938. H. Doc. 485.
Congress. House. *Alaska Native Claim Settlement Act Conference Report.* 92d Cong.,
    1st sess., December 13, 1971. H. Rept. 92–746.
Congress. House. Committee on Interior and Insular Affairs. *Inclusion of Lands in
    National Park, Forest, Wildlife Refuge, and Wild and Scenic Rivers Systems, Parts
    1–13.* 95th Cong., 1st sess., 1977.
Congress. House. Committee on Interior and Insular Affairs. Subcommittee on
    General Oversight and Alaska Lands. *Hearing on H.R. 39, H.R. 1974, H.R.
    2876, H.R. 5505 et al. to designate certain lands in the state of Alaska as units of the
    national park, national wildlife refuge, wild and scenic rivers, and national wilder-
    ness preservation systems, and for other purposes, H.R. 1454 to establish the Lake
    Clark National Park in the state of Alaska and for other purposes, H.R. 5605 and
    H.R. 8651 to establish Admiralty Island National Preserve in the state of Alaska and
    for other purposes.* 95th Cong., 1st sess. April 21–22, 1977.
Congress. House. Committee on Merchant and Marine Fisheries. *Alaska National
    Interest Lands — Part 2.* 96th Cong., 1st sess. 1979.
Congress. House. Committee on Merchant and Marine Fisheries. Subcommittee
    on Fisheries and Wildlife Conservation and the Environment. *Hearing on*

H.R. 39 to Designate Certain Lands in the State of Alaska as Units of the National Park, National Wildlife Refuge, Wild and Scenic Rivers and National Wilderness Preservation Systems, and for other Purposes. 95th Cong., 2d sess. March 16, and April 4, 6, 7, 1978.

Congress. House. Committee on the Public Lands. *Hearing on H.R. 5004 and H.R. 5401 Bills to Provide for the Protection of the Dall Sheep, Caribou, and other Wildlife Native to Mount McKinley National Park and for other Purposes.* 79th Cong., 2d sess. April 3, and May 22, 1946.

Congress. Senate. Committee on Commerce. Subcommittee on Oceans and Atmosphere. *Ocean Mammal Protection — Part 2.* 92d Cong., 2d sess., May 11, 1972.

Congress. Senate. Committee on Energy and Natural Resources. *Alaska Natural Resource Issues.* 95th Cong., 1st sess. 1977.

Congress. Senate. Committee on Indian Affairs. *Survey of Conditions of the Indians in the United States: Hearings Before a Subcommittee of the Committee on Indian Affairs — Part 36.* 74th Cong., 2d sess., 1939.

Congress. Senate. Committee on Interior and Insular Affairs. *Land Planning and Policy in Alaska: Recommendations Concerning National Interest Lands.* Report prepared by the Joint Federal-State Land Use Planning Commission for Alaska. 93d Cong., 2d sess., June 1974. Committee Print.

Congress. Senate. Committee on Territories. *Hearing on S.5716, A Bill to Establish the Mount McKinley National Park, in the Territory of Alaska.* 64th Cong., 1st sess., May 5, 1916.

Congress. Senate. *Proceedings of the Alaskan Boundary Tribunal.* Vol. 2. Document No. 162. 58th Cong., 2d sess., 1904.

Department of the Interior. National Park Service. *Administrative Policies for Natural Areas of the National Park System.* Washington, D.C.: Government Printing Office, 1970.

Department of the Interior. National Park Service. *Annual Report of the Director of the National Park Service to the Secretary of the Interior.* Washington, D.C.: Government Printing Office, 1916–49.

Department of the Interior. National Park Service. *Final Environmental Impact Statement: Gates of the Arctic National Park.* Alaska Planning Group. Washington, D.C.: Government Printing Office, 1974.

Department of the Interior. National Park Service. *Gates of the Arctic National Wilderness Park and Nunamiut National Wildlands, Alaska: Master Plan.* Open-file report prepared by Alaska Planning Group, December 1973.

Department of the Interior. National Park Service. *Recreational Resources of the Alaska Highway and other Roads in Alaska.* Washington, D.C.: Government Printing Office, 1944.

Department of the Interior. National Park Service. *Special Report on a Reconnaissance of the Kobuk-Koyukuk Headwaters Wilderness Area, Brooks Range, Northern Alaska.* Open-file report prepared by Office of Resource Studies, March 1969.

Department of the Interior. *Native Livelihood and Dependence: A Study of Land Use Values Through Time.* Special report prepared by North Slope Borough Contract Staff for the National Petroleum Reserve in Alaska, 1979.

Department of the Interior. *Opinions of the Solicitor of the Department of the Interior Relating to Indian Affairs, 1917–1974.* Vol. 1. Washington, D.C.: Government Printing Office, n.d.

Department of the Interior. *Report of the Secretary of the Interior by the Task Force on Alaska Native Affairs.* Washington, D.C.: Government Printing Office, 1962.

Federal Field Committee for Development Planning in Alaska. *Alaska Natives and the Land.* Washington, D.C.: Government Printing Office, 1968.

BOOKS, CHAPTERS, ARTICLES,
AND AUTHORED GOVERNMENT REPORTS

Abercrombie, T. J. "Nomads in Alaska's Outback." *National Geographic,* April 1969, 540–67.

Ackerman, Robert E. *The Archeology of the Glacier Bay Region, Southeastern Alaska.* Pullman: Washington State University, Laboratory of Anthropology, 1968.

Adney, Tappan. "The Sledge Dogs of the North." *Outing* 38, 1 (1901): 129–37.

Andrews, C. L. "Muir Glacier." *National Geographic,* December 1903, 441–45.

Atgood, Walter W. "Prospecting in Alaska." *The University of Chicago Magazine,* December 1910, 53–57.

Averkieva, Julia. "The Tlingit Indians." In *North American Indians in Historical Perspective.* New York: Random House, 1971.

Ballou, Maturin M. *The New Eldorado: Summer Journey to Alaska.* Boston: Houghton Mifflin Co., 1891.

Barry, Anne. "Now That You Own Alaska, Friends, What Are You Going To Do With It?" *Esquire,* April 1969, 119–25.

Beach, Rex. *The Iron Trail.* New York: Harper and Brothers, 1913.

Belasco, Warren James. *Americans on the Road: From Autocamp to Motel, 1910–1945.* Cambridge, Mass.: The MIT Press, 1979.

Belous, Robert. "Unsolved Problems of Alaska's North Slope." *National Parks and Conservation Magazine,* November 1970, 16–18.

Berger, Thomas R. *Village Journey: The Report of the Alaska Native Review Commission.* New York: Hill and Wang, 1985.

"The Bergs and Ice Cliffs of Glacier Bay." *Sunset* 126, 6 (1961): 63.

Berkhofer, Robert F., Jr. *The White Man's Indian: Images of the American Indian from Columbus to the Present.* New York: Alfred A. Knopf, Inc., 1978.

Bernstein, David A. "Bob Marshall: Wilderness Advocate." *Western State Jewish Historical Quarterly* 13, 1 (1980): 26–33.

Berry, Mary Clay. *The Alaska Pipeline: The Politics of Oil and Native Land Claims.* Bloomington, Ind.: Indiana University Press, 1975.

Birkedal, Ted. "Ancient Hunters in the Alaskan Wilderness: Human Predators and

Their Role and Effect on Wildlife Populations and the Implications for Re-source Management." Paper presented at the Seventh George Wright Society Meeting, Jacksonville, Florida, 1992.

Bista, Yupiktak. *A Report on Subsistence and the Conservation of the Yupik Life-style.* Bethel, Alaska: Yupiktak Bista, 1974.

Bohn, Dave. *Glacier Bay: The Land and the Silence.* Seattle: Sierra Club, Pacific Northwest, 1967.

Borbridge, John, Jr. "Native Organization and Land Rights as Vehicle for Change." In *Change in Alaska: People, Petroleum, and Politics,* edited by George W. Rogers. College, Alaska: University of Alaska Press, 1970.

Bosworth, Robert G. "Tlingit Subsistence in Glacier Bay, Alaska: Adapting to Change in Landscape and Bureaucracy." Paper presented at the Alaska Anthropological Association Meeting, Anchorage, Alaska, March 1987.

Bratton, Susan Power. "National Park Management and Values." *Environmental Ethics* 7, 2 (1985): 117–33.

Brooks, Alfred H. "An Exploration of Mount McKinley, America's Highest Mountain." In *Smithsonian Report 1903.* Washington, D.C.: Government Printing Office, 1904.

——. "The Mount McKinley Region, Alaska." *U.S. Geological Survey Professional Paper 70.* Washington, D.C.: Government Printing Office, 1911.

Brooks, Alfred H., et al. "Mineral Resources of Alaska." *U.S. Geological Survey Bulletin 773.* Washington, D.C.: Government Printing Office, 1925.

Brower, Kenneth. *Earth and the Great Weather: The Brooks Range.* San Francisco: Sierra Club, 1971.

Brown, Tom. *Oil on Ice: Alaskan Wilderness at the Crossroads.* San Francisco: Sierra Club, 1971.

Brown, William E. *Gaunt Beauty . . . Tenuous Life: Historic Resource Study for Gates of the Arctic National Park and Preserve.* Anchorage, Alaska: National Park Service, 1988.

——. *A History of the Denali-Mount McKinley Region, Alaska: Historic Resource Study of Denali National Park and Preserve.* Santa Fe: National Park Service, 1991.

Browne, Belmore. *The Conquest of Mount McKinley.* New York: G. P. Putnam's Sons, 1913.

——. "Where the White Sheep Range." *Outing Magazine,* May 1912, 131–43.

Brox, Ottar. " 'Conservation' and 'Destruction' of Traditional Culture." In *Circumpolar Problems: Habitat, Economy, and Social Relations in the Arctic,* edited by Gosta Berg. Oxford, U.K.: Pergamon Press, 1973.

Buddington, A. F. "Mineral Investigations in Southeastern Alaska." *U.S. Geological Survey Bulletin 783-B.* Washington, D.C.: Government Printing Office, 1926.

Burch, Ernest S., Jr., "The Caribou/Wild Reindeer as a Human Resource." *American Antiquity* 37, 3 (1972): 339–68.

——. *Eskimo Kinsmen: Changing Family Relationships in Northwest Alaska.* St. Paul, Minn.: West Publishing Co., 1975.

———. "Indians and Eskimos in North Alaska, 1816–1977: A Study in Changing Ethnic Relations." *Arctic Anthropology* 16, 3 (1979): 123–51.

———. "The Nunamiut Concept and the Standardization of Error." In *Contributions to Anthropology: The Interior Peoples of Northern Alaska*. Ottawa: National Museums of Canada, 1976.

Burroughs, John, et al. *Alaska: The Harriman Expedition, 1899*. New York: Dover Publications, 1986.

Cahalane, Victor. "The Evolution of Predator Control Policy in the National Parks." *Journal of Wildlife Management* 3, 3 (1939): 235–36.

Cahn, Robert. *The Fight to Save Wild Alaska*. Washington, D.C.: National Audubon Society, 1982.

Calvin, Jack. "Two Seal Hunters." *Alaska Sportsman*, May 1964, 30.

Cantwell, Robert. "The Ultimate Confrontation." *Sports Illustrated*, March 24, 1969, 67–76.

Capps, Stephen R. "A Game Country Without Rival." *National Geographic*, January 1917, 69–84.

———. "The Kantishna Region, Alaska." *United States Geological Survey Bulletin 687*. Washington, D.C.: Government Printing Office, 1919.

Case, David S. *Alaska Natives and American Laws*. Fairbanks, Alaska: University of Alaska, 1984.

Chance, Norman A. *The Eskimo of North Alaska*. New York: Holt, Rinehart and Winston, 1966.

Chase, Alston. *Playing God in Yellowstone: The Destruction of America's First National Park*. Boston: Atlantic Monthly Press, 1986.

Clark, Annette McFayden. *Koyukon River Culture*. Ottawa: National Museums of Canada, 1974.

Cline, Michael S. "Notes on the Observed Effects of a Winter Road Upon the Nunamiut Eskimos of Anaktuvuk Pass, with Predictions for their Future." In *Proceedings of the Twentieth Alaska Science Conference, College, Alaska, August 24 to 27, 1969*. College, Alaska: University of Alaska Press, 1970.

Coates, Peter A. *The Trans-Alaska Pipeline Controversy: Technology, Conservation, and the Frontier*. Cranbury, N.J.: Lehigh University Press, 1991.

Cohen, Michael P. *The Pathless Way: John Muir and American Wilderness*. Madison: University of Wisconsin Press, 1984.

Collins, George. *Operation Great Land*. Report prepared for the National Park Service, 1965.

Collins, George, and Lowell Sumner. "Arctic Wilderness." *The Living Wilderness*, Winter 1953–54, 5–15.

———. "Northeast Alaska: The Last Great Wilderness." *Sierra Club Bulletin* 38 (1953): 13.

Conover, Pat. "Alaska's Fishing Industry." *Alaska Life*, February 1947, 6–7, 28–31.

Conrad, David E. "Emmons of Alaska." *Pacific Northwest Quarterly* 69, 2 (1978): 59–60.

Cooley, Richard A. *Politics of Conservation: The Decline of the Alaska Salmon.* New York: Harper and Row Publishers, 1963.

Cooper, Bryan. *Alaska: The Last Frontier.* New York: Morrow, 1973.

Cooper, William S. "The Recent Ecological History of Glacier Bay, Alaska: I. The Interglacial Forests of Glacier Bay." *Ecology* 4, 2 (1923): 93–125.

———. "The Recent Ecological History of Glacier Bay, Alaska: II. The Present Vegetation Cycle." *Ecology* 4, 3 (1923): 223–45.

———. "The Recent Ecological History of Glacier Bay, Alaska: III. Permanent Quadrats at Glacier Bay: An Initial Report upon a Long Period Study." *Ecology* 4, 4 (1923): 355–72.

"Council on National Parks, Forests, and Wild Life." *Ecology* 5, 2 (1924): 185.

Cowan, Ian McTaggart. "Plant Succession and Wildlife Management." *Proceedings Second Alaskan Science Conference.* Fairbanks, Alaska: American Association for the Advancement of Science, 1951.

Crevelli, John P. "The Final Act of the Greatest Conservation President." *Prologue: The Journal of the National Archives* 12, 4 (1980): 173–91.

Crichton, Kyle. "Storm Over Alaska." *Collier's,* March 31, 1945, 20, 74–75.

Crisler, Lois. *Arctic Wild.* New York: Harper & Brothers, Publishers, 1958.

Curry, James E. "Displaced Alaskans." *Commonweal,* August 1, 1947, 381–83.

———. "Krug and the Indians." *New Republic,* April 25, 1949, 31.

Dannenbaum, Jed. "John Muir and Alaska." *Alaska Journal* 2, 3 (1972): 14–20.

Darling, F. Fraser, and Noel D. Eichhorn. *Man & Nature in the National Parks.* Washington, D.C.: The Conservation Foundation, 1967.

Dasmann, Raymond F. "National Parks, Nature Conservation, and 'Future Primitive.'" *The Ecologist* 6, 5 (1976): 164–67.

———. "Toward a Dynamic Balance of Man and Nature." *The Ecologist* 6, 1 (1976): 3–6.

De Laguna, Frederica. "Tlingit." In *Handbook of North American Indians.* Vol. 7. Washington, D.C.: Smithsonian Institution Press, 1990.

———. *Under Mount Saint Elias: The History and Culture of the Yakutat Tlingit.* Washington, D.C.: Smithsonian Institution Press, 1972.

Dixon, Joseph S. *Birds and Mammals of Mount McKinley National Park, Alaska.* National Park Service Fauna Series No. 3. Washington, D.C.: National Park Service, 1938.

Drucker, Philip. *Native Brotherhoods: Modern Inter-tribal Organizations on the Northwest Coast.* Smithsonian Institution. American Ethnology Bureau. Bulletin 168. Washington, D.C.: Government Printing Office, 1958.

Dryzek, John S. *Conflict and Choice in Resource Management: The Case of Alaska.* Boulder, Colo.: Westview Press, 1983.

Dufresne, Frank. *Alaska's Animals and Fishes.* New York: A. S. Barnes and Company, 1946.

———. "Alaska's Wildlife and Statehood." *Field and Stream,* December 1958, 62–63, 117.

———. "The Game and Fur Belong to All the People." *Alaska Sportsman*, April 1944, 16–18, 21.

Dunlap, Thomas R. *Saving America's Wildlife*. Princeton: Princeton University Press, 1988.

———. "Sport Hunting and Conservation, 1880–1920." *Environmental Review* 12, 1 (1988): 51–60.

Eidsvik, Harold K. "National Parks and Other Protected Areas: Some Reflections on the Past and Prescriptions for the Future." *Environmental Conservation* 7, 3 (1980): 185–90.

Erwin, Alexander M. "The Emergence of Native Alaskan Political Capacity, 1959–1971." *The Musk Ox* 19, 2 (1976): 3–14.

Fall, James A. "The Division of Subsistence of the Alaska Department of Fish and Game: An Overview of its Research Program and Findings 1980–1990." *Arctic Anthropology* 27, 2 (1990): 68–92.

Fienup-Riordan, Ann. *Eskimo Essays: Yup'ik Lives and How We See Them*. New Brunswick: Rutgers University Press, 1990.

Fleck, Richard F. "John Muir's Evolving Attitudes Toward Native American Cultures." *American Indian Quarterly* 4, 1 (1978): 19–31.

Foster, David. "Applying the Yellowstone Model in America's Backyard: Alaska." In *Aboriginal Involvement in Parks and Protected Areas*, edited by Jim Birckhead, Terry De Lacy, and Laurajane Smith. Canberra: Aboriginal Studies Press, 1992.

Fox, James L., and Gregory P. Streveler. "Wolf Predation on Mountain Goats in Southeastern Alaska." *Journal of Mammalogy* 67, 1 (1986): 192–95.

Fox, Stephen. *The American Conservation Movement: John Muir and his Legacy*. Boston: Little, Brown and Company, 1970.

Frome, Michael. "Hickel and the Arctic." *Field and Stream* 73, 6 (1969): 12–28.

Gabrielson, Ira N. "Crisis for Alaskan Wildlife." *Audubon Magazine*, November–December 1951, 348–53, 394.

Gardner, J. E., and J. G. Nelson. "Comparing National Park and Related Reserve Policy in Hinterland Areas: Alaska, Northern Canada, and Northern Australia." *Environmental Conservation* 7, 1 (1980): 43–50.

"Glacier Bay, Alaska Temporarily Withdrawn from Entry." *Ecology* 5, 2 (1924): 223.

Glover, James M. "Romance, Recreation, and Wilderness: Influences on the Life and Work of Bob Marshall." *Environmental History Review* 14, 4 (1990): 22–37.

———. *A Wilderness Original: The Life of Bob Marshall*. Seattle: The Mountaineers, 1986.

Goetzmann, William H., and Kay Sloan. *Looking Far North: The Harriman Alaska Expedition to Alaska, 1899*. Princeton: Princeton University Press, 1982.

Grant, Madison. "The Condition of Wild Life in Alaska." In *Smithsonian Report, 1909*. Washington, D.C.: Government Printing Office, 1910.

———. "The Condition of Wild Life in Alaska." Rev. ed. In *Hunting in High Alti-*

tudes: The Book of the Boone and Crockett Club, edited by George Bird Grinnell. New York: Harper and Brothers, 1913.

——. "The Establishment of Mount McKinley National Park." In *Hunting and Conservation*, edited by George Bird Grinnell and Charles Sheldon. New York: Arno Press, Inc., 1970. (Originally published in 1925.)

Grinnell, George Bird. *The Last of the Buffalo*. New York: Charles Scribner's Sons, 1892.

Grinnell, Joseph, and Tracy L. Storer. "Animal Life as an Asset of National Parks." *Science News Supplement*, September 15, 1916, 375–80.

Gubser, Nicholas. *The Nunamiut Eskimos: Hunters of Caribou*. New Haven: Yale University Press, 1965.

Gudgel-Holmes, Dianne. *Ethnohistory of Four Interior Alaskan Waterbodies*. Anchorage, Alaska: State of Alaska Department of Natural Resources, 1979.

Guthrie, Daniel A. "Primitive Man's Relationship to Nature." *BioScience*, July 1, 1971, 721–23.

Hall, Edwin S., Jr. "Interior North Alaska Eskimo." In *Subarctic*. Vol. 5 of *Handbook of North American Indians*, edited by June Helm. Washington, D.C.: Smithsonian Institution, 1984.

Harmon, David. "Cultural Diversity, Human Subsistence, and the National Park Ideal." *Environmental Ethics* 9, 2 (1987): 147–58.

Hartzog, George B., Jr. *Battling for the National Parks*. Mt. Kisko, N.Y.: Moyer Bell, Ltd., 1988.

Hatter, James. "The Status of Moose in North America." In *Transactions of the Fourteenth North American Wildlife Conference*. Washington, D.C.: Wildlife Management Institute, 1949.

Haycox, Stephen W. "Economic Development and Indian Land Rights in Modern Alaska: The 1947 Tongass Timber Act." *Western Historical Quarterly* 21, 1 (1990): 21–46.

Hensley, William L. "Arctic Development and the Future of Eskimo Societies." *Indian Truth* 47, 1 (1970): 1–8.

Hickok, David M. "Developmental Trends in Arctic Alaska." July 1, 1970. Arctic Environment Data Center, Anchorage, Alaska.

——. "Nunamiut Experience and Current Approaches to Subsistence Harvests Problems by the People of Anaktuvuk." February 1974. Arctic Environment Data Center, Anchorage, Alaska.

Higginson, Ella. *Alaska: The Great Country*. New York: Macmillan Co., 1908.

Hinckley, Ted C. *The Americanization of Alaska, 1867–1900*. Palo Alto: Pacific Books, 1972.

——. "The Canoe Rocks — We do not Know What Will Become of Us." *Western Historical Quarterly* 1, 3 (1970): 265–90.

——. "The Inside Passage: A Popular Gilded Age Tour." *Pacific Northwest Quarterly* 56, 3 (1965): 67–74.

Holzworth, John M. *The Wild Grizzlies of Alaska.* New York: G. P. Putnam's Sons, 1930.

Houston, Douglas B. "Ecosystems of National Parks." *Science,* May 14, 1971, 648–51.

Hoxie, Frederick. *A Final Promise: The Campaign to Assimilate the Indians, 1880–1920.* Lincoln: University of Nebraska Press, 1984.

Hunter, Celia. "Alaskan Wilderness: Going, Going — Gone?" *National Parks and Conservation Magazine,* November 1970, 11–15.

Huntington, Henry P. *Wildlife Management and Subsistence Hunting in Alaska.* London: Belhaven Press, 1992.

Ickes, Harold L. "Alaska's Natives Need Help." *New Republic,* July 24, 1950, 17.

———. "On Frisking the Alaska Indians." *New Republic,* May 9, 1949, 19–20.

Ingstad, Helge. *Nunamiut: Among Alaska's Inland Eskimos.* New York: W. W. Norton, Co., 1954.

International Work Group for Indigenous Affairs. *Arctic Environment: Indigenous Perspectives.* Document 69. Copenhagen: IWGIA, 1991.

Jacobson, Michael J., and Cynthia Wentworth. *Kaktovik Subsistence: Land Use Values Through Time in the Arctic National Wildlife Refuge Area.* Fish and Wildlife Service. Fairbanks, Alaska: Northern Alaska Ecological Services, 1982.

James, Susie. "Glacier Bay History." In *Haa Shuka, Our Ancestors: Tlingit Oral Narratives,* edited by Nora Marks Dauenhauer and Richard Dauenhauer. Seattle: University of Washington Press, 1987.

Joling, Dan. "Nunamiut Eskimos Welcome Return of Pilot Sig Wien." *Fairbanks Daily News-Miner* (Sunday Supplement), June 12, 1988.

Jorgensen, Joseph G. *Oil Age Eskimos.* Berkeley: University of California Press, 1990.

Kauffmann, John M. *Alaska's Brooks Range: The Ultimate Mountains.* Seattle: The Mountaineers, 1992.

———. "Noatak." *The Living Wilderness,* Winter 1974–75, 17–28.

Kennedy, Michael S. "Belmore Browne and Alaska." *Alaska Journal* 3, 2 (1973): 96–104.

Klein, David R. "Caribou, Alaska's Wilderness Nomads." In *Restoring America's Wildlife 1937–1987: The First Fifty Years in the Federal Aid in Wildlife Restoration (Pittman-Robertson) Act.* Department of the Interior. Fish and Wildlife Service. Washington, D.C.: Government Printing Office, 1987.

Klein, David R., and Robert G. White, eds. *Parameters of Caribou Population Ecology in Alaska: Proceedings of a Symposium and Workshop.* Biological Papers of the University of Alaska. Special Report No. 3. June 1978.

Koester, Susan H. " 'By the Words of the Mouth Let Thee Be Judged': The Alaska Native Sisterhood Speaks." *Journal of the West* 27, 2 (1988): 35–44.

Krause, Aurel. *The Tlingit Indians.* Translated by Erna Gunther. Seattle: University of Washington Press, 1956.

Lage, Ann. *George Collins: The Art and Politics of Park Planning and Preservation,*

1920–1979: An Interview Conducted by Ann Lage in 1978 and 1979. Introduction by Lowell Sumner et al. Berkeley: University of California Regents, 1980

Lantis, Margaret. "The Current Nativistic Movement in Alaska." In *Circumpolar Problems: Habitat, Economy, and Social Relations in the Arctic,* edited by Gosta Berg. Oxford, U.K.: Pergamon Press, 1973.

"The Last Treaty." *Harper's Magazine,* January 1975, 38.

Leatherbee, M. "Alaska: The Hard Country." *Life,* October 1, 1965, 76–77.

Leopold, A. Starker, and F. Fraser Darling. "Effects of Land Use on Moose and Caribou in Alaska." In *Transactions of the Eighteenth North American Wildlife Conference,* edited by James B. Trefethen. Washington, D.C.: Wildlife Management Institute, 1953.

———. *Wildlife in Alaska: An Ecological Reconnaissance.* New York: Ronald Press Company, 1953.

Leopold, A. Starker, et al. "Wildlife Management in the National Parks." *The Living Wilderness,* Spring–Summer 1963, 11–19.

Lopp, W. T. "Native Labor in the Alaskan Fisheries." *Pacific Fisherman* 12, 11 (1914): 16.

Loring, J. Alden. "Notes on the Destruction of Animal Life in Alaska." *New York Zoological Society Sixth Annual Report.* New York: Office of the Society, 1902.

McCloskey, Michael. "Wilderness Movement at the Crossroads, 1945–1970." *Pacific Historical Review* 41, 3 (1972): 346–72.

McKennan, Robert A. "Tanana." In *Subarctic.* Vol. 6 of *Handbook of North American Indians,* edited by June Helm. Washington, D.C.: Smithsonian Institution, 1981.

Mackintosh, Barry. *The National Parks: Shaping the System.* National Park Service. Washington, D.C.: 1991.

Mallet, Captain Thierry. "When the Caribou Failed." *Atlantic Monthly,* March 1928, 378–83.

Marshall, George. "Bob Marshall and the Alaska Arctic Wilderness." *The Living Wilderness,* Autumn 1970, 29–32.

———. "On Bob Marshall's Landmark Article." *The Living Wilderness,* October–December 1976, 28–30.

Marshall, Robert. *Alaska Wilderness: Exploring the Central Brooks Range.* 2d ed. Edited with introduction by George Marshall. Berkeley: University of California Press, 1970.

———. *Arctic Village.* New York: Literary Guild, 1933.

———. "Ecology and the Indians." *Ecology* 18, 1 (1937): 159–61.

———. "The Problem of the Wilderness." *The Scientific Monthly,* February 1930, 141–49.

———. "The Universe of the Wilderness is Vanishing." *Nature Magazine,* April 1937, 235–40.

Martin, Calvin. *Keepers of the Game: Indian-Animal Relationships and the Fur Trade.* Berkeley: University of California Press, 1978.

——— "Subarctic Indians and Wildlife." In *American Indian Environmental Religions,* edited by Christopher Vecsey. Syracuse: Syracuse University Press, 1980.

Marvin, Amy. "Glacier Bay History." In *Haa Shuka, Our Ancestors: Tlingit Oral Narratives,* edited by Nora Marks Dauenhauer and Richard Dauenhauer. Seattle: University of Washington Press, 1987.

Mekiana, Homer. *This is the Story of Anaktuvuk Pass Village.* Special Report of the Naval Arctic Research Laboratory. Barrow, Alaska, 1972.

Mendenhall, J. C. "Reconnaissance from Fort Hamlin to Kotzebue Sound, Alaska, by way of Dall, Kanuti, Allen (Alatna) and Kowak (Kobuk) Rivers." *U.S. Geological Survey Professional Paper 10.* Washington, D.C.: Government Printing Office, 1902.

Metzger, Charles. *The Silent River: a pastoral elegy in the form of a recollection of Arctic adventure.* Los Angeles: Omega Books, 1983.

Miller, Debbie S. "ANILCA was the best piece of lame duck legislation I can think of." *Wilderness,* Winter 1990, 30–31.

Mitchell, John G. "Where have all the tuttu gone?" *Audubon,* March 1977, 3–15.

Moore, Terris. *Mount McKinley: The Pioneer Climbs.* College, Alaska: University of Alaska Press, 1967.

Morse, Fremont. "The Recession of the Glaciers of Glacier Bay, Alaska." *National Geographic,* January 1908, 76–78.

Muir, John. "The Discovery of Glacier Bay." *The Century Magazine* 50, 2 (1895): 234–37.

———. *Letters from Alaska,* edited by Robert Engberg and Bruce Merrell. Madison: University of Wisconsin Press, 1993.

———. *The Mountains of California.* New York: Century, 1894.

———. *Travels in Alaska.* Boston: Houghton Mifflin Co., 1915.

"Mt. McKinley Mining People in Seattle in the Interest of Big Placer Project." *Alaska and the Northwest Mining Journal* 13, 9 (1919): 21–22.

Murie, Adolph. *The Wolves of Mount McKinley.* National Park Service Fauna Series No. 5. Washington, D.C.: National Park Service, 1944.

Murie, Olaus J. "Nature in the Arctic." *National Parks Magazine,* January–March 1958, 29.

———. "Wilderness Philosophy, Science, and the Arctic National Wildlife Range." In *Proceedings Twelfth Annual Science Conference.* Alaska Division, American Association for the Advancement of Science, 1961.

Nadel, Michael. "Wilderness Council in Alaska." *The Living Wilderness,* Summer–Fall 1963, 47.

Nash, Roderick. "The American Invention of National Parks." *American Quarterly* 22, 3 (1970): 726–35.

———. "The Strenuous Life of Bob Marshall." *Forest History* 10, 3 (1966): 18–25.

———. "Tourism, Parks, and the Wilderness Idea in the History of Alaska." *Alaska in Perspective* 4, 1 (1981): 1–27

———. *Wilderness and the American Mind.* 3d ed. New Haven: Yale University Press, 1982.

Naske, Claus-M. "Ernest Gruening and Alaska Native Claims." *Pacific Northwest Quarterly* 82, 4 (1991): 140–48.

"Natives: Even Hope is Scarce." *Business Week*, November 4, 1967, 152.

Nelson, E. W. "Charles Sheldon." *American Forests* 34 (November 1928): 659–60.

Nelson, Richard K. *Make Prayers to the Raven: A Koyukon View of the Northern Forest.* Chicago: University of Chicago Press, 1983.

Nelson, Richard K., Kathleen H. Mautner, and G. Ray Bane. *Tracks in the Wildland: A Portrayal of Koyukon and Nunamiut Subsistence.* Fairbanks, Alaska: University of Alaska, Cooperative Park Studies Unit, 1982. (Originally published in 1978.)

Newell, Alan S., Richmond L. Clow, and Richard N. Ellis. *A Forest in Trust: Three-Quarters of a Century of Indian Forestry, 1910–1985.* Bureau of Indian Affairs. Washington, D.C.: Government Printing Office, 1985.

Nixon, E. B., ed. *Franklin D. Roosevelt and Conservation.* Vol. 2. New York: General Services Administration, National Archives and Records Service, Franklin D. Roosevelt Library, Hyde Park, 1957.

Norris, Frank. *Gawking at the Midnight Sun: The Tourist in Early Alaska.* Anchorage: Alaska Historical Commission, 1985.

———. "Showing Off Alaska: The Northern Tourist Trade, 1878–1941." *Alaska History* 2, 2 (1987): 1–18.

Pack, A. N. "Admiralty's Bears." *Nature Magazine* 26, 8 (1935): 111–12.

———. "Alaskan Bears." *Nature Magazine* 20, 6 (1932): 257.

———. "The Bears of Admiralty." *Nature Magazine* 23, 1 (1934): 23.

Paneak, Simon. "We Hunt to Live." *Alaska Sportsman*, March 1960, 12–13, 55.

Parfit, Michael. "Alaska: Eleventh Hour for America's Wilderness." *The New Times*, September 18, 1978, 18–68.

Pearson, Grant H. *My Life of High Adventure.* Englewood Cliffs, N.J.: Prentice Hall, Inc., 1962.

Pender, Jane. "Alaskan Natives: Time of Crisis." *National Parks and Conservation Magazine*, November 1970, 23–27.

———. "Crisis on the North Slope." *Anchorage Daily News*, March 4, 1969.

Philp, Kenneth R. "The New Deal and Alaskan Natives, 1936–1945." *Pacific Historical Review* 50, 3 (1981): 309–27.

Pomeroy, Earl. *In Search of the Golden West: The Tourist in Western America.* New York: Alfred A. Knopf, Inc., 1957.

Price, Robert E. *The Great Father in Alaska: The Case of the Tlingit and Haida Salmon Fishery.* Douglas, Alaska: First Street Press, 1990.

Prindle, L. M. "The Bonnifield and Kantishna Regions." *U.S. Geological Survey Bulletin 314.* Washington, D.C.: Government Printing Office, 1907.

Rausch, Robert. "Notes on the Nunamiut Eskimo and Mammals of the Anaktuvuk Pass Region, Brooks Range, Alaska." *Arctic* 4, 3 (1951): 146–95.

Rearden, Jim. "Our Last Wilderness Revisited." *Outdoor Life*, March 1972, 59–61, 204–8.

——. "Subsistence, A Troublesome Issue." *Alaska Magazine*, July 1978, 5–6, 84–88.

Reed, John C. "Oil and the Arctic Tundra." *National Parks and Conservation Magazine*, November 1970, 4–7.

Reiger, John F. *American Sportsmen and the Origins of Conservation*. Rev. ed. Norman: Oklahoma University Press, 1986.

Roberts, Robert. "Shall We Ban States Fishermen?" *Alaska Life*, July 1940, 4–5, 14.

Runte, Alfred. *National Parks: The American Experience*. 2d rev. ed. Lincoln: University of Nebraska Press, 1987.

——. "Pragmatic Alliance: Western Railroads and the National Parks." *National Parks Magazine*, April 1974, 15–21.

——. *Trains of Discovery: Western Railroads and the National Parks*. Rev. ed. Niwot, Colo.: Robert Rinehart, 1990.

Sax, Joseph L. *Mountains Without Handrails: Reflections on the National Parks*. Ann Arbor: University of Michigan Press, 1980.

Schaller, George B. "New Area for Hunters." *Outdoor Life*, March 1958, 33–37.

Schroeder, Robert F., and Matthew Kookesh. *Subsistence Harvest and Use of Fish and Wildlife Resources and the Effects of Forest Management in Hoonah, Alaska*. Technical Paper No. 142. Juneau: Alaska Department of Fish and Game, 1990.

Schwantes, Carlos A. "Tourists in Wonderland: Early Railroad Tourism in the Pacific Northwest." *Columbia: The Magazine of Northwest History*, Winter 1993–94, 21–28.

Seaton, Fred A. "America's Largest Wildlife Area." *National Parks Magazine*, July–September 1958, 117–22.

Sellars, Richard West. "Manipulating Nature's Paradise: National Park Management Under Stephen T. Mather, 1916–1929." *Montana: The Magazine of Western History*, Spring 1992, 2–13.

——. "The Rise and Decline of Ecological Attitudes in National Park Management 1929–1940, Part I." *The George Wright Forum* 10, 1 (1993): 55–76.

——. "The Roots of National Park Management: Evolving Perceptions of the Park Service's Mandate." *Journal of Forestry* 90, 1 (1992): 16–19.

Seton, Ernest Thompson. *The Arctic Prairies*. New York: Charles Scribner's Sons, 1911.

Shankland, Robert. *Steve Mather of the National Parks*. New York: Alfred A. Knopf, 1951.

Sheldon, Charles. "Big Game of Chihuahua." In *Hunting and Conservation*, edited by George Bird Grinnell and Charles Sheldon. New Haven: Yale University Press, 1925.

——. *The Wilderness of Denali*. New York: Charles Scribner's Sons, 1930.

Sherwood, Morgan. *Big Game in Alaska: A History of Wildlife and People*. New Haven: Yale University Press, 1981.

———. "Specious Speciation in the Political History of the Alaskan Brown Bear." *Western Historical Quarterly* 10, 1 (1979): 49–60.

Slotkin, Richard. *The Fatal Environment: The Myth of the Frontier in the Age of Industrialization, 1800–1890.* New York: Athenaeum, 1985.

Smith, Philip S. "Mineral Industry of Alaska in 1924 and Administrative Report." *U.S. Geological Survey Bulletin 783-A.* Washington, D.C.: Government Printing Office, 1926.

Spearman, Grant. *Anaktuvuk Pass Land Use Values Through Time.* Prepared for North Slope Borough by Cooperative Park Studies Unit, University of Alaska. Occasional Paper No. 22. 1979.

Spencer, Robert F. *The North Alaskan Eskimo: A Study in Ecology and Society.* Smithsonian Institution. Bureau of American Ethnology. Bulletin 171. Washington, D.C.: Government Printing Office, 1959.

"A Sportsman's Paradise." *Alaska-Yukon Magazine,* January 1909, 285–87.

Stewart, B. D. *Annual Report of the Mine Inspector to the Governor of Alaska, 1922.* Washington, D.C.: Government Printing Office, 1922.

Stoney, George M. "Explorations in Alaska." In *Proceedings.* U.S. Naval Institute. Washington, D.C.: Government Printing Office, 1899.

Story, Isabelle F. *The National Parks and Emergency Conservation.on, D.C.: National Park Service, 1933.*

Streveler, Gregory P., and Bruce Paige. *The Natural History of Glacier Bay National Monument, Alaska.* Report prepared for the National Park Service, 1971.

Strong, Douglas Hillman. "The Indian and the Environment." *The Journal of Environmental Education* 5, 2 (1973): 49–51.

Stuck, Hudson. *The Ascent of Denali (Mount McKinley): A Narrative of the First Complete Ascent of the Highest Peak in North America.* New York: Charles Scribner's Sons, 1914.

Suttles, Wayne. "Coping with Abundance: Subsistence on the Northwest Coast." In *Man the Hunter,* edited by Richard B. Lee and Irven DeLore. Chicago: Aldine Publishing Company, 1968.

Taber, F. Wallace. "Hunting with Alaska's Nunamiute." *The American Rifleman,* February 1960, 23–26.

Tarr, Ralph Stockman, and Lawrence Martin. *Alaskan Glacier Studies.* Washington, D.C.: National Geographic Society, 1914.

"Ted's Troubles in the Tundra: Investigating Conditions of Alaska's Natives." *Time,* April 18, 1969, 22–23.

Trefethen, James B. *An American Crusade for Wildlife.* New York: Winchester Press, 1975.

Udall, Stewart L. "Nature Islands for the World." In *First World Conference on National Parks,* edited by Alexander B. Adams. Washington, D.C.: Government Printing Office, 1963.

Vanstone, James W. *Athapaskan Adaptations: Hunters and Fishermen of the Subarctic Forests.* Arlington Heights, Ill.: Harlan Davidson, Inc., 1974.

——. "Ingalik Contact Ecology: An Ethnohistory of the Lower-Middle Yukon, 1790–1935." In *Fieldiana: Anthropology*. Vol. 71. Chicago: Field Museum of Natural History, 1979.

Watkins, T. H. "The Perils of Expedience." *Wilderness*, Winter 1990, 23–84.

Weeden, Robert B. "Man in Nature." In *Alaska Public Policy: Current Problems and Issues*, edited by Gordon Scott Harrison. College, Alaska: Institute of Social, Economic, and Government Research, 1971.

——. "Oil and Wildlife: A Biologist's View." In *Transactions of the Thirty-Sixth North American Wildlife and Natural Sources Conference*, edited by James B. Trefethen. Washington, D.C.: Wildlife Management Institute, 1971.

West, Patrick C., and Steven R. Brechin, eds. *Resident Peoples and National Parks: Social Dilemmas and Strategies in International Conservation*. Tucson: University of Arizona Press, 1991.

White, Richard. "Native Americans and the Environment." In *Scholars and the Indian Experience: Critical Reviews of Recent Writing in the Social Sciences*, edited by W. R. Swagerty. Bloomington, Ind.: University of Indiana Press, 1984.

Whitney, Caspar, George Bird Grinnell, and Owen Wister. *Musk-Ox, Bison, Sheep and Goat*. New York: Macmillan Company, 1904.

Williss, G. Frank. *"Do It Right the First Time": The National Park Service and the Alaska National Interest Lands Conservation Act*. U.S. Department of the Interior. Atlanta: National Park Service, 1985.

Wilson, William H. "Ahead of the Times: The Alaska Railroad and Tourism, 1924–1941." *Alaska Journal* 7, 1 (1977): 18–24.

Wolfe, Linnie Marsh. *Son of the Wilderness: The Life of John Muir*. New York: Alfred A. Knopf, 1945.

——, ed. *John of the Mountains: The Unpublished Journals of John Muir*. Boston: Houghton Mifflin Co., 1938.

Wood, C. E. S. "Among the Thlinkits in Alaska." *The Century Magazine* 24, 3 (1882): 323–39.

Worster, Donald. "The Ecology of Order and Chaos." *Environmental History Review* 14 (Spring–Summer 1990): 1–18.

——. *Nature's Economy: The Roots of Ecology*. New York: Cambridge University Press, 1985.

——. *Under Western Skies: Nature and History in the American West*. New York: Oxford University Press, 1992.

Wright, George, Joseph Dixon, and Ben Thompson. *Fauna of the National Parks of the United States*, National Park Service Fauna Series No. 1. Washington, D.C.: National Park Service, 1932.

Wright, Sam. "Alaska's Wilderness Cries Out for a Plan." *The Living Wilderness*, Spring 1969, 3–6.

——. "Eskimo Village." *The Living Wilderness*, Winter 1970–71, 3–6.

——. "Koviashuktok: The Secret of the Eskimo's Wisdom." *American West* 8, 6 (1971): 16–19.

Young, S. Hall. *Alaska Days with John Muir.* New York: F. H. Revell Co., 1915.
Yupiktak Bista. *Does One Way of Life Have to Die So Another Can Live?* Bethel: Yupiktak Bista, 1974.

DISSERTATIONS AND THESES

Amsden, Charles Wynn. "A Quantitative Analysis of Nunamiut Eskimo Settlement Dynamics." Ph.D. diss., University of New Mexico, 1977.
Buske, Frank E. "The Wilderness, the Frontier and the Literature of Alaska to 1914: John Muir, Jack London, and Rex Beach." Ph.D. diss., University of California, Davis, 1976.
Matthews, Vincent Thomas. "A Case Study of a Homeland and a Wilderness: Gates of the Arctic National Park and the Nunamiut Eskimos." Master's thesis, University of Alaska, Fairbanks, 1990.
Specking, Joan Lynne. "The Alaska Railroad: Its Influence on the Promotion of Tourism in Alaska." Master's thesis, University of Washington, 1987.
Tollefson, Kenneth D. "The Cultural Foundation of Political Revitalization Among the Tlingit." Ph.D. diss., University of Washington, 1976.

NEWSPAPERS

Alaska Daily Empire (Juneau)
Alaska Fisherman (Wrangell)
Anchorage Daily News
Fairbanks Daily News-Miner
Ketchikan Daily News
Seattle Times
Southeast Alaska Empire (Juneau)
Tundra Times (Anchorage)

Index